Kṛtibodha Series
No. 2

General Editor
Dipti Tripathi

Kṛtibodha Series

The Kṛtibodha (Knowledge on Texts) Series is the project of the National Mission for Manuscripts to promote academic interest and scholarship in the area of manuscript studies. Previously unpublished and rare texts will be published as critical editions, with detailed introduction, analyses and commentaries under this series.

ŚRAUTA PRAYOGAKḶPTI
of
Ācārya Śivaśroṇa

आचार्य-शिवश्रोणविरचिता वाधूलशाखीया

श्रौतप्रयोगक्लृप्तिः

तस्येदं

विशदभूमिकया विविधाभिरनुक्रमणीभिश्च समलङ्कृतं
पाठविमर्शादिभिर्युतं समालोचनात्मकं संस्करणम्

प्रो. व्रजबिहारी चौबे

इत्याख्येन विदुषा संपादितम्

National Mission for Manuscripts

राष्ट्रीय पाण्डुलिपि मिशन
नई दिल्ली

तथा

डी० के० प्रिण्टवर्ल्ड (प्रा०) लि०
नई दिल्ली

ŚRAUTA PRAYOGAKḶPTI

(Belonging to the Vādhūla-Śākhā)

of

Ācārya Śivaśroṇa

Critically edited with detailed Introduction and various Indexes

by

Prof. Braj Bihari Chaubey

National Mission for Manuscripts

NATIONAL MISSION FOR MANUSCRIPTS
New Delhi

and

D.K. PRINTWORLD (P) LTD.
New Delhi

Cataloguing in Publication Data — DK
[Courtesy: D.K. Agencies (P) Ltd. <docinfo@dkagencies.com>]

Śivaśroṇa, *Ācārya*.
[Śrautaprayogakḷpti]
Vādhūlaśākhīyā śrautaprayogakḷptiḥ : tasyedaṃ viśadabhūmikayā vividhābhiranukramaṇībhiśca samalaṅkṛtaṃ pāṭhavimarśādibhiryutaṃ samālocanātmakaṃ saṃskaraṇam / Śivaśroṇaviracitā ; Vrajabihārī Caube.
p. cm. – (Kṛtibodha series ; no. 2)
In Sanskrit.
Digest of Hindu rituals according to the Vādhūla recension.
Includes index.
ISBN 9789380829005

1. Religious life – Hinduism. 2. Hinduism – Doctrines. I. Chaubey, B. B. (Braj Bihari), 1940- II. Title. III. Series: Kṛtibodha series ; no. 2.

DDC 294.544 22

ISBN 978-93-80829-00-5
First published in India in 2011

Published by:
National Mission for Manuscripts
No. 11 Mansingh Road
New Delhi - 110 001
Phone: (011) 2338 3894; *Fax:* 2307 3340
E-mail: director.namami@nic.in

Co-published by:
D.K. Printworld (P) Ltd
Regd. Office: Srikunj, F-52, Bali Nagar
Ramesh Nagar Metro Station, New Delhi-110 015
Phones: (011) 2545 3975; 2546 6019; *Fax*: (011) 2546 5926
E-mail: indology@dkprintworld.com
Website: www.dkprintworld.com

Printed by: D.K. Printworld (P) Ltd., New Delhi.

FOREWORD

The *Prayogakḷpti* is second in the Kṛtibodha series of NMM. This series was introduced as a means to bring to light critical editions of rare manuscripts. The first in this series was **Vādhūlagṛhyāgamavṛttirahasyam** of Nārāyaṇa Miśra edited by Prof. B.B. Chaubey.

The Vedic literature in our country consists of fourfold texts: Saṁhitā (collection of *mantra*s), Brāhmaṇa (for interpretation and application of *mantra*s during sacrifices), Āraṇyaka and Upaniṣad (texts dealing with spiritual matters). The relationship between the Saṁhitās and Brāhmaṇas is complex, because the Saṁhitās are only a collection of Vedic *mantra*s whereas Brāhmaṇas are texts which provide the guidelines for practical application of these *mantra*s during the sacrifices. Brāhmaṇas also deal with the spiritual (*ādhyātmika*), sacrificial (*ādhiyājñika*) and divine (*ādhidaivika*) interpretation of *mantra*s and rituals related with them.

There is another aspect of Brāhmaṇas which is known as Arthavāda. This is related to explaining the positive and negative aspect of the *mantra*s. Thus the Brāhmaṇas acquired the feature of description of sacrificial acts along with application of *mantra*s on the one hand and arthavāda of *mantra*s on the other. This feature gave to the Brāhmaṇas a unique and complex character which requires explanation for both, proper understanding and correct application.

It has to be kept in mind that the process of Vedic rituals (*Śrauta yāgas)* was not only complex but also lengthy. With the passage of time the need for specific guidelines and reference books of *Śrauta yāgas* was felt and texts dealing with the practical side of these sacrifices came into being. These texts, known as *prayoga-grantha*s, were designed as handbooks to explain the duties of different *ṛtviks* while performing *Śrauta yāga.* It would be erroneous to assume that the content of all *prayoga* texts is identical because, some texts were prepared keeping in view the duties of a particular *ṛtvik* in a particular *iṣṭi* or a *somayajña*. There were other *prayoga*-texts which were prepared keeping in view the order and sequence of the performance of sacrifices by different *ṛtviks* according to their own traditions. In these the divergent views of different *ācārya*s were also mentioned. It seems probable that a large number of *prayoga*-texts were composed by experts well-versed in Vedic tradition.

Śrautaprayogakḷpti of Vādhūla tradition is one such *prayoga*-text. It is based on the *Vādhūla Śrautasūtra*. The author is Ācārya Śivaśroṇa. It is a small text which was earlier on confused as a commentary on the *Vādhūla Śrautasūtra*.

Prof. B.B. Chaubey is an internationally acclaimed expert of Vedic literature who has painstakingly, with an eye for details, done a critical edition of *Śrautaprayogakḷpti.* Prof. Chaubey needs no introduction to the scholarly world. He has, with his academic pursuits, knowledge, application and dedication, carved a niche for himself amongst the hallowed world of experts in the field of Vedic literature. He has taken upon himself to bring to light still unknown texts of the Vādhūla Śākhā. The present text is a prayoga-text of this Śākhā.

It gives me immense pleasure to present before the scholarly world a critically edited version of *Prayogakḷpti* with a detailed introduction. The introduction as well as the indices have been diligently prepared by Prof. B.B. Chaubey. I hope with the help of experts the NMM will be able to publish many more such texts in this series.

I look forward to comments/reactions from scholars, which would serve as an input in improving the quality of publication.

1st January 2011

Dipti S. Tripathi
Director, NMM

PREFACE

Veda, comprising of threefold *mantra*s — *Ṛk*, *Yajus*, and *Sāman* — is the most ancient literature of the world. Though a large number of sacrificial terminologies coined by the seers themselves are found in them, but in their origin, they were related to cosmic sacrifice called *Sṛṣṭi-yajña*, as a result of which the universe is functioning in a proper system and will continue functioning for ever. Later on, to understand and to explain the functioning of the universe some ritualistic systems were introduced by the authors of the Brāhmaṇas, employing the *mantra*s to be uttered while performing the rituals. Before the compilation of the Brāhmaṇas, the original four Saṁhitās, too, seem to have been compiled on a ritualistic principle based on the principle of division of the four important *ṛtvik*s, viz. Hotā, Adhvaryu, Udgātā, and Brahmā. The entire activities, related to the rituals, were confined to the four groups of these principal *ṛtvik*s, which have been indicated in a *mantra* itself:

ऋचां त्वः पोषमास्ते पुपुष्वान् गायत्रं त्वो गायति शक्वरीषु ।
ब्रह्मा त्वो वदति जातविद्यां यज्ञस्य मात्रां विमिमीत उ त्वः ॥

— *ṚV* 10.71.11

But, as the main aim of the Brāhmaṇas was to explain the *ādhyātmika, ādhiyājñika* and *ādhidaivika* interpretations of the *mantra*s and rituals related to them, and not the mere ritualistic performances in a systematic order, it was not possible to perform a sacrifice only with the help of the Brāhmaṇas. As a result of this specific character of the Brāhmaṇas, a new type of Vedic literature, called Śrauta-sūtras, was composed keeping in view mainly the ritualistic performances of the sacrifices, leaving aside the *ādhyātmika, ādhiyājñika* and *ādhidaivika* interpretations of the *śrauta-yajña*s. The Śrauta-sūtras left out even the *arthavāda*s of the Brāhmaṇas.

In course of time, to make the Śrauta sacrifices easier, a new type of literature, called *Śrauta-prayoga*, was introduced by the later

*Ācārya*s. Actually, these *prayoga-grantha*s were handbooks to make easily understandable the duties of the different *ṛtviks* to be performed by them in various *śrauta-yajña*s. These texts were of different nature:

(i) Some *prayoga-grantha*s were prepared keeping in view the duties of a particular *ṛtvik* in a particular *iṣṭi,* or a *Somayāga*.

(ii) Some *prayoga-grantha*s were prepared keeping in view the order and sequence of performance of the *iṣṭi*s / sacrifices, by different *ṛtvik*s in their own tradition, mentioning different views of the *ācārya*s on the order and sequence of the rituals or any difference in other traditions.

A huge number of such *prayoga-grantha*s was composed by the later *Ācārya*s who were well-versed in Śrauta tradition, with a view to performing the individual rites on a particular occasion not as a part of long sacrifices.

A big number of such *prayoga-grantha*s is lying in several manuscript collections. But very few have been catalogued and more are still waiting for their cataloguing. In the second volume of the *Descriptive Catalogue of Sanskrit Manuscripts of Vaidika Saṁśodhana Maṇḍala*, Poona, Dr. T. N. Dharmadhikari has given a list of 1660 Śrauta *prayoga-grantha*s under 27 sections as: (i) *Miscellaneous Nibandhagranthas*, (ii) *Ādhāna*, (iii) *Punarādhāna*, (iv) *Agnihotra*, (v) *Pravāsa-vidhi*, (vi) *Darśapūrṇamāsa*, (vii) *Piṇḍapitṛyajña*, (viii) *Misc. Iṣṭis*, (ix) *Āgrayaṇa*, (x) *Cāturmāsya*, (xi) *Nirūḍha Paśu*, (xii) *Sautrāmaṇī*, (xiii) *Pitṛmedha*, (xiv) *Pravargya*, (xv) *Agniṣṭoma*, (xvi) *Atyagniṣṭoma*, (xvii) *Ukthya*, (xviii) *Ṣoḍaśī*, (xix) *Atirātra*, (xx) *Āptoryāma*, (xxi) *Vājapeya*, (xxii) *Ekāhas*, (xxiii) *Ahīna*s, (xxiv) *Agnicayana*, (xxv) *Kāṭhakacayana*, (xxvi) *Vihāra* and (xxvii) *Prāyaścitta*.

In other manuscript-collections, too, many manuscripts of *prayoga*s exist. Most of them still have not been even catalogued. But none of the catalogues, published so far, give any reference to the *Śrautaprayogakḷpti* of Vādhūla tradition.

In 1920 it came to the notice of Prof. Caland that some MSS of Vādhūla School written in Malayalam script had been discovered in Kerala by the Paṇḍits of Madras. One of such MSS entitled *Kalpāgamasaṁgraha* was sent to him. It was in Grantha script hence it was not very intelligible to him. However, he noticed that the MS consisted of three different parts, viz. (i) a complete text of *Kalpāgamasaṁgraha* of Āryadāsa or Ācāryapāda, (ii) *Prayogasandarbha* or *Prayogakalpanā* of Śivaśroṇa and (iii) a small part of the *Kārikā*s. Prof. Ikari understood the *Prayogakalpanā* as a commentary like the *Kalpasūtravyākhyā* of Āryadāsa on *Vādhūlaśrauta-sūtra* and referred to its author as Raghuśroṇa. After copying the entire text of the *Prayogakḷpti* and comparing it with the commentary of Āryadāsa, I found that the *Prayogakḷpti* was not a commentary but an original text under *prayoga*-category of literature, based on the *Vādhūlaśrauta-sūtra*. Since it was a small text, I thought to bring it out first before the commentary of Āryadāsa on *VādhŚS*.

Now it gives me immense pleasure to place in the hands of scholars the sixth text, viz. *Prayogakḷpti* of Śivaśroṇa under the project of bringing out critical editions of the texts belonging to the *Vādhūla Śākhā*, the other 5 titles having already been published are *Vādhūlaśrauta-sūtra* (1993), *Vādhūla-smṛti* with Hindi translation (2000), the *Vādhūla-Anvākhyāna* (2001), *Vādhūlayajña-prāyaścitta* (2001) and *Vādhūlagṛhyāgamavṛttirahasya* (2006).

I take this opportunity to express my sincere thanks to scholars and well-wishers who rendered their co-operation in several ways for the completion of the project which I had undertaken since long time. First of all I am very grateful to the authorities of the Government Oriental Manuscript Library, Madras; Adyar Manuscript Library, Madras; Oriental Institute, M.S. University, Baroda; Oriental Research Institute and Manuscript Library, University of Kerala, Thiruvananthapuram, from where I could get photostat copies of the MSS, which were in their possesion. I am very thankful to Pt. Nanaji Kale of Barshi who, taking great interest, directly sent one of his disciples to go to Baroda to get the MS copied down and kindly sent the photostat copy of the same to me.

I am grateful to Dr. T.N. Dharmadhikari, the former Director of the Vaidika Saṁśodhana Maṇḍala Pune, Dr. G.C. Tripathi, Dr. H.G. Ranade (alas! he is no more), with whom I always used to discuss the doubtful textual variants, whenever we met together whether in conferences, seminars or at any time when we got occasions to meet together. I am also thankful to Dr. Ghanashyam Uniyal who very sincerely helped me in checking the proofs.

I am heartily grateful to Prof. Dipti Tripathi, Director, National Mission for Manuscripts, Delhi and Dr. Vijay Shankar Shukla, Senior Research Officer, IGNCA for their kindly accepting this important work for its publication under Kṛtibodha Series. My Critical edition of the *Vādhūlagṛhyāgamavṛttirahasya* was also published as series No. 1.

I am also very thankful to Prof. Witzel, Prof. Yasuke Ikari and many other scholars whose scholarly works I consulted for the preparation of the text.

At the end, I would like to place on record my appreciation of the work done by Smt. Dr. Aruna Shukla, Shri Krishna Kumar Chaubey who assisted me in preparing various Indexes of the text, press copy, transcription and collation work and to Shri Yogesh Chaubey for composing and typesetting the work. I always wish them success in their life.

Varṣa Pratipadā, vs 2067
(16 March 2010)

Prof. B.B. Chaubey
Professor Emeritus, Panjab University
Director, Sangyan Vedic Studies
& Research Centre, Hoshiarpur
Former Director, VVBIS & IS (P.U.),
Hoshiarpur

CONTENTS

Foreword – by the General Editor **vii-viii**
Preface **ix-xii**
Scheme of Transliteration **xv**
Introduction **xvii-xlii**

1. Background xvii
2. Critical Apparatus Used for the Present Edition xviii
3. Nature of the MSS xix
4. Nomenclature of the text xx
    (i) *Prayogakḷpti*
    (ii) *Prayogakalpanā*
    (iii) *Prayogasandarbha*
5. Authorship of the Text xxi
6. Nature of the Text xxii
7. Arrangement and Division of the Text xxiv
8. Contents of the Text xxvii
9. Some salient features of the Text xxix

Text of the Śrauta Prayogakḷpti

प्रथमः प्रपाठकः	प्रस्तावना		**1**
	अग्न्याधेयम्	1.1.1 - 1.3.3	**2-12**
	पुनराधेयम्	1.4.1	9
	अग्निहोत्रम्	1.4.2 - 1.4.5	9
	अग्न्युपस्थानम्	1.5.1 - 1.5.3	11
द्वितीयः प्रपाठकः	पुरोडाशी	2.1.1 - 2.3.7	**13-26**
	याजमानम्	2.4.1 - 7	21
	ब्रह्मत्वम्	2.5.1 - 3	24
तृतीयः प्रपाठकः	चातुर्मास्यानि	3.1.1	**27-42**
	वैश्वदेवपर्व	3.1.1-3	27
	वरुणप्रघासपर्व	3.2.1-7	29

	साकमेधपर्व	3.3.1-3	33
	पितृयज्ञः	3.4.5	35
	चातुर्मास्ययाजमानम्	3.6.1-4	40
चतुर्थः प्रपाठकः	पशोर्याजनम्	4.1.4	**43-53**
पञ्चमः प्रपाठकः	ज्योतिष्टोमः	5.1-	**54**
	ऋत्विग्वरणम्		
	दीक्षणीयेष्टिः		
	सोमक्रयः	5.3.	60
	आतिथ्येष्टिः	5.3.4-5	62
	प्रवर्ग्योपसद्	5.4.1-3	63
	महावेदिविमानम्	5.4.4-7	65
	हविर्धानसंवर्तनम्	5.5.1-4	67
	वसतीवरीग्रहणम्	5.6.	70
षष्ठः प्रपाठकः	अग्निष्टोमः	6.1.1-6	**74 - 84**
	प्रयोगः	6.2-3	78

Index	I	व्याख्यात–पारिभाषिकपदानामनुक्रमणी	1 - 4
Index	II	उद्धृतमन्त्रानुक्रमणी	5 - 16
Index	III	उद्धृतपदानुक्रमणी	17 - 91

Scheme of Transliteration

Vowels

अ (a)	आ (ā)	इ (i)	ई (ī)	उ (u)	ऊ (ū)	
ऋ (ṛ)	ॠ (ṝ)	ऌ (ḷ)	ए (e)	ऐ (ai)	ओ (o)	औ (au)

Consonants

क (ka)	ख (kha)	ग (ga)	घ (gha)	ङ (ṅa)
च (ca)	छ (cha)	ज (ja)	झ (jha)	ञ (ña)
ट (ṭa)	ठ (ṭha)	ड (ḍa)	ढ (ḍha)	ण (ṇa)
त (ta)	थ (tha)	द (da)	ध (dha)	न (na)
प (pa)	फ (pha)	ब (ba)	भ (bha)	म (ma)

Semi Vowels

य (ya)	र (ra)	ल (la)	व (va)	ळ (ḻa)

Sibilants

श (śa) ष (ṣa) स (sa)

Aspirate

ह (ha)

Anusvāra and Visarga

ं (ṁ/ṃ) : (ḥ)

Ānunāsika

ँ (̃) e.g. अँ (ã) आँ (ā̃)

INTRODUCTION

1. Background

In the beginning of 1920 Prof. Caland, for the first time, came to know through the Report on the working of the peripatetic party of the Government Manuscript Library, Madras (1916-19) the existence of a manuscript called *Vādhūla-kalpavyākhyā*. Very soon he got a manuscript in Grantha script which was not very intelligible to him. However, he studied it and gave for the first time a detailed information about the *Vādhūlaśrauta-sūtra* (*VādhŚS*). The MS consisted of three different parts, viz. (i) *Kalpāgama-saṁgraha* of Āryadāsa, (ii) a very detailed part of the *Prayoga-sandarbha* or *Prayogakḷpti* of Śivaśroṇa, and (iii) a smaller part containing Gṛhya-rituals and some *Kārikās*. Caland was interested in bringing out the text of the *Vādhūlasūtra* on the basis of that MS. But, because the commentary was in piecemeal form, he found it impossible to subtract *VādhŚS* out of it. After one year, someone in Madras found an exhaustive fragment of the *Vādhūlasūtra* written in Grantha script. A Devanāgarī copy of the same was made available to Caland. On the basis of that MS, Caland published some extracts of the *VādhŚS* with the help from the *Kalpāgama-saṁgraha*. But, these extracts from *VādhŚS* were very small in number. In 1975 I also made up my mind to bring out a complete text of the *VādhŚS*. After working hard for 18 years, my edition appeared in 1993. After that I concentrated upon the *Vādhūla-anvākhyāna* and the same was published in 2002. At the time of working on *Vādhūla-anvākhyāna*, I had also copied down the entire texts of *Vādhūla-kalpāgama-saṁgraha* of Āryadāsa, *Prayogakḷpti* of Śivaśroṇa and *Vadhūlagṛhyasūtravṛtti*. It was in my mind to bring out the critical editions of all these texts. But, since the text of *Prayogakḷpti* of Śivaśroṇa was an independent text having nothing to do with the commentary of Āryadāsa, I first concentrated upon it, and now I am happy to announce the publication of that text before the scholars.

2. Critical Apparatus Used for the Present Edition

The following MSS have been used for the present critical edition of the *Prayogakḷpti* of Śivaśroṇa.

(i) ***M.*** A composite MS comprising of (i) *Vādhūlakalpa-vyākhyā* of Āryadāsa (pp. 1-377), (ii) *Prayogasandarbha* of Śivaśroṇa (pp. 377-498) and (iii) *Vādhūlagṛhyasūtra-vṛtti* of some unknown author (pp. 498-552), deposited in the Government Oriental Manuscript Library, Madras under No. R 2978; script—Devanāgarī; material—paper. It was copied from a Malayalam MS which was in possession of Nedumpilli Mana and was compared with M that of Kaḍaṅṅśśeri Mana by K.C. Venkata Subrahmanya Sastry on 13 October 1919.

(ii) ***AD***. A composite MS comprising of (i) *Vādhūla-kalpasūtra-vyākhyā* of Āryadāsa (pp. 1-772), (ii) *Śrauta-prayogakḷpti* of Śivaśroṇa (pp. 772-979) and *Gṛhyakalpasūtravṛtti* of some unknown author (pp. 982-1071), deposited in the Adyar MS Library, Madras, under No. TR6361 (Acc. No. 63371-73) in three parts. This MS is a copy of Madras MS No. R 2978, as it is clear from the colophon: मद्रपुरस्थराजकीय पुस्तकशालायां मूलमातृकायां विलिखितमिदं पुस्तकं on 18 November 1923.

(iii) ***B.*** A composite MS comprising of (i) *Vādhūla-Kalpavyākhyā* of Āryadāsa (pp. 1-211), (ii) *Prayogakḷpti* of Śivaśroṇa (pp. 212-313), deposited in the Oriental Institute, M.S. University of Baroda, under Acc. No. 13080. This MS is a transcript of MS No. R 2978, prepared in 1922. A hand-written copy of this B MS was prepared by Nana Kale of Barshi and a photostat copy of the same was supplied to me by him.

(iv) ***T.*** A composite MS comprising of (i) *Vādhūla-kalpa-sūtra-savyākhyā* (*Kalpāgama-saṁgraha*), (ii) *Prayoga-kḷpti* of Śivaśroṇa, and (iii) *Vadhūlagṛhyaprayoga*, deposited in the Oriental Research Institute and Manuscript Library, University of Kerala, Trivandrum, under Nos. 1083 (Sl. No. 16276) and T1147 (Sl. No. 12277), Devanāgarī script.

It may be pointed out that among these Devanāgarī paper MSS, M is the oldest one from which all have been transcribed. If a text is broken in M, it is shown broken in all the MSS.

Opening text is broken in all : M . . . वा भवन्त्यस्मै नमो वाधूलका-स्तुते . . . आपस्तम्बः प्रशिष्योभूद्यस्य वाधूलकस्य तु.

It appears that the first two *pāda*s and three syllables of the 3rd *pāda* of a Anuṣṭup metre are broken. Title of the text is not given in M. However, in AD it is given at the top of the page 771 by a later hand as 'श्रौतप्रयोगक्लृप्तिः'.

3. Nature of the MSS

(i) Madras MS (No. R. 2978) for the first time was transliterated into Devanāgarī from the Malayālam MS which was in possession of Nedumpilli Mana and was compared with the MS which was in possession of Kaḍaṅṅśśery Mana. Both AD and B were transcribed from M.

(ii) At the time of editing, I found that at many places there were some displacement of folios in all the MSS as given under :

a. The text beginning with अथ हुतेऽग्निहोत्रे [M p. 414, line 15; AD p. 837, line 5; B p. 243, line 10] and ending with तिसृभिराहवनीयोपायनं [M p. 416, line 1; AD p. 839, line 10; B p. 244, line 11], belonging to *Vaiśvadevaparvan*, due to displacement of folios, has come under *Brahmatva* (see fn. 2, p. 26).

b. The text beginning with °च्छिष्टमातच्य निधाय शाखामाहृत्य [M, p. 435, line 18; AD, p. 874, line 1; B, p. 261, line 3] and ending with होतुराहुतौ हुतायाम् [M, p. 440, line 1; AD, p. 882, line 1; B, p. 265, line 4] due to displacement of folios has come under *Paśubandha* in all the MSS. Actually, this text belongs to the *Varuṇapraghāsa* (see fn. 9, p. 29; fn 9, p. 46).

c. The text beginning with प्रणीतानिनयनमध्वर्योरेव [M p. 441, line 13; AD, p. 883, line 13; B, p. 266, line 2] and ending with आ गच्छेयुः [M, p. 443, line 1; AD,

p. 886, line 2; B, p. 267, line 6] has come wrongly under *Paśubandha* due to the displacement of folios. Actually this text belongs to the remaining part of the *Varuṇapraghāsa* [see fn. 9, p. 32].

d. Due to the displacement of folio in the original MS from which M was copied the text beginning with प्रणीतानिनयनं [M, p. 441, line 13; AD, p. 883, line 13; B, p. 266, line 2] belonging to the *Varuṇapraghāsa* has wrongly been copied under the *Paśubandha* (see fn. 18, p. 47).

4. Nomenclature of the Text

In the MSS we find 3 titles of the text, viz. *Prayogakḷpti, Prayogakalpanā* and *Prayogasandarbha.*

(i) ***Prayogakḷpti*** — The word *proyagakḷpti* occurs thrice in the very introductory part of the text (p. 1) : अतोऽस्मद्विधैः प्रयोगक्लृप्तिरेकान्ततो निश्चेतुमशक्या; यथामत्याधानादीनां प्रयोगक्लृप्तिर्वक्ष्यते, and ततो इदानीं प्रयोगक्लृप्तिः प्रस्तूयते. In the first and second cases, the word *prayogakḷpti* seems to denote the procedures of performing rituals. But in the third case, it is undoubtedly used for the title of the text. Nārāyaṇa Miśra, the author of the *VādhGVR* refers to this text in which many *prayoga*s have been discussed.[1]

(ii) ***Prayogakalpanā*** — This nomenclature does not appear anywhere in the body of the text. After giving the *anuvāka* number as अथ द्वितीयः in the 6th *prapāṭhaka,* MSS also give the title of the section as अथ प्रयोगकल्पना (p. 78), which, I think, is simply an indication of the beginning of the procedures of the ritual of the *Agniṣṭoma*. At the end of the 6th *Prapāṭhaka*, MSS give the colophon as: इति आचार्यशिवश्रोणस्य कृतिः प्रयोगकल्पना समाप्ता (vide p. 85).

---

1. प्रयोगक्लृप्तौ पूर्वस्यां प्रयोग बहुधोदिताः। समाचारानुसारेण प्रयोग इह कीर्त्यते ॥ *VādhGVR*. 1.4; ed Prof. B.B. Chaubey, National Manuscript Mission and D.K. Printworld, New Delhi, 2006.

Taking into consideration the nomenclature of the text,[1] as given in all the MSS in the beginning, I have accepted the reading *Prayogakḷpti* here also. The nomenclature given in the beginning by the author himself in the text has weightage over that of the scribe. The author cannot give two names of his work, one in the beginning and another at the end. Though, symantically there is no difference between the two words, yet it is proper to have *Prayogakḷpti* instead of *Prayogakalpanā* as the nomenclature of the text.

(iii) ***Prayogasandarbha*** — Another nomenclature of the text is given as *Prayogasandarbha* in all the three MSS at the end of the first *anuvāka*.[2] But in the introductory portion of the text the author attaches this title to a work of Ācārya Vādhūlaka.[3] From this statement of Śivaśroṇa, it appears that there might have been another *sandarbha*-text of Ācārya Vādhūlaka. But this text has not appeared so far. Efforts should be made to find out that text. From the reference to Vādhūlakācārya's *Sandarbha* by Śivaśroṇa, it is obvious that the said text was in existence, at least, up to the time of Śivaśroṇa. There were many *prayoga*-texts in existence belonging to each Śrauta tradition for the practical use of the ritualists. Any sacrifice could not be performed on the basis of the Śrautasūtra only. So, in each ritual-tradition such *prayoga*-texts must have been in existence. Śivaśroṇa must have consulted the *Prayogasandarbha*, prevalent in the Vādhūla-tradition. While mentioning the views of many *ācārya*s in the matters of ritualistic performances, Śivaśroṇa refers to the views of Vādhūlaka as authentic with the phrase अयमेवाचार्याभिप्रायः, etc.

5. Authorship of the Text

All the MSS unanimously mention Śivaśroṇa as the author of the text:

1. तत इदानीं प्रयोगक्लृप्तिः प्रस्तूयते। — *Prayogakḷpti*, p. 1.
2. इति शिवश्रोणस्य प्रयोगसन्दर्भे प्रथमः। — Ibid., p. 7, fn 3.
3. तथा तु मा व्यवहारोच्छित्तिरिति वाधूलकाचार्यसन्दर्भं नमस्कृत्य यथामत्याधानादीनां प्रयोगक्लृप्तिर्वक्ष्यते। Ibid. p. 1.

इति शिवश्रोणस्य प्रयोगसन्दर्भे प्रथमः at the end of the first *anuvāka* of the first *prapāṭhaka* and इति आर्यशिवश्रोणस्य कृतिः प्रयोगकल्पना समाप्ता at the end of the 6th *prapāṭhaka.* From this it is obvious that Śivaśroṇa is the author of the text.

Prof. Ikari refers to the name of the author of the text as Raghuśroṇa,[1] which, in my opinion, is due to wrong reading of the MSS in his possession. On which ground Prof. Ikari took Raghuśroṇa as the author of the text is not mentioned by him.

In the beginning of the 3rd *prapāṭhaka* all MSS give a very beautiful verse:

शोभनश्रुतिशरीरशिल्पवित्कल्पसूत्रकृदनल्पबन्धवे ।
श्रोत्रियाय शिवशब्दसमुदितश्रोणनामपरिशोभिने नमः ॥

This verse does not seem to be from the pen of the author, because salutation has been offered to Śivaśroṇa, the author of the text. Most probably this verse may have been composed by the scribe, someone among his students, to pay homage to his *guru*. According to this verse the author was a profound scholar of Vedas; he possessed the body shining with the knowledge of a *Śruti*, the Veda; he had the knowledge of *Śilpavidyā*; he was author of a *Kalpasūtra*; he was a brother of many; he had received the knowledge of the Veda through tradition; and his name was Śivaśroṇa. This verse gives a very authentic information about the scholarship of the author. His own *śākhā* was Vādhūla. Nothing more is available about the author. From the reference to a text *Prayogakḷpti*[2] by Narāyaṇa Miśra in his *VādhGVR*, it may be conjectured that he was prior to Nārāyaṇa Miśra.

6. Nature of the Text

The *Prayogakḷpti,* as its nomenclature indicates, is a *prayoga-grantha*, dealing with the sequence and procedures of Śrauta

1. Prof. Yasuke Ikari, 'A New Critical Edition of *VādhūlaŚS*'-1, Intro. p.16, fn. 45.
2. Vide, fn. 1, p. iv

sacrifices as prevalent in the Vādhūla-tradition. Prof. Ikari has referred to this text along with the *Vādhūlakalpasūtravyākhyā* of Āryadāsa as a commentary on the *VādhŚS*. But this view does not seem to be correct. The *Prayogakḷpti* is actually a *prayoga*-text dealing with the sequence and order of the Śrauta-rituals as prevalent in the Vādhūla-tradition. The aim of the author of the text is not to explain the *sūtra*s of the *VādhŚS*, but to present a systematic procedure of the rituals, so that one may perform the Śrauta sacrifices in proper systematic order. Explaining the word *kḷpti*, Āryadāsa, the commentator of the *VādhŚS,* takes it as denoting a *kalpa*. According to Āryadāsa, by word *kḷpti* one should understand a *kalpa,* because with the help of a *kalpa* only, one can understand the sequence of the ritualistic procedures. He says that references to the rituals and the applications of the *mantra*s in them are scattered throughout the *mantra*s and the Brāhmaṇas. The rituals, mentioned in one *kāṇḍa* in a specific order, are to be performed, but they are not performed in the same order in other *kāṇḍa*s. For example, at one place *śukramanthin-homa* has been prescribed before the *āgrayaṇa-graha*, but that *homa* is performed after taking of *āgrayaṇa-*, *ukthya-*, *dhruva-* and *āśvina-graha*s with the *prasthitacamasa*s. At many places only *mantra*s are given, but their Brāhmaṇa, prescribing their application, is not given. Similarly, 'दैव्या उपस्थाने छिद्रेषु' is prescribed in other recension, not given in one's own *śākhā*, but that is to be performed in one's own *śākhā*, too. Similarly, at places optional rituals have been prescribed, but which one of them is to be performed in one's own recension, must be mentioned. In such circumstances the text which gives specific instruction to be followed is called *Kḷpti*. Such *Kḷpti* cannot be made without the *Kalpasūtras*.[1] The ritualistic procedures as found in the *VādhŚS* must have undergone many changes including order of the rituals, omissions and additions of the rituals in course of time. At least, four sub-sections of the Vādhūlas had come into prevalence up to the time of Āryadāsa, who clearly mentions their names as —

---

1. कल्पाख्येन चाङ्गेन यज्ञस्य क्लृप्तिरभिधीयते। अत्राह–केयं क्लृप्तिर्नाम। उच्यते। मन्त्रब्राह्मणयोर्विसृतानां पदार्थानामभिप्रेतं कर्मण्यभिप्रेते वाऽवकाशे विनियोगः क्लृप्ति–शब्दवाच्यता – Āryadāsa on *VādhŚS* I.1.1.

Kauṇḍinya, Āgniveśya, Gālava and Śāṅkha.[1] Śivaśroṇa very politely accepts his little knowledge of rituals in comparison to the authors of the *sūtra*-texts. Even the *sūtrakāra*s were confused to know the real sense of the Vedic *mantra*s, what to say of persons like me, who does not have intelligence to know the meaning of the *mantra*s. In the matter of applications of the *mantra*s and sequence of the rituals, it is very difficult to decide. Therefore, one should perform the rituals after having consultations with experts in this matter. Śivaśroṇa had before him, the original work, *Prayogasandarbha,* prevalent in the Vādhūla-tradition, but contemporary variations in the performance were also before him. So, he wrote this text to make it clear which method he thought correct in the view of Vādhūla,[2] the propounder of the *śākhā*.

7. Arrangement and Division of the Text

The *Prayogakḷpti* follows the *prapāṭhaka*-division as followed in the *VādhŚS*. It is divided into six *prapāṭhaka*s. Since the MSS are broken in the beginning, no mention of the first *prapāṭhaka* is available. However, the end of the first *prapāṭhaka* is found mentioned in the MSS as under :

M. आधो(धा)नाख्यः प्रपाठकश्च समाप्तः (p. 394)

AD. आधो(धा)नाख्यः प्रपाठकश्च समाप्तः। (p. 802)

B. आधो(धा)नाख्यः प्रपाठकः॥ समाप्तः॥ (p. 227)

From the next *prapāṭhaka* onward, MSS do not mention the number of *prapāṭhaka*s, neither in the beginning nor at the end. There are displacements of folios in a large number. It appears that due to confusion caused by the displacement of the folios the scribe did not mention the beginning or end of the *prapāṭhaka*s. By mention of *prapāṭhaka* at the end of the first *prapāṭhaka*, it can definitely be said that the original text must have been divided into *prapāṭhaka*s. In the present edition, I have followed the *prapāṭhaka*-division and accordingly given their numbers.

---

1. के ते चत्वारो वाधूलाः। कौण्डिन्याग्निवेश्यगालवशाङ्खानां कल्पाः – *Kalpāgama-saṁgraha,* p. 3
2. See, *Prayogakḷpti*, p. 1.

Anuvāka-division — Each *prapāṭhaka* is sub-divided into *anuvākas*. But none of the MSS mention the word *Anuvāka* neither in the beginning nor at the end under the *prapāṭhakas*. They show the *anuvākas* in the beginning with phrase अथ प्रथम; अथ द्वितीयः, etc., and the end with इति प्रथमः, इति द्वितीयः, etc., without using the word *anuvāka*.

प्रथमः प्रपाठकः	अथ प्रथमः	इति प्रथमः
अग्न्याधेयः	अथ द्वितीयः	इति द्वितीयः
	अथ तृतीयः	इति तृतीयः
	अथ चतुर्थः	इति चतुर्थः
	अथ पञ्चमः	इति षष्ठः for इति पञ्चमः.
द्वितीयः प्रपाठकः	[अथ प्रथमः]	इति पुरोडाश्याख्यः प्रथमः
अथ पुरोडाशी	अथ द्वितीयः	इति द्वितीयः
	अथ तृतीयः	इति तृतीयः
	अथ चतुर्थः	[इति चतुर्थः]
	अथ पञ्चमः	इति पञ्चमः.
तृतीयः प्रपाठकः	अथ प्रथमः	[इति प्रथमः]
अथ चातुर्मास्यानि	[अथ द्वितीयः]	[इति द्वितीयः]
	[अथ तृतीयः]	[इति तृतीयः]
	अथ चतुर्थः	इति चतुर्थः
	अथ पञ्चमः	इति पञ्चमः
	अथ षष्ठः	इति षष्ठः
चतुर्थः प्रपाठकः	[अथ प्रथमः]	इति प्रथमः
[अथ पशोर्याजनम्]	अथ द्वितीयः	इति द्वितीयः
	अथ तृतीयः	इति तृतीयः
	अथ चतुर्थः	इति चतुर्थः
पंचमः प्रपाठकः	अथ प्रथमः	इति प्रथमः
[अथ ज्योतिष्टोमः]	अथ द्वितीयः	इति द्वितीयः
	अथ तृतीयः	इति तृतीयः
	अथ चतुर्थः	इति चतुर्थः
	अथ पञ्चमः	इति पञ्चमः
	अथ षष्ठः	इति षष्ठः

	अथ सप्तमः	इति सप्तमः
	अथाष्टमः	इति अष्टमो ज्योतिष्टोमः
[षष्ठः प्रपाठकः]	अथ प्रथमः	इति प्रथमः
[अथाग्निष्टोमः]	अथ द्वितीयः	इति द्वितीयः
	अथ तृतीयः	इति तृतीयः

Though all the MSS are unanimous in not using the term *anuvāka* as a sub-division under the *prapāṭhaka*s, I have used this term on the basis of *VādhŚS*.

***Paṭala*-division** — MS M displays another division within an *anuvāka* by putting sign („) without giving any number. I have given the number at each such place to show a sub-division which may be called *khaṇḍa* or *kaṇḍikā* under *anuvāka*s, as followed in the *VādhŚS* for the purpose of making reference easy.

Thus, the entire text of the *Prayogakḷpti* is divided into six *prapāṭhakas*, each *prapāṭhaka* into *anuvāka*s and each *anuvāka* into *khaṇḍa*s or *kaṇḍikā*s. This can be shown by the following chart:

Prapā	***Anu***	***Khaṇḍa***		***Prapā***	***Anu***	***Khaṇḍa***	
I.	1	9		IV	1	3	
	2	1			2	5	
	3	3			3	5	
	4	5			4	4	= 17
	5	3	= 21	V	1	8	
II	1	3			2	3	
	2	3			3	5	
	3	7			4	7	
	4	7			5	4	
	5	3	= 23		6	5	
III	1	3			7	1	
	2	7			8	2	= 35
	3	3		VI	1	6	
	4	5			2	6	
	5	2			3	4	= 16
	6	4	= 24				136

8. Contents of the Text

The text begins with the salutation to Ācārya Vādhūlaka and a laudation to Lord to grant knowledge for the accomplishment of the word and meaning, followed by a brief introduction, explaining the purpose of the text.

The first *prapāṭhaka* deals with the procedures of performing *Agnyādheya*, *Punarādhāna, Agnihotra* and *Agnyupasthāna* as prevalent in the Vādhūla tradition. In the very beginning, the sacrificer (*yajamāna*) should perform expiatory rites for becoming free from all sorts of sin. If there is some enmity with anybody, he should remove that by any means. If he has taken loan from anybody, he should return that, because a person who is under debt cannot perform any Śrauta sacrifice. If he is not able to return back the loan, he should assure the lender that at present he is unable to return it, but shall surely return back. Or, he should ask his sons or brothers to return the debt in time. This was the first code of conduct that he must obey. Before starting the *Agnyādheya*, he must see whether he has ample wealth for giving sacrificial fees to the *Ṛtvik*s and food to others. He must perform on *Upavasatha* day all rituals which have been prescribed for the *Darśapūrṇamāseṣṭi*. He must have *śamīgarbha- aśvattha*-wood for producing Agni by the ritual of *Araṇimanthana*. These are the preliminary essential rites which he must perform.

On the next day, sitting on a mat made of grass facing east, after having performed *prāṇāyāma* three times, both *yajamāna* and his wife invoke goddess Ākūti and then perform the ritual of the selection of priests called *Ṛtvig-varaṇa*. Then follows the preparation of places where *gārhapatya, anvāhāryapacana* and *āhavanīya* fires are to be set up. Materials belonging to soil and wood, required for *Agnyādhāna* are gathered. Then follow the purificatory rites of the *yajamāna* like *keśa-vapana*, nail-cutting, taking bath, and uttering of purificatory short sentences called *pāpmano vinihayaḥ* (*VādhŚS* XV.7.1-32). Then follows the setting up of the fire bringing it from the houses of different places as per desire of the sacrificer and worship of fire newly set up and sprinkling of it. This is called *amātyaparicaraṇa*. Then follows the *Amātyahoma*, partaking of the

Brahmodya by the *ṛtvik*s and worship of Agni with the chanting of *sāman*s. If chanting is not possible, he may recite the *yonimantra*s.

The second *anuvāka* prescribes the worship of *sabhya* and *āvasathya* fires daily throughout the life with *upasthāna mantra*s. The third *anuvāka* prescribes the uttering of *prāṇa-graha*s and *Pṛśni-graha*s and giving of sacrificial fees to the *ṛtvik*s. Two types of optional *vidhi*s, viz. *uddharaṇa-pakṣa* and *upasamedha-pakṣa* have been discussed. According to one view, the fires once set up are regarded as holy-ones up to the 12th day. After that they become wordly (*laukika*), not fit for offering oblations and worship. According to the other view, the setting up of fire through churning the two *araṇis* is for *āhavanīya* only, not for others, while for the setting of *anvāhārya-pacana*, *agni* is not produced through churning. It is brought from the house of others, as mentioned above. According to the other view, the three fires, once set up and kept burning up to twelve days, should be kept burning even beyond twelve days by putting *samidh*s into them. According to the author, in both the views option is equal. A person who wants to gain long life and is rich enough to continue the fires burning, he should do this. But a person who is not rich enough to continue it, he should do *Agnyuddharaṇa* and *Homa* with *mantra*s, but in other cases he may set-up fires silently without uttering *mantra*s.

The fourth *anuvāka* deals with *Punarādheya*, reinstallation of fires, which takes place, if the *Ādhāna* rite has not been successful. It is a kind of *prāyaścitta* to be performed, if the *gārhapatya* and *āhavanīya* fires have been extinguished, or discontinued. Another kind of *Punarādhāna* is also prescribed, if the fires, once set up, are extinguished and the sacrificer is not in a position to re-set them. This is called *Paroptapunarādheya*. After dealing with *Paropta-punarādheya,* the text deals with the procedures of *Agnihotra* in order of performance, also mentioning the differences in its performance among the *ācārya*s. The fifth *anuvāka* deals with the *Agnyupasthāna*. In this section the *Māhācamasopasthāna* and *Pravatsyadupasthāna* have been dealt with. It may be pointed out that the *Māhācamasopasthāna* is found only in the Vādhūla tradition, not in others. Thus, in the first *prapāṭhaka* mainly the procedures of *Agnyādheya, Punāradheya, Agnihotra* and *Agnyupasthāna* have been described.

The second *prapāṭhaka* deals with *Puroḍāśī,* another nomenclature of *Darśapūrṇamāseṣṭi* in three *anuvākas*, and the acts to be performed by the *yajamāna* himself, hence called *Yājamāna*, in the 4th *anuvāka*. The 5th *anuvāka* deals with the duties of *Brahman* priest, hence this section is called *Brahmatva.*

The 3rd *prapāṭhaka* describes the procedures of the constituents of the *Cāturmāsyeṣṭi*, viz. *Vaiśvadevaparvan* (3.1), *Varuṇapraghāsaparvan* (3.2), *Sākamedhaparvan* (3.3), *Pitṛyajña* (3.4-5) and the acts to be performed by the *yajamāna* in the *Cāturmāsya-iṣṭi* (3.6). How the *mantra*s, used in the *Prakṛti* of *Pitṛmedha*, are to be modified in the *Pitṛmedha* of *Cāturmāsya,* have been discussed. The act of modifying the wordings of the original *mantra*s to suit the context while using them in *Vikṛti-yāga*s, is called *Ūha*.

The fourth *prapāṭhaka* describes the rituals of *Paśuyāga* in four *anuvāka*s. Here also, the modifications and additions brought in the employment of *Prakṛti mantra*s to suit the context in the *Vikṛti-yāga*s have been prescribed.

The fifth *prapāṭhaka,* deals with the procedures of *Jyotiṣṭoma* beginning with the selection of *ṛtvik*s (*Ṛtvigvaraṇa*), *Dīkṣaṇīyeṣṭi* (5.1-2), *Somakraya, Ātithyeṣṭi* (5.3), and the *Pravargyopaṣad* (4). The remaining part of the 4th *anuvāka* is devoted to the measurement and preparation of *mahāvedī.* Then follows the *Havirdhāna-samvartana*, taking of two carts (*śakaṭas*) at the *mahāvedī* (5). The 6th *anuvāka* deals with *Vasatīvarīgrahaṇa*, a technical name of waters kept overnight, brought from a stream coming out of a hill by dipping a pitcher against the current before the sunset on the day before the pressing-day (*sutyā*).

The sixth *prapāṭhaka* deals with the rituals of remaining acts to be performed beginning with *prātaranuvāka,* the morning litany. In the 2nd and 3rd *anuvāka*s the *prayoga* of Soma-pressing has been given. Thus, the *Prayogakḷpti* deals with the procedures of performing rituals beginning with *Agnyādheya* to *Agniṣṭoma*.

9. Some Salient Features of the Text

(i) The text in the very beginning gives very important information not known before, through any other source, that

Agniveśya and Āpastamba were pupil and grand-pupil, respectively of Ācārya Vādhūlaka.[1] On the basis of this very information, Caland expressed his doubt about the placing of Vādhūla after Āpastamba and Baudhāyana by Mahādeva.[2] He questioned: when Āpastamba is said to be a grand-pupil of Vādhūla in the said verse, how can the former be placed earlier to the latter[3]? The information supplied by the present text establishes the anteriority of Vādhūla to the other Śrautasutrakāras, so far known.

(ii) While dealing with the ritualistic procedures of the Śrauta-sacrifices, Śivaśroṇa, at places, quotes the original *sūtra*s from the *VādhŚS*, e.g.:

अद्योपवसथ इत्यन्नमेव कुर्वीत। अपि ह गां पचेद् (*VādhŚS.* 1.1.7) — *Pra.* 1.1.2; अग्नीनाधास्ये (*VādhŚS.* 15.5.1) — *Prayoga* 1.1.7; सर्वकामोऽग्नीनाधास्ये (*VādhŚS.* 15.5.2) — *Prayoga.* 1.1.3; तत्ते ऋध्यताम्, तत्ते संवर्धतां कामः (*VādhŚS.*15.5.18) — *Prayoga* 1.1.3; अथातो विराजक्रमाः (*VādhŚS.* 3.1.28) — *Prayoga* 1.5.3; अथातो माहाचमसम् (*VādhŚS* 3.2.1)— *Prayoga* 1.5.3, etc.

(iii) The text deals with the ritualistic procedures of only the five main sacrifices, viz. *Agnyādheya, Puroḍāśī* (*Darśapūrṇamāseṣṭi*), *Cāturmāsyas Paśubandha Jyotiṣṭoma* and *Agniṣṭoma.* Remaining Śrauta-sacrifices, like *Agnicayana, Vājapeya, Rājasūya, Aśvamedha*, etc. have not been dealt with here.

(iv) In the performance of *Vikṛti-yāga*s some additions or modifications are to be made in the *Prakṛti mantra*s to suit the context of rituals to be performed. This is technically called *ūha*. Śivaśroṇa gives a large number of such *ūha-*

1. आपस्तम्बः प्रशिष्योऽभूद् यस्य वाधूलकस्य तु।
अग्निवेश्यगुरुः सोऽयमृषिरस्मानिहावतुङ्क — Prayoga. Intro. verse 1

2. *Prayogacandrikā* of Mahādeva Dīkṣita on *SatyāŚS* (XI-XVIII), Intro., p. 9; Publ. from Anandashram Sanskrit Series No. 53, Poona, 1927

3. See *Acta Orientalia*, I, p. 7. For detail see Introduction to *VādhŚS*, ed. B.B. Chaubey, pp. 57 ff.

*mantra*s while dealing with the *Pitṛyajña* under *Cāturmāsya.*

(v) While dealing with the ritualistic procedures of the Śrauta *yajña*s, Śivaśroṇa frequently gives gloss of many teachnical terms,[1] used throughout the text, e.g.:

अपानग्रहाः–अपानभृन्मन्त्राः (1.3.1)

अपिव्रताः–पुत्रा दुहितरोऽप्रत्ता भ्रातरोऽविभक्ताः। सपिण्डा इत्येके। (5.6.1)

आस्तावः–दक्षिणेन चात्वालं यत्र बहिष्पवमानेन स्तुवन्ति, यत्र ब्रह्माऽऽस्ते सदसि दक्षिणेन होत्रकान्। (5.8.1), etc.

(vi) Śivaśroṇa refers to some authorities in his work. In the very beginning, he refers to Ācārya Vādhūlaka, Agniveśya, and Āpastamba. Āpastamba is the author of the *Śrauta-*, *Gṛhya-*, *Śulba-* and *Dharma-Sūtras*. Agniveśya is the author of a *Gṛhyasūtra.* According to Āryadāsa, Agniveśya was propounder of one of the four sub-*śākhā*s of the Vādhūlas,[2] the other three being Kauṇḍinya, Śāṅkhya and Gālava. Śivaśroṇa once quotes the view of Kauṇḍinyas, according to whom, the two *praiṣa*s, related to putting the materials for *Anvāhārya-pacana* and *Agnyupasthāna,* are to be done by *Adhvaryu,*[3] whereas, according to Śivaśroṇa, *Agninivapana* is done by *yajamāna* silently.[4] *Adhvaryu* puts a piece of gold (*hiraṇyaśalka*) in the middle, and *yajamāna* offers homage to fire. He once mentions वाधूलकेषु in plural. Śivaśroṇa holds that among the Vādhūlakas an implement called *śulbiṇī* of a particular shape was used to cover the navel

1. For the complete list of such glosses see Index I.
2. चतुर्णां वाधूलानामिति। के ते चत्वारो वाधूलाः ? कौण्डिन्याग्निवेश्यगालवशाङ्खानां कल्पाः। तथा हि शुल्ब उक्तम्–वाधूलकाः सवाधूलाश्चत्वारो विहिताः क्रमादिति। — Āryadāsa on *VādhŚS* 1.1.5; Critical edition of the *Kalpāgama-saṁgraha* (under preparation).
3. प्रैषावुभावाध्वर्यौ वचनाद्ध्येतत् कौण्डिन्यानाम्। — *Prayoga.* 1.2.9
4. अग्निनिवपनं तूष्णीकं याजमानं च। — *Prayoga.* 1.2.9

of the *uttaranābhi* along with *karaṇī*.[1] This word is not found used elsewhere throughout the Vedic literature, published so far.

(vii) Śivaśroṇa does not mention any specific text on rituals by name. However, he once makes references to the texts like *Mantra, Brāhmaṇa, Samānatantra, Caratantra,* and *Nyāyaśāstra* as the sources of his work.[2]

(viii) Śivaśroṇa, at places, discusses the controversies regarding the performance of the rituals and at such places he refers to the different views of the *ācārya*s by simply using the phrase इत्येके, इत्यन्ये, इति केचित्, इत्यपरे. The list of such different opinions expressed by the phrases इति केचित्, इत्यन्ये, इत्यपरे and इत्येके is given here below for ready reference:

इति केचित्—'अहं त्वदस्मि' इत्याध्वर्यवमिति **केचिद्** – १.१.८

'यास्ते अग्ने शिवास्तनुवस्ताभिस्त्वामादधे' इति **केचिद्** समापयन्ति – १.१.९

प्रतीकग्रहणान्येतानीति **केचित्** – १.३.१

उदितहोमी जुहोतीति **केचित्** – १.४.३

केचिदत्र न प्राचीनावीतत्वमिच्छन्ति (१.४.४)

चरव्यानध्येतानपि विश्राव्य **केचित्** निदधति (२.२.१)

श्रृते **केचित्** पूर्वावदेये पूर्ववदेव तमभिपूरयन्ति (२.२.१)

केचिद् इडालेपादेवोपस्तृणन्त्यभिघारयन्ति च (२.३.४)

फाल्गुनशुक्लचतुर्दश्यामग्निहोत्रोच्छिष्टमातच्य निदधातीत्यादि प्रतिपद्यन्त इति **केचित्** –३.१.१

प्रतिप्रस्थाता आमिक्षाश्रपणीं च **केचित्** (३.२.३)

'पयो वामग्नी' इति पृथगेव मध्यमे परिधी अन्वारभ्य 'आ नू ह' इति **केचित्** (३.६.२)

---

1. उत्तरवेदेः पूर्वस्य करण्या अन्तिके शुल्बिणीनामोत्तरनाभिच्छादनार्थं वाधूलकेषु प्रसिद्धः कश्चिदाकृतिविशेषः। — *Prayoga.* V.4.6
cf शुल्बिण्या प्रावृत्य. — *VādhŚS* VI.13.55.

2. मन्त्रब्राह्मणसमानतन्त्रचरतन्त्रन्यायशास्त्रग्रन्थादिषु...। — *Prayoga* p. 1

सह यूपाहवनीयाभ्यामिति **केचित्** (४.२.२)
फलीकरणहोमं चात्र **केचित्** जुह्वति (५.२.२).
तथा सत्यविकृतः प्रैष इति **केचित्** (५.६.२)
आग्नीध्र एवाज्यानि गृह्णीयादिति **केचित्** (५.६.३)

इत्यन्ये— द्वयोरप्याग्न्याधेयिकमि**त्यन्ये** (१.३.१)
यजमानस्यैव कश्चिद् व्रतकाल **इत्यन्ये** (२.२.३)
यथोपपादमि**त्यन्ये** (२.३.४)
अनुयज्ञैरित्याध्वर्यवमि**त्यन्ये** (३.१.२)
प्रहरिष्यमाणमभिध्यायती**त्यन्ये** (३.४.२)
अतीत्य. . . या भावाल्लुप्यत **इत्यन्ये** (३.४.२)
'स्वधा नम' इत्यनुमन्त्रयत **इत्यन्ये** (३.४.५)
निर्वर्तनमन्थनमि**त्यन्ये** (४.२.१)
सह शामित्रेण **चेत्यन्ये** (४.२.२)
गौरित्येकेऽन्वाहार्य **इत्यन्ये** (४.३.२)
एका पयस्यायै **इत्यन्ये** (५.१.२)
समुच्चीयते ह **इत्यन्ये** (५.३.२)
दक्षिणाग्नावपि **इत्यन्ये** (५.४.२)
शाकलान्येवेध्मकाष्ठान्युपसत्स्वपि **इत्यन्ये** (५.४.२)
नैष स्नाननियम **इत्यन्ये** (५.६.१)
अग्नीदेवाधिश्रयणान्तं प्राकृतं तन्त्रं कुर्याद् **इत्यन्ये** (५.६.२)
अस्यैव कश्चित् प्रैष ब्रूयाद् **इत्यन्ये** (५.६.२)
तेषु पक्षेषु तयोः पक्षयोस्तदर्थान् आज्यसंयुक्ता लाजा **इत्यन्ये** (६.१.३)

इत्यपरे — न प्रतीकग्रहणम् **इत्यपरे** (१.२.१)
येषां पावमानेष्टिकम् **इत्यपरे** (१.३.१)
तमध्वर्यवे दत्त्वाऽन्यं ब्रह्मण **इत्यपरे** (१.३.२)
यथालाभमशनम् **इत्यपरे** (१.३.२)
शेषपक्षापेक्षमेतदुत्तरस्य पक्षान्तरत्वाय **इत्यपरे** (१.३.२)
अविशेषेण सर्वेषाम् **इत्यपरे** (१.४.३)

अध्वर्युर् **इत्यपरे** (१.४.५)

'धान्यमसि' इति च सर्वत्रानुषज्यत **इत्यपरे** (२.२.१)

सर्वत्रैतद् **इत्यपरे** (२.२.२)

न लुप्यत **इत्यपरे** (२.२.३)

यथापाठम् **इत्यपरे** (२.२.३)

यजमान **इत्यपरे** (२.२.३)

आज्यस्थाल्या **इत्यपरे** (२.३.४)

चतुर्धाकृतं चेद्व्यादिष्टं स्वभागं वेदेनोपस्तरणाभि...**इत्यपरे** (२.३.४)

होतैव **इत्यपरे** (२.३.४)

सादनमग्रेणैव परिहरणम् **इत्यपरे** (२.३.४)

न पर्याहरणम् **इत्यपरे** (२.३.५)

अग्नीत्समिधमाधायाग्नीन् संमार्ष्टि **इत्यपरे** (२.३.५)

समिष्टयजुषोऽनन्तरम् **इत्यपरे** (२.३.५)

पृथग्याजमानाः प्रकृत्यर्था **इत्यपरे** (२.३.७)

सकृद्वाच्यमानोऽभिमन्त्रयेत **इत्यपरे** (२.४.३)

अध्वर्युरेव **इत्यपरे** (२.५.३)

एवं 'वायव स्थोपायवस्थ' इति संदिग्धेष्वेकम् **इत्यपरे** (३.१.१)

दारुपात्रमेव **इत्यपरे** (३.१.१)

श्रुतमन्त्राभ्याम् **इत्यपरे** (३.१.१)

समुच्चय **इत्यपरे** (३.१.२)

स्तरणाभिघारणे **इत्यपरे** (३.१.२)

लोहितायसस्ताम्रमय अयोविकार कश्चिद् **इत्यपरे** (३.१.३)

शलल्यैव **इत्यपरे** (३.१.३)

वैश्वदेव एव प्रसुनियमो नोत्तरेषु पर्वसु **इत्यपरे** (३.२.१)

चतस्रो यथाप्रकृति **इत्यपरे** (३.२.१)

कल्याणकर्मणः सपिण्डा **इत्यपरे** (३.२.३)

पञ्चहोता अध्वर्योरेव **इत्यपरे** (३.२.४)

यथाप्रकृत्येव प्रेष्यन्नैवोहेद् **इत्यपरे** (३.२.४)

अध्वर्योरेव **इत्यपरे** (३.२.५)

न शमीवर्जं करीरसक्तूनां शेषकार्याणि विद्यत **इत्यपरे** (३.२.५)

न चास्य मन्त्रस्य ऊह इहे**त्यपरे** (३.४.३)

यथाप्रकृति **इत्यपरे** (३.४.५)

यावत्प्रयोगम् **इत्यपरे** (३.६.१)

आध्वर्यवम् **इत्यपरे** (४.१.२)

सह ब्रह्मयजमानाभ्यां च **इत्यपरे** (४.२.२)

अध्वर्युरेव **इत्यपरे** (४.२.३)

स्वयमेव परिक्रम्यात्याक्रम्य परिहृतामेवादायाश्रावयेद् **इत्यपरे** (४.२.५)

गोश्चान्वाहार्यश्च **इत्यपरे** (४.३.२)

नैवमूहेद् **इत्यपरे** (४.४.२)

अपरेणैव प्राग्वंशं पत्नीशालाया **इत्यपरे** (५.१.२)

अन्यद् **इत्यपरे** (५.१.३)

नैय्याग्रोधानि **इत्यपरे** (५.१.३)

ग्रामस्य दीक्षितः स्याद् **इत्यपरे** (५.१.४)

ग्रामे दीक्षितस्यैवैतन्मन्त्रद्वयम् **इत्यपरे** (५.१.४)

व्यवस्थितोऽयं विकल्प **इत्यपरे** (५.१.७)

एवं जपेद् **इत्यपरे** (५.१.८)

पूर्वं स्वयमेव जपित्वा उत्तरं वाचित **इत्यपरे** (५.१.८)

स्निहानं स्नेहमश्रुनिष्ठीवितम् **इत्यपरे** ५.१.८

तस्यैव चर्मण उत्तरार्धे तस्याभ्याशे प्रदेशान्तर **इत्यपरे** (५.३.१)

अत्र ग्रन्थ एवैष विकल्पनामात्राध्यायी **इत्यपरे** (५.३.५)

दीक्षामेवैताव् **इत्यपरे** (५.३.५)

अनुयाजविकारा **इत्यपरे** (५.४.१)

नैव क्वचिदभ्यादध्याद् **इत्यपरे** (५.४.२)

न तरेत्तु याजोऽर्धसमिद्भिश्च **इत्यपरे** (५.४.७)

नेत्यपरे (५.४.७)

यजमान एवोद्वपनानि निबाधत **इत्यपरे** (५.५.३)

प्रैषखण्डश्च **इत्यपरे** (५.६.१)
प्रयोजनमनसां प्रैष **इत्यपरे** (५.६.२
सर्वविरुद्धमाज्यग्रहणान्तं प्रतिप्रस्थातुर् **इत्यपरे** (५.६.३)
नात्र प्रणीता **इत्यपरे** (६.१.१)
पिष्टा एव प्रभ्वाज्यसंयुक्ता **इत्यपरे** (६.१.३)
पशुभ्य **इत्यपरे** (६.२.५)
यजमानेनापि सर्वैः सह जपनीया **इत्यपरे** (६.२.६)

इत्येके — य उत्तरो द्वादशाहस्तत्रैव ते नियमा **इत्येके** (१.३.२)
पञ्चममुन्नयनं पञ्चावत्तिनाम् **इत्येके** (१.४.२)
याजमानम् **इत्येके** (२.१.३)
तथोत्तरपूर्वमुत्तरेषां कपालानां निर्वर्तनप्रतिनोदने न स्तः **इत्येके** (२.२.१)
पुरोडाशविषयमेवाभिमर्शनम् **इत्येके** (२.२.१)
यथादेवतमभिचारम् **इत्येके** (२.२.३)
यजमान **इत्येके** (२.२.३)
एवमेकविंशति दारूण्यभ्याधेयानि **इत्येके** (२.३.१)
चतुर्धा कृत्व **इत्येके** (२.३.४)
अपरेण सर्वान् कर्तॄन् दम्पती च **इत्येके** (२.३.५)
अनेन मन्त्रेण होमानन्तरं निवर्तयेद् **इत्येके** (२.३.६)
यजमानभागप्राशनवर्जम् **इत्येके** (२.३.७)
प्राडेत्योपसमिधमादाय व्रतं विसृजेद् **इत्येके** (२.३.७)
अध्वर्युर् **इत्येके** (२.४.३; ४)
नैकस्याम् **इत्येके** (२.४.४)
अपेषणं पौष्ण**स्यैके** (३.१.१)
विकल्प **इत्येके** (३.१.१)
अध्वर्युरेवोभयानि पात्राणि सादयित्वा सहैव प्रोक्षेद् **इत्येके** (३.२.३)
पञ्चहोतुर् **इत्येके** (३.२.३)
अविभक्ता सपिण्डा **इत्येके** (३.२.३)

उभयोः पृथगेव फलीकरणहोम **इत्येके** (३.२.५)

अभिहोमो जुह्वासद्याज्यस्थाल्य अवदाय अपूर्वेण **इत्येके** (३.२.६)

नैव वेदिकरणम् **इत्येके** (३.३.२)

दारुपात्र्याम् **इत्येके** (३.३.२)

तेन नमस्कार **इत्येके** (३.३.३)

यथाप्रकृत्येव **इत्येके** (३.४.१)

नास्ति प्रच्छेदनाभिमर्शनम् **इत्येके** (३.४.१)

पात्र्याम् ए**के** धाना उद्वासयन्ति (३.४.१)

प्रणीतेऽग्नौ तस्याभिहिता भविष्यन्ति **इत्येके** (३.४.१)

यज्ञोपवीती**त्येके** (३.४.१)

अन्वाहार्यपचनम् **इत्येके** (३.४.२)

सकृदवहत्य त्रिष्फलीक्रियां भर्जनीया **इत्येके** (३.४.२)

उपभृति द्वे षट् गृह्णीते एकम् **इत्येके** (३.४.३)

नानाग्नेयविकारस्येदमभिघारणम् **इत्येके** (३.४.३)

'वर्षप्रविष्टस्तमङ्ध्वम्' **इत्येके** (३.४.३)

भर्जनानन्तरमेवोभयमम्बरीषान् मन्त्रेणोद्वासयेद् **इत्येके** (३.४.३)

अपरेण **इत्येके** (३.४.३)

यजमानस्य. . . ननं वर्जयित्वा **इत्येके** (३.४.४)

'स्वाहा' इत्यनुमन्त्रणमन्त्रो लुप्यत **इत्येके** (३.४.५)

अत्रापि **इत्येके** (३.५.१)

विकार **इत्येके** (३.५.१)

'आ देवपितृयजं वह' **इत्येके** (३.५.१)

उपभृत्येवम् **इत्येके** (३.५.२)

इति विक्रियेत **इत्येके** (३.५.२)

एवं 'देवान् पितृन् हविष' इत्यङ्गविकार **इत्येके** ह्वयति (३.५.२)

'देवपितृयज्यायै' नात्र विकार **इत्येके** ह्वयति (३.५.२)

'जेमानं महिमानं गमेयमि'ति महेन्द्रयाजिनाम् **इत्येके** (३.६.१)

वाजिनयागोऽपूर्वसान्नाय्यविकार **इत्येके** (३.६.१)

निस्तक्षणीय **इत्येके** (४.१.१)
खनन्**त्येके** उपरविभागान्वयात् (४.१.१)
शास्त्रप्रसिद्धमष्टग्रहणम् **इत्येके** (४.१.२)
'पृथिवीजन्मना आज्यस्थालीनाम्ना' इत्यूहित्वा सादयेद् **इत्येके** (४.१.२)
निस्तूष्णि **इत्येके** (४.२.१)
सहाज्यैश्चैके (४.२.२)
दृंहणवर्जमर्थलोप **इत्येके** (४.२.४)
न ध्रुवाम् **इत्येके** (४.२.४)
अर्थलुप्तमदानाधिश्रयणे चार्थलुप्ते **इत्येके** (४.३.१)
प्राशित्रपक्षे पुरोडाशस्य नास्ति परिहरणम् **इत्येके** (४.३.२)
दक्षिणस्या यौष्णः सव्यायाः श्रोण्या **इत्येके** (४.३.३)
वाचयिताऽध्वर्युर् **इत्येके** (४.३.४)
ग्रहणाभावादत्र नाभिमन्त्रणम् **इत्येके** (४.४.२)
'ध्रुवा' इति सन्नमयेद् **इत्येके** (४.४.२)
'अहम्' इत्येके सन्नमयन्ति (४.४.२)
न ते पक्षान्तरे नापि यजमानभाग प्राशनम् **इत्येके** (४.४.३)
तिस्र **इत्येके** (५.१.२)
अर्थविरुद्धमुपवेषोद्वासनम् **इत्येके** (५.१.५)
उपस्थापिता ब्रूयाद् **इत्येके** (५.१.६)
आमुष्यायण इति त्रिप्रवरमेके ब्रुवते (५.१.७)
अदितिमिष्ट्वा 'मरुतो यद्धवो दिवः' इति मारुती **इत्येके** (५.२.२)
कृष्णाजिनस्तरणमात्रमध्वर्युरेव **इत्येके** (५.३.३)
विमुच्यैवापरेण सोमवाहनमतिगमयेद् **इत्येके** (५.३.३)
तेनागत्येक्षोर् **इत्येके** (५.३.४)
शाकलानीध्मकाष्ठानि **इत्येके** (५.३.४)
पञ्च एव मुष्टयो न तूष्णीक **इत्येके** (५.३.४)
मन्त्रेण राजानं प्रपादयेद् **इत्येके** (५.३.४)

विकृतिविषयावेताव् **इत्येके** (५.३.५)

प्रस्तरेणैवोपसन्नह्य निदधाति **इत्येके** (५.३.५)

प्रयाजविकारास्ता वाचनिकोऽत्राघार **इत्येके** (५.४.१)

अथाध्वर्युर्वा तन्त्रं सर्वं कुर्याद् **इत्येके** (५.४.१)

अथाध्वर्युणैव निरुप्तस्याधिश्रयणमात्रमग्नीत् कुर्याद् **इत्येके** (५.४.२)

यथाप्रकृति **इत्येके** (५.४.२)

द्वाव् **इत्येके** (५.४.२)

उपांशुयाजनपक्षे एके सादयन्ति (५.४.२)

संसृज्यान्त्यायां प्रतिपादयेद् **इत्येके** (५.४.३)

तूष्णीम् **इत्येके** (५.४.३)

'पृथिवीजन्मनाऽज्यस्थालीनाम्ना' **इत्येके** (५.४.३)

प्रक्रमा एव **इत्येके** (५.४.३)

त्रीवेद्यन्तादपरतोऽर्धप्रक्रममवशिष्योत्तरवेदिं मिमीत **इत्येके** (५.४.५)

निरन्तरमेव दशकम् **इत्येके** (५.४.५)

निरन्तरमेव दशकव्यासम् **इत्येके** (५.४.५)

प्रदर्शनार्थयजुरादिवचनम् **इत्येके** (५.४.६)

प्राकृतोऽयं प्रैषखण्ड **इत्येके** (५.४.७)

तथोत्तरस्य हविर्धानस्य कुर्याद् **इत्येके** (५.५.१)

विमित एव विमितायामायतनप्रदेशाभ्यामधिकविस्ताराणि छदींषि कृत्वा तैरेव कुर्याद् **इत्येके** (५.५.१)

वर्त्मन्यां वर्त्मनि जुह्वच्चक्रमभिजुहुयाद् **इत्येके** (५.५.१)

तथा यूपार्थमनियम **इत्येके** (५.५.२)

नवच्छदीत्यादीनामन्यतमं क्रत्वर्थमपि **इत्येके** (५.५.२)

एकैकम् **इत्येके** (५.५.३)

आग्नीध्रियो धिष्णियो मध्ये आग्नीध्रागारस्य मध्याद्दक्षिणतोऽरत्निमात्र **इत्येके** (५.५.४)

सपिण्डा **इत्येके** (५.६.१)

हविरासादनस्थानं च वर्जयित्व **इत्येके** (५.६.२)
प्राकृतमधिश्रयणमात्रमग्नीत् कुर्याद् **इत्येके** (५.६.२)
प्राक्तने एव प्रस्तरतिरश्ची **इत्येके** (५.६.२)
अग्नीद् **इत्येके** (५.६.२)
स्वयमेव मन्त्रं ब्रुवन्नञ्जलिमात्रेण दम्पती उपस्थापयति **इत्येके** (५.६.३)
वसतीवर्य आज्येभ्योऽभ्यन्तरा **इत्येके** (५.६.४)
अध्वर्यवे राजानमित्येतत् कुर्याद् **इत्येके** (५.६.४)
दक्षिणेनोत्तरवेद्या **इत्येके** (५.६.५)
यजमानः प्रपादयेद् **इत्येके** (५.६.५)
'स्वाहोरोरन्तरिक्षात्' इति कनिष्ठिके **इत्येके** (५.६.५)
क्रीते राजनि प्राक् प्रवणात् प्रोह्य **इत्येके** (५.६.५)
अनित्याव् **इत्येके** (५.७.१)
अध्वर्युरेवानुदिशति **इत्येके** (५.८.१)
आधवनीयपूतभृतोर्योगः पात्रयागकाल **इत्येके** (५.८.१)
प्रातरेवोद्वास्य प्रवर्ग्यं प्रागाहवनीयस्य प्रणयनाच्छाखाहरणे वत्सापाकरणं च **इत्येके** (५.८.२)
बर्हिः संभरेत पूर्ववद् **इत्येके** (५.८.२)
वेदिकरणाभिमन्त्रणपरिस्तरणानि त्वग्नीत्कुर्याद् **इत्येके** (५.८.२)
पुरोडाशेडान्ते वाजिनेन चरेद् **इत्येके** (५.८.२)
ब्रह्मसदस्यन्ते ब्रह्मसदस्ययोरेवैष जप **इत्येके** (६.१.१)
फलकयोश्चर्म चर्मणि ग्राव्णो ग्रावसु राजानम् **इत्येके** (६.१.२)
माहेन्द्रस्य स्तोत्रे तार्तीयसवनीयान् **इत्येके** (६.१.२)
प्राशित्रहरणं पिष्टोद्वपनीं च प्रणीताप्रणयनं चैकेषाम् (६.१.३)
अथ हविष्कृदाह्वानाद् यवानवहन्याद् **इत्येके** (६.१.३)
पिष्टयवागूर् **इत्येके** (६.१.३)
प्रथममर्थलुप्तमन्त्रेण आलोडनं कुर्याद् **इत्येके** (६.१.४)
महावेद्याम् **इत्येके** (६.१.४)
सन्तर्पणं कलशात् निग्राभ्या **इत्येके** (६.१.५)

चत्वारोऽभिषोतार **इत्येके** (६.२.१)
उन्नेता कलशाद् **इत्येके** (६.२.१)
मनसेत्युपांशुत्वे पत्नीसंमनसैव **इत्येके** (६.२.१)
विप्रुड्ढोमेऽनुचरी **इत्येके** (६.२.३)
तद्व्याघारणमाग्नीध्रीयं होत्रीयं मार्जालीयं च नाभिजुहुयाद् **इत्येके** (६.२.४)
'इदम्' स्थाने प्राणादीन् निदध्यात्, 'इदम्' इत्येव **इत्येके** (६.२.५)
अनासिच्य **इत्येके** (६.२.५)
यावदुक्तम् **इत्येके** (६.२.५)
पशुभ्य **इत्येके** यथा अपां पशूनुन्मृजे इति (६.२.५)
ग्रहावकाशचरणं याजमानम् **इत्येके** (६.२.५)
अध्वर्युः प्रतिप्रस्थाता उभावपि द्वे द्वे **इत्येके** (६.२.६)
अध्वर्युर्यजमानश्च पूर्वया द्वारा प्रतिपद्येते **इत्येके** (६.३.१)
दशापवित्रेण परिमार्गो हिरण्यशल्कश्रयणं च प्रतिग्रहेषु **इत्येके** (६.३.२)
अध्वर्युरेव मन्त्रेण निष्क्रामति **इत्येके** (६.३.२)
द्वितीय **इत्येके** (६.३.२)

(ix) Besides giving the views of other ritualists by using the phrases इत्यन्ये, इत्यपरे and इत्येके in matter of ritualistic controversies, Ācārya Śivaśroṇa also gives the views of Vādhūlaka by using respectful phrases like आचार्याभिप्रेतः (५.२.२), आचार्याभिहितम् (५.१.५); आचार्येणेष्टम् (१.२.१; ६.१.६) and कल्पकाराभिप्रायः (५.८.१; २). If some views expressed by other *ācārya*s seem to go against the view of Ācārya Vādhūlaka, he expressly states नाचार्याभिप्रायः, नाभिप्रेतं वा इदमाचार्यस्य (२.३.४).

(x) At many places, Śivaśroṇa appears as giving his own judgement by using the terms ज्यायः, ज्याय इव, ज्यायान्,

ज्यायान् इव–

ज्यायः — एतदेव ज्यायः (१.३.२); अन्वासङ्ग एव ज्यायः (३.४.१); तदेव ज्यायः (३.४.१; ४.३.३; ४.२; ५.६.४; ६.१.२), एतदेव ज्यायः (३.४.४; ५.२; ५.४.७); परिहरणमेव ज्यायः (४.३.२); नवकं तु ज्यायः (५.३.५); स्नाननियम इति ज्यायः (५.६.१); अध्वर्युरिति ज्यायः (५.६.२); परिवाप इति ज्यायः न पिष्ट यवागूः (६.१.३); कलशादिति ज्यायः (६.१.५); पूर्वोक्तमेव ज्यायः (६.२.१); उन्नेतैवेति ज्यायः (६.२.१), प्राणमित्येव ज्यायः (६.२.५); यथापाठमिति ज्यायः (६.२.५); उभावपीति ज्यायः (६.३.२)।

ज्यायान् — सन्नाम एव ज्यायान् (३.२.४); तन्त्रमेव ज्यायान् (३.२.५); भाव एव ज्यायान् (३.३.२); पूर्वतनपक्षो ज्यायान् (३.४.१); द्वे इति ज्यायान् (३.४.२); अविकार एव ज्यायान् (४.४.२); स एव पक्षो ज्यायान् (५.१.७)।

ज्यायइव — ज्याय इवाभाति (४.१.२)।

—o—

॥ श्रीः ॥

[१]आचार्य-शिवश्रोणकृता वाधूलशाखीया

श्रौतप्रयोगक्लृप्तिः

॥ अथ प्रथमः प्रपाठकः ॥

[प्रस्तावना[१]]

आपस्तम्बः प्रशिष्योऽभूद्यस्य वाधूलकस्य तु।
अग्निवेश्यगुरुः सोऽयमृषिरस्मानिहावतु[२]॥ १॥

स्थित्युत्पत्तिलया भवन्ति जगतो यस्येच्छया सर्वदा
यद्रूपं ह्यभवच्चराचरमिदं यश्चापि सर्वालयम्।
यस्माद् यान्ति परां गतिं पटुधियो[३] [मोक्षात्मिकां] दुर्लभाम्,
सोऽस्मासु प्रतिपत्तिमर्थवचसोः[४] प्रज्ञां च दिश्यात् प्रभुः॥ २॥

कल्पसूत्रकाराणां वीतकल्मषाणां विदितवेदितव्यानां वेदार्थान् प्रति [सं-][५]शेरते मतयः, किमङ्ग पुनरलक्षधियां मादृशाम्। अतोऽस्मद्विधैः प्रयोग-क्लृप्तिरेकान्ततो निश्चेतुमशक्या। तथा तु मा व्यवहारोच्छित्तिरिति वाधूल-काचार्यसन्दर्भं नमस्कृत्य यथामत्याधानादीनां[६] प्रयोगक्लृप्तिर्वक्ष्यते, न तु ज्ञानाभिमानेन। अतो नास्माकमपराधः।

अभिहितोऽपि[७] प्रयोगो नास्माभिरेकान्ततो निश्चीयते। अतः पुनरपि सद्भिः सम्यग् विचार्यानुष्ठेयम्। [८]मन्त्रब्राह्मणसमानतन्त्रचरतन्त्रन्यायशास्त्रग्रन्थादिष्व-भिहितानि अविशेषाद्, [९]यथाबुद्ध्यस्माभिरुपसंह्रियन्ते। तत इदानीं प्रयोग-क्लृप्तिः प्रस्तूयते॥

१-१. Not given in MSS. Ad, however, gives the title of the text by some later hand as श्रौतप्रयोगक्लृप्तिः. २. M °हाचतुं, Ad °हावतुं. ३. M Ad broken between धियो and दुर्लभाम्. B does not show sign of broken text. ४. M °मर्थ प्रति पत्ति पत्तिमर्थचमसोः, °चमसोः has been corrected by later hand as (वच) सोः, Ad प्रतिपत्तिमर्थचम(वच)सोः. ५. M Ad B om. ६. M Ad B °धना°. ७. M °हितो वि, but वि corrected as पि, Ad °हितोऽपि वि. ८. M °चरत्तन्त्र. ९. M Ad °ध्य°.

[1] ॥ अथ अग्न्याधेयम् ॥

अथ प्रथमोऽनुवाकः[1]

अग्नीन् आधास्यमानः[2] प्रायश्चित्तादिभिः पूर्वमेव वीतकल्मषमात्मानं कुर्वीत। येनास्य विरोधः केनचित् कारणेन तेन चाविरोधम् आपादयेद् येनकेनचिदभ्युपायेन। यान्यृणान्युत्तमर्णत्वनिमित्तेनावस्थितानि[3], तानि च तस्मै दद्याद्, अनुज्ञापयीत वा। याश्चाग्न्याधेयदक्षिणा एका देया इत्येवमाद्याः, उपबर्हणं ददातीत्येवमाद्याश्च, यथासंभवं केनचिद्विकल्पेनोपकल्पनीयाः। ऋत्विजश्चोद्गातृपञ्चमा उद्गात्रका[4] वा, चत्वारो वरणाय अवस्थापयितव्याः। अन्नदानार्थानि साधनानि यथाशक्त्युपकल्प्य तस्याग्न्याधेयस्य[5] सुभिक्षतार्थैः[6] सुभिक्षताश्चाग्न्याधेयस्य कर्त्तव्याः[7]। अथेयमन्नदक्षिणा[8] इत्याग्रयणादीनां भूयिष्ठान्नदानमभिहितम्। भूयिष्ठदानाद्धि सुभिक्षता भवन्ति। अथ दानात् पुनरस्य उपबर्हणं ददातीति प्रतिपुरुषं विहिता॥ [१]

आ द्वादशं[9] ददातीति च सर्वेषाम् अस्मिन्नेव ब्राह्मणे विहिता। शाखान्तर आम्नाता एका देया[10], तिस्रो देया इत्युपक्रम्यापरिमितं देयमिति विकल्पा बहवः सन्ति। तेषु च सत्स्वपि भूयिष्ठान्नदानमभिहितम्। कल्पकारेणाप्येतदभिहितम्—अद्योपवसथ इत्यन्नमेव कुर्वीत, अपि ह गां पचेद् (वाधूश्रौ. १.१.७-८) इति। उपवसथो नाम याजमानीयेऽहनि प्रधानकर्म क्रियते, ततः पूर्वेद्युरुच्यते। यथा दर्शपूर्णमासयोर्यस्मिन् देवता यथा च सोमस्य यस्मिन्नैन्द्र आलभ्यते पशुः, एवमेवान्यत्रापि पूर्वेद्युरभिधीयत उपवसथशब्देन। अस्मिन् अन्नदाने श्रद्धायुक्तः स्यात्। मांसमप्यत्र कुर्वीत, गौरप्यालब्धव्या। आधास्यमानस्येच्छा[11] यदि संजायेत [तदैव][12] संभवोऽन्यथा हिंसाया दोष आशङ्क्येत। एवं त्रिचतुरः पराध्यें‍षु मासेषु।[13] [14][शमीगर्भा]रण्योश्चोपादानं कर्तव्यम् अग्न्युत्पत्तिसामर्थ्याय। शमीगर्भाभावे यस्य कस्यचिदश्वत्थस्योष्मणि यदश्व [. . . .][14] अशुभाभावार्थं कतिपयेषु दिवसेषु सकलं यथाकथञ्चिदादाय काले च मन्त्रेण [. . . .][15] शालार्थे विविक्ते प्रदेशे शौचवत्तरे [. . . .][16] मवका [. . . .][17] वन्तं कारयेत्।

१-१. M Ad B not mentioned. २. Ad B °मान. ३. M Ad B °निर्मलत्वेना°. ४. M Ad B उद्गातृका. ५. M Ad B तस्याधेयस्य. ६. M Ad B भिक्षि. ७. M Ad B कर्तव्यः. ८. M Ad अथेम°, B अथेमं नद°. ९. M Ad द्वादशेभ्यो, B द्वादशे. १०. B देयाः. ११. M Ad B आधस्य°. १२. M Ad B broken. १३. M Ad B मांसेषु. १४. M Ad B broken. १५. M Ad B broken. १६. M Ad B broken. १७. M Ad B broken.

पूर्वमेव द्वारे दक्षिणा [. . . .][१] **तां, अथ यथावर्णं वसन्तादिषु यदा**[२] **श्रद्धावित्ते**[३] **स्याताम्**[४], **तां रोहिण्यादिषु नक्षत्रेषु पर्वणि वा वाक्यशुक्लशुद्धवाससौ दम्पती शुचौ देशे दर्भेष्वासीनौ प्राङ्मुखौ शुद्धान्तःकरणौ भूत्वा तद्गतमानसौ**[४] **प्राणायामत्रयं कृत्वा** या पुरस्तात् प्र स्रवन्ती **इति श्रद्धामाहूय** आकूत्यै त्वा, कामाय त्वा **इत्येवमादिभिस्तिसृभिः** आकूतिं देवीम् [५]**इत्याकूत्यायावेदनं कृत्वा येनकेनचिद्विधानेन चतुरो वा महर्त्विजो वृणीयाताम्। ब्रह्मवरणे ह्येवाग्नीध्रो**[६] **वृतो भवति। उद्गातुरभावे त्रीनेव॥ [२]**

तत्र प्रार्थनामन्त्रं वा लौकिकं कृत्वाऽर्हयेत्। सोमाधान एव विधानेन वरणमिति केचित्। निदेशविहितैरेव[७] **मन्त्रैर्वृणीयात्**[८]**। तथेति प्रतिब्रूयुः। अश्वमेधे वा द्रष्टव्यः** त्वं मेऽध्वर्युरसि **इत्येवमादिभिः। सर्वेषु पक्षेषु वरणस्य**[९] **पुरस्तादुपरिष्टाद्वा मधुपर्कदर्शनं येनकेनचिद्विधानेन। तत उपव्याहरणमृत्विजां सकाशे। करिष्यमाणस्य कर्मणो व्याहरणं सङ्कीर्तनम्। तेषां वृतानामर्घ्यादिभिराराधितानां**[१०] **सन्निधौ**[११] **दर्भेषु प्राङ्मुख उपविश्य मनसा**[१२] **संकल्पयेत्** अग्नीनाधास्ये[१३] **(वाधूश्रौ १५.५.१) इति। अथ तदेव वाचा व्याहरेत्। तेषां च यथार्थं प्रतिवचनम्। अनुज्ञानादिकं वा स्यात् प्रतिवचनम्। अथवा तेषामेव सन्निधौ तथैवोपविश्य** सर्वकामोऽग्नीनाधास्ये[१४] **(वाधूश्रौ १५.५.२) (इति)**[१५] **मनसा त्रिः संकल्प्य तदेव वाचा त्रिर्व्याहरेत्। ते च प्रतिब्रूयुः**-तत्ते ऋध्यताम्, तत्ते संवर्धतां कामः **(वाधूश्रौ. १५.५.१८) इति। अथ पूर्वमेव कृतमायतनमग्न्यगारं**[१६], **विमितं वा दक्षिणया द्वारा प्रपद्यौदुम्बरीं च वैकङ्कतीं च शाखे आदाय तासां पश्चादा** [. . . .][१७] **निति** अपेत[१८] **इति मन्त्रान्ते** लोकमस्मै देवदत्ताय **इति यजमानस्य नाम गृह्णाति। प्राचीनावीतीत्युदजेदिति**[१९] [. . . .][२०] **उत्करे** [२१]**शाखे उदस्य**[२१] **स्फ्यमादाय समस्तमग्न्यगारं प्रागपवर्गमुद्धन्ति** उद्धन्यमानम् **इति। समस्तमेवाग्न्यगारं प्रोक्षति** शन्नो देवी **इति॥ [३]**

---

१. M Ad B broken. २. Ad यथा. ३. Ad वित्ते. ४. M Ad °मासनौ. ५. M Ad B broken. ६. M Ad B हैवाग्नेध्यै. ७. M Ad B °तैरल°. ८. M Ad om यात्. ९. M Ad B वरस्य. १०. M. Ad B °वृता नारर्घ्या°. ११. M Ad B सन्निभौ. १२. M Ad B मानसा. १३. M °ग्नीनाधानस्य, Ad , °ग्निनाधानस्य. १४. M Ad B °ग्नीनाधानस्य. १५. M Ad B om. १६. M. Ad B कृतं यतनम°. १७. M Ad B broken. १८. M B नित्यये°; Ad नित्युपे. १९. M B °वीतिप्युद°, Ad °वीतीप्युद°. २०. M Ad B broken. २१-२१. M शाखेऽप्यु°, Ad B शाखेप्यु°.

अथ स्फ्यमादाय गार्हपत्यस्यायतनं प्रदक्षिणं परिलिखति। ततः पुरस्ताद् ब्राह्मणस्यैकादशसु, राजन्यस्य द्वादशसु, वैश्यस्य चतुर्विंशत्यामपरिमिते चक्षुर्निमित आधेयः इति। वि[मित][१]स्त्रिभागोऽनेनान्तरालबहुना[२] समचतुरश्रं किञ्चिदाहवनीयादपरं तस्य च [. . . .][३] श्रोण्यामन्वाहार्यपचनस्यायतनं कल्पयेत् यथा श्रप्यमाणानि हवींषि संभवे[युः। परिमण्डलाकारं बृ][४]हद्गार्हपत्यस्यायतनम्, अर्धचन्द्राकृतिर्वा यथावकाशमन्वाहार्यपचनस्य, बाहुमात्रं समचतुरश्रमाहवनीयस्यापरिमितावकाशं वा यथार्थम्। यथार्थान्यवकाशान्येव[५] वा सर्वाणि चतुरश्राणि, सर्वाणि वा परिमण्डलानि। वेदिं च यजमानमात्रीम्। आहवनीयादेवापरतो मित्वा तस्यास्त्रिभागेन[६] मित्वा पश्चाद्बाहुं तस्या एवार्धं [७]पुरस्ताद्बाहुं मित्वा दक्षिणबाहुं[७] मित्वा दक्षिणबाहुद्विगुणां[८] रज्जुमुभयतःपाशां कृत्वा मध्ये लक्षणं करोति। दक्षिणबाहुमुभयतः शङ्कुं निहत्य शङ्कुद्वयेन पाशं प्रतिमुच्य लक्षणेन दक्षिणापायम्य लक्षणेन शङ्कुं निहत्य तस्मिन् पाशद्वयं प्रतिमुच्य लक्षणेन [९]श्रोण्याद् द्वावंसौ[९] दक्षिणं पार्श्वं परिलिखित्। एवं सा बाहुद्विगुणेनापरत एवमुत्तरत एवं सर्वत्र सन्नता वेदिर्भवति। ततो वेदेः[१०] परतोऽवशिष्टो विषयः पात्रसादनाद्यर्थो भवति। अथ गार्हपत्यस्यायतनं पुनरुद्धत्यावोक्षति। ता[११] निवपति वैश्वानर्ये रूपम् इति। तच्छर्कराः[१२] परिमिनुयात्। सिकता व्यूह्य तासामुपर्यूषान् निवपन् यददश्चन्द्रमसि कृष्णं तदिहास्तु इति चान्द्रमसं लक्ष्यं ध्यायेत्। यदिदं[१३] दिव इति निवपन् मन्त्रान्ते निवपनमात्रेण तदायतनं दध्ना मधुमिश्रेण परिप्लाव्य दर्भैः परिप्लावयेत्॥ [४]

एवमेवान्वाहार्यपचनस्यायतन उद्धननादि करोति। एवमाहवनीय-[स्यायतने][१४] यजमानो वा पूर्वोपात्ताननूपात्तपूर्वान्[१५] वा सन्निधावेव सते [१६]संभर्तुकामः सर्पिषा पाणी[१६] अभ्यज्य गत्वा संभरेत्। प्रजासृष्टानाम् इति सूदं पंकमनुपदासात् ह्रदात्; यस्य रूपं बिभ्रद् इत्यारण्येन वराहेण विहतां वपाम्; यत्पर्यपश्यत् इति पुष्करपर्णान्[१७] मन्त्रेण संभरेत्। इतरेषां पार्थिवानां त्रिः सकृत् सकृत् मन्त्रेण। याभिरदृंहज्जगत इति शर्कराः; अग्ने रेतः इति हिरण्यशल्कांश्च

१. M Ad B broken. २. M Ad B °नाग्न्यराळ°. ३. M Ad B broken. ४. M Ad B broken. ५. M Ad B °थार्थान्याव°. ६. M Ad B °भागो नमित्वा. ७. M Ad B °बाहु. ८. M Ad B °र्द्विगु° ९-९. M Ad B श्रोण्याद्यासौ. १०. M Ad B वेदः. ११. M Ad B का. १२. M Ad °र्कराभः, B. °र्करायः. १३. M Ad B om °दं. १४. M. Ad B broken. १५. M Ad B °पात्तपूर्ववान्. १६-१६. M B संभर्तुकाम सर्पितापाणी, Ad संभर्तुकामसमर्पिता पाणी. १७. M Ad B add इति.

शतमानं च; अश्वो रूपम् **इत्याश्वत्थम्**[१]; ऊर्जा पृथिव्या **इत्यौदुम्बरम्;** गायत्रिया[२] ह्रियमाणस्य, देवानां ब्रह्मवादम् **इति शम्याः पलाशम्;** यया ते सृष्टस्य **इति शमीम्;** यत्ते सृष्टस्य **इति वैकङ्कतम्;** यत्ते तान्तस्य **इत्यशनिहतम्;** चित्रियादश्वत्थात् **इति ब्रह्मौदनसमिधस्तिस्रः, इतरा सप्तदश;** अश्वत्थाद्ध-व्यवाहाद्, यो अश्वत्थ **इति द्वाभ्यामरणी आहृत्याग्न्यगारस्योत्तरपूर्वस्मिन् प्रदेशे तमभिनवं प्रक्षालितं घृताक्तं निधाय तस्मिन्नेतान् संभारान् सादयति सहैव** यं त्वा समभरं जातवेदः **इति। अथास्य सतस्यापरेणोदपात्रं भगवते जातवेदसे पाद्यत्वेन सङ्कल्प्य तत्रैवान्यदुदपात्रं निनीय अर्हणीयम् इति॥ [५]**

अथास्यैव समीपे किञ्चिदाप्यं प्रियमर्घत्वेन सङ्कल्प्य कस्मैचिद् ब्राह्मणाय दत्त्वा स्वयमेव केशश्मश्रू वपते वपे प्रवपे देवेन सवित्रा प्रसूतो ब्रह्मणा शंसितोऽहं[३] यानि म इत ऊर्ध्वं लोमानि ते[४] सन्तु **इति।** [५]**नखानि निकृत्य दतो**[६] **धावते। अथैनमद्भिस्तीर्थोदभिः**[७] **स्नानविधिना स्नापयित्वा नवनीतेन तूष्णीमभ्यज्य तूष्णीमेव सद्यः पिष्टेनाञ्जनेन सतूलया शरेषीकया आञ्ज्य देवयजनं प्रपाद्य परिमितैर्दर्भैः पुञ्जीलैस्तूष्णीमेव वपयति। अथै[नम्]**[८] [९]**एताभिरसृजमथैनमा-चमय्याथैनं मार्जयति** पवमानः सुवर्जन **इत्यान्तमेतेनानुवाकेन। अथोदपात्रमा-दायोभावुपनिष्क्रमय्य**[१०] **चतुष्पथ उदपात्रं प्रतिष्ठाप्य तत्रावेक्ष्यमाणमाधास्यमानं पाप्मनो** [११]**विनिधयः। ततो**[११] **गवालम्भमातिथ्यार्थं कुर्याद्यदीच्छेद् यजमानः। ब्रह्मौदनाग्निं ब्राह्मणस्य सोमयाजिनो गृहादाहरेद् ब्रह्मवर्चसकामः; राजन्य-स्यात्मीयमण्डलं प्रत्यभिषिक्तस्य गृहादिन्द्रियकामः; वैश्यस्य धनधान्यसमृद्धस्य गृहात्पुष्टिकामः। सकाम्यं** [१२][तं गृ]**हे पुरस्तादा**[दाय][१३] **पत्नीं गृहे पचनाग्नि-कार्ये विनियुज्योपादद्यात्। अकामतस्तु पुनरात्मीयादेव गृहात्पचनाग्नेर्व्याहृतिभि-र्गृह्णीयात्। सकामश्चाकामश्चाग्निं परिचरेद् अनेन विधानेन।** दिवि जाता **इति मार्जयित्वाऽग्निमुपसमाधाय** अदितेऽनुमन्यस्व **इत्येतैः परिषिच्य व्याहृतिभिर्व्य-स्ताभिः समस्ताभिश्चतस्रः समिधोऽभ्याधाय** ममाग्ने **इत्यनुवाकेनोपस्थाय** अदितेऽनुमंस्था **इत्येतैः परिषिच्य** दिवि जाता **इति मार्जयेत्। तदमात्यपरिचरणं नाम॥ [६]**

---

१. M Ad B °त्थः. २. M B °त्रीया. ३. M Ad B शंसिहोतोऽहं. ४. M Ad B त. ५. M Ad B अनखा°. ६. M Ad B ततो. ७. M Ad B तीर्थोनदद्यौ. ८. M Ad B broken. ९. M °रसृच°. १०. M Ad B वुनिष्टुमय्य. ११-११. M Ad °धं पतेत, B °धं...त. १२. M Ad B broken. १३. M Ad B broken.

अथामात्यहोमं जुहोत्यापूर्विकेण विधानेन। वाससा प्रतिच्छाद्य समन्वारब्धेष्वपि व्रतेषु यद्देवा देवहेडनम् इति कल्प आम्नातेनानुवाकेन। अनुवित्तिहोमायाज्यमतिशिनष्टि। तमग्निमन्वाहार्यपचनस्य स्थाने निधाय तत्र पितृभ्यो ददाति अद्याग्न्याधेयस्योपवसथ इत्युक्तेन विधानेन। अथवा तमग्निं समस्तमुद्धृत्यान्वाहार्यपचनस्योद्धते निधाय पिण्डपितृयज्ञं कृत्वा ततस्तस्मिन्-ग्नाविध्ममादीप्य सादयित्वौपवसथिकया[१] गवा पुनः पितृभ्यो ददाति। पिण्ड-पितृयज्ञयोर्विकल्प इत्यपरे। तत अमात्यहोमशेषेणाज्येनानुवित्तिहोमं जुहोती-त्युक्तेन विधानेन। उभयोरग्न्योरनुवित्तिहोमं हुत्वाऽऽहवनीये हुतामाहुतिं शूर्पादिना प्रतिच्छाद्य प्रत्यग्गत्वाऽमात्याग्निं सते समुप्य गार्हपत्यस्योद्धत अमात्याग्निं न्युप्याहृत्याधिवृक्षसूर्येऽस्तमनवेलायां ब्रह्मौदनाय प्रक्रमेत्। उद्धृतमग्निमुपस-माधाय परिसमूह्य पर्युक्ष्य परिस्तीर्य उत्तरतो बर्हिरुपस्तीर्य द्वन्द्वं पात्राणि सादयति। तत्र स्थालीं दर्वीं चोद्धरणसमर्थां च सतं निर्वपणसमर्थं प्रोक्षणीपात्र-मुलूखलमुसले पात्रीं च कंसादिमयीं स्रुवमाज्यस्थालीं च व्रीहींश्च शूर्पं च रोहितं चर्मानुडुहं च द्वौ हिरण्यशल्कौ मन्त्रवन्तौ, मन्त्रवतीश्च तिस्त्रः समिध इति। तूष्णीं प्रोक्षणीः संस्कृत्य तूष्णीमेव तानि प्रोक्ष्य चतुरश्चमसान्निर्वपेत्। तत् सुशृतं कृत्वाऽङ्गारेष्वेवावस्थिताया अनुद्वासिताया स्थाल्या बिलमवघार्याज्यं[२] संस्कृत्य स्रुवं संमृज्य दर्वीं च पात्रीं प्रक्षाल्य तस्यामुपस्तीर्य[३] हिरण्यशल्कमवधाय दर्व्यामुपस्तीर्य तथैवौदनमुपहत्याभिघार्य पात्रियामवधाय। एवमेवापरे॥ [७]

द्वे दर्व्यावुद्धृत्य ततो नियमेन यथाकाममुद्धृत्य व्यूह्य हिरण्यशल्कं प्रास्य बह्वाज्यमुपसिञ्चति। अथ ब्रह्मौदनुमुपतिष्ठते प्रवेधसे इति। तं ब्रह्मौदनं चत्वार आर्षेयाः सप्राशाः[४] प्राश्नन्ति। ब्रह्मौदनं प्रतिशिष्य तान् पादावाधास्यमान एव प्रक्षालयेत्। एते ब्रह्मौदनं पर्युपविश्य प्राश्नीयुः। ब्रह्मन् हुतमसि, ब्राह्मणान् भोजयत, अश्वं गोपायत, संभारान् संनिधत्त इत्येवमादि सम्यक् शिष्टया[५] पुत्रादौ प्रिये समत्वे सर्वमपश्यम्। कर्मापरिसमाप्तेरासजति। अथाध्वर्युः शयनकाले यजमानस्यारणी प्रयच्छति ऋत्वियवती स्थ इति। अग्निग्रहणं यजमानः करोति। अग्निग्रहणप्रभृत्याभिमन्त्रणादध्वर्युः। अरण्योरात्मानमभिनिवर्तनं याजमानमिति केचित्। ऊर्ध्वं याजमानमाहिरण्यप्रासनात्। अध्वर्युर्यजमानस्याञ्जलावादधाति। आधानमन्त्रं जपति। यजमानः स्वयमेवाभ्युपायेनाञ्जलावाधत्ते। भूर्भुवोऽमीषाम् इत्याधानमन्त्रः[६]। अञ्जलिस्थमेवाभिप्राप्य ततस्तूष्णीमेवायतने सादयति।

१. M Ad B °यित्वोप°. २. M Ad B विलन्नांगार्हाज्य. ३-३. M Ad B प्रक्षातस्यामुप°. ४. M Ad B शूपांसः. ५. M Ad B शिष्ट्या. ६. M Ad B °मिद्याधान°.

प्राशनवाचने आध्वर्यवे उपस्थानद्वयं याजमानम्। अहं त्वदस्मि **इत्याध्वर्यवम् इति केचित्॥ [८]**

अथाग्निमुपसमाधाय परिसमूह्य पर्युक्ष्य परिस्तीर्याहुतिषाहं कृत्वा जुहोति। उपस्थानमेवासति गाने। साम्न्यसति योनिभिः। सति च गाने साम्नां योनिभिर्वोपस्थानमित्यपरे। एवं सर्वत्र सर्वोपस्थानानि याजमानानि असति विशेष इत्यागमः। साममन्त्रं सर्वे ब्रूयुः। निवपान्वाहार्यपचनस्य संभारान् **इति प्रैषः। प्रैषावुभावाध्वर्यवौ, वचनाद्ध्येतत् कौण्डिन्यानाम्। यथा** प्रशास्तर्यज **इत्येके। अग्निनिवपनं तूष्णीकं याजमानं**[१] **च। विषुवति हिरण्यशल्कं सादयति अध्वर्युः, उपतिष्ठते**[२] **यजमानः। वामदेव्यं च सर्वेषाम्। उद्गात्रा आमहीयवेन**[३] **वामदेव्येन सहातिप्रयन्ति।** सूर्यमग्निमादधे, यास्ते अग्ने शिवास्तनुवस्ताभिस्त्वामादधे **इति केचिद् यजुः समापयन्ति॥ [९]** इति प्रथमोऽनुवाकः॥[४]

अथ द्वितीयोऽनुवाकः[५]

सर्वत्रादौ[६] **होमपरिसमूहनपर्युक्षणपरिस्तरणोपसमाधानालंकरणानि स्युरित्यागमः। गार्हस्थ्याश्रमप्रभृति सभ्यावसथीययोः सभागृहेऽग्निशालायां नित्यमाचार्येणेष्टं धारणम्।** नर्य प्रजां मे गोपाय **इत्येताभिरुपतिष्ठेत। प्रतीकग्रहणान्येतानीति**[७] **केचित्। श्रूयमाणैरेवोपतिष्ठेत। न प्रतीकग्रहणमित्यपरे। तूष्णीमग्निहोत्रे सर्वं कर्म मन्त्रवर्जं करोति। प्रतीचीं स्रुचमुन्मृज्य**[८] **प्राचीं चोन्मृज्य प्राञ्चं हस्तं कूर्चे निमृज्य प्रत्यञ्चं निमृज्यात्। उपस्थानं चोक्तेन विधानेन करोति॥ [१]** इति द्वितीयोऽनुवाकः[९]॥

अथ तृतीयोऽनुवाकः

पवमानेष्टिष्वद्य यज्ञाय रमताम् **इति पवमानेष्टिर्हविरिति। येषा**[१०] **पवमानेष्टिकमित्यपरे। उत्तरस्या अप्येवमेव। द्वयोरप्याग्न्याधेयिकमित्यन्ये**[११]**। निरुप्तेषु**[१२] **तेषु हविःषु** अग्निं होतारम् **इति वाचयित्वा प्राणग्रहांश्च पृश्नींश्च व्याचष्टेऽध्वर्युः। प्राणग्रहाः प्राणभृन्मन्त्राः,** अयं पुरो भुवः **इत्येवमाद्याः। पृश्नयो** वायुरसि

---

१. M Ad B यज°. २. Ad °तिष्ठने. ३ . M Ad B वाहीयमानेन ४. M B इति शिवश्रोणस्य प्रयोगसन्दर्भे प्रथमः; Ad इति शिवश्रोणस्य प्रयोगसन्दर्भे प्रथमः समाप्तः. ५. M Ad B अथ द्वितीयः. ६. M Ad B सर्वत्रादि°. ७. M Ad B. °ग्रहणान्येतानिति. ८. Ad °मुन्मृन्मज्य. ९. M B इति द्वितीयः; Ad इति द्वितीयः समाप्तः. १०. M Ad B मेषामिति पव°. ११. Ad °प्याग्नाधे°. १२. M Ad B निरुष्टेस्तेषु.

प्राणो नाम **इत्येवमाद्याः पञ्च समाः**[१]**। समासन्नेऽपानग्रहांश्च पृश्नींश्च हवींषि।** यन्म अग्ने **इत्यभिमृश्यापानग्रहांश्च व्याचष्टे। अपानभृन्मन्त्राः अपानग्रहाः।** प्राचीदिशाम् **इत्येवमाद्याः पृश्नयः**[२]। ऋतस्य[३] त्वा व्योमने **इति पञ्च चतुर्होतृस्थाने। दशहोतारं**[४] **ध्रुवायां व्याचष्टे। आज्यहविष्काणां त्रयाणां यागानां देवतोपांशुत्वात्** अब्धिरसि **इति चानुमन्त्रणमन्त्रः। त्रिरिडाया उपस्तृणानः**[५] **सकृदाज्यस्थाल्या उपस्तृणीते। द्विर्ध्रुवाया**[६] **अभि। पञ्चकृत्वोऽभिघारयंश्चतुर्ध्रुवायाः, सकृदाज्यस्थाल्याः। वाचनिकत्वे सर्वमाज्यस्थाल्यां** [७]**हविरुद्वासनोत्तरमग्नीदुदपात्रेणोत्कर उपसीदति॥** [१]

दक्षिणां प्रतिग्रहीतुम्[८]**। अत्राग्न्याधेयदक्षिणां केनचिद्विकल्पेन ददाति। एका वा गौर्देया सर्वेभ्यः, षट्, द्वादश वा, चतुर्विंशतिर्वा, शतं वा, सहस्रं वाऽपरिमितं वा। उपबर्हणं ददातीत्येवमाद्या वा। उपबर्हणानि**[९] **दत्त्वाऽश्वं ब्रह्मणे दद्यात्। येनाग्न्यायतनमाक्रान्तं तमध्वर्यवे दत्त्वाऽन्यं ब्रह्मण इत्यपरे। एका देया इत्येवमादिविकल्पोपादाने निहिताग्नेरेतमाधानानन्तरम्। द्वादशाहं समिद्धा अजस्रा** [१०]**अग्नयो भवन्ति**[१०]**। उद्धरणपक्षे व्यतीते**[११] **द्वादशाहे पूर्वयोरग्न्योर्लौकिकत्वम्। कर्मणि चोद्धरणमाहवनीयस्य, आहरणमन्वाहार्यपचनस्य। अथवा उपसमेधपक्ष एवायं विधिः। एते द्वादशाहं समिद्धाः समिन्धनीयाः सार्वकालं त्रयोऽग्नयः। एधान् प्रक्षिप्य न छादनीयाः। उद्धरणोपसमेधपक्षयोस्तुल्यो विकल्पः। आयुष्कामस्य गतश्रियश्च नियत उपसमेधपक्षः। उद्धरणाद्यग्निहोत्रार्थं समन्त्रकं, प्रायश्चित्तेऽनूद्यमाने मन्त्रेण** वाचा त्वा होत्रा **इति, इतरेषु कर्मसु तूष्णीमुद्धरणम्। दक्षिणाग्निस्त्वमात्यादाहार्यस्तूष्णीम्। उपसमेधपक्षे त्वाधातुमुद्धृत आहवनीयो नित्यो धार्यो नोत्स्रष्टव्यः। एवमाधातुमाहृतो दक्षिणाग्निः। तस्मिन् द्वादशाहे वर्तमानस्य व्रतमेतं** नानृतं वदती**त्येवमादि। भक्ताशनं सकृदशनं, यथालाभमशनमित्यपरे। अग्निहोत्रोच्छिष्टव्रतत्वं सद्योनिर्वापपक्षे। तच्च स्थाल्यामवशिष्टसंभवात्। शेषपक्षापेक्षमेतदुत्तरस्य पक्षान्तरत्वाय इत्यपरे। एतदेव ज्यायः। पक्षान्तरे च तूष्णीमग्निहोत्रशेषं निधायाप्याय्य व्रतयेदित्यपरे।**[१२] **द्वादशसु रात्रिष्वनु निर्वपेदित्यस्मिन् पक्षे** [. . . .][१३] **त्विष्टिषु**[१४] **य उत्तरो द्वादशाहस्तत्रैव ते नियमा इत्यन्ये॥** [२]

---

१. M Ad B समा. २. Ad प्रश्नयः. ३. Ad ऋतय. ४. M Ad B होतार. ५. M Ad B णाना. ६. M Ad B द्विध्रु°. ७. M Ad B हविरुद्यास°. ८. M Ad B °गृही°. ९. M Ad B °बर्हमानी देः. १०–१०. M Ad B अथयो भवति. ११. M Ad B व्यतीति. १२. Ad B व्रतयैदि°. १३. M Ad B broken. १४. M Ad B स्विष्टि°.

तथा सति [१]सर्वदोपस्थानादिविधिना न त्वशक्यं, तत्रैतदग्निहोत्राभावो वर्तते। सोमाधानेऽस्य चरितार्थतोच्यते[२]। दर्शपूर्णमासारम्भनिमित्ता एते होमाः। इष्टिं च तत्र सकृदेव क्रियेरन्। सकृदारम्भाभावः [३][. . . .] कस्य अन्वाधाना-[ख्यस्या][३]दः कर्मकलापस्योपलक्षणम्। भस्मोद्धरणस्य च तेषु संयोगात् प्रत्युपवसथं प्रवृद्धभस्मापनया औपवसथिकस्य व्यृद्धं प्रति तन्त्रतावचनात्, इतरेषु अश्मन्नूर्जम्[४] इति तु भेदेन कुर्वन्त्याम्नानभेदात्। बर्हिःसंहरणे परिदेश-नादुपगूह[त्यनुलोमं स ते माऽऽस्थात् इति। उर्वन्तरिक्षम][५]न्वित, देवगमं स्थ इति। रुद्राय गाम् इति तृणहस्ता मिथुनं गृह्णन्ति। अद्याग्नीषोमीयविकारश्चरुरूपात् शुचियाजविकारोऽन्त्य आग्नेयविकारः॥ ३॥ इति तृतीयोऽनुवाकः॥

अथ चतुर्थोऽनुवाकः

[पुनराधेयम्]

प्रसिद्धा आग्न्याधेयिकाः संभाराः। अथेतरे पुनर्निष्कृतो जीर्णः पुनः संस्कृतः, पुनरुत्स्यूतं [६]जीर्णं वासः[६] प्रोतं, पुनरुत्सृष्टोऽनड्वान्[७] जीर्णमुत्सृज्य पोषयित्वा कर्षणादिभिः पुनरपि जीर्णमुत्सृष्टः। प्रातराहुतिमपि यथोक्तं करोति। अत्रापि यस्य पदेऽग्निराहितस्तमध्वर्यवे दत्त्वा पुनरुत्सृष्टादीन् सर्वेभ्यो दद्यात्। परोप्तपुनराधेयं नाम। इयन्तं कालमग्नीनुत्सृज्याधास्यमिति यदाधानं तत् परोप्तपुनराधानम्। तस्यापि विधिर्यथोक्त एव। एतस्यां क्रियायां क्रियमाणायां तां दिशं न गच्छेत्। यदि गच्छेद् अन्यां दिशं प्रत्याऽस्तमयाद्[८] गच्छेत्[९]॥ [१]

[अग्निहोत्रम्]

अथाग्निहोत्रस्य प्रयोगो वक्ष्यते। पुराऽऽदित्यस्यास्तमयादुदयाच्चापि प्रत्या-गत्य[१०] अग्निहोत्रशालां परिसमूह्य गोमयेनोपलिम्पति। तं त्वा[११] इति यजमानोऽ-प्रतिषिद्धैः काष्ठैरग्निं मन्थीत, यथोक्तं च प्रविश्य [१२]आवेद्युपवेशनात् करोति। ततोऽध्वर्युः प्राण्यापान्य प्रजापतिः प्राची दिग् इति यज्ञपुरुषनमस्कारं [कृत्वा][१३] तीर्थेन प्रविश्याधानक्रमेणाग्नीन् समूह्य परिस्तीर्योत्तरेण गार्हपत्यमुपावहरणीयं कूर्चं निधाय वेद्यामुपसादनीयं च [करोति][१४]। अथाग्निहोत्रहवणीं स्रुवं समिधं

१. M Ad B सर्वदेवोप°. २. M Ad B चरितार्थोच्य°. ३-३. M Ad B broken. ४. M Ad B इमामूर्जम् , thus Tai.B 3.7.4.3. ५. M Ad B broken. ६-६. M Ad B जीर्णं जनः. ७. M Ad B °ष्टोध्वाज. ८. M Ad B प्रत्यस्तमयान्. ९. M Ad B give the sign of broken text after गच्छेत् क... १०. M Ad B अप्रत्यादित्यं. ११. M Ad ता, B त्वा. १२. M Ad B om. १३. M Ad B om. १४. M Ad B om.

मृन्मयीं स्थालीमुपवेषमभिद्योतनं च। उष्णोदकेन प्रक्षाल्य तीर्थेन प्रपाद्योपावहरणीयकूर्चे न्युब्ज्य द्वन्द्वशः [पात्राणि][१] सादयित्वा दक्षिणया द्वारा पय आनीयापरेण गार्हपत्यमुत्तरेणोत्करं च गत्वा तीर्थेन प्रपाद्यापरेण गार्हपत्यं सादयित्वा कामण्डलुकाभिरद्भिरुत्तानानि पात्राणि कृत्वा तूष्णीं त्रिः प्रोक्ष्य ऋतं त्वा सत्येन [परिषिञ्चामि इति][२] सायं परिषिञ्चति, सत्यं त्वर्तेन परिषिञ्चामि इति प्रातः। न वा परिषिञ्चति। ततोऽङ्गारान्निरूहणादि प्रतिपद्यते। यावद्भिर्हविः श्रप्यते तावतोऽङ्गारान्[३] इह व्यन्तान् करोति पृथक् करोति। गृह्णाति अग्निहोत्र-द्रव्यम्। अग्निहोत्रस्थाल्यां पय आनयति। ततो यथोक्तमङ्गारेष्वधिश्रयति। मूलतोऽभिद्योतनमापीड्य प्रागपवर्गमुदगपवर्गं वा स्थालीं संस्पर्शयन्तीव प्रातः पर्यग्नि कुर्यात्। दूरात् सायं दक्षिणा प्रतीचीं[४] प्रत्यभिद्योतनस्य निरस्यति। उदगुद्वासयति निष्टपयति। त्रिरिहान्तात्स्त्रुचमावेद्यासादनात् निदधाति। देवेभ्यः इत्यादिनाऽनुजानाति। यजमानः पूर्णान्वाऽनूचो वा चतुरुन्नयति। पञ्चममुन्नयनं[५] पञ्चावत्तिनामित्येके॥ [२]

अविशेषेण सर्वेषामेवेत्यपरे। अयं पक्षो युक्त इवाभाति। स्थालीगतमुन्नीतं चाभिमृशति सजूर्देवैर् इति। दशहोतारमुन्नीत एव ग्रहवर्जम्। अग्निं वैश्वानरम् इत्युद्यच्छति। प्रागग्राः समिधमादधाति। समिध्यादीप्तायामनादीप्तायां[६] मूलतो द्व्यङ्गुले जुहोति अग्निर्ज्योतिर्ज्योतिरग्निः[७] स्वाहा। सूर्यो ज्योतिर्ज्योतिरग्निः स्वाहा इत्युदितहोमी जुहोतीति केचित्॥ [३]

इहोक्तयोरनयोश्च ब्राह्मणोक्तयोरनयोश्च अविशेषेण वैकल्पिकमिच्छन्ति। स्त्रुचमनिधायैव प्राणिति यजमानः पूर्वेणाहवनीयं परीत्य। दक्षिणेनाध्वर्युर्गत्वा अपरेण गार्हपत्यं प्रागावृत्योपविश्य समिधमाधायानाधाय वा स्थाल्यामवशिष्टात्[८] स्त्रुवेणोपहत्य यथोक्तं हुत्वा पुनर्यथेतमागच्छति। प्रत्यवेक्ष्याध्वर्युर्दश-होतुराहुतिमनुद्रुत्य पूर्वाहुतेर्भूयोऽङ्गार एव जुहोति। समिधि स्त्रुचमधिधायैवापानिति। स्त्रुचमतिवाल्याग्नेरुपरि प्राग् गमयित्वा कूर्चे प्रागग्रां सादयति, तथा च यो हस्ते लिप्यते तथा प्रत्यग्रमुपमार्ष्टि। तं लेपं स्त्रुच उत्तरतः[९] कूर्चे प्रमार्ष्टि। तूष्णीमोषधीभ्यः सङ्कल्प्य तत एवमेव द्वितीयमुपमृज्य लेपं गृहीत्वा पितृभ्य इति सङ्कल्प्य यथोक्तं निमार्ष्टि। केचिदत्र न[१०] प्राचीनावीतत्वमिच्छन्ति। ततोऽत्रैवोत्तरतः कुड्याः समीपे कृतकर्तेऽसि कर्तेऽपोप्ते[११] कुड्ये जलप्रस्त्रवणार्थं

---

१. M Ad B om. २. M Ad B om. ३. M Ad तावतोऽङ्गतावतो. ४. M Ad B twice. ५. M Ad B °वर्त्तिना°. ६. M Ad B °दाप्तायां. ७. M Ad B om अग्निः. ८. Ad अविशि°, B अविसृ°. ९. M Ad B सूत्तरतं. १०. B om. ११. Ad प्राप्ते.

सुषिरवती[१] **द्वाराऽऽचम्याचम्याच्चुकारं शब्दमकुर्वन्** प्रजा ज्योतिर् **इति वा तूष्णीं वा प्राश्य पुनः समस्तमग्निहोत्रद्रव्यं स्रुग्गतं हस्ते गृहीत्वा आनीय यथोक्तं मन्त्रेण भक्षयित्वा द्विराचम्य स्रुचं द्विः संक्षाल्य आहवनीये त्रीन्निष्टप्य स्रुच्युदकमानी-योदगावृत्तसप्तं ध्यात्वा द्विरुद्दिश्य दक्षिणा पर्यावृत्य याज्ञिकानि काष्ठानि प्रक्षिप्य** [२]**उपवीजनेनोपवीज्याग्नीनाधानक्रमेण समिध्य स्रुग्गता आपो** [३]**निनीया-परेणात्मानं पूर्वेणोत्करं स्रुचमानीयोत्तरतः क्षेमे विधाय** ऋतं त्वा सत्येन **इत्यादिना पुनः परिषिञ्चति। ततो यजमानोऽग्न्यनुवीक्षणादि सर्वमनुवाकशेषं करोति॥ [४]**

तत्रानामग्रहणाद् यजमानायतन एव तिष्ठन् करोति। तत उपप्रयन्तो अध्वरम् **इत्यनुवाकद्वयेनोपस्थाय ज्योतिष्मन्तं त्वाऽग्ने इत्यादिना माहाचम-सेनोपतिष्ठते। अन्ते ब्रह्मवर्मेण**[४] **सायमनुवीक्षणेन प्रातर् एषः स्वयंहोमपक्षे विशेषः। स्वयमेव** देवेभ्यो हव्यं मह्यम् **इत्यनुजानाति। पत्नी शिष्यो वा यः कश्चिदध्वर्युर्वा** सं त आकुर्वन्तु **इति। तथैव गार्हपत्यहोमं स्वयमेव शीघ्रं गत्वा जुहोति। अध्वर्युरित्यपरे॥ [५]** इति चतुर्थोऽनुवाकः॥

अथ पञ्चमोऽनुवाकः

अग्नीनुपस्थास्यमानो[५] **भवति। यदि नक्षत्र आधत्ते माहाचमसेनोपस्थाया-नुवाकद्वयेनोपतिष्ठत आपर्वणं पर्वदिवसात्प्रागित्यर्थः। सर्वाधानपक्षे तु यथा-पाठमेव अग्निपावमानीभिरुपतिष्ठमान आद्ये दिवसे साग्निपावमानिकेना-नुवाकेनोपस्थाय ततः संवत्सरमनग्निकेनोपतिष्ठते। तत्र** उप त्वाऽग्न **इत्यतः प्राग् याजमाने**[६] **कृत्वाऽग्रेणाहवनीयं परीत्यापरेणाहवनीयं**[७] **गार्हपत्यं प्राङ् तिष्ठन्** उप त्वाऽग्ने **इत्यादि** तत्सवितुर्वरेण्यम् **इत्यादिभिरुत्तरेणाहवनीयं तिष्ठन्नुपस्थाय यथोक्तं गार्हपत्यमुपस्थायाशिष आशास्य** ज्योतिष्मन्तं त्वाऽग्ने **इत्यादिना माहाचमसोपस्थानाख्यं कर्म उत्तरविहारस्थ एव करोति॥ [१]**

तत्र समिन्धनमिहोक्तक्रमेण पूर्ववत् सहोपस्थानाभिवादनान्तमपरेण[८] **गार्ह-पत्यं स्थित्वा करोति। सप्तर्षिनमस्कारानन्तरं** वृष्टिरसि वृश्च मे पाप्मानम्, ऋतात्सत्यमुपैमि [९]**इत्युपस्पर्शनमभिवादनम्, तत्तदभिमृश्य। यत्रास्पष्टा**[१०] **मन्त्रो-क्तिः सर्वत्र** इमाम् **इत्युक्ते भूमिं प्रतीयात्।** वेदिमभिमृशामि **इति प्रसङ्गेनैतदुच्यते।**

---

१. M Ad B सुषिरपति. २. M Ad B उपजाने°. ३. Ad विनी°. ४. M Ad B °वर्णेन. ५. M Ad B °नुपास्यमानो; thus Vādhśs 1.19.1. ६. M Ad B प्राग्यज°. ७. M Ad B °नीय. ८. M Ad B °नाधिवद. ९. M Ad B इत्यपस्प°. १०. Ad यत्रस्पृष्टा.

सर्वत्र दक्षिणत उत्तरविहारं गच्छतामुत्तरतो वा दक्षिणविहारं गच्छतामग्रेणाहवनीयमार्गः, तथा दक्षिणाग्निं गच्छतां चापरेण गार्हपत्यं प्रातरप्येवं[१] करोति। तत्र मार्जनमुत्तानेन पाणिना। अनुवाकद्वयं ब्रह्मवर्मोपस्थानं च नास्ति। तत्र पयोऽभावे यवागूराज्यं दधिमांसमोदनं[२] तण्डुलः [३]सोमस्तैलं जलमितीमानि द्रव्याणि भवन्ति। तत्राज्येऽपां प्रत्यानयनकाले दर्भाग्रे प्रत्यस्यति। दधिसोमतण्डुलानामधिश्रयणं नास्ति। [४]तदभावेऽङ्गारनिरूहणमपां [५]प्रत्यानयनमुद्वासनमङ्गारप्रत्यूहणञ्चेत्येतानि न सन्ति। मन्त्रेणादाय बर्हिरिव निधाय अभिद्योतनपर्यधिकरणे करोति। सोमे रसं वा लतां वा गृह्णाति। तत्र श्रपणार्थं हिरण्यं निदधाति। केचिदधिश्रित्य पचन्ति। रसग्रहणपक्षे कुट्टयित्वा रसं गृह्णाति। लताग्रहणपक्षे छित्त्वा स्रुवेणैवोन्नयति। तैलेऽपां प्रत्यानयनमत्र नास्ति॥ [२]

[६]यावानोदने यावतोदकेन सम्यक् पच्यन्ते तण्डुलास्तावदपां प्रत्यानयने पय आनीय श्रपयति। हविःष्वप्सु सर्वं क्रियते। विशदद्रव्यमोदनाद्यपि स्रुवेणैवोन्नयति। प्रवत्स्यन् अग्नीन् प्रज्वाल्य अथातो विराजक्रमाः (वाधूश्रौ ३.१.२८) इत्यादि विधानेन याजमानोक्तेन प्रवासविधिना विराजक्रमैर्वा। अथातो माहाचमसम् (वाधूश्रौ ३.२.१) इत्यादिना माहाचमसेनोपस्थाय व्रजित्वा पुनरागच्छेत्। पथ्ये वा त्रिप्रादेशां समिधमादायागत्य येनोपस्थाय गतस्तेनैवात्रोक्तेन विधिनोपस्थाय तूष्णीं तृतीयं समिधोऽभ्यादधाति (वाधूश्रौ. ३.२.१९) इत्यादि च यथोक्तं करोति। बहुकालेनाप्येवं प्रवसतो दोषो नास्ति। यदि प्रवत्स्यदुपस्थानमनुपस्थाय प्रव्रजति यत्र स्मरेत्, तिष्ठन् अभिमुखो जपेत् इहैव सन् तत्र सतो वो अग्नय इति। प्रवसन्नग्न्युद्धरणकालमनशनेन (वाधूश्रौ. १.२२.२) इति[७] विधानेनोभयोः कालयोः भूर्भुवः सुवरग्नय आहोष्यमाणाः (वाधूश्रौ. १.२२.४) इत्यादि मन्त्रं प्राङ् वोदङ् वा तिष्ठन्नासीनो वा जपित्वा नित्येनोभयोः कालयोर्यथोक्तं जपति। स्वगृहाभिमुखोऽग्निहोत्रं यदा हुतं मन्यते तत्र यानि कर्माण्यनेन कर्तुमशक्यानि तान्यध्वर्युर्वा पुत्रो वा करोति। अमन्त्रकं पिण्डपितृयज्ञं, सर्वं समन्त्रकं च। समस्तं वा याजमानमस्मिन् पक्षे प्रवसदुपस्थानमेव। याजमानस्य सर्वं याजमानं वा अस्मिन् पक्षे देवेभ्यो मह्यम् इत्यनुज्ञानमपि यजमान एव करोति। प्रशास्तर्यज इतिवत् समाकृतं प्रैषं च। तथा पराग्निहोमं स्वयमेव जुहोति। अत्रोक्तान्युपस्थानानि कर्तव्यानि, विकल्प्यानि च॥ [३] इति पञ्चमोऽनुवाकः॥[८]

॥ इत्याधानाख्यः प्रपाठकः समाप्तः ॥[९]

---

१. M Ad B °प्येव. २. M Ad B °मांससमो°. ३. M Ad B स्तोम°. ४. M Ad B तद-भामङ्गारान्निरू°. ५. M Ad twice. ६. M Ad B यवान्नो. ७. M Ad B °मनश = प्येनेति. ८. M इति षष्ठः; Ad इति षष्ठः समाप्तः. ९. M आधोनाख्यो प्रपाठक; Ad °प्रपाठकश्च°.

॥ अथ द्वितीयः प्रपाठकः ॥[१]

॥ अथ पुरोडाशी ॥

अथ प्रथमोऽनुवाकः

अथ पुरोडाशी प्रारभ्यते। यज्ञोपवीत्यप आचम्य तीर्थेन प्रपद्य [२]प्राण्यापा-[न्याग्नीन]न्वाधायाग्निहोत्रोच्छिष्टमातच्य[३] निधाय शाखां छित्त्वाऽऽहृत्य तया वत्सानपाकृत्य गा अनुमन्त्र्य यजमानं चाभिमन्त्र्य शाखामुद्गूह्य बर्हिः संभारान् प्रस्तरादन्यानयुजो मुष्टीन् समन्त्रकान् लूत्वा सम्भृत्य यजमानस्य सर्वं लूता सम्भृत्य निधाय वेदं परिभोजनीयं[४] सकृदेकविंशतिर्वा[५] पालाशः खादिरो वा। तत्र त्रिप्रादेशाः परिधयो द्विप्रादेशा इध्मकाष्ठानि। ततः शाखां प्रादेशमात्रगतां छित्त्वा तत्र दर्भमयं त्रिगुणं शाखापवित्रं कृत्वा मन्त्रेणाग्नीन् परिस्तीर्य वत्सज्ञुं मूतकार्यमूर्ध्वाग्रं त्रिवृच्छिरसं[६] वा वेदं त्रिवेदिं[६] करोति, रत्नं धृत्वा संमार्ष्टी-त्यातः[७]। पौर्णमास्यां तु यथापाठमग्न्यगारपरिशोभनं[८] भस्मोद्वपनं पात्रप्रक्षालन-मिति च कृत्वाऽपराह्णे पितृभ्यो दत्त्वा तूष्णीं परिस्तृणीयात्। वेदं कृत्वा वेदिं कृत्वा पितृभ्यो दत्त्वाऽग्नीन्मन्त्रेण परिस्तीर्य वेदिमभिमन्त्रयत इत्यपरे। सान्नाय्य-पात्राण्युपावहृत्य [९]गा आयतीः[९] प्रतीक्ष्य यजमानञ्चाभिमन्त्र्य हुत्वाऽग्निहोत्र-मुत्तरेण गार्हपत्यं तृणानि संस्तीर्य तेषु द्वन्द्वं न्यञ्चि पात्राणि सादयेत्॥ [१]

सः [१०]तान्युत्तानानि कृत्वा शुन्धध्वं दैव्याय कर्मणे देवयज्यायै इति वा, तूष्णीं वा संस्कृताभिरद्भिः कामण्डलुकाभिरद्भिर्वा प्रोक्ष्य प्रसिद्धं सान्नाय्यं दोहयेत्। ततः प्रैषमभिमन्त्रणं प्रतिदोहमावर्तते। त्रिवृद्गृह्णतः कामधुक्ष इत्याद्या वर्तते। पूर्ववत् प्रातर्दोहाय वत्सानपाकुर्यात्, तूष्णीं वा दर्भैः प्रातर्दोहं दोहयन्। उदीचीनाग्रं पवित्रं निदधाति। प्रतिषिद्धवर्जं सर्वं कुर्यात्। अन्ते संक्षालानयनं नात्र धर्मपदविधानम्। अथाग्रेणाग्निं तृणानि संस्तीर्य तेषु द्वन्द्वं न्यञ्चि पात्राणि यज्ञायुधानि सादयति। स्फ्यादीनि सादयति। इतराणि[११] सादयति जुहूं च स्रुवं चोपभृतं च ध्रुवां च प्राशित्रहरणं चेडापात्रं च पुरोडाशमेक्षणं च पिष्टोद्वपनीं च प्रणीताप्रणयनं चाज्यस्थालीं च वेदं च दारुपात्रीं च मेक्षणं च चरुस्थालीं च

१. M Ad B om. २. M Ad B broken between प्राण्यापा [MSS मान्यप्रज्य] and न्वाधाय॰ [MSS पाधाय]. ३. M Ad B ॰तथ्यं. ४. M Ad B ॰भोजनी. ५. M Ad B ॰विंशतिं वा. ६-६. M Ad B त्रिवृच्छिरन सं वापेदं त्र्यवेदिं. ७. Ad B ॰त्यतः. ८. M Ad B ॰परि परिशोभनं. ९-९. M Ad B गायत्रयतिः. १०. M. तन्यु॰. ११. M Ad B त्वेतरा॰.

मदन्तीस्थालीं[१] चान्वाहार्यस्थालीं च समिधं च पत्नीसन्नहनं च वृषारवं चोपवेषं च। अयोदर्व्यादीनि अन्यान्यपि द्वन्द्वशः सादयेत्। अथ ब्रह्माणं दक्षिणत उपवेश्य पुरोडाशीयानाहृत्य निधाय पवित्रे आदाय प्रणीतापात्रमुत्तानं कृत्वा तूष्णीं कामण्डलुकाभिरद्भिः प्रोक्ष्य तत्राप आनयन्नाह—ब्रह्मन्नपः प्रणयिष्यामि इति। ता आनीता आपः परिगृह्य जपति—भूर्भुवः सुवर्देवस्य त्वा इति। ता उपादायोत्थाय मुखसंमिता अस्कन्दयन् हृत्वोत्तरेणाहवनीयं प्रबाहुगीषदिति[२] ॥ [२]

गता वा मन्त्रेण दर्भेषु सादयित्वाऽभिमन्त्र्य दर्भैः प्रतिच्छाद्य पवित्रे [३]आहरन्नेतीत्यादि प्रतिपद्यते। अग्निहोत्रहवण्यादीनि च तथैव प्रोक्ष्यादत्ते। वेषाय त्वा इति शूर्पादानमन्त्रम्। किञ्चित् पुरोडाशीयेभ्योऽधि निरस्यति। निरसीयन् तृणादीनि निर्वपति। उप्त्वाऽभिमर्शनमाध्वर्यवम्। याजमानमित्येके। रक्षायै त्वा नारात्यै इति हविरभिमन्त्रणम्। अग्ने हव्यं रक्ष इति गार्हपत्याभिमन्त्रणम्। उदिङ्गयति उत्कम्पयति, पाणिना चोर्ध्वं गमयति। सकृदेव मन्त्रस्त्रिरुदिङ्गनम्। त्रिर्वा च्छेदो मन्त्रस्य। अन्याभिरद्भिः प्रोक्षति। [४]जुष्ट्यावचनमन्त्रस्यावृत्तिः। हविष्कृदेहि इति ब्रुवन् प्रहरति। नायं प्रहरणमन्त्रः। उद्वादने चैकमन्त्रत्व-मनावृत्तिश्च, त्रयो वा मन्त्राः। उत्तुषान् उन्मुक्ततुषान्, पृथग्गततुषान्। मन्त्रेण विवेकमारभ्य सर्वान् वितुषीकृत्य सहैवाभिमृश्य उलूखले आवपन्नाह प्रैषम्। प्रेषिता पत्नी त्रिष्फलीकृत्य प्रब्रूयात्। अथैनान् प्रक्षाल्य प्रक्षालनमन्तर्वेदि निनीय पुनरेषूदकमासिच्य निदध्यात्[५]॥ [३] इति प्रथमोऽनुवाकः॥

अथ द्वितीयोऽनुवाकः

उपवेष उपधानार्थो नित्योऽन्यः शाखामूलम्। तेनाङ्गारनिर्वर्तनप्रतिनोदना-वर्त्तनानि कुर्यात्। प्रधिकं प्रधावुपधेययोरन्यतरत्। परिचितमितरत् परि-चिन्मन्त्रेण। परिचितान्दक्षिणपूर्वं पूर्वेण सपर्याहृत्योपदध्यात्। तथा दक्षिणापरम्। तथोत्तरपूर्वमुत्तरेषां कपालानां निर्वर्तनप्रतिनोदने न स्त इत्येके। सर्वत्र परिचिन्मन्त्रकाणि प्रदक्षिणं प्रागुदक्संस्थान्युपदधाति। विस्राव्य प्रेषणीयान् निदधाति। चरव्यानध्येतानपि[६] विस्राव्य केचित् निदधति। भूयस एधान् प्रक्षिपन्ति। मदन्तीरधिश्रयन्ति। तपन्ति च पिष्टोद्वपनीम्। धान्यमसि इत्येव मन्त्रेण प्रतिमुष्ट्यावपते[७]। भिन्ना एव मन्त्राश्चत्वारश्चतुर्णां मुष्टीनाम्। धान्यमसि इति

---

१. M Ad B मदन्ति°. २. M °दति. ३. M Ad B आहन्नैती°. ४. M Ad B मुष्ट्यावचन°.
५. M Ad B निदध्या:. ६. M Ad B चरव्यानद्ये तानवि. ७. M Ad B °प्रतिपुष्ट्या पत्तते.

च सर्वत्रानुषज्यत इत्यपरे। प्रपतितानन्ववेक्षते[१]। प्रैषमाह[२] संवपत पिष्टानि[२] तूनिकुरुताद् इति। प्रेषिता पत्नी दासी वा पिनष्टि। असंवपन्ति अमिश्रयन्ति पिष्टानि तण्डुलैः। न वा प्रैषैः, यदि कश्चित् पिनष्टि। पिष्टानि संवपन्ति। तप्तायां पिष्टोद्वपन्यां मुहुरालोड्याथ स्रुवेणाप आनयति। प्रणीताभ्योऽध्याहृता भूयसीरप आनयति मदन्तीभ्यः शनैःशनैः प्रम्णायन्। वीक्षमाणः परिप्रजनयति परितो गमयति। आनीता अपः संयौति मेक्षणेन। प्रम्णाय प्रमृद्य हस्तेन व्यावर्त्यादिशेन्मन्त्रेण। तूष्णीं पूर्वायतं प्रागायतं कूर्माकृतिं कृत्वा पुरोडाशमधिश्रयेत्। सर्वाणि कपालान्यभिप्रथयति। सर्वाणि छादयति। पुरोडाशं नातिप्रथयेत्। त्वग्ग्रहणम् अद्भिरभिमर्शनं त्रिष्कमसकृन्मन्त्रः। दधनि पूर्वमवदेये दधिपूर्वमुपनिधेयं श्रृते श्रृतम्। एवमासादनेऽभिघारणेऽभिमर्शने। प्रयाजशेषाभिघारेण स्विष्टकृदवदान इडावदाने च। श्रृते केचित् पूर्वावदेये [३][पूर्वव]देव तमभिपूरयन्ति। दध्ना [४]स्विष्टकृतः देवस्त्वा सविता इति चरुं चाभिमृशेत्। पुरोडाशविषयमेवाभिमर्शनमित्येके॥ [१]

अवज्वलनाभिवासने तु पुरोडाशस्यैव, तथा वेदेन संस्पर्शनम्। सर्वत्रैतदित्यपरे। संक्षालनं पिष्टपात्रीं पिष्टोद्वपनीम्। वेदेन वेदिं संमृज्य विमाय स्फ्यं च बर्हिश्चान्तर्वेदि निदधातीत्यादि प्रपद्यते। अन्तर्वेद्युदीचीनाग्रं बर्हिर्निदधाति। उत्करस्यार्जवे दक्षिणेन [५]ब्रह्माणमुत्तरेणोलूखलं स्थानं प्रहृत्य बर्हिःखण्डं सह पुरीषेणाहरेत्। अन्ते समस्तं इमां नरा इति जपः। समुद्धननं तूष्णीं हस्तेन हरणं संमार्जनं च। प्रैषेऽध्वर्युणोक्तेनाग्नीत् प्रैषार्थान् करिष्यन् मार्जयित्वा प्रोक्षणीरभिपूर्य तासां स्फ्यस्य वर्त्मन्नुपनिनीय तत्रैव मन्त्रेण सादयित्वोत्तरेण प्रणीता[६] अन्तरा प्रणीताश्चात्मानं च हृत्वोत्तर[७] एव प्रागाहुतिमिध्माबर्हिरुपसादयति। दक्षिणमिध्ममुत्तरं बर्हिः। अध्वर्युः स्फ्यं निहत्य मार्जयित्वा स्फ्यं प्रक्षालयति। अथाग्नीध्रः स्रुचः संमृज्य संमार्जनान्यग्नौ मन्त्रेण प्रहरति। तूष्णीं वा सञ्चर उदस्य सादयित्वा स्रुचः पत्नीसन्नहनाद्याज्यसादनान्तं करोति। अवान्तरावकाशेनावेक्षेते अध्वर्युरग्नीच्च। अग्नेर्जिह्वासि इति मन्त्रोऽवान्तरावकाशो वाचनेषु सर्वेषु। वाचयित्रोक्ते वक्ता ब्रूयात्। आत्मनश्छायामवेक्ष्य मन्त्रेणाज्यं पुनराहार्य[८] त्रिः सकृद्वोत्पूय प्रोक्षणीषु पवित्रे अवधायाज्यग्रहणादि

१. M Ad B प्रपतिता ननु अन्वपेक्षते. २-२. M Ad B माहा संवपति पीषान्. ३. M Ad give the sign of broken text between °देये and देवतम° (Ad देवताम°). ४. M Ad B दध्नान्विष्ट°. ५. M Ad B ब्राह्मणमु°. ६. M Ad B अन्तराप्रणीता twice. ७. Ad हुत्वो°. ८. M Ad B °हार.

प्रतिपद्यते। वरुणप्रदेशे[१] यत्राज्यं गृहीतं पवित्रे आदाय प्रोक्षणीशेषं निनीयाप उपस्पृशेत्। पवित्रे अपिसृजेत्। प्रदेशं लक्षयेत् साग्रं समाग्रं, प्राचः प्रागपवर्गान् दक्षिणतो मध्यत उत्तरत इति। समन्त्रकैस्त्रिभिर्मुष्टिभिः प्रागपवर्गैः समस्तां वेदिमास्तीर्याह—स्तृणीत बर्हिर् इति। त्रिवृत् त्रिगुणं बर्हिस्तृणन्ति॥ [२]

परिकर्मिणः सह पूर्वेण गुणेनानतिदूश्नम् अधिद्रष्टुमशक्यम्। पूर्वेण पर्याहृत्य दक्षिणं परिधिं परिदध्यात्। तथैव पुनः पर्याहृत्य प्रहरेत्। समिधावूर्ध्वाग्रे[२] तिरश्च्योर्ग्रहणं परिभोजनीयात्। स्तीर्णस्य[३] वा बर्हिषो मध्यमात् गुणात् सव्येनोपभृतं सादयेत्। प्रत्यङ् चरत्येव[४] हवींष्युद्वासयेत्। सर्वेषु पक्षेषु समन्त्रकमेवोद्वासनमुपस्तरणम्। पात्र्यां यवमयेषु हविःषु लुप्येतोपस्तरणमन्त्रः। न लुप्यत इत्यपरे। अभिघारयेत्[५] पुरोडाशं, सर्वतः सन्तर्पयेत्। उद्वास्यापि चरुमभिघारयेत्। यथापाठमित्यपरे। उत्तरस्योद्वासने सुरूपम् इति मन्त्रो लुप्यते। यथादेवतमभिघारमित्येके[६]। हविष्यासादयन्नवदानक्रमेण सान्नाय्ये सादयित्वाऽभिमृश्य मन्त्रेणानुपूर्वं हवींष्यभिघार्य दक्षिणेन ध्रुवां स्रुवं सादयित्वा साज्यस्रुवायां सादयेत्। यजमान इत्यपरे। वेदं सादयित्वा संसन्नं यज्ञं यज्ञसाधनेष्वभिमृशेत्। यजमान इत्येके। सर्वत्रैव प्रत्यगाशिषो मन्त्राः कर्मकरणाः कर्मवशादाध्वर्यवा एव यजमानेनापि सह जपनीयाः। अत्राध्वर्युर्व्रतमुपेयात्। यजमानस्यैव कश्चिद् व्रतकाल इत्यन्ये। स्रुचोऽभिमृशति। पृथक् पृथङ् मन्त्रमावृत्य सहैवासकृदेव [. . .][७]। व्याख्येयोऽत्र[८] ग्रहणे होमविधिः॥ [३] इति द्वितीयोऽनुवाकः॥

अथ तृतीयोऽनुवाकः

अग्नये दधाति। आहवनीये भूयस एधान् प्रक्षिप्य गन्धपुष्पैरलंकृत्य होतारमामन्त्र्य तस्मै देवतामभिधाय इध्मात् समिधमादधानो अग्नये समिध्यमानायानुब्रूहि इत्युक्त्वा त्रिषु प्र[णवेषु तिस्रः समिधोऽभ्यादधाति। अत][९] ऊर्ध्वं प्रतिप्रणवमेकैकमभ्यादधाति। अथवा आद्ये प्रणव एकामभ्याधाय अनन्तरे न्यासे तिस्रः। अत ऊर्ध्वं प्रतिप्रणवमभ्यादधाति। एवं पञ्चदश दारूण्यभ्याधेयानि। प्रतिप्रणवं तिस्रोऽभ्याधाय अत ऊर्ध्वं प्रतिन्यासं प्रतिप्रणवं पञ्च [अभ्याधेयानि . . .][१०]। एवमेकविंशतिदारूण्यभ्याधेयानीत्येके। सुव्यक्तान्येतेषामेक-

---

१. M Ad B °देशो. २. M Ad B समिधादू°. ३. M Ad B तीर्ण°. ४. M Ad B चरेत्येव. ५. M Ad °घातयेत्. ६. M Ad B °मभिधान°. ७. M Ad B broken. ८. M Ad B व्याख्ये यत्र. ९. M Ad B broken; cf VādhŚS 2.10.2-3. १०. M Ad B broken.

विंशतिपक्षे कल्पवाक्यानि सुयोज्यानि भवन्ति। आ जुहोत इति परिधानीयोपलक्षणं, नोपवाजनमन्त्रस्यावृत्तिः। आदीप्त इध्मे घ्रातहवन[१] इति श्रुत्वा ध्रुवाया अधि स्रुवेणोपहत्य वेदेनोपयत्य मनसा मन्त्रमन [. . . .][२] वते प्रजापतये संकल्प्य दक्षिणा तिर्यञ्चं सन्ततमृजुमाघारमाघारयेत्। सर्वेषु होमेषु प्रक्षेप्ता देवतां ध्यायेत्। भुवनमसि[३]=नमः इति जुहूपभृतौ प्रत्यञ्जलिं कुर्वन्नाहवनीयमुपतिष्ठते। सर्वत्र जुहूमुपभृत्यध्यूहन् पुरस्तात्प्रतीचीमध्यूहन् पश्चा प्राचीमुपावरोहेत्। सर्वत्रात्याक्रामन् सव्येनात्याक्रामन् पुनरत्याक्रामन् दक्षिणेनात्याक्रम्य प्रदक्षिणमावर्तते। प्रयाजत्रयायावशिष्योत्तरमाघारमाघारयेद्। उदञ्चं तिर्यञ्चमृजुम्[४]। सन्ततमृजुम् इन्द्राय संकल्प्य जुह्वा ध्रुवां त्रिः समनक्ति। त्रेधा मन्त्रं छित्त्वाऽनुषज्य, सकृदेव वा, समस्तेन मन्त्रेण बर्हिस्तीर्णाददीत[५]। अध्वर्युणाऽऽश्राविते अस्तु श्रौषट् इत्यग्नीत् प्रत्याश्रावयेत्॥ [१]

सर्वत्रैवं कुर्यात्। आश्रावण आद्यौ स्वरौ ब्रुवते। अस्तु श्रौषट् इत्याकारः। श्रावयेदिति चाध्यश्रौषट् इति च। अगानग्नीत् इत्याकारे ब्रूहीत्यूकार उदेहीत्येकारः आगुरित्येव याजान्तो वषट्कारं च। पृष्टो[६] होता स्वनाम प्रब्रूते। होतृषदने बर्हिः स्तीर्त्वाऽऽह सीद होतर् इति। एवं ब्रह्मयजमानयोश्च प्रागुपवेशाद् दक्षिणेनाहवनीयं ब्रह्मणः, ततः पश्चाद् यजमानस्य, तथा जघनेन पत्न्याः। सर्वाणि बर्हिःकार्याणि परिभोजनीयान्युक्त्वा[७] वेदिस्तरणं स्रुचावुभाभ्यां हस्ताभ्यां नासिकाया आर्जवे धारयित्वा तिष्ठन्नाश्रावयेत्। यत्र तिष्ठन्नाश्रावयेत् तत्रस्थ एव जुहुयात्। प्राचः प्रयाजान् यजति, प्रदिशं वा प्राङभिक्रम्याभिक्रम्य। तेषु वसन्ताद्या देवता यथाक्रमम्। अन्त्यस्य हेमन्तशिशिरौ। सर्वत्र वषट्कारप्रदाने यजमानः स्वाहेत्यनुमन्त्रयेत, अध्वर्युर्वा। सर्वं हुत्वा त्रीन्वा[८] स्रुचं धारयन्न क्वचिदग्नौ अत्यूहेत्। अथेदं शनैः प्रत्याहृत्य प्रतिसन्दध्यात्। आज्यभागाघारयोः[९] प्रबाहुक्त्वं जुहोति। मुखं चेत्येके। ध्रुवाया उपस्तरणाभिघारणे, प्रत्यञ्जनमाज्यस्थाल्याः समञ्जनं च सर्वं च मनुष्यसंबन्धं होमं च प्रागाघारादरण्योश्च[१०] वचनादन्यत् सान्नाय्याङ्गुष्ठप्रदेशिन्यौ, मा भेर्मा संविक्थाः इत्यवदातुमत्र[११] प्रेयात्। व्यतिषज्याङ्गुली भरतमुद्धर इत्यवदातुमारभेत। तिर्यक् पूर्वमन्वपेत् पुरस्तात्पश्चादन्येषां हविषां मध्यात्। पूर्वार्धादपरार्धादिति पञ्चावत्तिनाम्[१२]।

१. M Ad B घ्राताह°. २. M Ad B broken. ३. M Ad B abr; cf VādhŚS 2.10.9. ४. M Ad B om जु. ५. M Ad B स्तीर्णादादीत. ६. M Ad B वृष्टो. ७. M Ad B परिभोजनीयान्मु°. ८. M Ad B भीन्व°. doubtful. ९. M Ad B °भागावासयोः. १०. M Ad °दवरण्यो°. ११. M Ad B °मच. १२. M Ad B °वर्तिनां.

पञ्चावत्तिनश्च[१] **जामदग्न्यादयश्च। इदूशी पलाशमात्रं प्रथमा प्रदानात्। ततो ज्यायः** [२]**सौविष्टकृतमैडञ्च।** अनुब्रूहि **इत्युक्ते होता वाचं यच्छेदाऽनुवचनात्**[३], **अनूक्तायामध्वर्युश्चाश्रावणात्, श्रावितेऽग्नीदावृत्याश्रावणात्। प्रत्याश्राविते चाध्वर्युः** आ यज **इति वचनात्।** यज **इत्युक्ते होताऽऽवषट्कारात्। सर्वत्र विशदद्रव्यं प्रक्षिपन् स्रुग्गतादाज्यादाहुतिं प्रक्षेप्तुं**[४] **विस्राव्यावदानानि प्रक्षिप्य संस्रावणा[न्य]**[५]**भिजुहुयात्। मध्ये गोः प्रदक्षिणं मण्डलाकारः। प्रागपवर्गा वा प्रधानाहुतीर्जुहुयात् मध्य। एवं वा प्राचीरुपांशु याजयेत्॥ [२]**

सोमाय **इत्युपांशु,** अनुब्रूहि **इत्युच्चैः। तथा** विष्णवे **इत्यमावास्यायाम्।** सोमम् **इत्युपांशु,** यज **इत्युच्चैः। तथा** विष्णुम् **इत्यमावास्यायाम्। सान्नाय्ययोस्तूष्णीम्। प्रत्यञ्जनं चरोश्च।** अग्नीषोमौ यज **इति पौर्णमास्याम्,** इन्द्राग्नी यज **इत्यमावास्यायाम्। असन्नयत** इन्द्रम् **इति, सन्नयतो** महेन्द्रम् **इति महेन्द्रयाजिनः। उत्तरतः पुरस्तात् स्विष्टकृदवदानं तथा होमः। उत्तरत एवातिहाय पूर्वाहुतिरित्यभिहोमप्रतिषेधः। स्विष्टकृदवदानस्योपरि मेक्षणं प्रहरेत्। अत्याक्रम्य जुहूमद्भिः**[६] **पूरयित्वा अन्तःपरिध्यग्नावासिच्य**[७] **दक्षिणापवर्गं हुत्वा स्रुचं प्रक्षाल्य निष्टप्य पुनरद्भिः पूरयित्वा बहिःपरिध्युदगपवर्गं**[८] **जुहुयात्। प्राशित्राभिघारणं स्रुवदण्डेन। अवदानानि संभिद्यावत्तप्रदेशानां सन्धीनवखण्ड्य चत्वारि संभेदनानि सहैवादध्यात्। द्वितीयो होत्र इडां प्रयच्छन् वाचयेद्यजमानम्** सुरूपवर्षवर्ण **इति।** [९]**तत्रोत्तरानपि मन्त्रखण्डान् यत्र त्रयः। यजमानो ब्रूयात्** सा मे सत्याशीः **इत्युच्चैः। उपहूयमानायामिडायां वाचयेत्॥ [३]**

अत्रैव वा समस्तं प्रदायेडामपिसृजन्नध्वर्युः पूर्वेण होतारमत्याक्रम्य दक्षिणतो वेद्यामुपविशेत्। अङ्गुलैः प्रदेशिन्या अग्रे पर्वण्यनक्ति, अथ मध्ये। [१०]**केचिदिडालेपादेवोपस्तृणन्त्यभिघारयन्ति च। आज्यस्थाल्या इत्यपरे। उच्चैरुपहूयमानायां वाचयित्वा यजमानम्**[११] इ[मं] भागं [११]जुषस्व **इति जपित्वोपहूतः** पशुमानसानि **इत्युक्त्वा बर्हिःषदमष्टाकपालं करोति। चतुर्धा कृत्वेत्येके। नाभिप्रेतमिति वा इदम्**[१२] **आचार्यस्य। अथ** ब्रध्न पिन्वस्व **इति वाचयेत्।** [१३]**प्रवाचन-**

---

१. M Ad B °वर्तिन°. २. M Ad B सोविष्ट°. ३. M Ad B °वाचान्. ४. M Ad B स्तानेप्तुं. ५. M Ad B om. ६. M Ad B जुहूमन्त्रिः. ७. M Ad B °सीञ्च. ८. M repeat the text हुत्वा स्रुचं प्रक्षाल्य निष्टय पुनरद्भिः पूरयित्वा बहिः परिध्युदगपवर्गं before जुहुयात्. ९. M Ad B ततोत्तरा. १०. M Ad B °लेपाद्देव° [B °लो]. ११-११. M Ad B नमिभोगञ्जु°. १२. M Ad B वेद. १३. M Ad B पावाचन°.

माच्छिद्रिकोपादानम्[१]। पात्रियां समवहितात्पुरोडाशादग्नीध आदध्यात्। चतुर्धाकृतं चेद्व्यादिष्टं स्वभागं वेदेनोपस्तरणाभिघारणद्वयोरनुवादयोस्तन्त्रेण इत्यपरे। अग्नीद् व्यस्तदक्षिणोत्तरं पाणिद्वयमुत्करस्योपरि निधाय गृह्णीयात्। यथोपपादमित्यन्ये[२]। सविताघशंसात्पातु इत्यनुषङ्गः। यथापाठमित्यपरे। [३][अग्नीद्ब्रह्म-] होत्रध्वर्यवो[४] यजमानश्च चतुर्थ इडां प्राश्नीयुः। होतैवेत्यपरे। मार्जनं सर्वेषाम्। अथ प्राशित्रादग्रेणाहवनीयं परिहरेत्। अत्रैव वाऽतिहरेत्। परिहरणपक्षे नास्ति। [अति]हृत्योत्तरत एव सादनं, विनिविष्टो वा विकल्पः। व्यवेत्योपवेशनेऽतिहरणमव्यवेत्योपवेशने परिहरणम्। व्यवेत्योपवेशनं दक्षिण एव सादनमग्रेणैव परिहरणमित्यपरे। प्राशित्रप्राशनानन्तरं प्राङ् मार्जनाद् ब्रह्मभागं परिहरेत्। चतुर्धा क्रियापक्षे व्यादिष्टं ब्रह्मभागं तदानीमेव होत्रेऽध्वर्यव इति। यथा स्वं भागं प्रयच्छेत्। न त्वेतयोरसति चतुर्धाकरणे भागः। तच्चानभिप्रेतमिवाचार्यस्य। अपरेणात्मानं पूर्वेणोत्करमुदगावृत्तान्यष्टाकपालमुखानि सान्नाय्यान्तानि हवींष्युद्वासयेत्॥ [४]

अपरेण सर्वान् कर्तॄन् दम्पती चेत्येके। सर्वेषां द्रव्याणामेष एवोद्वासने मार्गः। प्रदर्शनमेतदित्यपरे। चतुर्णाम[शितु][५]मन्वाहार्यमन्वाहार्ये यज्जातीयं हविस्तज्जातीयैस्तण्डुलैस्तूष्णीं श्रपयेत्। तस्मिंच्छिष्टमाज्यमासिच्य[६] तत्र पत्नीं वाचयित्वा तमपरेण गार्हपत्यं पर्याहृत्य पूर्वेण ब्रह्माणं च यजमानं चातिहृत्यान्तर्वेद्यासाद्य[७] यजमानं वाचयित्वा ब्राह्मणा[८] अयं व ओदनस्तं यथाभागं प्रतिगृह्णीध्वम् इत्युक्त्वा अग्नीधे ब्रह्मणे होत्रेऽध्वर्यवे इति। यजमाने[९] व्यादिष्टे तमृत्विजः सप्तदशकृत्वोऽपान्य मन्त्रेण गृह्णीयुः। अथैनं पुनराहृत्यापरेणात्मानं पूर्वेणोत्करमुदञ्चमुद्वासयेत्। अन्वाहार्यादेवातिहरणम्। न पर्याहरणमित्यपरे। सन्ततिमनु तिस्रः स्रुवाहुतीर्हुत्वा होतुराहुतिं जुहुयात्। होतुरेवाहुतिरनन्तरं सन्ततेः प्रसवानन्तरमग्नीदग्निं[१०] संमृज्यासञ्चरे[११] तूष्णीं तृणान्युदस्येत्। अध्वर्युर्वा मन्त्रेणाग्नौ प्रहरति नारिष्ठहोमानन्तरम्। समिष्टयजुषोऽनन्तरमित्यपरे। समिधमाधाय स्रुचावादत्ते। अग्नीत्समिधमाधायाग्नीन् संमार्ष्टीत्यपरे। संमिनोति[१२] संगमयति। उद्ग्राभं च निग्राभं च इति प्राचीं जुहूमुदूहति। अथा सपत्नानिन्द्राग्नी

१. M Ad B give न after °दानं, but this is not wanted. २. M Ad B °पवाद°. ३. M Ad B broken; Cf VādhŚS 2.11.38. ४. M Ad B त्रनध्व°. ५. M Ad B broken cf. Kalpāgama on VādhŚS 2.10.32. ६. M Ad B तस्मिन्छुद्धिमा°. ७. M Ad B °द्यासद्य. ८. M Ad B ब्रह्मणा. ९. M Ad B °मानं. १०. M Ad प्रसवानन्तम°, B °सवादन्तम°. ११. M Ad B समृज्य सञ्चरेत्. १२. M Ad B संभिनत्ति.

इति प्रतीचीमुपभृतमपोहति। स्रुचा मध्यमं परिधिमन्वारभ्योत्तरतः प्रह्वस्तिष्ठन्नाश्रावयेत्। सूक्तवाकान्ते प्रस्तरं प्रहरेत्। यथापाठमित्यपरे। शाखां च सहते न प्रहरेत्॥ [५]

अनुप्रहृत्य बर्हिरध्वर्युः स्वगा दैव्या होतृभ्यः इति प्रेष्येत्। इमां पृथिवीमात्मानं हृदयदेशं [प्रत्यभिमृशते][१]। आयुष्पा इति नासिकां प्र[त्यभिमृशते][२]; चक्षुष्पा इति चक्षुषी, श्रोत्रपा इति श्रोत्रे। सकृदेव वा सर्वान् प्राणान् समस्तं मन्त्रमनुद्रुत्य। अभितः परिधी प्रहृत्याधस्ताच्चोपरिष्टाच्च मध्यमस्य[३] स्रुचा [अपः] संप्रगृह्णाति[४] सम्यक् प्रस्त्रावयन् गृह्णाति। आहवनीये जुहूं, जुह्वामुपभृतं ध्रुवायां संस्त्रावमुभयोः प्रश्च्योत्य स्फ्ये सादयति। स्फ्यान्तया संस्पर्शयति। मन्त्रान्तयैव होत्रे वेदं यजमानेनामन्त्रितं प्रयच्छेत्। उपांशु पत्नीसंयाजमन्त्रा उपांशुतरा देवता वेदः। तेषूपभृत्स्थानीयः पुरस्तात् परिश्रिते देवानां पत्नीर्यज इति यथाश्रुतम्। तेषु देवता अग्नीध आदधाति द्विपत्नीवते[५] सवे [. . .][६] परमेष्ठी प्रजापतिः। एवं सर्वेषु[७] यागहोमेषु चतुर्गृहीतं गृहीत्वा फलीकरणानोप्यापसलैः पर्यावृत्य इध्मपश्वाज्योलूखलमुसलम्[८] इति पिष्टलेपमनुवर्तयेत्, अनुजपेद्वा। अनेन मन्त्रेण होमानन्तरं निवर्तयेदित्येके। तत्र विश्वेदेवा देवताः। प्रसलैः आवृत्य देवं प्रदाय पत्नीं विस्रंसयेत्। समायुषा इत्यनुवर्त्य यथेतमेत्य नारिष्ठहोमान् जुहो[९][ति। नारिष्ठ]पूर्वेषु नारिष्ठो चतुर्थे सोम ऋषभं[१०] त्वा त्रिषूत्तरेषु यज्ञपुरुषः। अन्त्ये प्रजापतिराप्यायताम् इत्याज्यस्थालीस्थमाज्यं ध्रुवायामवनयति। वेदस्य तृणानि वेद्यां स्तीर्णेन बर्हिषा ध्रुवामुपसंगृह्य उत्थाय दक्षिणेन पदा वेदिमत्याक्रम्य ध्रुवयैव समिष्टयजुर्जुहोति। समङ्क्ता [बर्हिर्हविषा घृतेन इति ध्रुवायां][११] बर्हिरक्त्वा दिव्यं नभो गच्छतु इत्यनुप्रास्य स्वाहा वाते धा इत्यभिहुत्येध्मसन्नहनानि मन्त्रेणानुप्रहृत्य स्रुचा संस्त्रावं स्रुच आनीयाभिहुत्य प्रणीता आवृत्यार्धमन्तर्वेदि यजमानस्याञ्जलावानीय सादयित्वाऽद्भिः पूरयित्वा पूर्णपात्रे वाचयित्वा प्राच्यां दिशि देवाः इति पञ्चभिः पञ्चकृत्वः पुनरञ्जलावानीयातिशिष्टाः॥ [६]

आपोहिष्ठीयेन तृचेनाञ्जलावेवानयेत्। विष्णुक्रमादयोऽध्वर्युणाऽपि कर्तव्याः। यजमानभागप्राशनवर्जमित्येके[१२]। यजमान एव वा सर्वे। प्रवसति

---

१. M Ad B om. २. M Ad B broken. ३. M मध्यस्य. ४. Ad संप्रतिश्रृ॰. ५. M Ad B ॰पत्नीवर्जा. ६. M Ad B broken. ७. M Ad B सर्वे. ८. M Ad B ॰पश्वनान्यन्वाबलेमुसल. ९. M Ad B broken. १०. M Ad B ऋभवं. ११. M Ad B broken. १२. M Ad B ॰पाशवर्ज॰.

यजमानेऽध्वर्युणाऽपि कर्तव्याः। इहाम्नाता विकृत्यर्थाः। पृथग्याजमानाः प्रकृत्यर्था इत्यपरे। सर्वेषु पक्षेषु व्रतविसर्गो यज्ञविमोकः कपालविमोकश्चाध्वर्योः। उपवेषं चोदपात्रं चादाय उपप्रेत **इत्युत्परेत उभौ। मन्त्रमुक्त्वापसृजति। अध्वयुर्यजमानेन सहायः परिषिच्याप्रतीक्षमागत्य होतृषदनैर्वेदिमभिच्छाद्य व्रतं विसृजेत्। यजमानस्यायं व्रतविसर्गकालः। प्राङेत्योपसमिधमादाय व्रतं विसृजेदित्येके। प्रदक्षिणमावृत्य प्रत्यङ्ङुद्द्रुत्यान्वाहार्यपचने सर्व ऋत्विजो वरुणविमोकं कुर्युः॥** [७] इति तृतीयोऽनुवाकः॥

अथ चतुर्थोऽनुवाकः

[याजमानम्]

यजमानोऽपि यज्ञोपवीत्यप आचम्य विद्युदसि विद्य मे पाप्मानम् **इत्यप उपस्पृशति।** वृष्टिरसि वृश्च मे पाप्मानम् **इत्यन्ते प्रधानयागाद्यन्तयोर्वा। अथान्वाधायाग्निं गृह्णामीत्युद्यन्तमादित्यमनु समारोहन्तमग्निमुपस्थाय विक्रममाण इव दक्षिणतः स्थितेषु व्रतमुपेत्याद्भिरात्मानं मार्जयित्वा** अग्ने व्रतपते **इति समिधमादायारेचनेन प्राणानायम्यानुच्छ्वसन् पूरणेनात्मानमन्तरतः पूरयित्वाऽनृतात्[१] सत्यमुपेयात्। बर्हिषा पूर्णमासे व्रतमुपेयात्। वत्सैरमावास्यायाम्।** शिवा च मे **इति पूर्वस्मिन् परिग्राहे जपति। श्वोभूते पौर्णमास्यामपराह्णे पिण्डपितृयज्ञेन प्रचरेत्। आदित एव प्राचीनावीतं कृत्वा दक्षिणेनान्वाहार्यपचनं दक्षिणाग्रेषु दर्भेषु एकैकं पैतृयज्ञिकान् संभारान् सादयेत्॥** [१]

उदकुम्भमुलूखलमुसलं शूर्पं स्थालीं मेक्षणं दर्वीं सकृदाच्छिन्नं दशामिति। स्रुवं चाज्यस्थालीं चैके सादयन्ति पिण्डानामुपस्तरणाभिघारणार्थायेति[२]। अथैकं पवित्रं तिरस्कृत्य दक्षिणामुखः पितृपितामहप्रपितामहान् मनसा संकल्प्य स्थाल्यां निर्वपति। यथार्धपात्रं चरु स्यादविवेकं[३] विवेकवर्जः। सकृदेव वा वितुषीभावः। सकृदवहत्य सकृदेव फलीकृत्य यावतीभिः सम्यक् पाको भवति तावतीभ्यो न्यूना एकपवित्रा अप आनीयाधिश्रित्यैकपवित्रानेव तण्डुलानोप्य श्रपयित्वा नवनीतं प्रक्षिप्योद्वास्य दक्षिणत स्फ्येनोद्धन्ति[४]। दक्षिणतश्चेत् पिण्डदानमपरेणोद्धन्ति। अपरेण चेत् पिण्डदानं दक्षिणत एवोद्धन्ति। अपरेण पिण्डदानमित्यपरे। अथोल्मुकमादायेत्यादि प्रतिपद्यते। तृणमुष्टिं सकृदाच्छिन्नं दर्वी-

---

१. M Ad B °नृतत्. २. M Ad B °र्थाविति. ३. M Ad B VādhŚS 2.2.9, fn.11 अनपवेकं. ४. M Ad °ध्वन्ति.

सादनान्[१] पिण्डान् यथा चतुरश्चमसांश्चतुरः स्रुवान् इति। दर्व्यौ दक्षिणापवर्गाः। जीवत्पिता पिण्डद्वयं दद्यात् एतद्वः पितामहाः, एतद्वः प्रपितामहाः इति मन्त्रद्वयेन। विनिविष्टश्च मन्त्रविकल्पः[२]। एकेनैव मन्त्रेण पिण्डद्वयं दद्यात्॥ [२]

उदङ्ङावृत्य आतमितोरावेदनाद् [३]अनुच्छ्वसन्नसित्वाऽऽहवनीयमभिव्यनिति। व्यपगतोष्माणः पिण्डानभिपर्यावृत्य स्थालीगतमेवावजिघ्रति त्रिः[४] सकृन्मन्त्रः। दीर्घान् दशान् छित्त्वा मन्त्रेण पिण्डत्रये निदधाति। संसादयति[५]। विसर्जयति। मन आह्वयति। मत्वा ब्रूयात्। आहवनीयस्यार्धमेति मन्त्रेण। पात्रे चरुस्थाल्यां समस्यति। अथैतान्यायुधान्येकैकमुदाहरन्ति। अथान्वाहार्यपचने स्थालीपाकं श्रपयित्वा तस्मिन्नेव हुत्वा प्राश्नीयात्। अध्वर्युणा वा हुतं प्राश्योपवसेत्। श्वोभूते वाचं यच्छ इत्युक्ते वाग्यत आसीनो[६] हविष्कृदाह्वानात् अन्यत्र यज्ञसादनात्[७]। अधिनिहितेषु पवित्रेषु पुरोडाशीयेष्वध्वर्युणा वाच्यमानो धूः मन्त्रं ब्रूयात्। अग्निं होतारम् इति निरुप्यमाणं हविरभिमन्त्रयेत। अध्वर्युणा वाच्यमानः सकृदेवात्रैवाभिमन्त्रणं [८]मन्त्रयोर्विकल्पे इत्येकेनापि विकल्पः। निरुप्तेष्वेव सकृद्वाच्यमानोऽभिमन्त्रयेतेत्यपरे। उलूखलमुसलं दृषदुपलं च अध्वर्युणा युज्यमानमभिमन्त्रयेत, परेक्षेत वा। तथा सत्यध्वर्युणा दृषदुपलं परेक्षणीयं स्वेन स्वेन कर्मणा युज्यमानम्। पृथक् पृथगवघातेन युज्यमानमुलूखलमुसलम्। पेषणेन युज्यमानं दृषदुपलम्। एवं सति विमोकोऽपि स्वस्वकर्मणोऽन्ते, उलूखलमुसलस्यावघातान्ते, दृषदुपलस्य पेषणान्ते। सैव कपालानां विकल्पना यथा त्वमग्ने इति। निरुप्तानामभिमृशति[९]। अध्वर्युरित्येके। हविष्कृतमाहूयमानं मन्त्रेण प्रत्युत्थाय मन्त्रेणैवोपविश्य त्रिष्फलीक्रियमाणानामिति। तण्डुलेषु प्रक्षाल्यमानेषु जपित्वा परिग्रहणयोः जपित्वा स्फ्य उदस्यमाने जपेत्॥ [३]

अध्वर्युणा जप्यमान[१०] आज्यमसि इति निमीलयन्निवाज्यमवेक्षेत। तथाऽऽज्यग्रहानभिमन्त्र्य पवित्रयोरपिसृज्यमानयोः जपित्वा, बर्हिषि स्तीर्यमाणे जपित्वा, आस्तीर्यमाणां[११] वेदिमभिमन्त्र्य अस्मिन् यज्ञे इति परिधानारंभे जपित्वा, धत्त इत्यादींश्च परिधीयमानेषु जपित्वा, अग्निर्द्वेषांसि इत्यनुयुङ्क्त्वा, ऊर्ध्वयोः समिधयोरभ्याधीयमानयोर्जपित्वा, ध्रुवोऽसि इत्यादिभिर्वाच्यमानोऽपि

१. M Ad साधनात्. २. M Ad B °कल्पं. ३. M Ad B °न्नासित्वा°. ४. M Ad B त्रिष्कमसकृ°. ५. M Ad B संसाधय°. ६. M Ad B आसीता. ७. M Ad B °साध°. ८. M Ad B तालयो°. ९. M Ad B °प्तानभिमृ°. १०. M Ad B °मानम्. ११. M Ad B °स्तीर्यमा.

परिधीनभिमन्त्र्य मध्यमं परिधिमन्वारभ्याग्नियोगं जपित्वा, तिरश्च्योः साद्यमान-योर्जपित्वा, यन्मे अग्ने **इति** [१]**प्रस्तरमासाद्यमानमभिमन्त्र्यायं प्रस्तरं जपति। सर्वासु स्त्रुक्षु**[२] **प्रस्तरे साद्यमानास्वयं**[३] **मन्त्रः। नैकस्यामित्येके।** [४]**जुह्वामासाद्यमानायामुपभृति ध्रुवायां च** अग्नेरहम् **इत्यादिमन्त्रत्रयं जपित्वा** यन्मे अग्ने **इति मिथः स्त्रुचोऽभिमृश्यासन्नानि हवींष्यन्यानि च** अयं यज्ञः **इति संसन्नं यज्ञं यज्ञसाधनानि हवींष्यभिमृशति। अध्वर्युरित्येके।** अग्ने देवेद्ध **इतीध्ममाधीयमानम्। प्रत्याहवनीयमभिमन्त्र्य** उच्छुष्मा **इति वेदेनोपवीज्यमानम्। पूर्वस्मिन्नाघारे प्रजापतिं देवतात्वेन सङ्कल्पयेत्। सर्वेषु प्रदानेषु देवता ध्यातव्याः। आख्याता आध्वर्यवे**[५] **देवताः।** मनोऽसि **इति पूर्वमाघारमभिमन्त्र्य अग्नौ संसृज्यमाने** अग्ने वाजजित् **इति जपित्वा,** वागसि **इत्युत्तरमाघारमभिमन्त्र्याध्वर्युप्रवरे** अमर्त्यस्य ते होतर् **इति जपेत्॥** [४]

देवाः पितरः **इति च।** अहं देवेषु **इति चाश्राविते ब्रूयाद्,** अहं मनुष्येषु **इति प्रत्याश्राविते।** यज **इत्युक्ते** हविषां देवान् **इति।** ये यजामहे **इत्युक्त्वा** यथाभागं देवता **इत्युक्त्वा वषट्कृते देवतां ध्यात्वा** प्रतिमा तिष्ठ[६] **इत्युक्त्वा प्रथमे प्रयाज**[७] **एकं** प्रयाण **इत्यनुमन्त्र्य** वसन्तमृतूनाम् **इत्यनुमन्त्रयते॥** [५]

एवं सर्वेषु प्रयाजेषु अमुष्य **इत्यत्र द्वेष्यस्य नाम गृह्णाति। तथा** असौ **इति। सर्वत्र वषट्कारप्रदानेषु यत्र चाश्रावणादयो विद्यन्ते तत्र सर्वत्र निमित्तमङ्गी-कृत्यानुमन्त्रणानि प्रवर्तन्ते। प्राशित्रमवदीयमानम्** अग्निर्मा दुरिष्टात्पातु **इत्यभि-मन्त्र्य** आज्यायो यवमात्रात् **इति जपेत्। इडायामवदीयमानायां** मनुना दृष्टाम् **इति प्रति हविर्जपित्वा इडामाह्रियमाणामनुमन्त्रयते** सुरूपवर्षवर्ण **इति। अवान्तरेडाम-वदीयमानां** रन्तिरसि **इति। अथागत्येडामन्वारभ्य** जुष्टे जुष्टिं तेऽशीय **इत्युपांशु। उपाशीयमानाम्** उपहूतः **इति श्रुत्वा** वायुष्टेऽवतु **इति वायुं ध्यात्वा** सा मे सत्याशीः **इति अभिमन्त्र्य** ओम् **इति त्रिरुक्त्वा** उपहूतः पशुमानसानि **इति व्याहृत्य, यथेतं प्रत्येत्य यजमानायतन उपविश्य बर्हिषदमष्टाकपालं कृत्वा** ब्रध्न पिन्वस्व **इत्यनुमन्त्रयेत। अपि वा नीचा हस्तेन तमभिमृश्य जपेत्** आयुषः क्लृप्तिः **इति। अथोत्तान**[हस्तेन][८] ब्रध्न पिन्वस्व **इति। अथ** आग्निर्मा दुरिष्टात्पातु **इति**

---

१. M Ad B प्रस्तरासाद्य°. २. M Ad सुस्त्रु स्त्रुक्षु. ३. M Ad B साद्यस्वयं. ४. M Ad B जुह्वां सा°. ५. M Ad B चाध्व°. ६. M Ad B तिष्ठप°. ७. M Ad B याज. ८. M Ad B broken.

पूर्वस्मिन्। अग्नीध्रीयावदानेऽभिधाय उपहूतो द्यौष्पिता **इति जपित्वा** सविता-ऽघशंसात् **इत्युत्तरस्मिन्।** सविता माऽघशंसात् पातु **इति सानुषङ्गेण।** उपहूता पृथिवी माता **इति जपेत्। इडां प्राश्यावमार्जयते**[१] ॥ [६]

बृहस्पतिस्तनुताम् **इति। सादितमन्वाहारमभिमन्त्रयते** प्रजापतेर्भागोऽसि **इति।** मनो ज्योतिः **इत्यनुमन्त्र्याथानूयाजान्** बर्हिषः **इत्यादिभिः। अथाध्वर्युणा सह स्रुचावत्यूह्य**[२] **उज्जितीरनुमन्त्र्य** आशास्तेऽयं यजमानः **इति श्रुत्वा** एमा अग्मन्ना-शिष **इति जपित्वा** रोहितेन त्वा **इति प्रस्तरं प्रह्रियमाणमनुमन्त्र्य** [. . . .][३] **अथात्रैव [वाऽऽसीनो]**[४] **दक्षिणेन गार्हपत्यमासीनः पत्नीसंयाजाननुमन्त्र्येडां प्राश्य मार्ज-यित्वा प्राडेत्य ध्रुवामाप्याय्य समिष्टयजुर्हूयमानं** देवा गातुविदः **इत्यन्वारभ्यान्त-र्वेद्यासादितासु प्रणीतासु** [सदसि सन्मे][५] भूयाद् **इति जपित्वाऽञ्जलावानीता-भिर्हस्तौ प्रक्षाल्य [अथाप आचम्यापो न्युप्य**[६]] सदसि **इति पूर्णपात्रेऽभिधाय** प्राच्यां दिशि देवा **इत्यञ्जलावानीताभिरद्भिर्यथादिशं मार्जयित्वा** आपो हि ष्ठा मयोभुव **इति तृचेनातिशिष्टा आत्मनोऽञ्जलावानीताभिर्मुखं संमृष्टे** समिन्द्र णः, सं वर्चसा **इति। अथोपो[त्थाय दक्षि]**[७]**णं वे[द्यन्तमनु विष्णुक्रमान्,]**[८] विष्णोः क्रम **इत्यादि**[९]**[ना। य]दि चतुर्थेन मन्त्रेण चेत्, तिर्यक्**[१०] **कृषेत गोमतीं जपित्वा।** अयमात्मीयाद् गृहादनपायिनमिच्छन्तमुपवेषमाहर **इत्युक्त्वाऽनेनाहृतमुपवेषं** यं देवा मनुष्येषु **इत्यादयः। मन्त्रेण शाखामूलेनोपवेषोऽन्तरेण त्रिभिर्मन्त्रैः** येन संप्र **इति,** उपप्रेत **इति उपेत्य,** अव सृष्ट **इत्यवसृज्यापः परिषिच्याप्रतीक्षमागत्य व्रतं विसृज्य समिधमाधाय प्राण्यापान्यापानेनात्मानमन्तरतः पूरयित्वाऽऽह** इदमहं सत्यादमृतमुपैमि **इति। दक्षिणत उपविश्य** इदं हविर् **इति पयः पीत्वा यथा समुदिता ब्राह्मणाँस्तर्पयेत्॥** [७] [इति चतुर्थोऽनुवाकः।[११]] इति याजमानं समाप्तम्॥

[अथ पञ्चमोऽनुवाकः[१२]]

[अथ ब्रह्मत्वम्]

ब्रह्मा स्नातः शुचिवास[१३] **आचान्तः** भूपते **इति यजमानेन वृतो** अहं भूपतिर् **इति जपित्वा प्रयुज्य अजिनं वासो वा यज्ञोपवीतं कृत्वा आपोहिष्ठीयाभिराचम्य**

---

१. M Ad B प्राश्यवमा°. २. M Ad B स्रुचान्यूह्य. ३. M Ad B broken. ४. M Ad B broken. ५. M Ad B broken cf. VādhŚS 3.6.19. ६. M Ad B broken. ७. M Ad B broken. ८. M Ad B broken. ९. M Ad B broken. १०. M Ad °तिर्यकृ. ११. M Ad B om. १२. M Ad B om. १३. M Ad B °वाससा.

व्याहृतीभिः परिमृज्य प्रजापतिः प्राची दिग् **इति जपित्वा** [१]**प्राण्यापान्याग्निग्रहणमन्त्रद्वयं जपित्वा हस्तौ संमृश्य** बृहस्पतिर्ब्रह्मा **इत्यन्तरा वेदिं चोत्करं च प्रत्यङ् प्रपद्यापरेण वेदिमत्याक्रम्य दक्षिणं वेद्यन्तमनु गत्वा दक्षिणेनाहवनीयं प्रबाहुगिध्मसदन उपस्तीर्णानां शुष्काग्रं वा प्रतिच्छिन्नाग्रं वा मन्त्रेणादाय निरस्य अप उपस्पृश्य मन्त्रेणोपविश्य** देव सवितर् **इति जपति**। असौ **इत्यत्रात्मनो नाम गृह्णीयात्**। प्रणय यज्ञम् **इत्युपांशु जपन् प्रणवादिप्रसवमुच्चैर्ब्रूयात्। एवं सर्वेषु प्रसवेषु मन्त्रवत्कर्मसु येन केनचित् क्रियमाणेषु तस्य तस्य कर्मण आ समाप्तेर्वाग्यमः**[२]**। प्राशित्रमुभाभ्यां हस्ताभ्यां प्रतिगृह्य वेद्यां सादयित्वा अङ्गुष्ठोपकनिष्ठिकयाऽतिहाय दन्तान् मन्त्रेण जिह्वामूले निदध्यात्** ब्राह्मणस्योदरेण[३] **इति सहाद्भिः गिरति। अग्रेण दक्षिणजान्वेतां दिशं प्राचीमुदीचीं प्रति संक्षालं निनयेत्। प्राणाः स्वमन्त्रैर्यथालिङ्गम्**। अरिष्टा विश्वान्यङ्गानि **इति चोदितेषु स्थानेषु वाचयित्वा यथार्थमाभाषेत। वाग्यमनकालेऽपि यज्ञसिद्ध्यर्थमन्तर्हन्वेव ब्राह्मणेन संभाषेत॥ [१]**

समिष्टयजुरन्ते यथेतं निष्क्रम्यापरेण गच्छेत्। शकलौ प्रास्य[४] **वरुणविमोचनं कृत्वा यथार्थं गच्छेत्। एतेनैव विधानेन दर्शपूर्णमासविकाराणामपि ब्रह्मत्वं कुर्यात्। चातुर्मास्येषु तु वरुणप्रघासेषूभौ वेदी अत्याक्रम्यापरेण गच्छेत्। प्रणीतयोरग्न्योर्मन्त्रेणोपविशेत्**[५]**। उभयोः प्रणीतयोरूहेन प्रसौति** प्रणयतं, वर्धयतं, धत्त। इमां प्रणय **इति। नास्त्यूहोऽध्वर्युरेव प्रणयेदित्येके। परिग्राहप्रसवं चोहेत्। वेदिं** प्रिया स्योना नो स्तम्[६]**। अनन्तरयोरुपस्थयोः** अपां परिगृह्णीतम् **इति।** बृहस्पतिः परिगृह्णीतम्[७] **इति केचिदूहन्ति, अध्वर्युपरतां बृहस्पतिशब्दस्य मन्यमानाः। पितृयज्ञे पितृशब्दोऽन्वासङ्गः।** कर्मणे वां देवेभ्यः पितृभ्य **इत्यूहेत्।** बृहस्पतिर्ब्रह्मा [स यज्ञं पातु][८] स यज्ञपतिं पातु स मां पातु यज्ञन्यम् **इति। अपरेण पितृवेदिमत्याक्रम्य दक्षिणेन दक्षिणाग्निमुपविश्य** देव सवितर्[९] ओमहं मानुष **इति। प्रणीतासु प्रसवे** प्रणय यज्ञं देवताः पितॄन् वर्धयैतेन नाकस्य पृष्ठ अस्तु सप्तर्षीणां यज्ञं च धेह्योम् प्रणय **इति। परिग्राहे** प्रिया देवानां पितृणाम् **इति पितृशब्दोऽन्वासङ्गः। पक्षे विपर्ययेणाग्निं गत्वोत्तरतः उपविशेत्। अनुयाजेषु प्रसवे** स यज्ञं पाहि स पाहि मां पाहि यज्ञन्यम् **इति त्र्यम्बकैः प्रचरद्भिः सह**

---

१. M Ad B °पान्यग्नि°. २. M Ad B °वान्यमः. ३. M Ad B ब्रह्मणस्यो°. ४. M Ad B प्राश्य. ५. M Ad °णो.... शेदु°; B णोशेदु. ६. M Ad वेदिप्रियस्येनेन स्ताम् [B °प्रीय°]. ७. B गृहीतम्. ८. M Ad B om. ९. M Ad B सवितरेतः.

गच्छेत्। पशौ त्वपरेण वेदिमत्याक्रामेत्। प्रणीतेऽग्नावुत्तरवेदिमपरेणात्याक्रम्य मन्त्रेणोपविशेत्। प्रसिद्धमितरत् सर्वत्र कृत्वा कृतमन्वीक्षमाणः। यद्दक्षिणत एव स्यात् तत्रोक्तं च करोति॥ [२]

मैत्रावरुणदण्डे वाचनं, पशोर्मृत्यवे नीयमानस्यानुगमनं, रेवतीः **इति वपाश्रपणीभ्यामन्वारम्भः। संज्ञप्यमाने पशौ पुनरेत्य पृषदाज्यावेक्षणे वाचं यत्त्वा पशुमनवेक्ष्यासनम्। संज्ञप्ते पशौ** शमितार उपेतन **इति पुनः पशोरुपायनम्;** उर्वन्तरिक्षमन्विहि **इति पुनर्वपानुगमनं, वपाश्रपण्योः पुनः** अन्वपा रमयन्तु[१] गाव **इति मन्त्रं सन्नमयेत्।**[२] **वपान्ते चात्वाल आपोहिष्ठीयाभिर्मार्जनं पृषदाज्यरक्षणं पशुपुरोडाशस्य परिहृतस्य मनसा प्राशित्रप्राशनम् आप्राणसंमर्शनाद्भिः प्राशनम्। हृदयशूलप्रचार इति प्रायश्चित्तहोमश्च सर्वे ब्रह्मणः। अध्वर्युरेवेत्यपरे॥** [३] इति पञ्चमोऽनुवाकः[३] ॥ इति ब्रह्मत्वं समाप्तम्॥

[॥ इति पुरोडाश्याख्यः प्रपाठकः समाप्तः ॥][४]

---

१. Ad रस°. २. The text beginning with अथ हुतेऽग्निहोत्रे [M. 414, line 15; Ad p. 837, line 5, B p. 243, line 10] and ending with तिसृभिराहवनीयोपायनं [M p. 416, line 1, Ad p. 839, line 10; B p. 244] does not belong to *Brahmatva*. It is rather related to the *Vaiśvadevaparvan* under *Cāturmāsya*. So that text has been shifted to its proper place, i.e. *Cāturmāsya* (p 28, line 4, p. 29, line 1). The text, covering about four lines given after तिसृभिराहवनीयोपायनम् in the above MSS, deals with the *Brahmatva*, hence it follows after 'अन्वपा रमयन्तु गावः' इति मन्त्रं सन्नमयेत्. With this description ends the *Brahmatva* of the present text. ३. M Ad B Anuvāka number not given. ४. M Ad B om.

[1] ॥ अथ तृतीयः प्रपाठकः ॥

॥ अथ चातुर्मास्यानि ॥[1]

[2][अथ प्रथमोऽनुवाकः]

[वैश्वदेवपर्व][2]

शिशिरादौ वनमुपोष्य तेषु तरुणदर्भेषु संजातेषु फाल्गुनशुक्लचतुर्दश्यामग्निहोत्रोच्छिष्टमातच्य निदधातीत्यादि प्रतिपद्यन्त इति केचित्। पञ्चदश्यामित्यपरे। अस्मिन् पक्षे यजनीयेऽहनि वैश्वदेवश्च पौर्णमासी च स्याताम्। तत्राग्निहोत्रोच्छिष्टमातच्य[3] निधाय यज्ञोपवीत्यप आचम्य तीर्थेन प्रपद्य प्राण्यापान्य प्रजापतिः प्राची दिग् **इति यज्ञपुरुषाय नमस्कृत्याभ्याधायोत्परेत्य[4] पलाशशाखामाच्छिनत्ति। तत्र** इषे त्वोर्जे त्वा **इति प्राकृतस्योपलक्षणम्। एवं** वायव स्थोपायव स्थ **इति सन्दिग्धेष्वेकमित्यपरे[5]। प्रस्तरमात्रं प्रसूमयम्। अन्येषु मुष्टिष्वनियमाः। त्रेधा सन्नहनं तूष्णीं, समस्तसन्नहनं समन्त्रकम्। तदुपगूहनान्तं कृत्वा प्रसिद्धमारम्भणीयाया बर्हिर्लुनाति। तत्रार्वाक् परिदेशनातन्त्रम्। ततश्चोद्यमानादिसादनान्तं मन्त्रविपरिणमनं[6] च। मन्त्रं पुरुषसंस्कारं चाभ्याधानं च वचनात्। अथ परिस्तरणादेरान्तादावृत्तिः।** अग्निं होतारम् **इति वाचयित्वा प्राणग्रहादयो व्याख्येयाः। व्यावर्तने** यथाभागं व्यावर्तध्वम् **इति दक्षिणपिण्डं विच्छिन्द्यात्[7] अथेतरो** यथाभागं व्यावर्तेथाम् **इति। एवं पुरोडाशग्रहणे[8] सर्वत्र**

१-१. M Ad B None of the MSS mentions the serial number of the *Prapāṭhaka.* Instead following benedictory verse—

शोभनश्रुतिशरीरशिल्पवित्कल्पसूत्रकृदनल्पबन्धवे।

श्रोत्रियाय शिवशब्दसमुदितश्रोणनामपरिशोभिने नमः ॥

is given. This verse, in no way, is from the pen of the author. Most probably, this verse belongs to the copyist who himself composed it in the honour of Śivaśroṇa, the author of the *Prayogakḷpti*, highlighting the excellent knowledge of Śrauta rituals of the author. After the benedictory verse the title of the Chapter is wrongly given as अथ पितृयज्ञः प्रारभ्यते instead of 'अथ चातुर्मास्यानि प्रारभ्यन्ते'. As the topic, dealt here, belongs to the Cāturmāsya rituals, I have accordingly given the title as 'अथ चातुर्मास्यानि'. २-२. M Ad B om. ३. M Ad B °मासच्य. ४. M Ad B °त्पत्यै. ५. M Ad B सन्दिग्धेष्वेवमि°. ६. M Ad B °परिणांश्च. ७. M Ad B °पिण्डमवि°. ८. M Ad B °गणे.

चरु इत्यूहः। यन्म अग्ने इति हवींष्यभिमृश्य प्राणग्रहांश्चोत्तरांश्च[१] पृश्नींश्च व्याचक्षीत। दश-होतारं[२] चतुर्होत्रर्थं प्रत्याम्नातः। संस्थितायामारम्भणीयेष्ट्यां[३] वेदं कृत्वाऽभि-मन्त्र्याग्नीन् कृत्वा परिस्तीर्य दोहनाय गा आयतीः प्रतीक्षमाणः इह वो विश्वेदेवा इति। [४]अथ हुतेऽग्निहोत्रे प्रसिद्धं दोहयेत्। पात्रासादनकाले[५] वाजिनपात्रमा-मिक्षापात्रमाशयपात्रं च सादयेत्। अविकृत्या प्रोक्षणमन्त्रः, न वा। नाग्नेय-विकारेषु जुष्ट-शब्दं स्वे स्वे स्थाने चरुस्थालीमपिश्रित्य तिरःपवित्रमप आनीय मारुतस्य कपालान्यभिधायामिक्षापात्रमधिश्रित्य तिरःपवित्रं प्रातर्दोहमानयेत्। स्वयैव स्थाल्या श्रृतमधिश्रयेत्। एककपालं पुरोडाशमात्रमुपदध्यात्। पुरोडाशं कूष्माण्डमात्रं कुक्कुटाण्डमात्रं वा, यथाप्रकृति वा। चरव्यानपयच्छन् पृथक् पौष्णस्यापयच्छति। पुरोडाशार्थान् पिष्ट्वा तूष्णीं पौष्णान् पिंष्यात्। अपेषणं पौष्णस्यैके। मारुतमधिश्रित्य तप्ते पयसि श्रृताप्ये सायंदोहं दध्यानीय उद्वास्याग्निनाऽऽमिक्षां श्रपयित्वा वाजिनं कृत्वा प्रतापे निदधाति। मेक्षय चरून् इत्यूहेत्। अलङ्कुर्वन्त्यानुपूर्वं हवींषि गन्धपुष्पेनाज्येन वा। भूयसोपस्तरणं चालङ्कारः। स्वरूपापादनं वा सर्वेषां हविषाम्। उपस्तीर्णाभिघारितामामिक्षा-मुद्वासयति कांसे[६] वा चमसे वा। दारुपात्र्यामेवेत्यपरे। तथा कांसे वा चमसे वोपस्तीर्यैकैकं पात्रमुद्वास्याभिघार्य बह्वानीयापिपृष्ठं कुर्यात्। समभिघार्य [७]हवींष्याहृत्य सादयेत्। सान्नाय्यमन्त्रद्वयेनामिक्षां सादयित्वा आमिक्षा मयि श्रयताम्, मां धिनोतु इत्यभिमृशेत्। विकल्प इत्येके। श्रुतमन्त्राभ्यामेवेत्यपरे। वाजिनमाधायोत्करे विशये वा सादयेत्। निर्मन्थ्येन चरति॥ [१]

शकलादानादिनाऽभिहोमान्तेन उपांशुधर्मः। सावित्रश्च एककपालश्च त्र्यवत्तश्चैककपालकेऽस्यानुमन्त्रणं प्राकृतं प्रत्यानमेत्। समुच्चय इत्यपरे। [८]अनुयज्ञैः इत्याध्वर्यवमित्यन्ये। पर्यावृत्तं पुरोडाशं स्त्रुचा[९] सादयेत्, न हस्तेन। याज्यानुवाक्याभ्यां प्रत्यृचमभिहोमः। ताश्चतस्त्र आहुतयः। आमादेककपाल-स्येडामप्यवद्येत्। सन्ततिमनु विष्टम्भान्वारोहान्। आच्छिद्रिकोपादानपक्षे अनाज्ञातम् इति तिस्त्रः स्त्रुवाहुतीरनु वाजिनस्य। प्रणीताभ्य उपस्तरणाभि-

---

१. M Ad B °पनग्रहाश्चोत्तरश्च पृश्नीन्. २. M Ad B दशहो [B °होतु]. ३. M °मरंभणी°. ४. The text beginning with अथ हुतेऽग्निहोत्रे and ending with तिसृभिराहवनीयोपायनं, as referred to in f.n. 3 on p. 26, has been wrongly put under *Brahmatva* due to displacement of folios, I have given this text here as it deals with the *Vaiśvadevaparva*. ५. M Ad पात्रसदन°; B पात्र सा°. ६. M Ad B कः सो. ७. M Ad B हविष्या°. ८. M Ad B अनुयज्ञेरि°. ९. M Ad B स्त्रुचं.

घारणेनोपारंभः। उप त्वाग्ने दिवेदिवे **इति तिसृभिराहवनीयोपासनम्**[१]**। स्तरणाभिघारणे इत्यपरे। अन्तर्वेदि तिष्ठन् वाजिभ्य आश्रावयेत्। दिग्भ्य**[२] **उच्छेषयेत्। दिशो हुत्वा भक्षायोच्छिनष्टि। किञ्चिदुपादाय घ्राणभक्षं**[३] **भक्षयेयुः सर्वे**[४]**। यजमानः प्रत्यक्षं भक्षयेत्॥** [२]

संस्थामनु [हविषो निवर्तयते][५]**। तस्य पौर्णमासान्ते वा निवर्तनम्। लोहितायसस्ताम्रमय अयोविकारः कश्चिदित्यपरे। वपनमेव परिवर्तनम्। वपनार्थो विभागः केशानाम्। शलल्यैवेत्यपरे। समानेऽहनि वैश्वदेवपौर्णमासौ पञ्चदश्यां वैश्वदेवस्य काले। पौर्णमास इत्यपरे॥** [३] इति प्रथमोऽनुवाकः॥

[अथ द्वितीयोऽनुवाकः]

[वरुणप्रघासपर्व]

सर्वेषु पर्वसु [अर्धकक्षमुपो][६]**षति। ग्रीष्मे वरुणप्रघासार्थं कक्षमुपौषत्, शरदि साकमेधार्थम्, यथार्हं शुनासीरीयाय। वैश्वदेव एव प्रसूनियमो, नोत्तरेषु पर्वस्वित्यपरे। चतस्रश्च स्थाल्यो दोहनार्थाः। यज्ञायुधानामेकतयाधिकानि**[७] **दक्षिणविहारार्थानि। तान्येतानि भवन्ति — स्फ्यश्च वैकङ्कतश्चाग्निहोत्रहवणी**[८]**श्च शूर्पञ्च शमीपर्णानि च करीरसक्तवश्च मेष्यै च लोमानि मेषस्य च।** [८]**चतस्रो यथाप्रकृतीत्यपरे। आज्यस्थाली इध्मानां द्वावग्निप्रणयिनीयौ यवाः करम्भपात्रं मेषमेष्यार्थाः। ऐषीकं शरमयं, करीरसक्तवः करीरफलानि चूर्णीकृतानि, मेषमेष्योर्लोमानि नानैव निधेयानि वरुणप्रघासार्थम्। श्वोऽषाढाभिः पौर्णमासीत्यग्निहोत्रोच्छिष्टमातच्य**[९] **निधाय शाखामाहृत्य वत्सानपाकृत्य बर्हिर्द्वयमध्वर्यवे लुनीयात्। वचनादन्यतस्तूष्णीम्। तल्लक्षणं विहारार्थम्। अथेध्मद्वयं सन्नय्य शाखापवित्रं निष्पाद्य वेदौ कृत्वाऽभिमन्त्र्य गार्हपत्यं चान्वाहार्यपचनं च परिस्तीर्य गा आयतीः प्रतीक्ष**[ते। एता मरुतो][१०] वरुणश्च रमयन्तु गाः **इत्यूहित्वा**

---

१. M ॰योपायनम्, B ॰योपानयनम्. २. M Ad B दिग्य. ३. M Ad B ॰पक्षं. ४. M Ad B सर्व. ५. M Ad B broken; thus VādhŚS 4.4.21. ६. M Ad B broken; cf. VādhŚS 4.1.1. ७. M Ad B केतयादनि. ८–८. M Ad B होत्र . . . ण्याक . . . चतस्रो. cf. VādhŚS 4.5.2 ९. The text beginning with च्छिष्टमातच्य निधाय शाखामाहृत्य [M p. 435, line 18; Ad p. 874, line 1; B p. 261, line 3] and ending with 'होतुराहुतौ हुतायाम्' [M p. 440, line 11; Ad p. 882, line 1; B. p. 265, line 4] due to displacement of folios, is given under Paśubandha in all the MSS. Actually, it belongs to the *Varuṇapraghāsa,* so it has been placed here at its proper place under *Varuṇapraghāsa.* १०. M Ad B broken.

हुतेऽग्निहोत्रे दोहमारभेत बहु दुग्धि इत्यातः। प्राङ् मारुत्याः कृत्वा वारुण्याश्च करोति। तदेव पवित्रमुद्धाय तावान् मारुतं चाननुसृजेत्। अथ बहु दुग्धि मरुद्भ्यो वरुणाय हविः इत्युक्त्वा वत्सेभ्यो देहि इत्यादि प्रतिपद्यते। विप्रुषामनुमन्त्रणतन्त्रं स्रंक्षालनान्तम्[१]। पृथगामन्त्रणश्चावर्तते[२]। तथाभिद्योतनप्रत्यानयने तन्त्रम्। पर्यग्निकरणं प्रतिष्ठापनं तु युगपदेव यथासम्भवम्। आतञ्चनं पृथगेव मन्त्रस्यानावृत्तिः। तथा पात्राभ्यामभिधानतन्त्रम्। तथा प्रातर्दोहं दोहयित्वा पूर्वेणाहवनीयं त्रयोदशाङ्गुलान्तराले वेदिं मिनुयात्॥ [१]

तयोः पशोरुत्तरा दार्शिकी दक्षिणा पाशुक्या समानायामा पशुबन्धस्येव चात्वालोत्करौ। तन्त्रमुक्तम्[३]। तयोः स्तम्बयजुषी हविष्यसौ[४] वेदाभ्यां वेदी संमृष्टस्तूष्णीं प्रतिप्रस्थाता। एवं सर्वत्र सहक्रियायां स्तम्बयजुराज्यग्रहणमेव प्रतिप्रस्थातृकर्मणा। तूष्णीकत्वमित्येके। वेदिं मिमाय स्फ्यदानात्प्रभृति प्रागुत्तरस्मात् परिग्रहात् कुरुतः। [५]अध्वर्युरेव करणं जपति। संनमयन् इमे नराः कृणुत वेदी एत्य इति। हर इति चाह सर्वत्र। प्रतिवचनाश्रावणप्रैषाः सहक्रियामध्वर्योरेव। गच्छन्नागच्छंश्च प्रतिप्रस्थाताऽध्वर्युं परिगृह्णीयात्। अपरेणात्मानमुत्तरेणाध्वर्युं, प्रतिप्रस्थातारमपरेणोत्तरवेदिमध्वर्युं च प्रतिप्रस्थातुः संचारः।[५] पशाविवोत्तरस्यां वेद्यामुत्तरवेदिं न्युप्य शूर्पेणावतृणैर्वा प्रच्छाद्याध्वर्युरुत्तरवेदिकस्यावृता प्रहरति। षड्ढोतृहोमवर्जमधर्मकं प्रतिप्रस्थाता दक्षिणस्यां वेद्याम्। सधर्मकमधर्मकमित्यपरे। अपरेणोत्तरवेदिं परीत्यान्तरेण वेदी प्रत्यङ् गत्वाऽपसलैः पर्यावृत्य दक्षिणमिध्मं सादयित्वा प्रावृत्य यथेतं गच्छेत्॥ [२]

एवमुपयमनीहरणं चाधर्मकम्। पक्षे सधर्मकत्वेऽप्युपयमन्यसन्नोपस्नानमतिमुक्तयश्चेत्येतावान् प्रतिप्रस्थाताऽध्वर्युश्च[६] वैतमूहेन्न किञ्चिदधर्मकत्वे। अथ तावग्नी परिस्तृणीतः। अग्रेणाग्नीदध्वर्युः[७] दर्भान् परिगृह्य, दक्षिणमग्निं प्रतिप्रस्थाता परिस्तृणीयात्। अथाग्रेण गार्हपत्यं तृणानि संस्तीर्य तेषु यथास्थानं[८] पात्राणि सादयतः — स्फ्यं प्रोक्षणीपात्रं स्रुवं स्रुच आज्यस्थालीमामिक्षापात्रं वेदमिति। प्रतिप्रस्थाता आमिक्षाश्रपणीं च केचित्। अध्वर्युरेवोभयानि पात्राणि सादयित्वा सहैव प्रोक्षेदित्येके। पञ्चहोतुरित्येके। अध्वर्युरेव यवोदनं मृदित्वा तेन [९][प्रति]पुरुषं करम्भपात्राणि करोत्येकमतिरिक्तम्, यावन्तो गृह्या भवन्ति। गृह्याः

१. M संक्षालयविमर्ज्य, Ad संक्षालविमात्रर्वर्ज्य, B संक्षाल विमर्ज्य; thus VādhŚS 4.5.23. २. M Ad B पृथगाममन्त्र°. ३. M Ad B °मुत्कर:. ४. M Ad हरिष्यसौ. ५–५. M Ad B text beginning from अध्वर्युरेव to संचारः repeated. ६. M Ad B °स्थातरध्वर्युश्च. ७. M Ad B °णाग्नीन्दध्वर्युः. ८. M Ad °स्थं. ९. M Ad B om प्रति; cf. VādhŚS 4.5.40.

पिता पुत्रा भ्राता चाप्रत्ता दुहितारश्च[१]। अविभक्ताः सपिण्डा इत्येके। कल्याणकर्मणः सपिण्डा इत्यपरे। यवोदनेन मृदितेन मेषीमध्वर्युः करोति, मेषं प्रतिप्रस्थाता। लोमानि चाश्लेषयतः। अध्वर्युरेवोभयं कुर्यात्। अथ कपालोपधानाद्यध्वर्युः प्रतिपद्यते। वेदौ सवेदौ परिवासय **इति मन्त्रसन्नामः। प्रतिप्रस्थाता पवित्रे आदाय प्रोक्षणीः संस्कृत्य पात्राणि प्रोक्ष्य प्रोक्षणीशेषं निधायैन्द्राग्नकपालोपधानानन्तरं तिरःपवित्रं पय आनीय मारुत्यर्थमधिश्रित्यैन्द्राग्ने अधिश्रित्य[२] दध्यानीय मारुतीमामिक्षां परिश्रपयेत्। अथाध्वर्युर्वारुणीश्रपणादि प्रतिपद्यते। हविर्भिः सह करम्भपात्राण्यपि पर्यग्निकुर्यात्। प्रतिप्रस्थाताप्याज्यानि[३] निरुप्याधिश्रित्य पर्यग्निकृत्वोपास्ते। अथाप्यग्निनयनान्त उभौ स्फ्यावादाय परिग्रहणयोयोपने[४] कुरुतः। अध्वर्युरेवावस्कम्भनं प्रैषं च। प्रैषानग्नीत्[५] कुर्यात्। प्रतिप्रस्थाता स्वयंमेव दक्षिणविहारे। पत्नीसंबन्ध एवाग्नीत् कुर्यात्॥** [३]

साऽप्युभयमाज्यमवेक्षेत। अग्नेर्जिह्वाऽसि **इत्यध्वर्युणावेक्ष्य प्रतिप्रस्थातावेक्षेत। मेषमेष्यौ शमीपर्णानि करीरसक्तूंश्चामिक्षापात्रयोरेवावदध्यात्। शतादधिकानि शमीपर्णान्येकैकस्मिन् पात्रे निवपेत्। नवाजिनद्वयमेकस्मिन् पात्रे कृत्वा निधाय[६] सादयेत्।** ध्रुवा असदन्, यन्म अग्ने पञ्चहोता **इत्युभयोः। पञ्चहोता अध्वर्योरेव इत्यपरे। निर्मन्थ्योऽध्वर्योरेव। अध्वर्युरेव संप्रैषमाह—** अग्नीध्यां समिध्यमानाभ्यामनुब्रूहि **इति। यथाप्रकृत्येव प्रेष्येन्नैवोहेदित्यपरे। सन्नाम एव ज्यायान्। एवं सर्वत्राग्न्यभिधायिनां वा शब्दानाम्।** उच्छुष्मो अग्ने **इत्युभयोः।** पत्नि कति ते जाराः **इति पृष्टा यावन्तो जारास्तेषां संख्यां निर्दिशेदेक इति वा, त्रय इति वा। संख्यां निर्दिश्य** असौ मे जारः **इति। पुनस्तेषां नामानि निर्दिशेत्। अथ यं द्विष्यात् तं** वरुणो [७]गृह्णातु **इति[७] ब्रुवन् प्रतिप्रस्थाता यजमानेन द्वेष्यान् जारान्[८] ध्यायति[९]। न वा पत्नीं पृच्छन्ति। करम्भपात्राण्येकातिरिक्तानि कृत्वा हरति।** यद् ग्रामे यदरण्ये **इति याज्यामुभौ दम्पती ब्रूयाताम्। ब्रुवन्तीं पत्नीं वाचयेत् अनुच्छिन्दञ्छिरसः शूर्पम्। स्वाहाकारान्ते करम्भपात्राणि वरुणाय हुत्वा शूर्पमनु प्रास्येत्। ततो दम्पती** अक्रन् कर्म **इति यथास्थं[१०] स्थानं नयति यजमानायतनम्[११]। यजमानं जघनेन गार्हपत्यं[१२] यथेतम्। संमार्ष्ट्यग्नीदग्निं[१३] दक्षिणम्। अग्निजघनेनोत्तरवेदिं गत्वा यथास्थं स्फ्येध्मसन्नहनम्।**

---

१. M Ad B दुहितरश्चा°. २. M Ad °न्द्राग्नेऽधि°. ३. M Ad °ज्यान्निरू°, B °ज्यानिरू°. ४. M Ad B °योर्योपने. ५. M Ad B °ग्नीन्. ६. M B विधाय, Ad निधाय. ७–७. M गृह्णाति, Ad गृह्णानि. ८. M दारान्. ९. M Ad B जायति. १०. M Ad B यथास्वं. ११. M Ad B °यतना. १२. M Ad B गार्हपत्नीं. १३. M Ad B °मार्ष्ट्यग्निन्द°.

अध्वर्युरेव प्रवरं प्रवृणीते अग्नी देवौ होतारौ देवान् यजेतां विविद्वांसौ[१] चिकित्वदा च वहताम् **इति॥ [४]**

प्रत्याश्रावणादौ साधारणकर्मण्यौत्तरविहारिकमेव स्फ्यमग्निं धारयेत्। अध्वर्योरेवाश्राव्य प्रेष्येत्। अभिघारणात्[२] प्राङ् मेषमेष्यौ व्यतिहरणम्। उपभृत्यन्ततः[३] प्रतिप्रस्थाताऽभिघारयति। अनुब्रूहि **इति वाऽध्वर्योरेव। आज्यभागयोर्यजति च। एवं सर्वत्र सहक्रियां स्वाहेत्यनुमन्त्रणमुभयोरेव। अध्वर्योरेवेत्यपरे। उपवेशनं व्यापारादुपरमा ऐन्द्राग्नादित्यभिविधिः। न शमीवर्जं करीरसक्तूनां शेषकार्याणि विद्यन्त इत्यपरे। दारूणि जघनेनोत्तरां वेदिमाहृत्य तस्यां निधाय स्विष्टकृतमवदाय यथेतमाहृत्यायतने सादयित्वैवमेवाहृत्येडामवद्येत् प्रतिप्रस्थाता। सोऽपि हस्तादुद्गतं गन्धमाघ्राय प्राणेन मार्जयते। सन्नह्याद्यध्वर्योरेव[४]।** ब्रह्मन् प्रस्थास्यामः समिधावाधायाग्नीदग्नी सकृत्सकृत् समृड्ढि **इति प्रेष्येत् सूक्तवाकाय च। अथ** इदं ब्रूहि **इति।** अनुप्रहर संवदस्व **इत्यग्नीत्।** अगा३नग्नीत् [५]श्रावय स्वगा दैव्या होतृभ्यः[५] **इत्यध्वर्योरेव। बर्हिरनुप्रहरणाभ्युपयो वाजिनभक्षान्त उभौ होत्रे दत्तः। पत्नीसंयाजाद्यध्वर्योरेव। ध्रुवाऽऽप्यायनात् फलीकरणहोमं चाज्यस्थालीभ्यां चतुर्गृहीतं गृहीत्वा सर्वफलीकरणानोप्योभयानीध्मप्रवृश्चनान्यभ्याधाय जुहुयात्। उभयोः पृथगेव फलीकरणहोम इत्येके। तन्त्रमेव ज्यायान्। तुल्यैषा [६]नारिष्ठहोमानां विकल्पना। ध्रुवाऽऽप्यायनादि स्रुचः[७] सम्पद्यते तथा कल्पयेत्। तथा सत्रकर्ममध्येऽग्निहोत्रं हुत्वा ... न्येकं प्रथमे पर्याये द्वे मध्ये द्वे उत्तमे इत्येके॥ [५]**

[८]**प्रणीतानिनयनमध्वर्योरेव। अथवाऽवभृथपात्रसादनादि प्रतिपद्यते। पात्राणि स्फ्यमग्निहोत्रहवणीं स्रुवं जुहूमाज्यस्थालीं वेदमिति। सादयित्वा पवित्रे आदाय** यजमान वाचं यच्छ **इत्युक्त्वा** कर्मणे वाम् **इति हस्तौ मार्जयित्वा प्रोक्षणीः संस्कृत्य पात्राणि प्रोक्ष्याज्यं निरुप्य पर्यग्निकृत्वा स्फ्येनावस्कभ्य संप्रेष्यति** स्रुवं च स्रुचश्च संमृड्ढि **इति। अथवा स्रुवं च स्रुग्जुहूमाज्यस्थालीं वेद-**

१. B °द्वांसोचिकित्वा. २. M Ad B अभिकार. ३. M Ad B उपभृत्यव्यन्ततः. ४. Ad °ह्याध्व°. ५-५. M Ad °स्वगदैर्व्याहृतभ्य, B °हत्यभ्य. ६. M Ad नारिषुगोमानामविकल्पना. ७. M Ad स्रुगः. ८. The text beginning with प्रणीतानिनयनमध्वर्योरेव [M p. 441, line 13; Ad p. 883 line 13; B p. 266 line 2] and ending with आ गच्छेयुः [M p. 443, line 1; Ad p. 886, line 2; B p. 267, line 6] has come wrongly under *Paśubandha*, due to displacement of folios. Actually, it belongs to the remaining part of the *Varuṇapraghāsa,* and *Anīkavatīṣṭi,* hence it has been placed here at its proper place.

मिति। संमृज्याज्येनोदेहि इति प्रैषेत्। अथ पञ्च स्रुवं च संमृज्य पत्नीमवेक्षयेत्। अथाध्वर्युरग्नीत्सहितोऽन्वीक्ष्य यजमानं चावेक्षणं वाचयित्वाऽऽत्मनश्छायामवेक्ष्योत्पूय[१] स्रुवमाज्यस्थाल्याज्यं निष्कासतुषानित्यादीनादायावभृथं[२] गच्छेद् उरुं हि राजा इत्येतामु च त्रिरनुब्रुवन्। अत्र पत्नीयजमानावूर्णासूत्रमये[३] मेखले तूष्णीं पर्यस्येते[४]। अभिहोमो जुह्वा[५]सद्याज्यस्थाल्य अवदाय अपूर्वेणेत्येके। चतुर्गृहीते जौह्वैर्मन्त्रैर्ध्रुवैराज्यभागयोस्तूष्णीमुपस्तरणाभिघारणे कुर्यात्। अग्नीवरुणाभ्यां समस्यनिष्कासान् सकृदवदाय द्विरवघारणम्। सकृदेवेत्येके। द्विरिति ज्यायान्। अनूयाजार्थं चतुर्गृहीतं तूष्णीमर्धस्रुवैः। ब्रह्मन् प्रस्थास्याम इत्येतावदुक्तं [६]प्रवत्स्यतोऽनुयजति॥ [६]

[७][प्रव]सेतापीत्यपरे। देवौ यज यज इत्याद्यैः यज इत्येवेतरस्मिन् किन्दून्बिन्दून् संप्रकिरति। तुषादुत्तरसिचावुत्तरीये वाससी दम्पत्योरध्वर्यू न्यस्यतः वासोभ्यामप्सु न्यस्ताभ्यामुभौ स्वयमेव स्वके शरीरे अभिनि[वेष्टयेते दशामेखले स्व][८]यमेव विस्रंसयेते। [९]पृष्टीर्धावतः पृष्ठे शोधयतः। [प्रतिप्रस्थाता][१०] उन्नयति तीरत आगमयति। एकैकां समिधं बहुसमित्प्रमाणां कुर्वाते[११]। तथैवाभ्याधत्तः एनौ दम्पती स्वं स्वमग्निम्। उपस्थापयत्यध्वर्युः। पूर्वमग्निमौत्तरवेदिकं विसृजति। शकलयोः संभारे नह्य पशाविव॥ [७] इति द्वितीयोऽनुवाकः॥

[अथ तृतीयोऽनुवाकः]

[साकमेधपर्व]

[अनीकवतीष्टिः]

सायमग्निहोत्रं हुत्वाऽभ्याधानप्रभृत्याप्रणीताभ्यां कृत्वाऽऽदित्योदयमाकांक्षेत्। उद्यता गभस्तिमताऽनीकवतस्यारभेत। अपि वा यत उदयत उदयेन प्रधानया गच्छेयुः।

[गृहमेधीयेष्टिः]

[१२]. . . . वपायोगो वा प्रहरणकाले परिधीन् निवर्तयति, पृथक् प्रेरयति। शयं बर्हिर्यथास्तीर्णमेव शाययितस्य। [१३]आगृहमेधीयसमाप्तेर्न समिष्टयजुषा सहानु-

१. M Ad B °वेक्ष्यात् पूय, [B °यूय]. २. M Ad B तुषानित्यादियावभृथं. ३. M Ad B °माना पूर्णा°. ४. M Ad B पर्याग्नीस्वेते. ५. M Ad B जुह्वासद्यादा°. ६. M Ad B पास्यतोनु°. ७. M Ad B broken before सेवापी°. ८. M Ad B broken, cf. VādhŚS 4.8.34. ९. M Ad वृष्णिर्धा°. १०. M Ad B om; cf. VādhŚS 4.8.36. ११. M Ad B कुर्वते. १२. M Ad B the opening part of the *Gṛhamedhīyeṣṭi* is broken. १३. M Ad B मागृह°.

प्रहरणाः। अथ गृहमेधीयस्य सायमभ्याधाय प्र [. . .][१] **त्यवे** [२][. . . **अभि**]-**मन्त्र्याग्नीन् परिस्तीर्य वेदमभिमन्त्र्य स्फ्यमग्निहोत्रहवणीं स्रुवं जुहूमुपभृतमाज्यस्थालीं चरुस्थालीं मेक्षणमिडापात्रमोदनोद्धरणाय दारुपात्रीं चेति पात्राणि सादयित्वा** [३]**ब्रह्माणमत्र मन्त्रेणोपवेशयेत्। सति वेदिकरणे पवित्रे आदाय यजमा**[न . . .][४] **मा त्वा कर्मणे हस्तौ वर्जयित्वा प्रोक्षणीः**[५] **संस्कृत्य पात्राणि प्रोक्ष्य सर्वासां स्वानां गवां दुग्धे सम्यगवहितैस्तण्डुलैर्गृहमेधीयतण्डुलाभ्यादानं**[६] **श्रपणमाज्यं**[७] **निरुप्याधिश्रित्य पर्यग्निकृत्वा वेदिं करोति॥** [१]

बर्हिष[. . . .][८]**स्तम्बयजुर्हरेद् उद्धननकर्मवर्जम्**[९]**। नैव वेदिकरणमित्येके। भाव एव ज्यायान्।** प्रोक्षणीरासादय स्रुवं स्रुचौ संमृढ्याज्येनोदेहि **इति प्रैषः। स्रुवं च स्रुचौ च संमृज्य सादयित्वा पत्न्यवेक्षितेनाज्येनोदेत्याथ** अग्नेर्जिह्वासि **इति चावेक्ष्य यजमानमेवेक्षमाणं** [. . . .][१०] **मवेक्ष्योत्पूय शृतस्योदनस्य त्रीन्** [११]**राशीनुपस्तीर्णाभिघारितान् उद्धरति पात्रत्रये। दारुपात्र्यामित्येके। प्रथमोद्धृतं व्यूहमदधानं कृत्वा श्लक्ष्णीकृत्य तत्र ध्रौवैर्मन्त्रैश्चतुर्गृहीतं गृह्णानश्चतुर्थे स्रुवे भूय आनयेत्। इतरयो**[१२][**रुप**]**सिञ्चेत्। अथ वेदिं प्रोक्ष्य**[१३] **निनीय प्रोक्षणीशेषमुदूह्य प्रोक्षणीपात्रं यथास्थानं परिधीन् निधायाग्नियोगं कृत्वा तूष्णीं स्रुचौ सादयित्वौदनान् सादयन् ध्रुवामन्ते**[१४] **प्रथमोद्धृतं मध्यत आसादयेत्। तूष्णीं दक्षिणतश्चोत्तरतश्च . . .**[१५] **ध्रुवाभाजनमभिघार्य दक्षिणेन ध्रुवाभाजनं मन्त्रेण स्रुवं सादयित्वा ध्रुवाभाजने चातिरिक्तमुत्तरेण वेदं सादयित्वा व्रतमुपैति॥** [२]

ध्रुवासन्नां विष्णो पाहि, यन्म अग्न **इति ध्रुवाभाजनमभिमृश्य तत्र चतुर्होतारं सग्रहं व्याख्याय उच्छ्र**[**यणे**-][१६]**नोपावाज्य**[१७] अग्नीदग्निम् **इति प्रेष्य संमृष्टेऽग्नौ प्रवरं प्रवृत्य** अश्विनावध्वर्यू **इत्यश्विभ्यां ब्राह्मणेभ्यश्च नमस्कृत्याज्यभागादि प्रतिपाद्य, तेन नमस्कार इत्येके। प्राक्स्विष्टकृत्संस्रावाभिहोमात् सर्वान् परिधीन् सह संगृह्य तूष्णीमनुप्रहृत्य तान् संस्राव्येडामनुपस्तीर्णाभिघारितामवदायोपहूतायामिडायामुत्तरमोदनमग्नीधे समस्तमुपोहेत्, नावद्येत्। दक्षिणं ब्रह्मणे परिहरति। स्थाल्यामवशिष्टमध्वर्युयजमानौ नियोगतः प्राश्नीयाताम्। अन्य ऋत्विजो ब्राह्मणाश्च यथाकामम्। अन्यपक्वं पत्नी प्राश्नीयात्।**

१. M Ad B broken. २. M Ad B broken. ३. M Ad B ब्राह्मण॰. ४. M Ad B broken. ५. M Ad B णी. ६. M Ad B मेधीभ्यादा. ७. M Ad B श्रपयन्नाज्यं. ८. M Ad B broken. ९. M Ad B उद्धननक . . . नवार्जं. १०. M Ad B broken. ११. M Ad द्राशी, B दशि. १२. M Ad B broken. १३. M Ad B प्रेक्ष्य. १४. M Ad B ॰मन्त्रे. १५. M Ad B broken. १६. M Ad B broken. १७. M Ad B नोपलाज्य.

यजमानश्च गृह्या भृत्याश्चाञ्जनाभ्यञ्जनादिभिरभिपूजिता आशिता गायन्तो हसन्तश्च क्रीडमाना एतां रात्रीं जाग्रयति स्वाद्वन्नं भुञ्जाना पिबन्तश्च। वत्साश्चैतां रात्रीं मातृभिः सह वासयेयुः। आज्येनानीय प्रयन्ते। निहितं यजमानः स्वयमेवैतां रात्रीं रक्षेत्। औषसमग्निहोत्रं हुत्वा दर्विहोमिकमाज्यं संस्कृत्य स्रुवं च दर्वीं च संमृज्य तस्यामुपस्तीर्य निष्कासेन दर्वीं पूरयित्वाऽभिघार्य जुहोति। यजमानस्य रवथे रु-शब्देन[१] साकं [. . . .][२]ख्यातम्। अतिमुक्त्यन्ते महाहविषस्तन्त्रमुपक्रमेत। ऋजु शेषः॥ [३] इति तृतीयोऽनुवाकः॥

[अथ चतुर्थोऽनुवाकः]

[पितृयज्ञः]

अथ पितृयज्ञः प्रारभ्यते। अम्बरीषं भर्जनपात्रमभिवान्याऽन्यवत्सा[३] यस्या नास्ति स्ववत्सः इक्षुशलाका[४] च मूलच्छिन्ना वेदिर्दक्षिणाग्नेर्दक्षिणपूर्वस्यां दिशि तल्प्यावकाशा तत्प्रमाणा पुरुष[संमिताप्र-][५]वति दिशि [६]चतुःस्रक्तिः सर्वतः समान्वेक्षणा च[७] क्वचित् प्रवणा द्राघीयान् प्राकृतात् प्रादेशप्रमाणात् कशिपुस्तरित्र्याकार[८] उपबर्हणं शिरोपधानं दर्भमये वा भाक्ते।

अथ प्रयोगः। गार्हपत्यान्वाहार्यपचनयोरभ्याधाय[९] बर्हिः संभरेत् समूलम्। देवस्य त्वा **इत्यभ्रिमादाय** देवेभ्यः पितृभ्यो जुष्टं देव[ानां पितृणां परि]षूतं[१०] देवेभ्यः पितृभ्यस्त्वोर्ध्वबर्हिभ्यः **इत्येवं सर्वत्राङ्गं प्रधानार्थेषु स्वार्थे देवशब्दे पितृशब्दमन्वासंजयेत्। यथाप्रकृत्येवेत्येके। अन्वासङ्ग एव ज्यायः।** अवर्ढति मा रिषम्[११] **इत्याच्छिनत्ति। यथाप्रकृत्येवेत्येके। तदेव ज्यायः[१२]। नास्ति प्रच्छेदना-भिमर्शनमित्ये[के। प्रणी]यमाणो[१३] यजमानशब्दमपोहेत्।** वेदोऽसि विन्द पुष्टिम् **इति दक्षिणेन गार्हपत्यं तृणानि संस्तीर्य तेष्वेकैकशः पैतृयज्ञिकानि[१४] यज्ञायुधानि सादयेत्। षट् कपालान्यम्बरीषं च मन्थपात्रं च सादयेत्। धानापात्रं च। पात्र्यामेके धाना उद्वासयन्ति। पवित्रादानं कृत्वा** अपः प्रणे[ष्यामि, वाचं][१५] यच्छ **इत्येव ब्रूयात्। अथैनाः प्रणीय पैतृयज्ञिका वेदेरुत्तरतः सादयेत्। यथा वेदिमध्ये सादितस्याग्नेः। प्रबाहुग् उत्तरतो ब्रह्मयजमानौ दक्षिणाग्नेरभितः प्रणीताः।**

---

१. M Ad B शब्दे. २. M Ad B broken. ३. M Ad °वान्यान्य वत्सां. ४. M Ad B इक्ष्वाकुशलाका. ५. M Ad B broken. ६. M Ad B om चतुः. ७. M Ad B समान्वः. ८. M कशिधास्तरि. Ad कश्चिद्यास्तरिद्याका. ९. M Ad °पचयोर°, B °पचनोर°. १०. M Ad B देव . . . ष्कृतं. ११. B रिषीमीत्या°. १२. M Ad B न्याय. १३. M Ad B broken. १४. M Ad B °यज्ञिका यज्ञा°. १५. M Ad B broken.

ब्रह्मयजमानौ च प्रागग्निप्रणयनात्। प्रणीतेऽग्नौ तस्याभिहिता भविष्यन्तीत्येके। ऊहेन हस्तौ संमृज्याग्निहोत्र[हवण][१]यां दक्षिणतः प्राचीनावीती[२] सोमाय पितृमते व्रीहीन् निर्वपेत्। यज्ञोपवीतीत्येके॥ [१]

पितृभ्यो बर्हिषद्भ्यो यवान्। पितृभ्योऽग्निष्वात्तेभ्यश्च यवानेव। वैश्वानरं ज्योतिः इत्याहवनीयं परेक्षते। अन्वाहार्यपचनमित्येके। प्रहरिष्यमाणमभिध्याय-तीत्यन्ये। अतीत्य [. . . .][३] या भावाल्लुप्यत इत्यन्ये। आदित्यास्त्वा[४] इति दक्षिणतः सादयेत्। दक्षिणत एवावघ्नन्ति। न यवानामवघातोऽनवहता एव भर्जनीयाः[५]। सकृदवहत्यान्तरेण त्रिष्फलीक्रियां भर्जनीया इत्येके। अवघातपक्षे प्रागावपनात्[६] तन्त्रम्। कृष्णाजिनादानादि ऊर्ध्वं च हविष्कृदाह्वानात्। [दक्षिणार्धे][७] कपालान्युपधाय दक्षिणार्धे दक्षिणाग्नेरम्बरीषं प्रथमेन कपालमन्त्रेणैवोप्य यवान् भर्जयति। तेषामर्धाः फुल्ला धाना भवन्ति। सक्तूनितरान् धानान् कुर्वन्ति। तान् पुरोडाशीयपेषणानन्तरं पिनष्टि। तत्र कृष्णाजिनादानात्प्रागधिवपनात् तन्त्रम्। कालेऽम्बरीषाधिश्रयणमात्रं कृत्वाऽधिश्रिते पुरोडाशयवानोप्याम्बरीषे तान् भृष्ट्वा फुल्लानर्धानां धानार्थान् निधायार्धान् सक्त्वर्थान् पिनष्टि। पूर्वतनपक्षो ज्यायान्। प्राक् पेषणादुत्तरार्धे गार्हपत्यस्य प्रतिपुरुषं [८]त्र्यम्बका[नवघ्नन्त्ये-][९] ककपालम्। तूष्णीं श्रपयेत्। प्रतिपुरुषमिति व्याख्यातम्। अथ पुरोडाशीयान् पिष्ट्वा सक्तून् पिंषेत्। पुरोडाशमधिश्रित्याज्येन धानाः संयुवन्ति। अभिवान्यायै दुग्धेऽर्धपात्रे सक्तूनोप्य शलाकया सकृदुपमथ्य सर्वाणि हवींषि पर्यग्निकुर्यात्॥ [२]

पत्नीवर्जं प्रेष्येत्। [१०]उ[त्तर]तोऽग्नौ प्रोक्षणीरिध्माबर्हिश्च सादयेत्। तदा-नीमेवान्वाहार्यपचने स्रुचः संमृज्यात्रैव सादयित्वा पत्न्यनवेक्षितेनाज्येनोदेत्याधि-श्रित्यान्वाहार्यपचनस्यान्ते सादयेत्। अथ अग्नेर्जिह्वासि इत्यवेक्ष्य[११] यजमान-मवेक्षमाणं वाचयित्वाऽऽ[१२]त्मनश्छायामवेक्ष्यो[दीचीनाग्राभ्यां पवित्राभ्यामाज्य-मुत्पूय][१३] उपभृति द्वे षट् गृह्णीते। एकमित्येके। द्वे इति ज्यायान्। सर्वत्रान्त्यस्य मन्त्रस्यावृत्तिः। अत्रैवाज्येन सादयित्वा पुरोडाशमुद्वास्यान्वाहार्यपचनस्यार्धं हरेत्। [१४]आज्यानि धानाश्च[१४] संयुतांस्तत्समीपे हरेत्। तथा मन्थं पुरोडाशोद्वासना-

---

१. M Ad B broken. २. M Ad B °वीति. ३. M Ad B broken. ४. M Ad B अदित्यात्वे°. ५. M Ad B °नीयः. ६. M Ad B वाशावपनात्. ७. M Ad B broken. ८. M Ad B त्र्यम्ब°. ९. M Ad B broken. १०. M Ad B broken. ११. M Ad B °सीर्यवेक्ष्य. १२. M Ad B °त्मनच्छाया°. १३. M Ad B °क्ष्योत्. . . . तग्नि उप°. १४-१४. M Ad B °ज्यनाधानेश्च.

नन्तरम्। [. . . .][१] **द्वा सादयेत्। यथार्थं तन्त्राणामूहः। तथा सति मन्त्रस्योपस्तरण-मधस्तादुपाञ्जनं चार्थलुप्ते। उभयोश्च भस्मोदूहनम्**[२]**। धानानां तूहो, न मन्त्रस्य।** स्योनं वः सदनं करोमि[३] = सीदतामृते[४] प्रतिष्ठित, यवानां मेधाः सुमनस्यमानाः, आर्द्राः प्रथस्तनवो भुवनस्य = [५]जनयित्र्यो मतीनाम्, सुरूपा वो वसुविदः पशूनां तेजसा पितृभ्यो बर्हिषद्भ्यो जुष्टा अभिघारयामि, आत्मन्वत्यः सोम घृतवत्यो हि भूत्वा पितॄन् गच्छत सुवर्विन्दत[६] = कामान्। **नानाग्नेयविकारस्येदमभिघारणमित्येके।** खमङ्ध्वं [७]त्वचमङ्ध्वम् **एव** आत्मानं पशुषु प्रविष्ट्य[स्तमङ्ध्वम्][८] आत्मानं वर्षप्रविष्टंस्तमङ्ध्वम् **इत्येके। न चास्य मन्त्रस्य ऊह इहेत्यपरे।** स विन्दति लोकम् **इति सर्वत्र यजमानशब्दमपोहेत्। भर्जनानन्तरमेवोभयमम्बरीषान् मन्त्रेणोद्वासयेदित्येके। अर्थलुप्तमुभयस्य मन्त्रेणोद्वासनमित्यपरे। आच्छिद्रिको-पादानमत्र क्ष** [. . .][९] **नादग्निं** [. . .][१०] **वेद्यै सादयित्वोपसमाधाय तस्या स्तम्बयजुः मनसा मन्त्रमनुद्रुत्य हरेत्। अपरेणाग्निं बर्हिर्निधाय प्रहरेत्। तस्या एवोत्तरत उत्करः।**[११] **प्राकृत एवोत्कर**[१२] **इत्यपरे। प्राकृतत्वेऽग्रेणाहवनीयं हरेत्। अपरेणेत्येके॥** [३]

सर्वेषां द्रव्याणामृत्विजां[१३] **यजमानस्य** [. . .][१४] **ननं वर्जयित्वेत्येके। एतदेव ज्यायः। अथोदकुम्भमाहृत्य दक्षिणेंऽसे निदधाति। प्रोक्षणीश्चाहृत्यास्याग्नेरपरत आहृत्य। यद्यग्नेरुत्तरतो बर्हिरिध्मं तु पृथक् पृथक् सादयेत्। अत्रैव प्रोक्षणी-रासादयेदिध्माबर्हि** [. . . .][१५] **कः। अथ** प्रोक्षणीरासादय **इत्याद्यास्त्रुग्व्यूहनात् करोति, धरुणप्रोक्षणवर्जम्। अथोदकुम्भमादाय परिषेक्ता कश्चन बलवान् परिषिञ्चन्नपसलैस्त्रिरग्निं पर्येति। निधाय यथायतनं कुम्भं प्रतिपथं त्रिः पुनः परिद्र[वति। मुष्टिनाऽभिच्छादयति]**[१६] **प्रस्तरं सकलं बर्हिः स[कलम्]**[१७]**।** उरु यज्ञाय **इत्यादिभिर्मुष्टिमभ्यन्तरतः[परि]**[१८]**स्तृणन् पर्येति बर्हिः।** उरु [यजमानाय][१९] **इति द्वितीयं बर्हिः। तत** उरु [यज्ञपतये][२०] **इत्येव तृतीयम्। तृतीयेन सह प्रस्तरादन्यत् परिसमापयेत्।** [२१]**एतदेव त्रिवृतत्वम्**[२१]**। निधाय प्रस्तरं प्रतिपथं त्रिः**

---

१. M Ad B broken. २. M Ad B भस्मेदू. ३. M Ad B abr. ४. M Ad B सिद°. ५. M Ad B abr. ६. M Ad B abr. ७. M Ad B तच°. ८. M Ad B broken. ९. M Ad B broken. १०. M Ad B broken. ११. M Ad B उत्तर. १२. M Ad B उत्तर. १३. M Ad B ऋत्युजां. १४. M Ad B broken. १५. M Ad B broken. १६. M Ad B broken. १७. M Ad B broken. १८. M Ad B om. १९. M Ad B om. २०. M Ad B om. २१-२१. M Ad B °देवास्त्रिवृत्त्वं.

पुनः परिव्रुत्य प्रस्तरमादाय [१]**[प्राङुत्सृप्य परि]धीन् परिधाय परिधिषु वाचयित्वाऽग्निं युक्त्वा परिहाप्य तिरश्च्योः सादनम्। अपरेणाग्निं तूष्णीं प्रस्तरं सादयित्वा स्त्रुगादीनि सादयेत्। तत्र स्वैर्मन्त्रैः स्त्रुचः सादयित्वाऽथेतराणि यथास्थानमासाद्य** ध्रुवा असदन् **इति स्त्रुचोऽभिमृश्य** यन्म अग्ने **इति हवींष्यभिमृश्य** [२]**[षड्ढोतारं व्या]ख्याय स्त्रुवेणानुपूर्वं हवींष्यभिघारयन् यजमान-शब्दमपोहेत्। धानासु पूर्ववदूहः। दक्षिणेन ध्रुवायामरिक्तं ध्रुवायां सादयित्वा वेदं सादयन् यजमानशब्दमपोहेत्** स विन्दतु लोकम् **इति॥ [४]**

अथास्मात्[३] **समिधमाधाय** अग्नये देवेभ्यः पितृभ्यः समिध्यमानाय **इत्युक्त्वा** [. . . .][४] **वः समिधेभ्यो दध्यात्। तृतीये प्रयाजे**[५] **सर्वं**[६] **समिधेभ्यो दधाति। अनूयाजसमिधमतिशिष्याद्**[७]**। वेदेनोपवाजयन् यजमानशब्दमपोहेत्** उच्छुष्मो अग्न एधि **इति। आघारप्रभृति समानमेतावदेव। नाना**ऽग्नीदग्निं सकृत्सकृत् संमृड्ढि **इति प्रैषः। यज्ञपतिशब्दमपोहेत्।** [८]**आ श्रावय इत्याश्राव्य**[८] सीद **इत्येतावत्प्रवरो होतुर्वचनं च नास्तीति। त्रीन् प्रयाजानिष्ट्वोपभृत्यर्धं समानीयोत्तमं प्रयाजं यजति। परिश्रयन्ति यथा परिश्रयणस्यान्तर्वर्तिनः सर्वे कर्तारः स्युः। अतिचङ्क्रम्य पुनरत्याक्रामति।** अनु स्वधा कुरु **इति तृतीयमक्षरं प्लवते।** आ स्व[धा **इति आश्राव्य]**[९] **द्वन्द्वे** अस्तु स्वधा **इति। तृतीयमेव** ये स्वधा **इति** आद्यस्वधा नमः **इति चाद्या।** स्वाहा **इत्यनुमन्त्रणमन्त्रो लुप्यत इत्येके।** स्वधा नमः **इत्यनुमन्त्रयत इत्यन्ये। यथाप्रकृतीत्यपरे। मध्येऽपसव्यं मण्डलाकारं प्रधानाहुतीर्हुत्वा अग्निं कव्यवाहनं**[१०] **दक्षिणार्धेऽतिहाय पूर्वार्धे** [. . .][११] **जुहोति। तान्यवघ्रातान्यत्रैवोपपात्रे संप्रकिरति।** मार्जयस्व **इति च प्रैषोऽञ्जलौ चावदान-माध्वर्यवमितरत्सर्वं याजमानं बहुवचनश्रवणे सर्वे कुर्युः। ऋजुधा चरन्ति। दैववद्यथाप्रकृत्येवाश्रवणादि कुर्वन्ति। विपर्यन्ति। यथाप्रकृत्येव**[१२] **[प्रयाजा]नूयाजौ यजेत्।** देवा यज यज **इत्याद्ये** यज **इत्येवान्त्ये शयन्ते**[१३] **पत्नीरसंयाज्य**[१४] **समृद्धिहोमान्यृध्वा चेति। स्त्रुवाहुतीर्हुत्वा**[१५] **फलीकरण-होमाद्यर्वाक् ध्रुवाऽऽप्यायनं**[१६] **कृत्वा समिष्टयजुर्वर्जम्। स्त्रुक्संस्त्रावहोमान्तं**

---

१. M Ad B broken before धीन् [MSS ॰धन्]. २. M Ad B broken. ३. M Ad B अथेस्मा. ४. M Ad B broken. ५. M Ad B प्रणयः. ६. M Ad B सर्वः. ७. M Ad B ॰धमिति॰. ८-८. M Ad B शक . . . . श्रव्य. ९. M Ad B broken. १०. M Ad B ॰हन. ११. M Ad B broken. १२. M Ad B broken. १३. M Ad B शःयन्ते. १४. M B पतीरसं॰, Ad प्रतीरसं. १५. M Ad B चाहुती॰. १६. M Ad B ॰प्यायनात्.

कृत्वा हविःशेषान् [. . . .][१] **प्राजापत्ययाऽऽहवनीयस्यार्धमेति॥ [५]** इति चतुर्थोऽनुवाकः॥

अथ पञ्चमोऽनुवाकः

पितृशब्दान्वासञ्जनपक्षेऽङ्गप्रधानार्थेषु देवशब्दे स्वार्थे पितृशब्दे अन्वासञ्जयेयुः। प्रधानार्थे देवशब्दे तस्य स्थाने पितृशब्दं प्रयुञ्जीरन्। अविकारो [अ][२]**ङ्गार्थे। तद्यथा** देवेभ्यः पितृभ्यो जुष्टम्, [देवानां पितृणां][३] परिषूतम्, देवेभ्यः पितृभ्यस्त्वोर्ध्व[४]बर्हिर्भ्यः, देवपितृबर्हिर्भ्यस्त्वा[५], देवपितृबर्हिः शतवलिश, देवपितॄन्[६] गमयसि, यज्ञं तनुवै देवानां पितृणामात्मना, देवानां पितृणां ब्रह्मणा देवा **देवेष्वन्यार्थो देवशब्दः। नात्र पितृशब्दोऽन्वासङ्गः। अत्रापीत्येके।** कर्म[णे वः][७] पितृभ्यः शकेयम्, तं धूर्व, पितृणामसि सस्नितमं पितृहूतमम्, हुवे पितॄन् यज्ञियान् 'आयान्तु पितरः सुमनस्यमानाः'[८], 'नयन्तु[९] देवाः' **इत्यङ्गित्वाद-विकारः। विकार इत्येके।** इदं पितृणाम्, इदं पितृभ्यः, कव्यास्तृप्यन्तु, पितरः कव्यस्य मे। अन्यदेवायुवम् **इत्यविकारः।** देवपितृयुव **इत्यपि।** प्रियाय कर्मणे देवपितृयज्यायै पितृपीतये[१०] वः, स इदं पितृभ्यः कव्यं शमिष्व, पितृभ्यः शुन्धध्वम्, आ पितृयजं वह, आ देवपितृयजं वह **इत्येके॥ [१]**

निर्वपामि देवपितृयज्यायै, देवेभ्यः पितृभ्य ऊर्जे सीद, सुभूर्देवानां पितृणां धाम्नेधाम्ने, देवेभ्यः पितृभ्यः ध्रुवायाम्। प्रियं देवानां पितृणाम्, अनाधृष्टं देवपितृयजनम् **इति। उपभृत्येवमित्येके।** पितृणां विष्ठामनु, पितॄन् गच्छ देवानाम् **इति विक्रियेतेत्येके।** पयस्वती देवानां धेनुः, पृथिवि देवपितृयजनि, देवपितृ-यजनात् पृथिव्याः देवपितॄन्, बर्हिरूर्णाम्रदसं त्वा, स्वासस्थं देवेभ्यः पितृभ्यो युनज्मि त्वा [. . .][११] **न पित्रियेण[१२] हव्याय कव्याय चास्मै। पितृशब्दोऽन्वा-सङ्गः[१३]।** कव्याय च **इति नियोगतो वाच्यं सर्वत्रैव प्रधानार्थे। यथा** प्रियं देवानाम् **एवं** प्रिया देवानाम् अग्नये, देवेभ्यः पितृभ्यः **इति** योगतः सिद्धम्। एवं देवान्, पितॄन् हविष **इति। पितृशब्दोऽन्वासङ्गपक्षे। एवं** देवान् पि[तॄन् हविष इत्य][१४]ङ्गविकार **इत्येके ह्वयति।** देवपितृयज्यायै **नात्र विकार इत्येके। एतदेव**

---

१. M Ad B broken. २. M Ad B broken. ३. M Ad B om. ४. M Ad B broken. ५. M Ad B °बर्हिर्मात्वा. ६. M Ad B पितॄं. ७. M Ad B broken. ८. M Ad B °मानां. ९. M Ad B नीयन्तु. १०. M Ad B °पितये. ११. M Ad B broken. १२. M Ad B °येणव. १३. M Ad B °ङ्गति. १४. M Ad B broken.

ज्यायः। ब्रह्म देवाः पितरोऽवीवृधन्, यं देवाः पितरः कल्पयन्। स्वाहाकृत्वाऽऽह त्रिरेकदेवान् पितृन्॥ [२] इति पञ्चमोऽनुवाकः॥

अथ षष्ठोऽनुवाकः

[चातुर्मास्ययाजमानम्][१]

अथ याजमानानि। आरम्भणीयवैश्वदेवयोस्तन्त्रेणान्वादधत् अग्निं गृह्णामि **इत्यूहेत्। अद्य श्वो** यज्ञाय रमताम् **इति।** इमामूर्जं [पञ्च][२]दशीमारम्भणीयं वैश्वदेवहविरित्यूहेत्। **पृथगेवोहेत्। आरम्भणीय[३] अनुमन्त्रणानि** अन्नादो भूयासम् **इति पुरोडाशानां,** दब्धिरसि **इति चरोः। अथ** वैश्वदेवस्यान्नादो भूयासम् **इति। आद्यतृतीययोः** दब्धिरसि **इति चरूणाम्।** इन्द्रियाव्यन्नादो भूयासम् **इति मारुतस्य** [. . .][४] **इत्यामिक्षायाम्,** जेमानं महिमानं गमेयम् **इति महेन्द्रयाजिनामित्येके।** वृत्रहा भूयासम् **इत्येककपालस्य। सूत्रान्तराद्वा गमयित्वाऽन्यप्राकृतानामनुमन्त्रणमुपांशुयाजविकारवर्जम्। वाजिनयागोऽपूर्वसान्नाय्यविकार इत्येके। यजमानायतने [प्रागावृ][५]त्त उपस्थं कृत्वोपविश्य वाच्यमानो वपनमन्त्रान् भूयाद्। देवव्रतानि चरन्नमांसमश्नाति, अन्यत्र यज्ञसदनात्[६]। न स्त्रियमुपैति, अन्यत्रर्तोः। पल्पूलनं रजकधवलिकरणम्। अधःशायीति खट्वादि प्रतिषेधः। प्रासादमञ्चादावपि न शयीतेत्येके[७]। अमृन्मयपायीत्यभ्यपहा [८][. . . उ]पलक्षणमिति क्षेमा। अशूद्रोच्छिष्टं प्रयच्छेदन्यात्मदासात्[९]। स्वयं पादौ प्रक्षालयेत[१०], नान्येन पादप्रक्षालनं कारयेत्। भक्ताशी सकृदाशी। प्रथमे त्वेव संवत्सरे व्रतचर्या। यावत्प्रयोगमित्यपरे। वरुणप्रघासानामपि चातु[र्मास्येषु][११]। तत्र** इमामूर्जं चतुर्दशीं वहतु वरुणप्रघासा हविः **इत्यूहः। पूर्वस्मिन् परिग्राहे द्विवदूहेत्।** शिवे च मे शं च मे स्तम्, स्योने च मे सुषदे च स्तम्, ऊर्जे सत्ये स्तम् **इति। दक्षिणस्या दक्षिणत उपवेशनम्। दक्षिणाग्निप्रणयनस्य सधर्मकत्वे** कविर्यज्ञस्य वित[नुतः पन्थां ना]कस्य=[१२] हव्यं वहथ याथ दूतावितः प्रचेता अमुतः सनीयांसौ[१३] **इत्यूहेत्।।** [१]

उत्तरस्मिन् परिग्राहे[ऽनुमन्त्रण][१४]मिति षट्कृत्वं चतुःशिखण्डे युवती

---

१. MSS do not give the heading. २. M Ad B broken. ३. M Ad B °णीया. ४. M Ad B broken. ५. M Ad B broken. ६. M Ad °साध°, B °साधनं. ७. M Ad B शयित्येके. ८. M Ad B broken. ९. M Ad B °दासाय. १०. M Ad B °यत. ११. M Ad B broken. १२. MSS do not show sign of abridged text. १३. M Ad B सनीयसवि°. १४. M Ad B broken.

सुपेशसौ घृतप्रतीके [**भवनस्य मध्ये**][१] मर्मृज्यमाने [**महते सौभगाय**][२]मह्यं दुग्धं यजमानाय कामान् **इति योयोपने जपेत्। दुहाथाध्वर्योराज्यमवेक्ष्य प्रतिप्रस्थातुरपेक्षते।** पञ्चानां त्वा वातानाम्' **इति सर्वेष्वाज्यग्रहणानुमन्त्रणेषु** त्वा-**शब्दस्य स्थाने** वां-**शब्दं निदध्यात्।** इमौ प्राणौ चापानौ च यजमानमपि गच्छताम्[३]। यज्ञे ह्यभूवन् पोतारः[४] पवित्राणि हव्यशोधन[ानि **इति**][५] **विसर्गे जपेत्।** चतुःशिखण्ड **इत्युक्तम्।** वयुनानि वसतात् **इति स्तीर्यमाणे,** मे दुहाताम्[६] **इति स्तीर्णयोर्जपेत्।** दुग्धम् **इति वा;** धर्तारौ, धरुणौ, धरीयांसौ **परिधीयमानेषु।** अग्निर्भेषांसि **इत्यग्नियोगे।** यं वामग्नी पितरौ चरन्तौ अग्नी योनौ द्वेष्टि सौतानग्नी[न्][७]सन्दहताम् **इति समिधो नाराधीयमानयोः।** ध्रुवौ स्थः[८], उग्रौ स्थः, अभिभवौ स्थ **इति परिध्यनुमन्त्रणानि।** युनज्मि वां ब्रह्मणा[९] = जातवेदसौ; इन्धाना वां सुप्रजसः; पयो वामग्नी **इति पृथगेव मध्यमे परिधी अन्वारभ्य** आ नू ह **इति केचित्।** [. . . .][१०] **त्रिभिः** विशो[११] यन्त्राभिः, विशो यन्त्रा नुदमाना अरातीः, सीदन्त्यो देव्यः सुकृतस्य लोके, धृत्यः स्थ विधृत्यः स्थ, प्राणान् मयि धारयत, प्रजां मयि धारयत, पशून् मयि धारयत **इति तिरश्चीषु साद्यमानासु।** यन्मे अग्ने **इत्यन्तरित्वाऽध्वर्योः प्रस्तरं साद्य[मानासु]**[१२] **पुनस्तथैव जपेत्।** इमौ प्रस्तरावुभयस्य धर्तारौ प्रयाजानां तौ दधत, तयोः स्रुचोर् असि **इति प्रस्तरयोः;** जुह्वोरारोहतं पथो, जुहूरेव[१३]। हिरण्यपक्षे, अजिरे सा भृताङ्गे वहाथोम् **इति। उपभृतोः** अवभृद्भ्यां सपत्नान् **इति॥ [२]**

[१४][. . . .]**ति।** यन्मे अग्न [अस्य यज्ञस्य][१५]रिष्याद् **इति जपित्वा ध्रुवाम्। अथ दक्षिणस्यामेव जुह्वोरुपभृतोश्चान्ततः पृषदाज्यग्रहण्यां हविःषु च जपेत्। नैन्द्राग्नेन जपित्वा मारुत्या जपेत्। वारुण्यामन्ततः। संसन्नं यज्ञमभिमृशेत्। इध्मावाधीयमानावभिमन्त्रणे** [१६][उच्छुष्मा]वग्नी यजमानाय स्तं निशुष्मावभि-दासते **इति।** अग्ने वाजजित् **इत्यभ्यूह्यावर्त्य** मनः स्थः प्राजापत्यं मनसा मा भूतेनाविशतम् **इत्याघारानुमन्त्रणम्।** वाक् स्थ ऐन्द्री सपत्नक्षयणी वाचा मेन्द्रियेणाविशतम् **इत्युक्तयोर्वाङ्मनःपरौ मूर्धन्निप्रेव** [. . . .][१७] **उत्तरस्यां वेद्यां**

१. M Ad B om. २. M Ad B om. ३. M Ad B गच्छन्तु. ४. M Ad B पोतार. ५. M Ad B broken. ६. M Ad B दुह उताम्. ७. M Ad B broken. ८. M Ad B add ध्रुवः after स्थः. ९. M Ad B ब्राह्म°; text abr. १०. M Ad B broken. ११. M Ad B पिशो. १२. M Ad B broken. १३. M Ad B जुहूदेव. १४. M Ad B broken. १५. M Ad B broken. १६. M Ad B broken. १७. M Ad B broken.

स्त्रुचौ व्यूह्याथ दक्षिणस्यां व्यूहेत्। रोहितेन वामग्निर्देवतां गमयतु, हरिभ्यां वामिन्द्रो देवतां गमयतु, [1]एतशेन वां सूर्यो देवतां गमयतु[2] **इति प्रस्तरप्रहरणानुमन्त्रणौ।** वेदौ स्थः वित्ती स्थः विदेय; कर्मणी [स्थः करुणे स्थः क्रि][3]यासम्; सनी[यांसौ][4] स्थः, सनितारौ] स्थः सनेयम्; [घृतवन्तं कुलायिनं रायस्पोषं सहस्रिणं][5] वेदौ दत्तां वाजिनम् [इति][6] **वेदानुमन्त्रणम्॥** [३]

यथोक्तकाले तु शुनासीरीयं कुर्वन् यथोक्तं करोति॥ ४[7]॥ इति षष्ठोनुऽवाकः॥

॥ इति चातुर्मास्ययाजमानं समाप्तम्॥

॥ इति चातुर्मास्याख्यस्तृतीयः प्रपाठकः समाप्तः[८]॥

---

१. M Ad B गमयित्वेतशे°. २. M Ad B गमयित्विति. ३. M Ad B broken. ४. M Ad B broken. ५. M Ad B abr. ६. M Ad B om. ७. M Ad B put this Kaṇḍikā after इति चातुर्मास्ययाजमानं समाप्तम्. ८. M Ad not mentioned.

[1] ॥ अथ चतुर्थः प्रपाठकः ॥

॥ अथ पशोर्याजनम् ॥

अथ प्रथमोऽनुवाकः

[2] संवत्सरे द्विः सकृद् वा नित्येन पशुबन्धेन यक्ष्यमाणः प्रोष्ठपद्यां[3] माघ्यां वाऽमावास्यायां वे[दिं करोत्य][4]भ्यगारे। ततोऽन्यत्र वेदेरवसाय[5] यज्ञोपवीतं कृत्वा मन्त्रेणाचम्य प्राण्यापान्य[6] प्रजापतिः प्राचीर्दिक् इति जपित्वा तीर्थेन प्रपद्याग्नीन् विहृत्य यूपाहुत्या[7] सहापरेण[8] त्र्यरत्निं चतुररत्निं[9] वा पालाशं स्वाद्योनेरूढं बहुपर्णं [10]बहुशाखमसुषिरमक्रिम्णं परिष्वङ्गपराध्यर्प्रादेशावमपरि-[माणमनक्षसङ्गंवृ][11]श्चति यथा स्थानपक्षो न सज्येत। प्राञ्चं वोदञ्चं वा प्रप्रापयति पातयति। शाखानुगुण्येन[12] प्रसूदयति। प्रवृश्चति विगतशाखं करोति। यूपार्थत्वात् मन्त्र-स्यावृत्तिः। परिवासयति छिनत्ति। चषालच्छेदनेऽपि मन्त्रत्रयमिति। यूपं चषाल-शकलाभ्याच्छादने प्रथमशकलं यूपावटेऽव[दधाति][13], प्रथमशकलं स्वरु। स चाग्निष्ठाया निस्तक्षणीय इत्येके। अथ पिण्डपितृयज्ञं कृत्वा, इष्टिपक्ष इष्टिं कृत्वा वेदिं मिमीते रथावकाशाम्[14], रथप्रमाणाम्। अष्टाशीतितमाङ्गुल-पार्श्वमानीं च चतुःशताङ्गुलपश्चिमबाहुं षडशीत्यङ्गुलपूर्वरज्जुं, पूर्वरज्ज्वोर्मध्ये[15] यूपावटीयः शङ्कुः परिणाहाभ्यां मनागुपरमति। खनन्त्येके उपरविभागान्वयात्[16]। तां[17] विमाय समन्ततः स्पन्द्यया परितनोति। अथ तूष्णीं दक्षिणतो ब्रह्माण-मुपवेश्य तस्याः स्तम्बयजुर्हृत्वा[18] उत्तरस्मात् परिग्रहात् स्फ्यमुदपात्रमित्यादि प्रतिपद्यते। उत्तरेणाहवनीयमुत्तरस्माद्वेद्यन्ता[त् . . . .][19] चात्वालकालं शम्यामात्रं चात्वालात् परिणाहतो निम्नतश्च। तमपरेणोत्करः॥ [१]

अतः प्रभृति तयोरन्तरेणैव सर्वेषां प्रपदनं[20] निष्क्रमणं च वा। शम्यानिधाने मन्त्राः। अनुलेखन इत्येके। यूपावटीयाच्छङ्कोरर्धप्रक्रमे शम्यामात्री चतुःस्रक्ति-

---

१. None of the MSS gives the number of the Prapāṭhaka. २. M Ad B तथा. ३. M °पाद्यां. ४. M Ad B broken. ५. M Ad B वेदवसाय. ६. M Ad प्राणा°. ७. M Ad B °हुत्वा. ८. M Ad B सहोप°. ९. M Ad B चतुरेतिं. १०. M Ad B शाखानसु°क्रिणं. ११. M Ad B broken before श्चति [MSS °त्]; cf. VādhŚS 5.1.8-9. १२. M Ad B शाखानुपुण्येन. १३. M Ad B om. १४. M Ad B °काशाः. १५. M Ad B °रज्जो°. १६. M Ad B °राविभाभत्व°. १७. M Ad B कां. १८. M Ad B °यजुर्हुत्वा. १९. M Ad B broken. २० . M Ad B प्रवद°.

रुत्तरवेदिः। तत्र पु[रीषं][१] यजमानोऽन्वारभेत। मन्त्रं च ब्रूयादित्येके। मध्य उत्तरवेद्या न्युप्तेन पुरीषेणोत्तरनाभिं करोति सुष्ठु श्लक्ष्णामनग्नामप्रकाशाम्। ऊर्णास्तुका वेद्यन्तरा[२] शृङ्ग्योरुपात्ता। यथोपपादमित्यपरे। पौतुद्रवाः परिधयः प्रादेशमात्राः, प्रोक्षण्यः, [३][पञ्चगृहीतमाज्यम्। षड्ढोतारं मनसाऽनुद्रुत्यान्वा]-ख्यातिं जुह्वदिध्ममभिजुहुयात्। निरुक्तायामाद्यायामृचीध्ममुद्यच्छन्ते परिकर्मिणः। एकस्फ्यया आग्नीध्रो यथालिङ्गमनुदिशमुत्तरनाभिं प्रोक्षति। व्याघरणानि सर्वाणि प्रागपवर्गाणि। मध्यापवर्गाणीत्येके। स्रुचमुद्गृह्णाति। ससंस्रावान् संभारान्नि-वपति। विनियुक्त [४][उपयच्छन्त्युप]यमन्यः सिकता प्रथमः। सीद योनिम् इत्युच्यमाने पुरस्तात्प्रत्यगावृत्त इध्मं सादयेत्। उपस्थानं[५] याजमानम्। आध्वर्यवमित्यपरे[६]। अग्निमुपसमाधायालंकृत्य तूष्णीं परिस्तीर्यातिमुक्तीर्जुहुयात्। अत्र प्राकृतमन्त्रं प्रक्रमे मध्यमवर्जम्। त्रीनग्नीनन्वाधाय व्रतमुपेयात्। अध्वर्युरन्वाहितेष्वेवाभ्याधाय बर्हिः संभृत्य प्लक्षशाखामिडसूनं[७] चोपकल्प्य वेदं कृत्वा परिस्तृणीयात्। आच्छिद्रिकोपादानपक्षे प्रातः स्तम्बयजुषो वेदकरणम-पकृष्येत। अथ पात्राणि सादयेत् स्फ्यं चाग्निहोत्रहवणीं [च][८] जुहूमुपभृतं च स्रुवं च स्वधितिं च प्रणीताप्रणयनं च सर्वार्थत्वे प्रणीतानाम् आज्यस्थालीं च वेदं च समिधश्च पत्नीसन्नहनं च वसाहोमहवनीं च प्लक्षशाखां चेडसूनं[७] च रशनाद्वयं च मैत्रावरुणदण्डं च हिरण्यशल्कांश्च[८] कुम्भीं च शूलं च वपाश्रपण्यौ च यच्चान्यदेवंजातीयकानि[९] सर्वाणि संसाद्य पवि[त्रेण . . . .][१०] ब्रह्माणमुपवेश्य सर्वार्थत्वे प्रणीतानां प्रणीताः प्रणीय, प्रणीताऽभावेऽपि यजमान वाचं यच्छ इत्युक्त्वा हस्तौ मार्जयित्वा [. . . .][११] पर्यग्नि कृत्वा दधि चोपनिधाय सहोत्तरपरिग्रहादि प्रतिपद्यते। यथासमाम्नातं प्रैषं प्रसि[द्धं . . . .][१२]। स्रुवं संमृज्य स्रुवमन्त्रेण स्वधितिं संमृजेत्। स्वधितिरसि इत्यूहित्वा अथवा स्रुवस्वधिती जुहूपभृतौ प्रसिद्धं संमृज्य उपभृज्जुहूध्रुवासि इति ध्रुवामादाय प्रसिद्धं निष्टप्य प्रजां योनिं[१३] चक्षुः श्रोत्रं गोष्ठाद्रयिं[१४] मा निमृक्षं संमार्ज्मि इति संमार्ष्टि। प्रसिद्धमित्येव ज्याय इवाभाति। प्रसिद्धमाज्यग्रहणम् [. . . .][१५] प्रसिद्धं जुह्वां गृहीत्वोपभृति न्यायप्रसिद्धं चतुर्गृहीतं गृह्णीयात्। शास्त्रप्रसिद्धमष्टग्रहणमित्येके।

---

१. M Ad B broken. २. M Ad B वेत्वन्त°. ३. M Ad B broken before ख्याति; cf. VādhŚS 5.2.1-6. ४. M Ad B broken; cf. VādhŚS 5.2.8. ५. M Ad B °पस्तानं. ६. M Ad B अध्व°. ७. M Ad B इडसूनुं. ८. M Ad B om च. ९. M Ad B °कास्म नि. १०. M Ad B broken. ११. M Ad B broken. १२. M Ad B broken. १३. M Ad B योनेश्च°. १४. M Ad B गोष्ठुद्रयिं. १५. M Ad B ग्रहणा . . . . न्नति.

ध्रुवायां पृषदाज्यग्रहणं तत एव वनस्पती हृदयाभिघारणे पृथगेव वा तयोरर्धमाज्यस्थाल्याः किञ्चिदाज्यं पात्रान्तर आसिच्य निदध्यात्। तृतीयं च पूर्वमाज्यं दधिसंसृष्टं हृदयाभिघारितं [. . . .][१] **वति ज्याय इवाभाति। आज्य-स्थाल्याज्यध्रुवा कार्येति दिष्टं न ग्रहणमन्त्रा नार्वाञ्चो ध्रुवासंस्काराः। प्रसिद्धं जुहूमुपभृतो सादयित्वा उपभृन्मन्त्रेण ध्रुवां सादयेत्, ध्रुवामन्त्रेणाज्यस्थालीम्।** पृथिवीजन्मनाऽऽज्यस्थालीनाम्ना **इत्यूहित्वा सादयेदित्येके। प्रसिद्धं स्रुचः सादयित्वा तूष्णीं** [. . . .][२] **न्येव। प्रसिद्धमा होतुर्व्याख्यानाच्चतुर्होतुः स्थाने दशहोता। क्लृप्तचषालः प्रतिमुक्तचषालः प्रक्षालितस्तीर्थेन प्रपादितः पूर्वेण यूपावटमुपनिहितः स्यात्॥ [२]**

सह यूपशकलौ स्वरुणा रशनया मैत्रावरुणदण्डे च प्रोक्षण्यस्तूष्णीकाः पृथिव्यै [त्वा, अन्तरिक्षाय त्वा,][३] दिवे त्वा **इति मूलमध्याग्रेषु पराञ्चं यूपं प्रोक्षेत्। अपोऽवनयति प्रोक्षणीनामुच्छिष्टाः। विषूचीनाग्रं**[४] **व्यस्ताग्रम्। अव-स्तरणादिहोभयोः प्राचीनावीतित्वं दक्षिणमुखत्वं च। अग्निष्ठाया एवाञ्जनम्। अग्निष्ठमन्त्रेणोक्त्वा तूष्णीं सर्वमनक्तीत्यपरम्।** अ[. . . .][५] **वनितः प्रतिभाति। पृथ्वीं वा तीक्ष्णां वाऽध्वर्युरनक्ति। यजमान इत्यन्ये। अध्वर्युणा मन्त्रेणाज्यसिक्ते यजमानो हस्ताभ्यां सर्वमनक्तीत्यपरम्। आन्तमनक्ति। नोपरमनक्ति। अञ्जनादि-यूपमध्वर्युयजमानौ न विसृजतः। आशकलावगूहनं स्रुवं स्थापयति। यथाऽऽहवनीयेऽनूर्जमिता स्यात्। उत्काशयति उद्दीक्षयति। दृंहयति दृढयति। प्रवयति अस्यत्यास्यति परिव्यये रशनागुणे॥ [३]** इति प्रथमोऽनुवाकः॥

अथ द्वितीयोऽनुवाकः

अथ पशुं [६]**सिक्तरेतसमन्तरेण चात्वालोत्करौ प्रपाद्य उत्तरे यूपं प्रत्यङ्मुखं स्थापयित्वा च** [. . . .][७] **र्वन्। पशोः**[८] **पृष्ठे बर्हिषी निधायोपर्युपरि कदमन्तरेण शृङ्गे विकर्षेत्। प्रज्ञाते उपलक्षिते यथा पुनरप्यादीयेयातां शकलम् अभिमन्थन-शकलं वृषाणौ वृषणस्थायौ शकलद्वयमेव तस्याभिमन्थनस्याभितो निदध्यात्।** घृतेन[ाक्तौ **इति स्वरुं स्वधितिं च।**][९] **तेनाञ्जन् युगपदेवानक्ति। ततः शकलेषु समन्त्रकामधरारणिं निधाय मन्त्रेणान्यामुत्तरारणिमवदध्यात्। प्रजातिभिरात्मानं प्रति निवर्तयते। अधरारण्यां यजमानोऽयं प्रथमो मन्थति। प्रेष्यति चेत्यपरे।**

---

१. M Ad B broken. २. M Ad B broken. ३. M Ad B broken. ४. M Ad B °नाग्रा. ५. M Ad B broken. ६. M B सितरे Ad. ७. M Ad B broken. ८. M Ad B वशोः. ९. M Ad B broken; cf. *VādhŚS* 5.5.12.

निर्वर्तनमन्थनमित्यन्ये। परिवर्तनं मन्थति। बलवन्तः कुशलाः परिकर्मिणः। जातायानुब्रूहि इति जात आह। प्रह्रियमाणायानुब्रूहि इति प्रहरिष्यन्। अक्ष्णया शृङ्गं दक्षिणं सहास्येन पशोः परिहरति। परितो बध्नाति। युनक्ति यूपरशनायाम्। यूप इत्यपरम्। न प्रोक्षणीनां मन्त्रेण संस्कृतिः। मन्त्रेण [१][प्रोक्ष्य पा]ययित्वा तत उत्तराणि [२]वक्षप्रोक्षणपृष्ठप्रोक्षणनिपाय्य प्रोक्षणानि तूष्णीकानि कृत्वा निधाय पात्रम् अग्नये समिध्यमानाय इत्यादि प्रतिपद्यते। जुह्वा जुहूगतेनाज्येन पशुं समनक्ति सं ते प्राणः इति। ललाटे संयजत्रैः इति, ककुदि सं यज्ञपतिः इति, दक्षिणा[३] समङ्गानि [४][इति, गच्छ]न्ताम् इति मनसा क्रियापदं स्मरेद् वाक्यपरिपूरणायेति। निस्तूष्णीत्येके। स्रुच्येकादशाय प्रयाजायाज्यमतिशिष्य दश प्रयाजानिष्ट्वा कः स्वधितिहस्तम् इति ब्रुवन्नत्याक्रम्य स्वरुं च स्वधितिं चादाय विषूचीनाग्रे कृत्वा मन्त्रेण युगपत् स्रुच्यनक्ति। बिले स्वरुं स्रु[चः स्व] [५]धितिं[६] युगपदेव[७] मन्त्रेण। पशुं संमृज्य विशेषेण स्वधितिना ललाटं प्रति पशोरुन्मृज्य शमित्रे स्वधितिं प्रयच्छन्नुपलक्षयेत्। तामश्रिं यया पशुः समत्तो नैतयावदास्यामि इति शमित्रे प्रादर्शये॥ [१]

नैतया विशसितव्यमिति। पर्यग्नयेऽनुब्रूहि इत्यध्वर्युणा उक्तेऽग्नीदाह[वनी-यादुल्मुकमादायान्तरा चात्वालोत्करौ निष्क्रमय्य प्रस] [८]लैस्त्रिः पर्यग्नि कुर्यात्। सह यूपाहवनीयाभ्यामिति केचित्। सहाज्यैश्चेत्येके। सह शामित्रेण चेत्यन्ये। सह ब्रह्मयजमानाभ्यां चेत्यपरे। पशुमेवेत्याचार्याभिप्रायः प्रतिभाति। तस्मिन् पक्षे विस्रस्य पशुं पर्यग्निकृत्य[९] यथास्थानमुल्मुकं[१०] निधाय यथेतमपसलैस्त्रिः[११] परीत्य तदेवोल्मुकमादायाग्नीध्रः[१२] प्रथमो गच्छेत्तमन्वगितरे। तीर्थेन निष्क्रम्या-श्राव्य संप्रे[ष्य वपाश्रपणीभ्यां पशुम] [१३]न्वारभ्यापरेण शामित्रावभिगश्चेदग्रेण

१. M Ad B broken. २. M Ad B पक्ष°. ३. M Ad B broken between दक्षिणा and अङ्गानि. ४. M Ad B broken. ५. M Ad B broken. ६. M Ad B °धितिन्त. ७. M Ad B °पद्देव. ८. M Ad B broken between दाह and लैस्त्रिः [M Ad B लेत्रिः] cf. VādhŚS 5.5.18. ९. Due to displacement of the folios in the original MS from which the Madras MS was copied, the text between पर्य[ग्निकृत्य and यथास्थानमु dealing with *Cāturmāsya* covering 5 pages from M p. 435, line 18; Ad p. 874, line 1, to M p. 440, line 11; Ad p. 882, line 1 has been wrongly copied down here in MSS. The text beginning with यथास्थानं up to the end of the Prapāṭhaka belongs to the remaining part of the *Paśubandha*. १०. M Ad B स्थानमुन्दुकं. ११. M Ad B मवसलैस्त्रीं. १२. M Ad B °ग्नीध्रं. १३. M Ad B broken; cf. *VādhŚS* 5.5.24-26.

वश्यश्चात्वालस्योत्तरे [१]शामित्रदेशस्तस्योत्तरस्मिन् प्रदेशे मन्त्रेण बर्हिषोऽन्यतर-त्प्राचीनाग्रं वोपास्योपरि पशुं शाययन्ति।[२] प्रैष उक्ते[३] यथेतरत्तूष्णीं पुनर्गच्छेयुः। मन्त्रेणाध्वर्युयजमानौ[४]। पान्नेजनमुदकं पादप्र[क्षालनार्थं][५]माप्यायनार्थं च। आप्यायतेऽध्वर्युः[६] पत्नी वा। अध्वर्युरभिषिञ्चेत्॥ [२]

पत्न्यभिमृशेद्यथालिङ्गं पत्न्याः। व्रताभिरद्भिरभिषिच्य पत्नीं वाचयेद् आप्यायनमन्त्रान्[७] या ते प्राणान् इति वर्जयित्वा। पदः[८] संनिधाय मार्जयति प्रक्षालयति। श्रोण्योर्निनयत्यध्वर्युः। निनीता[९] अपोऽनुमन्त्रयते। अध्वर्युरेवेत्यपरे। कवोत्तानम् ईषदुत्तानम्। दक्षिणेन नाभिमावर्तते[१०], तत्प्रति बर्हिषा त्वचमुप-संगृह्णाति[११]। सह बर्हिषा[१२] आच्छ्यति[१३] शनैरेव वा दर्शनात्। उपस्थादितरच्च बर्हिर्द्वेधा छित्वा तस्य स्थविमखण्डस्याग्रद्वयं पशोर्लोहिते[१४] त्वचो[१५] दूरतो मन्त्रेण निरस्येत्[१६]। शिष्टस्य [१७][अ]पि बर्हिषः खण्डस्य मूलं छित्वा तेन परिवासनम्। यत्र वपा परिवासिता तं प्रदेशं प्रतियौति अपिदधाति। अतोऽन्येनापि दर्भेण दृढं विधाय दर्भान्तरेण वपाद्रव्यं संवेष्ट्य सम्यक् प्रक्षाल्य मन्त्रेणोल्मुके प्रतितप्य शामित्रदेशमुल्मुकान् मातरिश्वनो घर्मोऽसि इति संप्रकृष्य संविधूय उप समादध्यात्॥ [३]

अथाग्रेण शामित्रं वपां पर्याहृत्योल्मुकप्रथमा आगच्छेयुर्वपाश्रपणी अन्वा-रम्भमाणास्तीर्थेन मन्त्रत्रयेण सर्व आहवनीयसमीपं वपाहोमान्तमुभयोः। [१८]अथो-ल्मुकमाहवनीयसमीपे विसृज्य वपामन्त्रेणान्तमेऽङ्गारे प्रतप्यान्तरा यूपाहवनीयं चाहृत्य प्रतिप्रस्थाता गच्छेत्। तत्राङ्गारनिरूहणाधिश्रयणदृंहणान्यर्थलुप्तानि। दृंहणवर्जमर्थलोप[१९] इत्येके। अर्थलोप एव ज्यायान्। तस्यां श्रप्यमाणायां विशिष्टं

---

१. M Ad B °त्तरगोमित्र°. २. B °यन्ती. ३. M Ad B उत्ते. ४. M Ad B °मानो. ५. M Ad B वोदप्र . . . मा°. ६. M Ad B तोऽध्वं. ७. M Ad B भाव्या°. ८. M Ad B वदसन्नि. ९. M ताः विन्यनु, Ad °ताः निन्यनु, B ताः नुम. १०. M Ad र्तत. ११. M Ad संग्रष्णौदि. १२. M Ad B repeat त्वचमुत्संग्रष्णौदि सह वर्हिषा. १३. M Ad B आज्यति. १४. M Ad B वशो°. १५. M Ad B क्त्वो. १६. M Ad B निदस्येत्. १७. M Ad B broken. १८. Due to displacement of the folios in the original MS from which the Madras MS was copied, the matter between वपाहोमान्तमुभयोः M p. 441, line 13, Ad p. 883, line 13 and ending before अथोल्मुकमाहवनीयसमीपे [M p. 443, line 2, Ad p 886, line 2] belonging to Varuṇapraghāsa has wrongly been copied down under Paśubandha. That text has been put at proper place under Varuṇapraghāsa vide p. 32 fn. 8. The text beginning with अथोल्मुकमा constitutes the remaining part of the Paśubandha. १९. M Ad B दृंहणवज्जनान्नार्थं.

बर्हिःखण्डमुपास्यैतां[१] श्रप्यमाणां घृतेनाप्याययेत्। सम्यक् श्रपणाय तस्यां मन्त्रवत्पर्यग्निकरणद्वयं तन्त्रेण कृत्वा तूष्णीमभिघार्य इदमिन्द्रियम् **इति दक्षिणायां श्रोण्यामासाद्य वपां** मयि श्रपयताम् **इत्यभिमृश्य** यस्ते शुष्म **इत्यभिघार्य, वपामभिघारयेत्। न ध्रुवामित्येके। अथाज्यभागौ[२] यजति, यद्यत्र यजेत्॥** [४]

अग्नय आज्यस्यावदीयमानस्यानुब्रूहि **इत्याज्यं गृह्णानश्चतुरत्याक्रम्याश्रावयन्नग्नय आज्यं प्रस्थितं प्रेष्य वषट्कृते हुत्वा सोमायाज्यस्य** सोममाज्यम् **इति सौम्यमाज्यभागमिष्ट्वा, अथ वपाया उपस्तीर्य हिरण्यशल्कमवधाय** इन्द्राग्निभ्यां छागस्य[३] **इति प्रैषमुक्त्वा जुह्वा[४] उपरि स्रुवेण[५] वपां संप्रलुम्पन् विस्त्रंसयन् यथा संप्रप्लुता जुह्वां पतेत्। अथ हिरण्यशल्कमवधायाभि** स्वाहा देवेभ्यः **इति प्रतिप्रस्थात्रा हुते मन्त्रेणाध्वर्युर्वषट्कृते वपां जुहोति** देवेभ्यः स्वाहा **इति। प्रतिप्रस्थाताऽऽघार्य वपाश्रपणी अन्तरा यूपं चाहवनीयं चातिहृत्योत्तरतस्तिष्ठते प्रतिप्रस्थात्रे प्रदाय स्रुचावादाय दक्षिणत एव तिष्ठन्नाह**—इन्द्राग्निभ्याम् **इति। प्रति परिहृत्य वपामत्याक्रम्याश्रावयेदित्येके। स्वयमेव परिक्रम्यात्याक्रम्य परिहृतामेवादायाश्रावयेदित्यपरे। आद्य एव पक्षो ज्यायानिवाभाति।** स्वाहा देवेभ्यः **इति प्रतिप्रस्थात्राहुते मन्त्रेणाध्वर्युर्वषट्कृते वपा जुहोति। प्रतिप्रस्थाता जुहोति।** देवेभ्यः स्वाहा **इति अध्वर्युरित्येके। वपाश्रपणी प्रहरति [६][प्रति]प्रस्थाता। सर्वे मार्जयन्ते चात्वालप्रदेशे चात्वाले [७]वोदकमासिच्य॥** [५] इति द्वितीयोऽनुवाकः॥

अथ तृतीयोऽनुवाकः

प्रैष उक्तेऽग्नीत्पात्राणि संसादयेत् कपालादीनि नव, प्राशित्रहरणं च। हविर्यज्ञविधपक्षे मेक्षणं च पिष्टोद्वपनीं[८] च प्रणीताप्रणयनं च। सवविधपक्षे दारुपात्रीं च मदन्तीस्थालीं[९] चोपवेषं च वृषारवं च। पुरोडाशीयानाहृत्य निधाय पवित्रे आदाय प्रणीताः प्रणयेत् सवविधपक्षे। पक्षान्तरे यजमान[१०] वाचं यच्छ **इत्युक्त्वा हस्तौ मार्जयित्वा** वेषाय त्वा **इत्यग्निहोत्रहवणीं शूर्पमित्यादाय निष्टप्य हविर्निरूप्य निधाय पुरोडाशीयान् प्रोक्षणीः संस्कृत्य प्रोक्षणं कुर्वन् सर्वाभिः पात्राणि प्रोक्ष्य व्रीहीनवहत्य कपालान्युपधाय पिष्टानि कृत्वा प्रणीताभ्योऽध्याहरेत्येतावदुक्त्वा समुप्य संयुत्यासंक्षालननिनयात् करोति। प्रतिप्रस्थाताऽपि**

---

१. M Ad B °स्येतां. २. M Ad B °भाग्नौ. ३. M Ad B जागरस्येति. ४. M Ad B स्रुवा. ५. M Ad B °वेणापां. ६. M Ad B om. ७. M Ad B वोकमा°. ८. M Ad विष्टो°. ९. M Ad B °दन्ति°. १०. M Ad B °मानः.

पुरोडाशस्य हविष्कृदन्ते पशुं विशास्ति शासयति। विशसनाय शमितारं[१] प्रेष्येत्। विशसनादिश्रपणान्तं[२] शमितृकर्म। स चाङ्गान्यु[द्धरेत्][३]। यथैषामाकृतिराविः स्यात् तथा गात्रंगात्रमस्यानूनमुद्धरेत्। उद्धृतानि कस्मिंश्चिद् विदले काष्ठे वा लतायां वा न्युप्य[४] त्रीणि त्रीणि तथा संकल्प्योपलक्षयेत्। एकचरमसहायं तेषु[५] त्रित्व-संकल्पो नास्ति। अध्यूध्निमूढता सासह [. . . .][६] न्युद्धृत्य मेदश्चापक्षाय काष्ठस्यान्ते मिथ आसिच्य[७] सम्यक् प्रक्षाल्यावदध्यात्। प्रागेव विशसनात् शामित्रमुप समाधाय द्यौरसि इति कुम्भीमादाय विश्वधाया[८] इत्यधिश्रित्य दृंहस्व[९] इति दृंहित्वा वोपधि केनचित् पात्रेण द्यौः स्थः पृथिवी स्थ इत्यादाय[१०] अवधाय[११] कुम्भ्यामवनयेद्[१२] दृंहणम्। अर्थलुप्तमदानाधिश्रयणे चार्थलुप्ते इत्येके॥ [१]

तत उद्धृत्यावदानानि[१३] यथोक्तं कुम्भ्यामवधाय श्रपयेत्। अथ श्रिते पशावग्नीत् पात्र्यां पशुपुरोडाशमुद्वास्यालंकृत्य वेद्यामासादयेद्यथाऽध्वर्युः। यस्ते शुष्म इत्यभिघार्य यन्मे अग्ने इत्यभिमृशेत्। अत्राज्यभागाभ्यां चरति यदि पुरस्तादकृतौ स्याताम्। अथ प्रतिप्रस्थाता व्रतमुपेत्य यथोक्तं देवतासौविष्टकृते अवदाय, सन्धाय स्रुचावध्वर्यवे प्रयच्छेत्। अथाध्वर्युः स्रुचावादायात्याक्रम्या-श्राव्य यथोक्तमुभयमिष्ट्वाऽत्याक्रम्य स्रुचं पूर्णं द्विर्निनीय यथायतनं स्रुचौ सादयित्वा प्राशित्रमवद्येद् हविर्विधपक्षे। पक्षान्तरेऽवदायैव प्राशित्रम् इडामव-खण्ड्यावदानानि संभिद्याभिघार्य प्रत्यङ् वाऽऽवृत्य सहैव पात्र्येडां होत्रे प्रयच्छेत्। इडार्थमवत्तामवान्तरेडामवदायावशिष्टं बर्हिषदं कृत्वा तत्र यजमानं वाचयित्वा पुनः पात्र्यामवधायाग्नीध आधाय प्राश्नन्ति। मार्जयन्ते। अथ प्राशित्रं परिहृत्य पुरोडाशं परिहरेत् प्राशित्रपक्षे। पक्षान्तरे पुरोडाशमेव। प्राशित्रपक्षे पुरोडाशस्य नास्ति परिहरणमित्येके। परिहरणमेव ज्यायो यदि वपान्ते न नीता स्यात् सा। अन्यथा शुद्धम्। गौरित्येकेऽन्वाहार्य इत्यन्ये। गौश्चान्वाहार्यश्चेत्यपरे। ज्याया-निवैष पक्षः। अत्रानाज्यकेन फलीकरणहोमं चरित्वा पिष्टलेपमनुवर्त्य[१४] विष्णु-क्रमैश्चरित्वा सवविधपक्षमुलूखलमुसलं परेक्ष्य कपालानि विमुञ्चेद् यदि प्रागपि मुक्तानि स्युः॥ [२]

---

१. M Ad B °तारः. २. M Ad श्रवणान्तरं, B °श्रवणानन्तरं. ३. M Ad B broken. ४. M Ad B नुज्य. ५. Ad त्रिषु. ६. M Ad B broken. ७. M Ad B आसच्य. ८. M Ad B °धाय. ९. M Ad B °हस्य. १०. M Ad B °दय. ११. M Ad B विश्वधा°. १२. M Ad B °नये. १३. M Ad B °दानि. १४. M Ad विष्टलोप, B विष्टलोम°.

अथ प्रेषितोऽग्नीत्[१] प्लक्षशाखां पर्णसूनं[२] चाग्रेण शामित्रमाहृत्य तीर्थेन प्रपाद्यान्तरा यूपं चाहवनीयं चाहृत्य दक्षिणान्ते वेद्याः पर्णसूनं[३] निधाय तस्योपरि प्लक्षशाखां निदधाति। अथ प्रतिप्रस्थात्रा[४] पृषदाज्यस्योपहत्य यथोक्तसमुदितेऽध्वर्युर्मन्त्रेण पशुं पर्यग्निकृत्वा हृदयशूलेन[५] हृदयं संस्पृश्य तं प्रज्ञातं निधाय प्रतिप्रस्थातुः पृषदाज्यमादाय हृदयमुत्तमं कृत्वा सं ते मनसा इति पशुमभिघारयेद्, यथा पूर्वहृदये पतित्वा सर्वेष्ववदानेषु पतेत्। अथैतं पशुमन्तरा यूपं चाहवनीयं चाहृत्य स्थाल्या उद्धृत्य दक्षिणतः प्लक्षशाखायाः प्रत्यवदानं निष्कलिवनिष्ठुवर्जं मन्त्रेणासाद्य हृदयं मयि श्रयताम्, जिह्वा मयि श्रयताम् इत्यनुपूर्वमेव मन्त्रेणाभिघारयेत्। आसादनसंमर्शनाभिघारणमन्त्रा [६]देवतानामेव, न स्विष्टकृदिडार्थयोः। दक्षिणस्या यौष्णः[७] सव्यायाः श्रोण्या इत्येके। तदेव ज्यायः। अथ यन्मे अग्ने इत्यनुपूर्वमेवाभिमृशेत्। अथ प्रतिप्रस्थाता जुहूपभृतोर्वसाहोमीयाम्[८] इडापात्रमाज्यस्थालीद्वयं प्राकृतीमपूर्वां च स्रुवं स्वधितिमन्तरा यूपं चाहवनीयं चाहृत्य दक्षिणत आसीनो जुहूपभृतोः ध्रुवाज्यादुपस्तीर्य मनोतायै हविष इति प्रेष्येत्। हृदयादीनामुत्सादनप्रदेशेभ्योऽनुपूर्वं स्वधितिना द्विरवदाय यूष्णोपसिच्य मेदो यूषन्नवधाय तेन जुहूं प्रोर्णोति। अभिघार्य प्रत्यज्य स्विष्टकृदर्थं गुदतृतीयम्। अथ त्र्यङ्गाणां यथोक्तमुपभृत्यवदाय[९] यूष्णोपसेचनादि कृत्वा न प्रत्यज्य वसां वसाहोमीयायां विस्राव्यापूर्वाज्यस्थाल्या अभिघार्यानस्थिकेऽवधाय यूष्णोपसिच्यावत्तं मन्त्रेण पशुमभिमृश्य श्रीरसि इति केनचित् पार्श्वेन वसाहोमीयं प्रयुत्य स्रुचोः पञ्चहोतारं व्याख्यायावत्तं प्रति परिहृत्य स्रुग्द्वयं प्रतिसन्धायाध्वर्यवे प्रयच्छेत्॥ [३]

ते आदायाध्वर्युरुत्तिष्ठन् प्रैषादि प्रतिपद्यते। अथ [१०][पञ्चहो]तारमुक्त्वा [११][प्रति]प्रस्थाता मन्त्रेण वसाहोमं जुहोति। अथाध्वर्युर्वषट्कृते हविर्हुत्वा वनस्पतये इति ब्रुवन् स्रुवेण पृषदाज्यस्योपहत्य[१२] जुह्वामानीयाश्राव्य प्रैषमुक्त्वा वषट्कृते जुहुयात्। यद्यनत्याक्रम्याश्रावणेति तु प्रदक्षिणमावृत्य [. . .][१३] मेदस्य[१४] अग्नीध आदधाति। पृथगुपस्तीर्णाभिघारिते प्राश्नन्ति। मार्जयन्ते। ब्रह्मा च वक्षः प्राश्य मार्जयते[१५]। पार्श्वे प्रतिप्रस्थाता। सन्ततिमनु तिस्रः स्रुवाहुतीर्हुत्वा प्रेष्यति

---

१. M Ad B °ग्नीन्. २. M Ad B °सूननं. ३. M Ad B °सूनुं cf. VādhŚS 5.8.32. ४. B °स्थाता. ५. M Ad B °शूलौ. cf. VādhŚS 5.8.43. ६. M Ad B दैवता°. ७. M Ad B दौष्ण. ८. M Ad B °मृतावसाहोमि°. ९. M Ad B °वद्वय. १०. M Ad B broken. ११. M Ad B om. १२. MB °दाज्यसो. १३. M Ad B broken. १४. M Ad B मेतस्त. १५. M Ad B °यन्ते.

अग्नीदौपयजान[ङ्गारानाहर][१] **इति। अथ ध्रुवायै वाऽनूयाजान् यजत्युपभृतैवौं[२]-[पयजान् . . .]। इहाप्याज्ये**[२] मैत्रावरुणेन सह यज **इति ब्रूयात्। उपयष्टा प्रतिप्रस्थाता गुदतृतीयस्य निहितस्य प्र**[३]**[च्छेदम]संभिन्दन्नसंगमयन्नन्यस्य प्रयच्छेत्।** [४]**अन्यस्यैकदेशमितरेणासंगमयन् अथवा संभेदनमकुर्वन् प्रच्छिन्द्यात्। अपर्यावर्तयन्, पर्यावर्तमानमकुर्वन् एकादशभिर्मन्त्रैर्यथाक्रममेकादशकृत्वं प्रैषं [कृत्वा]**[५] **तेषु जुहोति। हस्तौ निमृज्योपयष्टा** तनूत्वचम् **इति यजमानं वाचयेत्। वाचयिताऽध्वर्युरित्येके॥ [४]**

अनूयाजानिष्ट्वोपपरिक्रम्य स्वरुसमीपं गत्वा स्वरुमुद्धृत्य जुह्वामक्त्वा[६] **तस्यामवधाय तया पुरस्तात् प्रत्यङ् तिष्ठन् जुहोति। अथागत्य वाजवतीभ्या-मित्यादि प्रतिपद्यते। उत्तानमिडामदधद् उपस्तीर्य द्विरादायाभिघारयेत्। नीच्या अग्नीधे द्विरादधाति। शँय्वन्तमेतत् कृत्वाऽऽज्यस्यैव फलीकरणहोमं हुत्वा पिष्टलेपमनुवर्त्य प्राजापत्यं हुत्वा प्राड्त्य ध्रुवामाप्याय्य त्रीणि समिष्टयजूंषि हुत्वा प्रणीताः पर्याहृत्य तासु यजमानं वाचयित्वा ता यजमानस्याञ्जलावानीय** अयं ते योनिः **इत्यादि प्रतिपद्यते हविर्यज्ञविधपक्षे। पक्षान्तरे फलीकरणे होमवर्जम्॥ [५]** इति तृतीयोऽनुवाकः॥

अथ चतुर्थोऽनुवाकः

'शिवा च मे' **इति पूर्वस्मिन् परिग्राहे जपित्वा वृणीत औत्तरवेदिक आदित्यं प्रत्यग्निमुपतिष्ठमानः। अद्य** यज्ञाय रमताम् **इति सन्नमयेत्। अथाग्नीनन्वाधाय पूर्वपरिग्राहं जपन्** इमामूर्जं प्रतिपदमष्टमीं पञ्चदशम् **इति तां तिथिं लक्षयित्वा** पशुबन्धं हविर् **इत्यूहित्वा व्रतमुपेयाद्**[७] **हविर्यज्ञविधपक्षे। पक्षान्तरेऽनुपेत्य वतं प्रेषितो वाचं यच्छेदागत्य प्रोक्षणात्। अथोत्तरस्मिन् परिग्राहे** इमामूर्जम् **इति जपित्वाऽऽज्यमवेक्ष्याज्यग्रहणमभिमन्त्रयन् प्रसिद्धमेव** [८]**जौहवानभिमन्त्र्यौपभृतांश्चतुरः। अथ पृषदाज्ये** सुवीर्याय त्वा **इति चतुर्भिश्चतुरो दधिवर्जं** भूरस्माकम् **इति॥ [१]**

चतुर्भिराज्यस्थालीमभिमन्त्रयेत्। ग्रहणाभावादत्र नाभिमन्त्रणमित्येके। तदेव ज्यायः। अथ यत्र प्रस्तरे [९]**अपिसृजतीत्यादि प्रतिपद्यते, प्रसिद्धं जुहूपभृतोः**

---

१. M Ad B °यजनानिति. २–२. M Ad B °भृतैवो...रिहाप्यन्ये; [Ad °भृतौ]. ३. M Ad B प्र...संभन्द°. ४. M Ad B °नस्येक°. ५. M Ad B broken. ६. M Ad B °मक्ता. ७. M Ad B °मुपयेधा. ८. M Ad B जाहवान°. ९. M Ad B अविसृ°.

सादने जपित्वा पृषदाज्यग्रहण्याम् अवाहं[1] बाध इति जपेत्। ध्रुवा इति सन्नमये-दित्येके। नैवमूहेदित्यपरे। यो मा वाचा इत्याज्यस्थाल्याः। अहम् इत्येके सन्नमयन्ति। अविकार एव ज्यायान्। अञ्जनादि यूपं यजमानोऽनुसृजेदा स्वरो-रवगूहनात्। त्वां गावोऽवृणुत राज्याय इति ब्रह्मणा वाचितो ब्रूयात्। प्रयाजा-निष्ट्वाननुमन्त्र्यमाणः प्रसिद्धांस्त्रींस्त्रींरभिमन्त्र्य चतुर्थेनोत्तरांश्चतुरः पञ्च-मेतरान्। एवमेवैकः[2] प्रयाण इत्यादीनपि ब्रूयात्।[2] अथ पशुमुदञ्चं नीयमानं वपा-श्रपणीभ्यामन्वारभमाणं गत्वा संज्ञपनाय[3] प्रैष उक्ते प्रदक्षिणमावृत्य नाना प्राणः इति। पुनरागत्य तीर्थेन प्रपद्य पृषदाज्यं मन्त्रेणावेक्ष्य पशोः प्राङ्मुख आसित्वा हुते संज्ञप्तहोमपेषलैः पर्यावृत्य[4] शमितार उपेतन इति पशुमुपेत्य पाशप्रतिमोचने गत्वाऽपः प्रतिषिच्याप्रतीक्षं पुनरागत्याङ्गारेषु संप्रकृष्टेषु प्रदक्षिणम् उर्वन्तरिक्ष-मन्विहि इति पुनरेत्य तीर्थेन प्रपद्य उप त्वाग्ने[5] इति तिसृभिराहवनीयमुपेत्याथ यथेतं प्रपद्य दक्षिण आसीनः स्वाहाकृत्यानुमन्त्रणादि कुर्यात्। इन्द्रियावी भूयासम् इति वपानुमन्त्रणम्। अथ प्रेषितो वाचं यत्वोलूखलमुसलं परेक्ष्य यथाप्रकृति पशुपुरोडाशस्य वृत्रहा भूयासम् इति॥ [२]

दैक्षयज्ञविचारपक्षे अग्नेरहं देवयज्ययाऽऽयुष्मान् यज्ञेन प्रतिष्ठां गमेयम् इति पशुपुरोडाशस्विष्टकृतः। अथ दक्षिणा नयेद्यदि वपान्तेन नीता स्यात्। दक्षिणा सवविधे पक्षे विद्यात् तत्रापि गौरिति क्वचित्। पक्षान्तरेऽपि गोः समुच्चयोऽन्वाहार्येणेति। अफले फलीकरणहोमे हुते पिष्टलेपानुवर्तते। यजमानभागं प्राश्य प्रणीता निनीय विष्णुक्रमांस्तु क्रमेत सवविधे। न ते पक्षान्तरे नापि यजमानभागप्राशनमित्येके। अथोलूखलमुसले विमुच्य कपालानि विमुञ्चेद् यद्यविमुक्तान्युद्वासनकाले स्युः। अथ यन्मे अग्ने इति हविरासन्नम[6]-भिमृश्य अयं यज्ञः समसदद्धविष्मान्[7] इत्यासन्नां हविरभिमृशेत्। [8]वपावद्ध-विरभिमन्त्र्य वनस्पतेरहं[9] देवयज्ययाऽऽयुष्मान् इति वनस्पतिभागमभिमन्त्रयेत। प्रसिद्धं स्विष्टकृदनुमन्त्रणम्। प्रसिद्धान्यनुमन्त्रणानि[10]। प्रसिद्धं मार्जनम्। अत्र याज्यानुमन्त्रणेषु प्रसिद्धं प्रथमानुमन्त्रणम्। [11]['देवी]द्वारामहमुषासनक्तयोः, अहं जोष्ट्रियोः, अहं बर्हिषो वा ऋतीनाम्[12] 'अहं देवयज्यया प्रजावान्' इति

१. M Ad B अवादहं. २-२. M Ad B repeated. ३. M Ad B संज्ञाप°. ४. M Ad B °वृशामुता°. ५. M Ad B त्वाण. ६. M Ad B °रासनमभि°. ७. M Ad B °दध्मविष्ट्वान्. ८. M Ad B °वन्धवि°. ९. M Ad B °तेऽयन्देव°. १०. M Ad B °सिद्धानुमन्त्र°. ११. M Ad B om. १२. M Ad B रिती.

यथालिङ्गं प्रथमविकारेषु। 'ऊर्गाहुत्योरहं तिसृणां तिसृणां देवीनाम्, अहं नराशंसस्य, अहं देव पशुमान् भूयासम्' **इति यथालिङ्गम् मध्यमविकारेषु।** 'दैव्ययोर्होत्रोरहम्, वनस्पतेरहम्, अग्नेः स्विष्टकृतोऽहं प्रतिष्ठां गमेयम्' **इत्युत्तमविकारेषु यथालिङ्गम्। अथ स्रुग्व्यूहनादि प्रतिपद्यते॥** [३]

न त्वत्र प्रणीतामार्जनं विष्णुक्र[१]**मश्च सवविधे॥** [४] इति चतुर्थोऽनुवाकः[२] ॥

॥ इति पशोर्याजनाख्यश्चतुर्थः प्रपाठकः समाप्तः ॥[३]

---

१. M क्रमञ्च, Ad B क्रमं च. २. M Ad B इति चतुर्थः. ३. M Ad पशोर्याजनं समाप्तम्॥

॥ अथ पञ्चमः प्रपाठकः ॥

॥ अथ ज्योतिष्टोमः ॥

[अथ प्रथमोऽनुवाकः][१]

[ऋत्विग्वरणम् दीक्षणीयेष्टिश्च]

ज्योतिष्टोमेन यक्ष्यमाणः पुरस्तादेव संभृतसंभार उपकल्पितदक्षिणो ब्राह्मणाननूचानान्[२] बन्धुसम्पन्नान् नियमव्रतचारिणः संशितव्रतान् [३]परीक्ष्याहूय तेषां य आत्मनो [४]नेदिष्ठस्तमध्वर्युं प्रथमं वृत्वा तद्वशानन्यान्[५] वृणीत। ब्रह्माणमेव[६] वा प्रथमं वृत्वा यथोपपादमितरान्। ते च को यज्ञः, क[७] ऋत्विजः, को[८] दक्षिणा इति पृच्छन्तः प्रतिजानीयुः। अमुकेन यज्ञक्रतुना यक्ष्ये इति संकल्प्याथ तेषां सन्निधावुच्चैर्व्याहरेदन्येषां च ऋत्विजां दक्षिणाविकल्प एकविंशतिर्द्विविंशतिरिति[९]। अकुनखिनमाङ्गिरसमध्वर्युं वृणीत, अकिलासिनं वासिष्ठं ब्रह्माणम्, अखण्डं वैश्वामित्रं होतारम्, अकवारमयास्यमुद्गातारम्। नव शिष्टान् भृगूनङ्गिरसो वा। तेष्वनियतमा वाऽसंभवे, न त्वेव न यजेत। नित्येन ज्योतिष्टोमेन सकृद्यजेत, प्रतिवर्षं वा। संकल्पितव्रतो यजमानः स्यात्। संकल्पितव्रतस्याप्यसंभवे तन्निष्क्रयाय वैश्वानरीष्टिः कार्या। अग्निष्टोमं प्रथमाहोऽतिरात्रो[१०] वाऽपीत्यपरम्। पयसी धेनुव्रतदुहौ दीक्षितवसने क्षौमे, अन्ये वाऽनुपहतोऽसंभवे सतूला अनन्तर्गर्भा[११] सा वा शरेषीकशरतरुणाञ्जनसमर्था पुञ्जिलानि समूहः योक्त्रं मौञ्जं मेखला त्रिवेणी शरमयी नस्कूजनी[१२] शङ्कुः कण्डूयनसमर्थः, कृष्णविषाणा त्रिवली, पञ्चवली वा, दण्डो यक्ष्यमाणस्य मुखेन संमितः। पुरस्तादेव प्रागुदक् प्रपन्ने शुद्धे देशे प्राग्वंशं करोति॥ [१]

द्वादशप्रक्रमायां दिक्ष्वतीकाशवन्तम्। चतुर्दशीमुपात्तदिगन्तरेणोदीचीनं पत्नीशालं करोति। उत्तरेण यज्ञशालं परिश्रिते करोति। पूर्वं यजमानायापरं पत्नियैव सह क्रियायाम्। जघनेन प्राग्वंशं पत्नियै। कालान्तरे क्रियायामुभयोः पक्षयोः। अपरेणैव प्राग्वंशं पत्नीशालाया इत्यपरे। प्राग्वंशकाल एवोद्देशेन

---

१. M Ad B om. २. M Ad °णानान्तूचा°. ३. M Ad B वरीक्ष्याः°. ४. M Ad B नेदृष्टस्तम°. ५. M Ad B °दन्यान्. ६. M Ad B ब्राह्म°. ७. M Ad B om. ८. का + उ. ९. M Ad B °शतिमि°. १०. M Ad B माहारो प्रथमाहोरोति°. ११. M Ad B असन्तर्गभाः°. १२. M Ad B नस्तूज°.

शालामुखीये यूपावटीयं च शङ्कुं निहत्य तयोः पृष्ठ्यामातनुयात्। संभारानुपकल्पयंश्चतुष्टयानि कपालान्युपकल्पयेदेकादश[१] नव दशाष्ट च। पञ्चदश चतस्रश्च स्थालीरेका प्रायणीयोदयनीययोरेका सौम्यस्य द्वे व्रतयोः। एका पयस्यायै इत्यन्ये। तिस्र इत्येके। पद्धरण्येका चतस्रश्च सोमस्थाल्यः[२] पञ्चैकधनार्थाः। ये व्रतयोस्ते एवाशिरे दधिघर्माय। चतस्रश्च स्थाल्यो देविकाहविर्भ्यः[३]। पञ्च कलशाः प्राग्वंश एकः, सोदञ्चनो मार्जालीय एकः, आग्नीध्रिय एकः, द्वावाधवनीयपूतभृतौ। तयोः समान उदञ्चनः। पञ्च कुम्भा वा द्वावप्सुदीक्षायै, क्रयायैको, घर्मोद्वासनायैको, वसतीवरीभ्य एकः। चतस्रः कुंभ्यो मदन्तीभ्य एका, तिस्रः पशूखाः[४], बहवः शरावाः[५], अम्बरीषं च। सवनीयार्थं सर्वं यथा प्राग् द्विगुणमुपकल्पनीयम्। अथ[६] दारुमयाणि[७]। चमसौ व्रतप्रदानौ सोमासन्द्यौदुम्बरी। तस्या नाभिदघ्नाः पादा भवन्ति अरत्निमात्राणि॥ [२]

[८]शीर्षण्यान्यनूचीनानि। सा मौञ्जीभी[९] रज्जुभिः युक्ता[१०] भवति। एकसराभिः [११]कादृशस्तूच्चैस्तेन सम्राडासन्दी[१२] द्वे हविर्धाने अनसी प्रतियुक्तचक्रे[१३], तयोरुच्चैस्तरं[१४] सनीडम्। तदेव सोमवाहनमन्यदित्यपरे। प्रचरणी स्रुक् पालाशी, ऊर्ध्वमुपराद् यजमानेन संमितौ स्थूणौ द्वे अधिषवणफलके औदुम्बरे त्रिप्रादेशे अध्यर्धप्रादेशव्यासे, उदङ्कद्रोणकलशौ चौदुम्बरौ। कलशयोरुदङ्क एवोदचनो महापरिधयश्च। अनियतवृक्षाणि चोर्ध्वपात्राणि षट्तयानि। नैय्यग्रोधानीत्यपरे। बैल्वं [शुक्रपात्रं][१५] द्वे एकं नि [१६][. . .] न्येकादशाग्रबिलानि प्रादेशमात्राणि प्रादेशपरिणाहान्युलूखलाकाराणि कुडुम्बभारबिलानि[१७]। आश्वत्थे अ[श्वशफ][१८]बुध्ने उभयतोमुखे एकादश चमसा नैय्यग्रोधाः। उत्सरुमन्तः कुडुम्बभारबिलाः[१७] द्वितर्यः कार्ष्मर्य[मयाः परिधय][१९]श्च पञ्चदश दारुर्नानावार्क्ष्यः स्त्रीवृक्षी वदरे पाटलिची वामलकी शिंशपा जम्बू इत्येवमादाय बहुतया काष्ठकला[पा आ][२०]सनार्था भूयस्यश्च[२१] तृणकलाप्यः[२२] काष्ठानि सदोहविर्धानाग्नीध्रसंमानाय सन्ततश्च। देवयजं दूरतः परिश्रयन्ति दुर्जननिरोधाय। चत्वारि कृष्णाजिनानि, रोहितं चर्मैकं, दौघटकटौ, व्रीहयश्च

---

१. M Ad B °कल्पये एका°. २. M Ad B °ल्या. ३. M Ad B देविकोह°. ४. M Ad B पशूखन्. ५. M Ad B शरवाः. ६. Ad अथवा. ७. M °मायाणि. ८. M Ad B °र्षण्यन्तू°. ९. M Ad B °जीभि. १०. M Ad B °न्यूका. ११. M Ad B °तच्चै°. १२. M Ad B °सनी. १३. M Ad व्रति°, B व्रती°. १४. M Ad B च्चैस्करं. १५. M Ad B broken. १६. M Ad B broken. १७. M Ad B कुडुम्बधार°. १८. M Ad B broken. १९. M Ad B broken. २०. M Ad B broken. २१. M Ad B भूयस्यं. २२. M Ad B °लाव्यः.

यवाश्च छागादयश्च क्रयार्थाः संभाराश्च। परिकर्मिणो बहवो यज्ञविदो वश्याः[१] **सुवृत्ताः। अध्वर्युर्मन्त्रेणाचम्य प्राण्यापान्य** प्रजापतिः **इति जपित्वा कर्माण्यारभते। एवं सर्व ऋत्विजः स्वे स्वे कर्मादौ कुर्वन्ति॥ [३]**

अथ प्रवर्ग्याः संभृत्य यूपं स्पृष्ट्वा[२] **कृत्वाऽनख आशितो भूत्वा स्नाहीति देवयजनमभिप्रयाति समारूढाग्निभिररण्यस्यैव**[३] **वा। ग्रामस्य दीक्षितः स्यादित्यपरे। अथेम्** अवस्यवे[४] त्वा **इति दीक्षिष्यमाणोऽपरेण शालामवस्यति। वचनाद्यनुक्रमणमप्सुदीक्षायाः पूर्वत्वोपलक्षणमित्यपरे। ग्रामे दीक्षितस्यैवैतन्मन्त्र-द्वयमित्यपरे। तथा सति देवयजने दीक्षिष्यमाणे देवयजनाभिमन्त्रणादि प्रति-पद्यते। न प्रयाणावसानमन्त्रौ ब्रूयात्। क्षत्रियं देवयजनं याचेद्, यस्य**[५] **मण्डले तद्देवयजनम्। अथ चेन्न याचेद् देवान्**[६] **देवयजनं याचेत् सत्रीन् हिरण्यशल्का-नादायेत्यनेन। अथाध्वर्युः पादौ प्रक्षाल्य शाखे आदाय पूर्वेण द्वारा प्रपद्य मन्त्रेण प्रागपवर्गं व्युदजेत् प्राचीनं च शालाया आवेद्यन्तात्। असमारूढेष्वेवाज्यं संस्कृत्य स्रुक्स्रुवं संमृज्य समारोप्याग्नीन्** [७]**गच्छेद्, अजस्रैर्वा मथित्वाऽग्नीन्**[७] **विहरेत्। समारोपणे अजस्रपक्षे यथास्थानं निवपेत्। पितृभ्यो दानं पिण्ड-पितृयज्ञः। यदृणमवश्यदेयमुत्तमर्णाय तद्यथोत्साहं प्राग्दीक्षायै दद्यात्। अथ यदपनेतुमशक्यम्, अपनेतुमशक्यमुत्तमर्णमनुज्ञापयेत्। यद्यनुज्ञापयितुमशक्यं तत्पुत्रादावुपनयति प्रतिमोचयति। यद्वा स्वेनावश्यं कर्तव्यं तत्पुत्रादावासच्य स्वयं वैदिक एव प्रवर्तेत** इमामूर्जम् **इति॥ [४]**

यस्यां तिथौ दीक्षा तां निर्दिशेद् दैक्षणीयं हविर् **इति चोहेत्। अत्र दम्पत्यो-**[८]**र्वतोपायनमप्सुदीक्षा पूर्वत्वे लुप्यते पत्न्याश्च सन्नहनम्।** मधवे स्वाहा **इति द्वादशाहुतयो**[९] **जुह्वा सकृद्गृहीतेन होतव्याः। अन्येऽप्येवंविधाः।** वृत्रहा भूयासम् **इति हविरभिमन्त्रणं नास्ति। अन्वाहार्यहरणं पत्नीसंयाजान्तायामस्यामिष्ट्वा फलीकरणहोममत्राचार्याभिहितं क्रियते, नान्यत्। किन्तु न यज्ञविमोककपाल-विमोकौ, व्रतविसर्जनमिति च कुर्वीरन्। अर्थविरुद्धमुपवेषोद्वासनमित्येके। तथोत्तरयोरिष्ट्योः कृतानुकरपक्ष उत्तरेणैव शालामभ्याशे परिश्रितान्तरे प्रति-प्रस्थाता कृतानुकरस्तूष्णीं पत्नीं दीक्षयेत्। उत्तरस्मिन्नपि गोदाने तान्येव** [१०]**दर्भपुञ्जीलानि यानि दक्षिणस्मिन्। प्रत्यभिमर्शनं याजमानमित्येके। क्षुरगन्धि**

---

१. M Ad B पश्याः. २. M Ad B पृष्ट्वा. ३. M Ad B °रजस्यैव. ४. M Ad B om °वे त्वा. ५. M Ad B तस्य. ६. M B देवान् twice. ७–७. Ad om. ८. M B दम्पत्योद्व्रतो°. ९. M Ad B °तयोर्जु°. १०. M Ad B गर्भपु°.

क्षुरपथं करोति। अप आशयन्[१] मन्त्रमपि वाचयेदित्येके। अभिषेकाद्याञ्जनान्तं याजमानम्। अहतं वासः। क्षौमाभावेऽन्यत्। सकृदेव मन्त्रमुक्त्वा दक्षिणं पूर्वाङ्गं[२] तथा सव्यं दक्षिणं दक्षिणमनु निरस्यति। अथैनं सर्वैः सह मन्त्रैर्दर्भपुञ्जीलैः। अथैनम् अश्मन्मे इति वाचयित्वा अपो देवास इत्येनं सव्ये पाणावभिगृह्य शालां प्रपादयेत्॥ [५]

अष्टर्चेन पावमानेनाहवनीयमुपस्थापयेत्। उपस्थापिता प्रब्रूयाद् इत्येके। अस्मिन्नवसर इष्टिपूर्वकं च दीक्षणीयाध्रौवं[३] दीक्षाहुतिषु प्रतिपादयेत्। अप्सुदीक्षापूर्वकत्वे शालाप्रयाणेऽयमवसरः। फलीकरणहोमानन्तरं दीक्षाहुतयो होतव्याः। मूलकल्पाभिहिते ब्रह्मदीक्षा कैशी च विकल्प्येते। कृष्णाजिना-सर्पणादियाजमानमुपवेशनं तूष्णीकं प्राङ्मेखलादि सर्वं क्रियेत। देवपत्नी ब्रह्मपत्नी ऋतुदीक्षासु कैशिनी च विकल्प्येते। वाससा प्रोर्णवञ्छिरसोऽधस्ताद् वाससि[४] च[५]दशायां कृष्णविषाणा प्रबध्नाति। बन्धनाद्याध्वर्यवमाचमसप्रदानात्। हस्तौ प्रतपत्याहवनीये[६]। चमसेऽधि हस्तौ द्वयं निधाय 'स्वाहा यज्ञं मनसा' इति मन्त्रमुक्त्वाऽन्ते सहैव सर्वा अङ्गुलीर्निपिचति[७] विकुञ्चति। सह वा च्छन्दो दीक्षायाः। चतस्रः प्रदेशिन्यौ द्वौ चाङ्गुष्ठौ प्रसारयति। पत्न्याः कृतानुकरपक्षे सर्वे मन्त्राः [. . .][८] समानरूपाणामेव लोपो नान्येषाम्। यथा शालाप्रपदनं सन्नहन-मुपनिषद इति समनरूपं [. . .][९] लुप्यत[१०] इत्यपरे। कृष्णाजिने अध्यूहितो दीक्षितस्योपरि स्वयमध्वर्युश्च दीक्षिते वादः सत्ये सुतरां प्रवृत्तिः परोक्षं मनुष्यनामकथनं पर्यायशब्दैरभिधानम्। अथ यानि नामानि नियोगतः प्रत्यक्षवचनीयानि विचक्षणेति तेषामुपरिष्टाद् दध्यात् देवदत्त विचक्षण, यज्ञदत्त विचक्षण इति। यान् गुरू[न्][११] ते चनसितेन तेषामुपरिष्टाद् दध्यात् अप्सुमित्र चनसित, ब्रह्मदत्त चनसित इति। कृष्णाजिनान्मा निर्यौषीत्॥ [६]

निर्गतकृष्णाजिनः कदापि मा भूत्। दण्डस्पष्टोऽस्तु, न विस्मरणीयः, सदा सन्निहित एव स्यात्। अन्तःशालं शालाभ्यन्तरेति। अमूमसावित्यत्र[१२] नाम ब्रह्मण्यादामुष्यायणन्त्या[१३] ब्राह्मणो[ऽदीक्षिष्टा][१४] ता वामिन्द्राग्निभ्याम् इति आमुष्यायण इति त्रिप्रवरकमेके[१५] ब्रुवते यथा ब्राह्मणो देवदत्तो वासिष्ठः

१. M Ad B आयशन्. २. M Ad B °पूर्वमाङ्. ३. M Ad B °णीयाध्रौवं. ४. Ad B वाससी. ५. M B चि. ६. M Ad B व्रत°. ७. M Ad B °र्निचति. ८. M Ad B broken. ९. M Ad B broken. १०. M Ad B ल्स्यते°. ११. M Ad B broken. १२. M Ad B जून्नसा°. १३. M Ad B ब्रह्मव्यादा°. १४. M Ad B broken. १५. M Ad B इत्यप्रवरके मके.

शाक्त्यः[१] पाराशर्यः तमिन्द्राग्निभ्याम्[२] इति[३]। ओन्नक्षत्राद् उदितनक्षत्रकालात्[३]। [४]आत्मन्नग्निमाहवनीयं[४] समारोहयते। अग्नेरुपरि मन्त्रेणापन्नादपि [५]स्पृणन्नभि-प्राणिति। व्रतचमसं सोमचमसवद्दर्भैरद्भिः प्रक्षाल्य निदध्यात्। संवेशनयजुः सकृदेव, असंवेशने यजुश्चान्त्ये प्रबोधने तथा प्रतिपर्यावर्तनं पर्या-वर्तनयजुरावर्तते। तेषामर्थान्तरेण व्यवधाने व्रतविधानम्। मार्जनादि मार्जनान्तं व्रतयित्वा वाचमुपाकरोति। सनिरुपकल्पितः। अनुकल्पितदक्षिणस्य[६] न इति। व्यवस्थितोऽयं विकल्प[७] इत्यपरे। पूर्वस्मिन् पक्ष उपकल्पिताभिर्दक्षिणाभिः सहाभ्यधिकं सनिलब्धं नीयेत्। स एव पक्षो ज्यायान्। यन्मन्यते तत्प्रत्याख्यास्यतीति तं प्रतिपथं ब्रूयात्। प्रतिगृह्णाति। उस्त्रादयो जातिवचनम्। प्रपतनं मरणम्। वल्यौ रज्ज्वा वा बद्ध्वा[८] म्रियेत। संशरणं सर्वसाधारण्येन व्याधिना मरणम्। अविज्ञातव्याधेर्निश्चेष्टीभूतस्य मरणम्। पौरुषो वा वधः पुरुषचैतन्यात्। महादेवो वा महादेवानुचरभूतावेशो वा हन्यात्॥ [७]

या[९] नद्धकं म्रियेत बन्धनप्रतिबद्धा म्रियेत। येयं प्रपतिता नष्टा म्रियेत वा, नैनामुपाकुर्यान्न मिश्रयेद्[१०] दक्षिणाभिरेनां न गोष्ठे आत्मीयैः पशुभिर्मिश्रयेत्। दक्षिणाभूतैरपि सन्निहितामेव रक्षितुमनुब्रूयाद्[११]। अनृत्विजे प्रसर्पकाय[१२] दद्यात्। योगः प्रस्थानं कदाचिदापद्येत। तप्त्वेति व्रतोपलक्षणम्। तप्तं व्रतयित्वा इति। मध्यन्दिनमध्यरात्रयोरपि व्रतम्। नास्तित्वं दर्शयितुमित्यपरे। समारोपणं पृथगरणीष्वजस्रैर्वा प्रयातीत्यन्ये। यदा वा सायं समवस्यन्ति तदाऽवसानमन्त्रं[१३] ब्रूयात्। उषित्वा प्रयन्प्रयाणमन्त्रमुक्त्वा प्रयायात्। वहन्तीरपः पर्यातुमशक्याः शक्याश्चेत् पर्यायोत्संवाहयेयुः संप्रवाहयेयुः। आप्येन पुरुषेण वोत्तारयेत्, नैवापः स्वयमवगाहेत, विशातयेत्। सन्ततमापरस्मात् तीरात् तेष्वपारे तीरे उदकान्ते यदुच्छिष्येत तन्न्यसेत्। अवधृतनिश्चयो निरावधं यत्र यष्टुं शक्यमिति मन्यते तत्र देवयजनाभिमन्त्रणादि कुर्यात्। अमेध्यं क्लीबं[१४] पश्येद् यच्चान्यदमेध्यमिति। लोके प्रसिद्धमित्यपरे। अभिवृष्टो जपति ऊर्गस्यन्नाद्यमूर्जम् इति प्रतिपद्य सर्वं वाचितम्। एवं जपेदित्यपरे[१५]। पूर्वं स्वयमेव जपित्वा उत्तरं वाचित इत्यपरे। स्निहानं स्नेहमश्रुनिष्ठीवितमित्यपरे[१६]। नासिकाश्मश्रुनिष्ठी-

---

१. M Ad B शाक्यः. २. M Ad B °मिन्द्राणिभ्यां. ३-३. M Ad B ओमित्यनक्षत्रान् कालाद् आदित°. ४-४. M Ad B आ नग्निमाह°. ५. M Ad B स्पृजन्नाभि°. ६. M Ad °स्यान, B °स्थान. ७. M Ad B विकल्पयित्य°. ८. M Ad B बन्धा. ९. M Ad B यो. १०. M Ad B °र्यान्निश्रये. ११. M Ad B रक्षितमनुष्याद्. १२. M Ad B सर्वताय. १३. M Ad B °मन्त्रणं. १४. M Ad B क्ली बा. १५. M Ad °त्यरे. १६. M °त्यरे.

वितम्। सेभुं[1] शिंघाणिकारे मूत्रपुरीषकारणेष्वाचमननिमित्तेष्वाचम्यानुमन्त्रण-मसुत्यस्याह्नां परिसमाप्ते दीक्षितस्यादीक्षितव्रते वर्तेत॥ [८]

पत्न्या[2] अप्येतत् सह दीक्षायाम्॥ [९] इति प्रथमोऽनुवाकः॥

अथ द्वितीयोऽनुवाकः

अन्त्ये दीक्षादिवसे रोहितं चर्म [3]पल्पूलयित्वोत्तरलोम विघ्नन्ति। विघातो नाम बलवद्विसार्य तस्यान्तेषु समन्ततः शङ्कूनां निघातः। उष्णीषचतुर्थानि सोमार्थानि आदित्यप्रक्षेपणार्थं[4] चरुं सुपर्णं स्पन्द्या रज्जुः[5] सोमवाहनयोजनार्थां[6], राजासन्दी, [7]अरुणपिशङ्गैकहायनी चतुःशराव ओदनः बल्बजस्तुका-नामान्तःसरः किञ्चित् तृणजातम्। श्वोभूते प्रातरेव प्रायणीयारम्भः। आदावेवा-स्या द्वारः संवृण्वन्ति। इदमादिष्वन्वाघातं न विद्यते। देवतापरिग्रहार्थत्वे विद्यत इत्यपरे। पत्नीमिह दीक्षायामध्वर्युर्दीक्षयेत् उपहूता इति सह तस्या[8] अपि पूर्वाणि कर्माण्यनुजानीते। अनुज्ञाने चानुज्ञानं च न स्तः सह। दीक्षायां दम्पत्योराप्यायन-काले[9] तेभ्यस्तण्डुलानपयच्छति। यत्नतो निदध्यादुदयनीयार्थम्। प्रायणीय-स्याधिश्रयान्तं प्रतिप्रस्थातैव कुर्यादित्यपरे। भूय आज्यं निर्वपेत्। सर्वं श्रिते चरावानीय तत्पुनराज्यस्थाल्यामवस्कन्दयेत्। ध्रुवादवस्राव्य[10] तेन ग्रहणादि कृत्वा प्रचरेत्॥ [१]

पथ्या स्वस्त्याद्यर्थमेव चरावानीयावस्रावयेदित्येके। सर्वमिति ज्यायः। पत्नीसन्नहनमेतदादिषु लुप्यते। तथा दम्पत्योर्व्रतोपायनमित्येके। वैकल्पिका-वेतावाज्यभागौ। अभावः[11] प्रायेणानयोराचार्याभिप्रेतः। उपांशु याजविकाराः। पशावपि[12] प्रधानयागादभिमन्त्रणम्[13]। उपांशु देवताकल्पं च। दीक्षणीयादीना-मुपसदन्तानां[14] तन्त्रस्वरभिन्ना[15] मन्दादुच्चरितं दीक्षणीयायां, मन्दतरं[16] प्रायणीयायां, मन्दतममातिथ्यायाम्, उपांशु उपसत्स्वित्येके। प्रधानविषयोऽयं भेदः। तन्त्रं सर्वेषाम्, उपांश्वित्यपरे। अदितिमिष्ट्वा मरुतो यद्ध वो दिवः इति मारुती [. . .][17] इत्येके। अतिवालयतो निदध्यात्। फलीकरणहोमं चात्र केचित् जुह्वति। नैष आचार्याभिप्रायः। अतीकाशवद्धिरण्यमवदधाति। अङ्गुलीयकादि

---

१. M B सेभः, Ad सेभ्यः. २. M Ad B पत्या°. ३. M Ad B वन्मूल°. ४. M Ad B °प्रेपक्ष°. ५. M Ad B रजः. ६. M Ad B °तयोर्जना°. ७. M Ad B अरुणापिङ्गलैक°. ८. M Ad B तस्य°. ९. M Ad B °त्योरप्यापयमनकाले. १०. M Ad B लुलाकादवस्राप्य. ११. M Ad B °भावं. १२. M Ad B पश्वापि. १३. M Ad B °गादब्दिम°. १४. M Ad B दीक्षयिणीया°. १५. M Ad B °स्वरा°. १६. M Ad B मन्दं. १७. M Ad B broken.

चतुर्गृहीते सर्वं प्रायणीयाज्यशेषमवनयति। तृतीयमन्त्रं द्विरावर्तयेत्। सर्वं[१] वा मन्त्रजातं चतुरावृत्य[२] चतुर्गृह्णीयात् सहिरण्येन। प्रणीतानिनयनं तूष्णीकम्। प्रायणीयस्थालीमुत्स्विद्य सम्यङ् निर्णिज्य तस्यामवयातान् तण्डुलानोप्य प्रायणीयाया एव वेदं मेक्षणमिति स्थाल्यामवधाय स्तीर्णमेव बर्हिस्तया सहोपनह्य मध्यमे स्थूणाराजे [३]शकलीकृत्यानुवेष्ट्य निदधाति। स्फ्यमुदपात्रं [४]पद्धरणीमादायाध्वर्युयजमानौ। तत्र राजक्रयणीमानयन्ति। तामभिमन्त्रयेते चिदसि इति। मन्त्रोक्तिर्बन्धनमात्रम्, पदि बन्धनम्। एवमनुमदतोऽध्वर्युयजमानौ। अथैनां तावेव प्रदक्षिणं परिक्रामतः। अथातः पश्चात् स्थित्वाऽध्वर्युः प्रति प्रैषमाह। प्रेषितः परिक्रर्मी प्राचीमुदीचीमुत्क्रमयते॥ [२]

तस्या[५] अभ्युत्क्रामन्त्याः [६]सक्थ्नोऽधस्तादभिपद्य वस्व्यसि[७] इत्यादिभिः षड्भिर्मन्त्रैः। अभिगृह्णात्युभाभ्यां हस्ताभ्यां यत्रास्याः सप्तमं पदमाहितम्। हिरण्यमभि तत्रस्थ एव हिरण्ये परिलिखति। अपोद्धृत्य हिरण्यं खनित्वा[८] संवपेत्। प्रतिसंवपनं मन्त्रावृत्तिः। खननं तूष्णीकम्। यावन्मूतं यावत्क्लिन्नम्। संकाशयति समीक्षयति। स्वयमेव मन्त्रमुक्त्वा यजमानेनापि पत्नी स्वयमेव मन्त्रं ब्रूयात्। समीक्षितमेतस्मिन् कूपे यतः पदपांसव उदात्ताः॥ [३] इति द्वितीयोऽनुवाकः॥

अथ तृतीयोऽनुवाकः

[सोमक्रयः]

राजा विचितो[९] भवति। रोहिते चर्मन्नधिलोमकस्यां पार्श्वे वासः प्रत्युदीर्णं च। तस्यैव चर्मण उत्तरार्धे तस्याभ्याशे प्रदेशान्तर इत्यपरे। क्रयदेशेऽपो निधाय तासामन्तिके दक्षिणतो ब्रह्मण आस्ते। अङ्गुष्ठे सौवर्णमङ्गुलीयमाबध्याङ्गुष्ठाग्रमेकैकेनाङ्गुल्यग्रेण सन्धाय पर्यायशः, तेन मुष्टिना पञ्चकृत्वो मन्त्रमावृत्य मुष्टीन् राज्ञो मिमीते। महानाम्न्या प्रदेशिन्या कनीयस्या मध्यमया कनीयस्या मुष्टिक्रमो याजुषे माने। तथैव पञ्चकृत्वस्तूष्णीं मध्यमया कनीयस्या प्रदेशिन्या महानाम्न्या प्रदेशिन्या तूष्णीं माने मुष्टिक्रमः[१०]। अथ प्रदेशिन्या मध्यमया महानाम्न्या कनीयस्या प्रदेशिन्येति याजुषे माने, कनीयस्या महानाम्न्या मध्यमया प्रदेशिन्या कनीयस्येति तूष्णीं माने, दशकृत्वो मिमानोऽर्धवेलां प्रजाभ्यस्त्वा इत्युपसमूहति॥ [१]

---

१. M Ad B सर्वा. २. M Ad B °वर्त्य. ३. M Ad B कशली°. ४. M Ad B पन्धरणीमित्या°. ५. M Ad B तस्य. ६. M Ad B स्नुप्नोदस्ता°. ७. M Ad B वस्फ्यसी°. ८. M Ad B खात्वा. ९. M Ad B °पि चि°. १०. M Ad B मुष्टिकामः.

चर्मण्यवशिष्टानंशूंश्चर्मण्यवहत्य मिमीते। राज्ञोऽपि सृष्टिमिच्छेत्। उपन्यस्यति वाससोऽन्तान् संगमय्य दशादिना बध्नीयात्। अनुग्रन्थति विस्त्रंसयति। समायत्य सम्यगुपरि बध्वा चर्मणि सादयेत्। सोमविक्रयिणोऽभ्याशे सादनान्तं कृत्वाऽग्रेण यूपावटं[१] पलाशशाखां निहत्य समुपनद्धं राजानं तस्यामासज्य मनाक् तूष्णीमासीत। तत्र तत्र यत् क्षिप्रम् इति वा त्वरध्वम् इति वा कुरुत इति वा क्रयसंबन्धं कञ्चित् कञ्चित् ब्रूयात्। तं सोमविक्रयिणं संकल्प्य सर्वं कुर्वीत संपादवर्जम्। कला गोः षोडशांशः[२], शफोऽष्टमभागः फलानि क्षीरं दुग्धमात्रं, पयः शान्तफेनं शीतं, प्रतिधुक् पुनः प्रस्नुतोपात्तं, शर आविर्भूतस्नेहं, शृतं पक्वम्। वयांसि[३] निष्क्रयमाणानि, अधिदेयानीत्येके। एनं सोमविक्रयिणमाह-[४]अन्यया परिपालयिष्यामो नव ऋषभः प्रगृहाण प्रसारय आवृत्तया[५] आवृत्तेति वा। तस्याः पृष्ठेन सोमविक्रयिणमभिभवन्निव प्रकर्षेण बाधेत॥ [२]

आत्मानं प्रत्यावर्त्यान्वर्जति विसृजति। तामेतामजां सोमविक्रयी लभते। सैकहायनी। तानीतराणि[६] राजक्रयणानि यजमानस्यैव भवति। यजमानः शुक्लामूर्णास्तुकामादाय दशापवित्रस्य मध्ये बध्नीयाद् येन सोमं पुनन्ति। तं प्रतीक्षते। यजमानस्य दक्षिण ऊरावा सादयतोऽध्वर्युयजमानौ। राजानमेनमागतं प्रति स्वयमेवापोर्णुते[७] प्रावरणमपनयति। स्थानादिभ्योऽनुदिशतोऽध्वर्युयजमानौ। राजानमादायोत्तिष्ठति यजमानः। एतदाद्यासन्नोपस्थानान्तं स एव कुर्यात्। कृष्णाजिनस्तरणमात्रमध्वर्युरेवेत्येके। तत्र नीडे सोमवाहनस्य अपरेण सोमवाहनं पर्यानीय[८] दक्षिणतस्तिष्ठन् राजानं सादयेत्। सोमवाहनं पर्यानह्यति। दक्षिणपूर्वस्यां दिशि दशातो बध्नीयात्। तयोराळं कृष्णाजिनेऽवदध्यात्। अभिमन्त्रयेते अध्वर्युयजमानौ। अपरेण सोमवाहनं पर्यानीय दक्षिणमनड्वाहं युञ्ज्यात्।[९] विमुच्यैवापरेण सोमवाहनमतिगमयेदित्येके। अवगूहनार्थो मन्त्रः। अभिदधाति। [१०]शुगूबन्धनमामुञ्चेत्। उपस्तंभनाभिमर्शनं सकृदेव। विष्टम्भः परिणाहः। विष्टम्भनार्थं तिर्यक् स्थापितं काष्ठं द्रुपदाख्यमनुष्ठानफलकं यद्यन्ततोऽधितिष्ठेत्। स्पन्द्या शकटयोजन्यभिधानी वा। सुब्रह्मण्योम् इति ब्रूयात्। नवकृत्व इत्येके। छदिः शकटस्यान्वारभेते अध्वर्युयजमानौ स्पन्द्यामस्पृशन्तौ। आहवनीयादुल्मुकादानम्[११], उपस्तभ्नाति उपस्तंभनीम्। स्थूणां दत्त्वा शकटं

---

१. M Ad B °वटा.. २. M Ad B षडाशांश. ३. M Ad B पयांसि. ४. M Ad B °णमाहन्य या. ५. M Ad B आवत्तया, cf. VādhŚS 6.8.39 (fn. 4 : प्रत्यावर्त्तया). ६. M Ad B कानीत°. ७. M Ad B मेवोपो°. ८. M पर्यायानीय, B °र्याय. ९. M B पुज्या°. १०. M Ad B श्रृग°, शुल्ब. ११. M Ad B °दुन्मुका°.

स्थापयति। उन्मुक्तो वरुणस्य **इत्यभिधानीमपनयेत्। उपचारणतः उपस्तंभतः पूर्वं युक्तं विमुञ्चेत्॥** [३]

[आतिथ्येष्टिः]

गृह्णाति निर्वपति। बर्हिः संभरन् काशमयं प्रस्तरं गृह्णीयात्। इक्षुपत्रे तिरश्च्यर्थे। तेनागत्येक्षोरित्येके[१]**। कार्ष्मर्यमयान्**[२] **परिधीन् कुर्यात्। शाकलानीध्मकाष्ठानीत्येके। निर्वापकाले पत्नी प्रविश्यान्वारभेत।** अनुमन्यस्व **इति चोक्त्वा** अनुमन्ये **इति प्रब्रूयात्। मन्त्रमुष्टयो मन्त्रवन्तः। षष्ठस्तूष्णीकः। पञ्चैव मुष्टयो न तूष्णीक इत्येके। सर्वेषु सावित्रोऽनुषक्तव्यः। सर्वेषु निगमेषु विष्णुशब्द एवोच्चार्यः। इतरमप्यनड्वाहं**[३] **मन्त्रेणैव विमुच्य तत्रैव स्थापयित्वा दक्षिणामुखं वाचं**[४] **विसृज्य प्राञ्चं राजानमुपावरोप्य उत्तरेण शकटं परिक्रमय्य सम्राज्ञि प्रपादिते** या ते धामानि **इति पूर्वया द्वारा प्रपादयेत्। दक्षिणेनाहवनीयं सम्राडासन्द्यां सम्राज्ञि सादिते अपरेणाहवनीयमेति। गमय्यापरस्यामासन्द्यां मन्त्रेण राजानं सादयेत्। पूर्वमेव पूर्वया द्वारा प्रपादिते रज्जूत्तरेणाहवनीयं स्थिते सम्राजं प्रपाद्यापरेणाहवनीयं मन्त्रेण राजानं प्रपादयेदित्येके। तूष्णीं सम्राज्ञः पूर्वमुदपात्रं निनीय मन्त्रेण राज्ञो निनयेत्। अग्नीध आधानं प्राशित्रस्य ब्रह्मणे परिहरणं होतुराहुतिरित्येतावद्वाचनिकं क्रियेत, नान्यत्किञ्चित्। ध्रुवाऽऽप्यायनमप्राकृतमन्त्रकम्।** [५]**तानूनप्त्रमापादयितुं विगृह्णाति विविधं गृह्णाति। पञ्चभिर्मन्त्रैः पञ्चकृत्वो गृह्णन् अन्ते सर्वं वाऽवनयेत्।**[६] **तानूनप्त्रं प्रति विनयन्ते, संज्ञानमेतत्। घृतं हिरण्यं च चमसमुपस्पृशन्**[७] **ते शपथं कुर्वन्त्याकर्मपरिसमाप्तेः** अन्योऽन्यस्मै न द्रुह्याम: **इति वदन्तः। मन्त्रेण घृतं हिरण्यं च न स्पृशन्ति। तत ऊर्ध्वं न मिथो द्रुह्येत् पुराऽऽकर्मपरिसमाप्तेः**[८]**। अतिवाचयति पूर्वं मन्त्रमतीत्य वाचयति। अनेन तानूनप्त्राज्येन सहापराह्णे तप्त्वा व्रतं प्रयच्छति। देवोपसदनमपि प्रातरेवानुपसदमेव वा व्रतमस्मिन्नहन्यपराह्णे सम्पद्यत इति मन्त्रलिङ्गोपपत्तिः॥** [४]

तथा सति त्रिव्रतमस्मिन्नहनि दैक्षं प्रातरनूपसदं द्विर्दैक्षं[९] **चतुःस्तनत्रिस्तनद्विस्तनैकस्तनान्यानुपूर्वोपसत्सु। कति पय अवान्तरदीक्षाव्रते**[१०]**।**

---

१. M Ad B तेनादयस्ये°. २. M काष्मर्य°. ३. M Ad B °नध्वाहं. ४. M Ad B वोपसृज्य. cf.; VādhŚS 6.10.3. ५. M Ad B तानूनपूमा°. ६. M Ad B वपनयेत्. ७. M Ad B °मुपमृश°. ८. M Ad B °समाप्तः. ९. M Ad B द्वि दैक्षं. १०. M Ad B वाक्याक्षाव्रते; cf. VādhŚS 6.11.7.

स्तनचतुष्के वत्सायैकस्तनमात्रमवशेषयेत्। कतरत्पूर्वं करिष्यामः इत्यादिरदृष्टार्थो मन्त्रो वाच्यः, नैष मन्त्रो वाच्यः। अत्र ग्रन्थ एवैष विकल्पनामात्राभिधायी इत्यपरे। समिधं यज्ञियस्य वृक्षस्य प्रोक्षितामादत्ते। सर्वत्रैवं समिच्चोदनायां संतरां सम्यक्तरां समायच्छते, दृढीकरोति अशिथिलीकरोति। तप्तव्रतः उष्णव्रतो भवति। ततः प्रभृति मदन्तीभिरुष्णाभिरेव मार्जनादिरुदकार्थम्। आऽवान्तरदीक्षाविसर्गात्पूर्वं व्रतनं ये देवाः इति प्राक्तनमन्त्रम्। एतत्समारूढा एव अवान्तरदीक्षायामेव समारूढाः। ततः प्रभृति व्रतकाले समारोपणविसर्गौ न भवतः। स्वे दक्ष इत्यत्र समारोपणम् अहं त्वदस्मि इति वा। अवान्तरदीक्षाविसर्गकाले विसर्गः। अवान्तरदीक्षोपादानविसर्गाभ्यां तु विकल्प्येते[१]। विकृतिविषयावेताविति एके। समुच्चीयेते हेत्यन्ये। दीक्षामेवैताविति अपरे। तत उत्तरेण वेदिमत्याक्रम्य वेद्य [. . .][२] स्तेष्वासक्तानंशूंस्तत्रैवाधातुं स्रुग्व्यूहना[दि][३]वाचनिकमध्वर्योः। यजमानस्यापीत्यन्ये। परिधीनां[४] प्रस्तरस्य चाञ्जनं तूष्णी[म्।. . .][५] षु स्रुक्षु निह्नुवते। द्यावापृथिवीभ्यां नमस्काराञ्जलिं कुर्वन्ति। किमित्युष्णा भवन्ति। ताभिराद्रव[६] इत्याध्वर्यवं तृ[णग्लाभं][७] प्रस्तराय प्रस्तरेण उपसन्नह्यासहनादिकं संस्कारं कृत्वा निदधाति[८]। तृणग्लाभं तृणकलापीम्। अन्यां काञ्चिन्मुष्टिमात्रमसिदादानादिना संस्कृत्याप्रस्तराय अप्रस्तरणाय। प्रस्तरेणैवोपसन्नह्य निदधातीत्येके। मदन्तीभिराग्नीध्राहृताभिर्मार्जयते॥ [५] इति तृतीयोऽनुवाकः॥

अथ चतुर्थोऽनुवाकः[९]

[प्रवर्ग्योपसद्]

अत्रैवातिथ्यानन्तरं शीघ्रमयं प्रैषो वक्तव्यः। अस्मिन्नहनि बहूनि कर्माणि कर्तव्यानीत्यनुपरमेण शीघ्रं पदार्थाः कर्तव्याः। अतिरात्रः प्रथमयज्ञो प्रवर्ग्यत्वमुक्ते[१०] च सर्वदोपसदो घर्मवानाघारः। प्रयाजविकारास्ता वाचनिकोऽत्राघार इत्येके। तयोरुभयोः पक्षयोः ये प्रकृतावङ्गप्रधानार्थास्त इह प्रवर्तन्ते। अनूयाजविकारा इत्यपरे। तत्रापि तत्तुल्यमुपांशुयाजविकारा आस्युः। आघारेणात्रेतरा

---

१. M Ad B ०ल्पेते. २. M Ad B broken. ३. M Ad B broken. ४. M Ad B परिधिनां. ५. M Ad B broken. ६. M Ad B ०द्राव. ७. M Ad B broken; cf. VādhŚS 6.11.30. ८. MSS wrongly show the sign of close of the Kaṇḍikā here, and beginning of the next Kaṇḍikā from तृणग्लाभं in new para, cf. VādhŚS 6.11.30-32. ९. M B अथ चतुर्थः; Ad अथ तुरीयः. १०. M B ०मुक्त्वे.

अङ्गेज्याः परिसंख्याताः[१], तथा सति ये प्रकृतावङ्गार्थाः प्रधानार्थाश्च [२]सन्निपत्योपकारिणस्त इह धर्माः प्रवर्तेरन्। अस्मिन्पक्षे स्तम्बयजुषोऽर्वाक् पदार्थानां प्रेषितोऽग्नीत्[३] कर्ता स्यात्। आज्याधिश्रयणमात्रमपूर्वं कृत्वोपास्ते। अथाध्वर्युर्वा तन्त्रं सर्वं कुर्यादित्येके॥ [१]

अध्वर्युणैव निरुप्तस्याधिश्रयणमात्रमग्नीत् कुर्यादित्येके। अपरे प्रवर्ग्यानन्तरमध्वर्युणा प्रेषितोऽग्नीद्[३] गार्हपत्याहवनीययोरभ्यादध्यात्। दक्षिणाग्नावपीत्यन्ये। नैव क्वचिदभ्यादध्यादित्यपरे। प्रागेवातिथ्यान्ते स्तीर्णादन्यत्तृणकलापिमन्त्रेण संभृता वेदिस्तरणाय प्राक्तन एव प्रस्तरतृणकलाप्या सह[४] नद्धः प्राक्तनमेव वेदिपरिधिस्तिरश्च्यपि चतुर्दश दारुरिध्मः सह परिधिभिः। यथाप्रकृतीत्येके। शाकलान्येवेध्मकाष्ठा[५]न्युपसत्स्वपीत्यन्ये। तत आहवनीयं परिस्तृणीयाद्। द्वावित्येके। दक्षिणाग्निमपीत्यन्ये। स्फ्यं चाग्निहोत्रहवणीं च जुहूं चोपभृतं च स्रुवं चाज्यस्थालीं च प्रणीताप्रणयनं चोपांशुयाजनपक्षे एके सादयन्ति। पवित्रे आदाय ब्रह्माणं दक्षिणत उपवेश्य प्रणीताः प्रणयेत्। उपांशुयाजविकारत्वे पक्षान्तरेष्वप्रणीयैव प्रणीताः यजमान वाचं यच्छ इत्युक्त्वा हस्तौ मार्जयित्वा मदन्तीभ्य आसिच्य प्रोक्षणीः संस्कृत्य पात्राणि प्रोक्ष्यातिशिष्टा निधायाज्यं निरुप्याधिश्रित्य पर्यग्निकृत्वा मदन्तीषु भूयसीरप आनयेत्। अथाध्वर्युर्व्यूह्य बर्हिः स्तम्बयजुर्हरेत्। उद्धननं च बर्हिषोऽन्तरालेषु[६] योयोपनं[७] च। प्रेषितोऽग्नीन्म[८]दन्तीभिरद्भिः संपूर्य प्रोक्षणीः सादयित्वेध्माबर्हिरुपसाद्य मन्त्रेण स्रुवं संमृज्य तूष्णीं स्रुचौ संमृजेदपूर्वपक्षे। पक्षान्तरेषु यथाप्रकृति वेदेन संमार्गः। वेदस्य प्रच्छिद्यानुप्रहरेद्वोदस्येद्वा समस्तमन्त्यायामुपसदीति। वेदेनैव संमृज्यान्त्यायां प्रतिपादयेदित्येके॥ [२]

विभज्य सप्तधा परिवासनानि सर्वत्र संमृजेत्। प्रतिपादयेच्चेत्येके। पत्नीमुपनिषदनुपनिषदौ[९] वाचयित्वा पत्न्यवेक्षितेनाज्येनोदेति[१०]। अथाध्वर्युराज्यानि गृह्णन्नुपांशुयाजविकारत्वे ध्रौवैर्मन्त्रैस्त्रीणि चतुर्गृहीतानि गृह्णीयात्। तूष्णीमित्येके। प्रयाजविकारत्वे जौहवैः। अपूर्वत्वेऽनूयाजविकारत्वे च तूष्णीम्। अनुयाजविकारत्वेऽनुमन्त्रणानि सुवीर्याय त्वा इत्यादीनि, अपूर्वत्वे तु न सन्ति। वेदप्रोक्षणं[११] बर्हिष्येव। प्रोक्षेत् स्तरणबर्हिष्ये तृणकलाप्या च। स्रुक्सादनकाले यथाप्रकृति जुहूपभृतौ सादयित्वा ध्रुवामन्त्रेणाधिकृतेनाज्यस्थालीं सादयेत्।

---

१. M Ad °संघ्याता. २. M Ad °वत्वो°. ३. M Ad B °ग्नीन्. ४. M Ad B सहन्. ५. M Ad B काष्ठान्यप°. ६. M Ad °राळेषु. ७. Ad B om योपनं. ८. M Ad B ग्नी मद°. ९. M Ad B °षदानुनिष°. १०. M Ad B पत्नी अवे°. ११. M Ad B वेदं प्रो°.

पृथिवीजन्मनाऽऽज्यस्थालीनाम्ना **इत्येके। अपूर्वपक्षे त्वाज्यस्थालीमेव मन्त्रेण सादयेत्। तूष्णीमितरे।** ध्रुवाऽसदत् **इत्यपूर्वपक्षे, पक्षान्तरेषु** ध्रुवा असदन्[1] **इति। पत्नीराज्यस्थाल्यां व्याचष्टे। सर्वास्तूष्णीम्। उपांशुयाजविकारत्वे षष्ठप्रणवे सर्वमिध्ममभ्यादध्यात्। उत्तरत्रोपवाजनं बर्हिश्च शकलं चादायोत्तरतस्तिष्ठन्** [2]**प्रवरायाश्राव्य शकलं प्रास्य** सीद होतर् **इत्येतावद् अञ्जलिं कुर्यात्। प्रसूतः स्रुचावादाय यथोक्तं कुर्यात्। उपांशुयाजविकारत्वे मध्ये प्रदक्षिणं मण्डलाकार-माहुतीर्जुहुयात्। मध्य एव वा प्राचीः। तथाऽपूर्वत्वे प्रयाजविकारत्वे प्राचीरभि-क्रमन् वर्गक्रमेण**[3] **वा पुरस्ताद्दक्षिणत पञ्च जुहुयात्। अनूयाजविकारत्वे मध्यादुपक्रम्य प्रतीचीरन्ते प्राचीराहुतिः संस्रावेण संभिन्द्यात्। अनुमन्त्रणमु-पांशुयाजविकारत्वे** दब्धिरसि **इति। सर्वेषां याजविकारत्वे** अग्निं देवानां प्रीणामि स मा प्रीतः प्रीणातु, सोमं देवानां, विष्णुं देवानाम् **इति॥**

अनूयाजविकारत्वे प्रजावान्पशुमानायुष्मान् यज्ञेन **इति। नास्त्यपूर्वत्वेऽनु-मन्त्रणानि, यावदुक्तमेतावत ऊर्ध्वं कुर्यात्। उपांशुयाजविकारत्वे पुनः पक्षान्तरे त्वरमाणा इवोपसद्भिः प्रचरेयुः, नाकृतमाद्रियेरन्। सव्येन हस्तेन धनुरिव धारयन् दक्षिणेन हस्तेन समस्ताङ्गुलिना स्रुवमादायास्यन्निवोपसदं जुहुयात्। अनुमन्त्रणं याजमानम्। अत्र त्रिस्तनव्रतं प्रयच्छन् मध्यरात्रे चैव व्रतयन् द्विस्तनव्रतं मध्याया-मुपसदि। तथैकस्तनमुत्तमायामुपसदि। एकस्तनं**[4] **व्रतं विभज्य तत्रोक्तयोः कालयोर्व्रतयेत्। सायं प्रातरेव उपसदङ्गमपि व्रतमित्यपरे। पूर्वाह्ण एव पौर्वाह्णिक्यौ प्रवर्ग्योपसदौ कुर्यात्।** [5]**अपराह्ण एवापराह्णिक्यौ।** [३]

[महावेदिविमानम्]

एतां रात्रिं प्रति प्राचीं दिशं स्पाशयन्ते। कृत्स्नायां रात्र्यामनन्यव्यापार-दिगुपलक्षणमेव यतन्त इत्येके। दृष्ट्वा प्राङ्मुखः स्थित्वा कृत्तिकाद्यानामु-दितनक्षत्राणामार्जवे पुरुषं स्थाणुं वा स्थापयित्वा तत्र शङ्कुं निहत्य यत्र च स्थित्वा पश्यति तत्र च निहत्य तयोः [6]**शाङ्क्वोरुपस्पन्द्यामायम्य प्राचीं दिशं जानीयात्। प्राग्वंशार्थमादरेणानुपलक्षितायामपि दिशि नियोगतो निश्चिनु-यादित्यपरे। तथोपात्तया दिशा प्राग्वंशस्य पूर्वस्मात् स्थूणाराजन् पञ्चसु प्रक्रमेषु वेद्यन्तार्थं शङ्कुं निहत्य ततः पुरस्तात् षट्त्रिंशत्सु यूपकालं निहन्यात्।**

---

१. M Ad B असदग्नीति. २. M Ad B प्रपराया°. ३. M Ad B वर्मक्र°. ४. M Ad B त्वेक°. ५. M Ad B स्वपरा°. ६. M Ad B शाक्वोप°.

प्रकृतिभिरुपक्रमः। सर्वमितरत्तुल्यम्। स्पन्द्या मानरज्जुस्तस्याः पाशादेकोनचत्वारिंशत्सु प्रक्रमेष्वरत्निषु वा निरञ्छनं[१] कुर्यात्॥ [४]

कल्पपक्षे प्रक्रमाः शुल्बपक्षे[२]ऽरत्नयः। निरञ्छनमत्र[३] श्रोण्यर्थम्। निरञ्छता[४] त्रिष्वंसार्थं लक्षणं कुर्यात्। लक्षणद्वादशसु पाशान्तरं तं पाशं यूपावटीये प्रतिमुच्येतरं प्रथमनिहते निरञ्छनेन दक्षिणावायम्य लक्षणशङ्कुं निहन्यात्। स दक्षिणांसः[५]। विपर्यस्तौ पाशौ प्रतिमुच्य निरञ्छनेनोत्तरो रज्जुमायम्य लक्षणे शङ्कुं निहन्यात्। स उत्तरांसः[६]। अथैनां स्पन्द्याऽक्ष्णया मानं मिमाय समन्ततो दर्भमय्या स्पन्द्यया परिनह्य[७] पृष्ठ्यामातनोति। चात्वालोत्कराग्नीध्राणां कल्पपक्षे यावन्तः प्रक्रमास्तावन्तः[८] शुल्बपक्षेऽरत्नयः। तृतीयं वेद्या आग्नीध्रीये मध्ये न भवितव्यम्। प्रक्रमा एवेत्येके। पञ्चारत्नि चतुरश्रमाग्नीध्रागारम्। तस्यार्जवे दक्षिणे वेद्यन्ते तत्परिमाणमेव मार्जालीयम्। ततो यूपकालाच्छङ्कोरपरतः[९] सर्वत आयामविस्तराभ्यां दशपदोत्तरवेदिः शतपदपक्षे। त्री वेद्यन्तादपरतोऽर्धप्रक्रममवशिष्योत्तरवेदिं मिमीत इत्येके। तदेव ज्यायः। प्रथमनिहताच्छङ्कोरुत्तरवेद्या अर्धप्रक्रममात्रमवशिष्य नवकं समचतुरश्रं हविर्धानं मिमीते निरन्तरमेव दशकमित्येके[१०]। नवकं तु ज्यायः। प्रथमनिहताच्छङ्कोः पूर्वतोऽर्धप्रक्रममवशिष्य सदो मिमीते। निरन्तरमेव दशकव्यासमित्येके। तच्च स्यादुदगायतं विस्तारार्थमेव दक्षिणतः पृष्ठ्याया उत्तरतस्त्वधिकमात्रेणोत्सेधत्वादौप्तापेक्षम्[११]। धिष्णियानामन्तरालानां चोदकपृष्ठ्याया अर्धचतुर्दशमात्रेण भवितव्यम्। तेऽर्धपञ्चमप्रक्रमा उत्तरेणाच्छावाकस्य धिष्णियं संचारेण भवितव्यम्। तदनुरूपमुदग्वर्धयेत्॥ [५]

शुल्बपक्षे[१२] किष्कुभिर्मिताया वेद्याः प्रथमनिहताच्छङ्कोर्द्वयोः किष्कोर्नवव्या[सं][१३] सार्धं दक्षिणतः पृष्ठ्याया इतरदुत्तरतस्तदर्धाष्टककिष्कुक्षेत्र[१४]-धिष्णियानामन्तरालसञ्चाराणां च प्रभवे वा अष्टौ[१५] दक्षिणतः पृष्ठ्यायाः षडुत्तरतः। अस्मिन्पक्षे सर्वतो मध्यत औदुम्बरी मिता स्यात्। पृष्ठ्यायाश्च दक्षिणत किष्कुमात्रे होतुर्धिष्णियं पृष्ठ्यायामितरयोः पक्षयोः। शुल्बपक्षे [. . . .][१६] हविर्धानं स्तम्बयजुर्नाम्ना धर्मान् गृह्णाति। वेदिशब्दवाच्यायां महावेद्यां सर्वे वेदित्वापादनार्था धर्माः प्रवर्तन्ते। प्रदर्शनार्थं यजुरादिवचनमित्येके। तथा सति

---

१. M Ad B नीरा°. २. M Ad B शुत्पक्षे. ३. M Ad B मात्रव श्रो°. ४. M Ad B °ञ्छना. ५. M Ad B °णासः. ६. M Ad B °रासः. ७. M Ad B परितत्य. ८. Ad oms प्रक्रमास्तावन्तः. ९. M Ad B °काल्याच्छ°. १०. M Ad B °त्येक. ११. M Ad B°मावपोत्सत्वा°, doubtful. १२. M Ad B °पक्षके. १३. M Ad B broken. १४. M Ad B °ष्टकमिष्कु°. १५. M Ad B दष्टौ. १६. M Ad B broken.

वेदमभिमन्त्र्य वेदिं संमृज्य उत्तरतोऽत्रैवापवर्जयेत्। स्फ्ये[नोद्धत्य चात्वाल-][1]काले निदध्यात्। दक्षिणतो महावेद्यै [2]ब्रह्मैवोपविशति तूष्णीम्। एवं यजमानश्च समुद्धन्ति। प्रेत्याग्नीध्रश्च हरेत्। कृण्वन्ति वेदिं स्थ [लानि]च निम्नानि पूरयित्वा स्थाणुंश्चावृत्य[2] पांशुभ्योऽन्यत्सर्वं कुर्युः। वेदिप्रदेशं हृत्वा उत्तरवेद्यां सादयति। उत्तरवेदेः[3] पूर्वस्य करण्या अन्तिके शुल्बिणी नामोत्तर-नाभिच्छादनार्थं वाधूलकेषु प्रसिद्धः कश्चिदाकृतिविशेषः। अर्धव्रतम् अर्धस्तनव्रतम्, सकृद्दुग्धमेकस्तनव्रतं द्वेधा विभज्यार्धस्तनव्रतं प्रयच्छेत। एतदेव एतस्मिन्नेवकाले पूर्वाह्ने। एवं विपरीतमाज्यानि गृह्णीयात्॥ [६]

[4]सौरीं हुत्वेध्ममादीपयन्ति[4]। उद्वासनानन्तरमग्निप्रणयनमारभेत। अत्रैवाग्नये तृतीयमुपनिवपन् व्यवच्छिन्नेध्मं निवपेत् भस्मनि, नाग्नेरुपरि। मन्त्रवदुत्तरं परिग्राहं परिगृह्य मन्त्रेणैव योयुपित्वा पूर्वेण शालामवस्कभ्य संप्रेष्येत्। प्राकृतोऽयं प्रैषखण्ड इत्येके। नेत्यपरे। एतदेव ज्यायः। प्रोक्षण्यस्तूष्णीकाः पवित्रान्तर्हिता[5] आपः। इध्मस्तु शाकलोऽअग्नीषोमीयार्थः। बर्हिः संभरणकाल उपादातव्यम्[6]। प्रोक्षणायात्रैवोपादीयते। द्विः प्रोक्षणीकत्वं चास्य धर्मो वाचनिकः। शाकलत्वं सह परिधिभिः। परिधीन् परिहाप्येत्येके। न तरेत्तु याजोऽर्धसमिद्धिश्चेत्यपरे। एतत्सारं बर्हिर्महावेदिस्तरणार्थम्। प्रोक्षणं च सर्वमप्राकृतस्तूष्णीकम्। आसन्नमुपरवकाले महावेदिकं बर्हिः प्रोक्षति। तृणकलापी[7] पृष्ठ्यास्तरणार्था। एधा आहवनीयाग्निसमिन्धनार्थाय। प्रोक्षिताः पृष्ठ्याः प्रथमनिहतात्प्रभृत्या यूपावटीयान्मध्यसूत्रम्॥ [७] इति चतुर्थोऽनुवाकः॥

अथ पञ्चमोऽनुवाकः

[हविर्धानसंवर्तनम्]

हविर्धाने शकटे प्रतियुक्तचक्रे यत्र हविर्धीयतेऽभिषुतोऽनभिषुतश्च सोमः, तीर्थेन प्रपद्य तयोर्दक्षिणमग्रेणाहवनीयं पर्याहृत्य तथैवोत्तरतः प्रथमनिहताच्छङ्को-ररत्निकमात्रे प्राक् स्थापयित्वा उत्तरमुत्तरेणाहृत्य तथैवोत्तरतः स्थापयेत्। सांकाशिने समीचीने, संकाशस्थिते वा, बन्धनादि विस्त्रस्य सम्यक् निर्णिज्य पुनर्बद्धां रराटीयं पुरस्ताच्छादनार्थं प्रत्यानह्य[8] तृतीयं च्छदिरुद्दधति। तृतीयमु-

---

१. M Ad B broken; cf VādhŚS 6.13.54. २-२. M Ad B Text from ब्रह्मोप° to समुद्धन्ति repeated after स्थाणुश्चावृ. ३. M Ad B °वेदो. ४-४. M Ad B सौरहित्वेध्ममनीपयन्ति. ५. M Ad B om ता. ६. M Ad B °तव्यः. ७. M Ad B °लापि. ८. M Ad B प्रत्यन°.

परिष्टाच्छादनार्थमुपरिष्टादुद्धाय परिश्रयन्ति। दक्षिणतश्चोत्तरतश्च परिगृह्णन्ति। तथोत्तरस्य हविर्धानस्य कुर्यादित्येके। विमित एव विमितायामायतनप्रदेशाभ्यधिकविस्ताराणि च्छदींषि कृत्वा तैरेव कुर्यादित्येके। तूष्णीं संस्कृतमाज्यं स्रुक्स्रुवौ च [१]संमृष्टावेवंजातीयकेषु प्रोक्षण्यस्तूष्णीकः सपवित्राश्च। वर्तन्यां वर्त्मनि जुह्वच्चक्रमभिजुहुयादित्येके। प्राचोत्तानेन पदेनाक्षं पत्नी उपानक्ति। चक्रमुद्वृह्य यत्र चक्रं बद्धं तत्र तथा दक्षिणतस्तूष्णीं पदमवशेषयेत्। उत्तरस्योपात्तनाय अत्यूहति प्रयच्छति। तत्रापि सर्वं तुल्यम्। कृत्स्नं पदं तत्रैव विनियुञ्जीत। उत्सर्जनेऽनुपलब्धे विनियोगत उत्सर्जनप्रायश्चित्तं वाचयेदेव। अनुमन्त्रयेत। अध्वर्यू वारयतश्च काले यत्र स्थातुमहतः नभ्यस्थे नभ्यफलके स्थिते कृत्वाऽरत्निमात्रपृष्ठ्याया व्यपेत मिथः समीचीने। अपरेणाहवनीयं परिहाप्य जघनेन ऋचा[२] मेथ्यनपसर्पणार्था शकटस्यैव तया सहाक्षमीषां वा बध्नाति। एवं मिताऽत्र[३] हविर्धानं मितं कुर्वन्ति नवकं दशकं वा। उदीचीनकर्णा स्थूणा[४] उच्छ्रयति चेदेतयोर्द्वारोः[५] पृष्ठ्याया अभितोऽरत्निमात्रे तासु वंशानुद्धाय छदींष्युद्दध्युः[६]॥ [१]

पुरस्तात् तिर्यग्रराटीयमपरतः तृणं वा सीव्यति छादयति ऊर्ध्वाग्रैर्दर्भैः कुशलतया ग्रन्थिरहितामेव। द्वार्बाहू कुर्वन्तौ सीव्यतः। अथापरौ[७] द्वार्बाहू तूष्णीं सीव्यतः। नेत्यपरे। अथ सर्वत्र परिश्रयन्ति। प्रसलैः प्रागपवर्गं द्वारौ परिहाप्य अभिमृशतोऽध्वर्यू। अभ्यन्तरमुपरवार्थमादेयम्। तथा यूपार्थमनियम इत्येके। अवटमभ्येतोऽध्वर्युयजमानौ। प्रक्षाल्य प्रपाद्याग्रेणाहवनीयं पर्याहृत्य स्वस्थानं प्रत्युपनिहितामौदुम्बरीं चाभ्येतः। सर्वाणि तामन्वितराणि च प्रक्षाल्य तीर्थेन प्रपाद्यानि यैर्दक्षिणतः पृष्ठ्याया अर्थस्तानि चाग्रेणाहवनीयं पर्याहर्तव्यानि। पुरुषाश्च प्रक्षालितपादा आचान्तास्तीर्थेन प्रवेशयेयुः। तथा दूशीकवः परिकर्मिणोऽन्ये च ये प्रयोजनवन्तः दक्षिणतो व्याप्रियमाणा अग्रेणैवाहवनीयं परीयुः। तथा ततश्चोत्तरत आगच्छन्ति। औदुम्बरीस्थूणामध्यमासदनमूर्ध्वमुपरवाद्[८]। यजमान अत्रानीतां[९] क्रियमाणाप्युदगात्रोच्छ्रियमाणामध्वर्युणा सह कुर्यात्। विषूके विशाखे स्थूणायाः कर्णयोरन्तराले मन्त्रान्ते हिरण्यस्योपरि जुह्वन् भूय आज्यमासिञ्चेत् यावतान्तमन्ववस्रावयेत्। भूमिगत आज्ये स्वाहा करोति। अथ प्राचीनकर्णा स्थूणा उच्छ्रित्योदीचो वंशानुद्धाय ऐन्द्रमसि इति

---

१. M Ad B संमृष्टामे°. २. M Ad B संचा. ३. M Ad B °मित्रात°. ४. M Ad B °स्तूणा. ५. M Ad B चेद्वे°. ६. M Ad B °दींष्युंद°. ७. M Ad B °अपरो. ८. M Ad B °मुपरद्यज. ९. M Ad B आत्रीतां.

दक्षिणं[१] **छदिरभिनिधाय** विश्वजनस्य छाया[२] **इत्युत्तरतः किञ्चित्। अथेतराणि तूष्णीमधि निदध्युः। अकामानामनियतानि**[३] **छदींषि क्रत्वर्थानि, कामिनां तु यथाकामं**[४] **नियमः। नवच्छदीत्यादीनामन्यतमं क्रत्वर्थमपीत्येके। दक्षिणेन दक्षिणान्युत्तराण्यधराणीतराणि**[५]**। अन्तर्वर्तान् कुर्वन्ति। छदिःसन्धिषु सर्वेषु तृणावर्तान् प्रत्यवस्यति। तेऽन्तर्वर्तादुदीचीनं**[६] **सदो वर्धयन्ति, न समचतुरश्रं कुर्वन्ति। उदगायतं कुर्वन्ति॥** [२]

उत्तरतो वा पृष्ठ्याया वर्धयन्ति। 'परि त्वा गिर्वणो गिरः' **इत्यभितः परितः समुच्छ्रयन्ति। परिश्रयणमन्त्रेणाध्वर्युरारभेत। तथेतराणि। परिकर्मिणः प्रसलैः प्रागपवर्गं द्वारद्वयवर्जं परिश्रयन्ति। द्वौ द्वौ बाहू मन्त्रेण सीव्यतः। एकैकमित्येके। तदाग्नीध्रागारं कृत्वा परितः परिश्रित्य दक्षिणतो द्वारं कुर्वन्ति, तथोत्तरतः। मार्जालीयस्य दक्षिणतोऽपरेणोपरवानासीनो**[७] **यजमानः पदाङ्गुष्ठाभ्यां निबाधते नीचैर्बाधते। भूमिमुदस्तात्पांसूनित्येके। तदेव ज्यायः। अध्वर्युरेव निबाधनं**[८] **कुर्यादित्येके। यजमान एवोद्वपनानि**[९] **निबाधत**[१०] **इत्यपरे।** अध्वर्यो किमत्र **इत्युक्तो** भद्रम् **इत्यध्वर्युराह,** तन्नौ सह **इति यजमानः।** यजमान किमत्र **इत्युक्तो** भद्रम् **इति यजमानः,** तन्नौ सह **इत्यध्वर्युः। एवं सर्वत्र यं यमध्वर्युर्जहाति तं तं यजमानः संमृशति। प्रोक्षणमत्र सकृदेव सर्वेषाम्। अपनयनप्रस्कन्दनावस्तरणा-भिहोमेष्वावृत्तिर्यथा नापसर्पतस्तथा कुर्यात्। पर्यूहनं च दृढिम एव। बर्हिषा परि च स्तृणाति। परि चाधिषवणचर्म**[११] **त्रिप्रादेशायामविस्तरम्। प्रादेशोऽधः-प्रमाणमूर्ध्वलोमाधोअक्ष**[१२] **यथार्थप्रमाणमाखरं कल्पयेत्। यावन्ति सोमपात्राणि स्रुचश्च साद्येरन्। एतस्मिन्काले दक्षिणस्य हविर्धानस्योपस्तम्भनस्य पूर्वार्धे बर्हिर्मुष्टिं निबध्नीयात्। स्तोत्रोपकरणाय नवानि बध्नीयात्। स्रुग्धारणार्थादेव प्रस्तरात् स्तोत्रोपकरणार्थं बर्हिराददीत्॥** [३]

आग्नीध्रियो धिष्णियो मध्य आग्नीध्रागारस्य मध्याद्दक्षिणतोऽरत्निमात्र इत्येके। धिष्णियाः सर्वे प्रादेशप्रमाणा अरत्न्यन्तराला येष्वन्तरालः संभवः। अग्निचित्यायां त्वरत्निप्रमाणाः प्रादेशान्तरालाः। प्रत्यङ्ङासीनो धिष्णियान् निर्वपेत्। ततो मध्यात् प्राक् प्रक्रमत्रये वा पृष्ठ्यायां होतुर्धिष्णियम्, अरत्निमात्रे

---

१. M Ad B भुक्षि; cf. VādhŚS 6.17.3. २. M Ad B श्चये°. ३. M Ad B °तानिशच्छ°. ४. M Ad B °कामाग्नियम. ५. M Ad B °क्षिणान्युपकरत्यध°; cf. VādhŚS 6.17.5. ६. M Ad B °चीना. ७. M Ad B °सिनो. ८. M Ad B °धनमेव. ९. M Ad B °वपन. १०. M Ad B °धने. ११. M Ad B °वर्म. १२. M Ad B °अधत्रक्ष.

वा दक्षिणतः पृष्ठ्यायां दक्षिणेन प्रशास्तुरुत्तरेण ब्राह्मणाच्छंसिनः पोतृनेष्टॄच्छावाकानां च। अन्ततो मार्जालीयस्य धिष्णियां निर्वपेत्। उपस्थापयति यजमानम्। अनूयाजस्यान्वत्रैव केचिद् अनुदिशन्ति। अनूकशब्दं च वाक्यशेषं तेष्वनुवर्तयन्ति॥ [४] इति पञ्चमोऽनुवाकः॥

अथ षष्ठोऽनुवाकः

[वसतीवरीग्रहणम्]

सर्वे[१] ऋत्विजो विविधं गच्छन्ति स्नानाय। पुनर्देवयजनमागच्छन्ति[२]। नियोगतोऽत्र[३] सर्वैः स्नातव्यम्। नैष स्नाननियम इत्यन्ये। स्नाननियम इति ज्यायः। कुम्भो दृढिष्ठो परिकृष्टवासतीवरः[४]। ग्रहणकाले[५] कूर्चापिहितेन गृह्णीयात्। उत्क्षुभ्य[६] वहन्तीरपः कृत्वाऽऽत्मनश्छायामौदकीं कुर्यात्। अपिव्रताः पुत्रा दुहितरोऽप्रत्ता भ्रातरोऽविभक्ताः। सपिण्डा इत्येके। ग्रावाणः पञ्च सोमांशुसवनाः[७], वायव्यान्यूर्ध्वपात्राणि, समवशमनं सम्यगवधानं, गार्हपत्यं प्रत्युदयनं पत्न्यास्तथा [८]अनःप्रवर्तनम्। यत्रानोऽभिष्टव्यवहारस्तत्रैव[९] प्रवर्तनम्। प्रैषखण्डश्चेत्यपरे॥ [१]

प्रयोजनमनसां प्रैष इत्यपरे। स्तृणन्त्यध्वर्युपुरुषा अन्ये च परिकर्मिणः। कृत्स्नां महावेदिं नैरन्तरेण उदगपवर्गं तूष्णीं हविर्धान आग्नीध्रिये मा[१०] तावदिति बाहुल्येन स्तृणन्ति धिष्णियोत्तरवर्जम्। हविरासादनस्थानं च वर्जयित्वेत्येके। अर्धस्तनव्रतं विभज्य निहितं प्रयच्छेत्। अथाग्नीत्प्रेषितः पूर्वं वैसर्जनहोमार्थमधिश्रयेत्। अथाध्वर्युरेव पाशुकं तन्त्रमारभेत, प्रतिप्रस्थाता वा। प्राकृतस्यैवाज्यस्य प्राकृतमधिश्रयणमात्रमग्नीत् कुर्यादित्येके। अग्नीदेवाधिश्रयणान्तं प्राकृतं तन्त्रं कुर्यादित्यन्ये। तदेव[११] ज्याय इवाभाति। तथा सति अग्नीदभ्याधाय बर्हिः संभरेत्। प्राक्तने एव प्रस्तरतिरश्ची इत्येके। इध्मस्तु शाकलः पूर्वमुपात्तः[१२] प्रोक्षितश्च। परिधयः प्राक्तना एव। गार्हपत्यान्वाहार्यपचनाहवनीयान् परिस्तीर्य वेदिमभिमन्त्र्योत्तरेण गार्हपत्यं पाशुकानि पात्राणि सादयित्वा पवित्रेण यन्ति येषां पुरोडाशार्थास्ताः। अथ दक्षिणमंसमभिनिवर्त्य हस्तौ मार्जयित्वा प्रविश्य[१३] शालां प्रोक्षणीं संस्कृत्य पात्राणि प्रोक्ष्यातिशिष्टाः पूर्वेण गार्हपत्यं निधाय वेदं परिवासय **इत्युक्त्वाऽऽज्यं निरुप्याधिश्रित्य दधि च**

---

१. M Ad B सर्वर्त्वि°. २. M Ad B °देवयजमानमागच्छति. ३. M Ad B °तेऽत्र. ४. M Ad B परिष्टवा°. ५. M Ad B °कालः. ६. M Ad B उक्षु°. ७. M Ad B सोपांशु°. ८. M Ad B सनांप्र°. ९. M Ad B °नोऽभिष्ट्यवहा°. १०. M Ad B मास्ता°. ११. M Ad om त. १२. M Ad B °त्तं. १३. M Ad B प्रवभ्य.

पर्या[णीय][१] **प्रैषखण्डमाह** प्रोक्षणीरासादयेध्माबर्हिरुपसादयाज्येनो[२]देहि पृषदाज्याय दध्याहरेहि यजमान **इति। अग्नीदित्येके। तथा सत्यविकृतः प्रैष इति केचित्। अस्यैव कश्चित् प्रैष ब्रूयादित्यन्ये। अध्वर्युरिति ज्यायः। प्रतिप्रस्थात्रे प्रोक्षणीः स्फ्यस्य वर्त्मनि सादयति यत्रावस्कभ्य प्रैष उक्तः॥** [२]

तत इध्माबर्हिरुत्तरेणाहवनीयं सादयेत्। अथ स्रुचः संमृज्यात्रैव सादयित्वा पत्न्यवेक्षितमाज्यं हृत्वाऽऽहवनीयेऽधिश्रित्योत्तरेण प्रोक्षणीः सादयित्वा अग्नेर्जिह्वासि **इत्यवेक्ष्य यजमानावेक्षित**[३] **आत्मनश्छायामवेक्ष्यापूर्य**[४] **प्रोक्षणीषु पवित्रे निधाय पुनराहृत्य प्राग्वंश** [५]**एवाज्यं निदध्यात्**[५]**। पत्न्यवेक्षितमाज्यं पुनर्मन्त्रेण गार्हपत्यं** [६]**वाऽधिश्रित्योत्तरेण गार्हपत्यं मन्त्रेण सादयित्वा** अग्नेर्जिह्वासि **इत्याज्यग्रहणान्तं**[७] **करोति। यजमानश्चावेत्यावेक्षेत। आद्य एव पक्षो ज्यायान्। आग्नीध्र एवाज्यानि गृह्णीयादिति केचित्। अध्वर्युरेव सर्वत्र। तन्त्रं प्रैषश्च खण्डतो वाच्यः। आज्याधिश्रयणमात्रमग्नीधः प्रैषार्थश्च प्रतिप्रस्थातुरिति केचित्। सर्वत्राज्याधिश्रयणान्तमग्नीधोऽन्यत् सर्वमविरुद्धमाज्यग्रहणान्तं प्रतिप्रस्थातुरित्यपरे। परसूत्रप्रसिद्धश्च पुराणगार्हपत्यं पत्नीयजमानावुपस्थापयति। अध्वर्युर्मन्त्रं वाचयेत्। स्वयमेव मन्त्रं ब्रुवन्नञ्जलिमात्रेण दम्पती उपस्थापयतीत्येके। तथा सति मन्त्रलिङ्गविरोधः। प्रागावृत्त उपविशतीत्यपिव्रता दम्पती च वाससा प्रतिच्छन्ना अध्वर्युरन्वारभमाणः। अथ ब्रह्मोत्तरेणाग्नीध्रीयं धिष्णियमुत्तरेण च सदः परीत्य पूर्वया द्वारा शालां प्रपद्योत्तरेण शालामुखीयं गत्वाऽपरेण वेदिमत्याक्रम्योपस्थे राजानं कृत्वा दक्षिणेन शालामुखीयमसित्वा**[८] **वैसर्जनहोमानन्तरं होतुरुत्थानमनु राज्ञा सहोत्थाय यथेतं निष्क्रम्य होत्रध्वर्यू दम्पती उत्तरेण गच्छन्त राजानं परिहरेत्। तथा वसतीवरीः पात्राण्याज्यानि चोत्तरेणाग्निं परिहृत्याग्रेण गार्हपत्यं प्रसलैः पर्यावृत्य गच्छतां दक्षिणतः॥** [३]

प्राङ् [९]**गच्छन्मन्त्रेणान्वगिवाग्रे गच्छतामग्निरभ्यन्तरोऽथ राजाऽथाज्यान्यथ वसतीवरीरथ ग्रावाणोऽथ वायव्यानि। वसतीवर्य आज्येभ्योऽभ्यन्तरा इत्येके। कर्तृषु दम्पती आभ्यन्तरावथाध्वर्युरथ होताऽथ ब्रह्माऽथोद्गाता। सर्वत्रैवमर्धिभ्यो मुख्यास्तृतीयिभ्योऽर्धिनः पादिभ्यस्तृतीयिनो मुख्यानुपूर्व्या मिथः। पुरुषाः सर्वे मन्त्रेणाग्निप्रथमाः पूर्वया द्वारा निष्क्रम्योत्तरेण सदः परीत्याग्नीध्रागारं प्रविशन्ति। ब्रह्मा सर्वेभ्यः पूर्वं सह राज्ञा प्रविश्योत्तराग्नीध्रीयं**[१०] **धिष्णियं परीत्यापसलैः**

---

१. M Ad B पर्य. २. M Ad B °दयोऽज्मनो. ३. M Ad B om °त. ४. M Ad B °पूय. ५-५. M Ad B एव ज्यायः ज्यानि ज्यायात्. ६. M Ad B वोऽधि°. ७. M B °ग्रहणाणत्तं. ८. M Ad B °मासित्वा. ९. M Ad B गच्छन्. १०. M Ad B ध्रियं.

पर्यावृत्य दक्षिणतस्तिष्ठेत्। अथाध्वर्युरग्निं सादयित्वा अनुरब्धेष्वपि वृतेषु[१] नयवतीं हुत्वाऽत्रैव द्रोणकलशं च वसतीवरीश्च यत्नतो निदधायाज्यान्यादायोत्तरेणाग्नीध्रीयं धिष्णियं परीत्याहवनीयं प्रति गच्छतां ब्रह्मा दक्षिणतो गत्वाऽध्वर्यवे राजानं संप्रदायापरेणाहवनीयं गत्वा दक्षिणत आहवनीयस्योपविशेत्। उत्तरवेदिं गच्छतां दक्षिणतो गत्वा प्रसलैः प्रर्यावृत्यादशहोतुर्व्याख्यानादुत्तरेणाहवनीयं राजानं धारयन् स्थित्वाऽध्वर्यवे[२] राजानमित्येतत् कुर्यादित्येके। तदेव ज्यायः। अग्रेणाज्यानि परीत्याध्वर्युः प्रोक्षणीरादाय प्रदक्षिणमावृत्य प्रत्यङ्ङुद्रुत्य धरुणेऽपोऽवोक्ष्य पुनरागत्याग्रेणाज्यान्युद्धृद्रुत्य [...][३] प्रोक्षणादि प्रतिपद्यते॥ [४]

वेदिशब्देन हविःसादनप्रदेश इव लक्ष्यते। स चाग्रेण जघनेनोत्तरवेद्याः। दक्षिणेनोत्तरवेद्या इत्येके। बर्हिषि[४] बर्हिषि उन्नयति। अवनिनयनं[४] चात्र स्तीर्णस्यैव बर्हिषो दक्षिणोत्तरम्। द्वयोः[५] श्रोण्योर्निनयनम्। तत्रैव स्रुवाहुत्यां संप्रयच्छन्नारभ्य यथेत अप उपस्पृश्य पूर्वया द्वारा राजानं प्रपादयेत्[६]। सर्वत्राप उपस्पृशेत्। आज्यं स्पृष्ट्वा सोममुपस्पृशन् सोमं वा स्पृष्ट्वाऽऽज्यं स्पृशन् यजमानः प्रपादयेदित्येके। संप्रदानादि नियोगतो यजमान आऽङ्गुलीनां विसर्जनात्। इदमहम् इत्यादिरुपावर्तनमन्त्रः। उपोत्तानं[७] चेमं लोकं मनसैवाञ्जलिं करोति। नमो देवेभ्यः इति स्वधा पितृभ्यः इत्यञ्जलिं करोति। पितृभ्यो दक्षिणमवाञ्चं कृत्वा सव्यमुत्तानं प्राचीनावीति दक्षिणमुखश्च। उपवीतविपर्यासे हस्तप्रक्षालनं सर्वत्रैव। अनुवीक्षते[८] आकाशं स्वर्गलोकमभिध्यायन्। अस्पर्शयन्निव पाणिद्वयं निधायाङ्गुलीर्विसृजति। सर्वमन्त्रान्ते सह सर्वा [९]विसृजेत। स्वाहा यज्ञं मनसा इति मध्यमिके, स्वाहा द्यावापृथिवीभ्याम् इत्युपकनिष्ठिके, स्वाहोरोरन्तरिक्षात् इति कनिष्ठिके इत्येके। क्रीते राजनि प्राक् प्रवणात् प्रोह्येत्येके। अत्र वा वृश्चे तथा सति वृक्णे यूपे यूपावटखननम्। नैवात्र व्रश्चनमित्येके। अथ यथोक्तं पाशुकं कर्म प्रतिपद्यते॥ [५] इति षष्ठोऽनुवाकः॥

अथ सप्तमोऽनुवाकः

आण्डीवलत्वादिगुणयुक्तोऽग्नीषोमीयः। नित्यावित्यत्र वाऽऽज्यभागौ। अनित्यावित्येके[१०]। अनुमन्त्रणं[११] वपाया इन्द्रियावी भूयासम् इति॥ [१] इति सप्तमोऽनुवाकः॥

---

१. M Ad B पृतेषु. २. M Ad B स्थित्यध्व°. ३. M Ad B broken. ४-४. M Ad B °बर्हिसून्नत्यवानि°. ५. M Ad B धो. ६. M Ad B प्रपेद°. ७. M Ad B उपात्तनं. ८. M Ad B °वीक्षिते. ९. M Ad B °पिसृ°. १०. M Ad °नित्याधित्यके; Ad B त्येके °धिके. ११. M Ad B °मन्त्रव°.

अथाष्टमोऽनुवाकः

अन्युप्तधिष्णियाननुदेशेन[१] एकत्रैव तिष्ठन्ननुदिशेत्। यजमानोऽध्वर्युं चानुदेशयति। अध्वर्युरेवानुदिशतीत्येके। स एव कल्पकाराभिप्रायः। आस्तावो दक्षिणेन चात्वालं यत्र बहिष्पवमानेन स्तुवन्ति, यत्र ब्रह्माऽऽस्ते सदसि दक्षिणेन होत्रकान्, यत्र हारियोजनीभिश्चरति, यत्र धानाभिः पितृकार्यं कुर्वन्ति मार्जालीयसमीपे, यत्र निर्मन्थ्येन चरति। उत्तरेणोत्तरवेदिं पत्नीसंयाजनं यन्ते। पश्वाज्यशेषेण तरांसि जुहोति। निपदः काले निपदनकाले शयनकाले आग्नीध्रे वसतीवरीः सादयित्वा राजानं चातिहृत्यैव सादयेयुः। आधवनीयपूतभृदाख्यौ कलशौ बहुशः परीक्षितौ ह्लदौ प्रक्षालितौ पूर्वया द्वारा हविर्धानं प्रपाद्योत्तरस्य हविर्धानस्य नीड आधवनीयं कृतेण्ड्वं[२] न्युब्जति। प्रउगे पूतभृते कृतेण्ड्वमाग्नीध्र एकं सोदचमसापिधानं निमिनुयात्। तथा मार्जालीये ते चत्वारो पूतभृताकारमहान्तः[३] कलशाः। तदानीमेव चतस्रः स्थालीरेकधनार्थाश्च सम्यक् परीक्ष्य प्रक्षाल्य निदध्यात्। आधवनीयपूतभृतोर्योगः पात्रयागकाल इत्येके॥ [१]

महापरिधयो द्राघिष्ठाः परिकृष्टाः परिणाहेन च महान्तः। अत्र सवनीयार्थं गार्हपत्याहवनीययोरभ्याधाय शाखां छित्त्वा यजमानस्य व्रतदुहो वत्समपाकुर्यात्। प्रातरेवोद्वास्य प्रवर्ग्यं प्रागाहवनीयस्य प्रणयनाच्छाखाहरणं वत्सापाकरणं चेत्येके। बर्हिः संभरेत पूर्ववदित्येके। नाचार्याभिप्रायः। अथेध्मं सह महापरिधीन्[४] पूर्वमेवेतर इध्म उत्तरः। अथ वेदं कृत्वाऽभ्याहितावग्निं परिस्तीर्य वेदमभिमन्त्रयेत। असति साधारणे तु वेदकरणाभिमन्त्रणेन तन्त्र उपक्रमकाल एव। वेदिकरणाभिमन्त्रणपरिस्तरणानि त्वग्नीत् कुर्यादित्येके। प्रैषानुपूर्वा दोहयेत् पयस्यायै धर्मवत्। इतरत्सर्वमधर्मकम्। इन्द्रः पयस्यायै[५] देवता। सायंदोहः पयस्येत्येके। न चात्रातञ्चनमित्यन्ये। आमिक्षैव पयस्यातञ्चनं कुर्याच्च काले। प्रातर्दोहं दोहयेत्। पुरोडाशेडान्ते वाजिनेन चरेदित्येके। सायंदोह एव प्रायः कल्पकाराभिप्रायः[६]। दधिग्रहाय शुक्लं दध्युपकल्पयेत्। आदित्यग्रहाय च॥ [२] इत्यष्टमोऽनुवाकः॥[७]

॥ इति ज्योतिष्टोमाख्यः पञ्चमः प्रपाठकः समाप्तः ॥[८]

---

१. M Ad B °या सदेशन. २. M Ad B कृत्वेण्व; cf VādhŚS 6.28.25. ३. M Ad B भूकार°.४. M Ad B °धीनि. ५. M Ad B वयस्या°. ६. M Ad B कल्पकराभिप्राया°. ७. M B इत्यष्टमो ज्योतिष्टोमः ; Ad इति अष्टमे ज्योतिष्टोमः. ८. M Ad B om.

[१]॥ अथ षष्ठः प्रपाठकः ॥

॥ अथाग्निष्टोमः ॥

अथ प्रथमोऽनुवाकः[१]

अपराह्णे पशुमालभ्यास्तमिते वपया[२] प्रचर्य मनागपवनीयरात्रेरवदानैः प्रचर्य पशुं परिसमाप्य कर्मशेषं च कृत्वाऽऽग्नीध्रीय उषित्वा रात्रेर्दशसु मुहूर्तेष्वतीतेषु तृतीयावशिष्टायां रजन्यां यज्ञवाट् रक्षिणो यजमानपुरुषा दम्पती ऋत्विजः परिकर्मिणश्च संबोधयन्ति। तेषां सम्बोधितानां दम्पती हस्तपादान् प्रक्षाल्याचम्य प्रविशतः। इतरेषामपि ये प्रयतास्ते[३] तथैव प्रविशन्ति। ये त्वप्रयतास्ते स्नात्वा प्रक्षालितोपवा[४]तान्यक्लिष्टानि वासांसि परिधायाचम्य प्रविशन्ति। [५]सर्व ऋत्विजोऽभ्रप्रभृत्यनुवाकं[६] जपित्वा तीर्थे प्रपद्यन्ते। ब्रह्मसदस्यन्ते ब्रह्मसदस्ययोरेवैष जप इत्येके। जोषंकृतेषु तूष्णीमेव कृतेषु प्रारब्धेषु। तूष्णीं शब्दोऽत्र लक्षणयोपांशुत्वप्रकर्षवचनः। राजानं प्रपाद्य प्रेष्येत्। प्रेषितोऽग्नीत् पात्रसादनानि प्रतिपद्यते। उत्तरेणाहवनीयं पाशुकानि पात्राणि सादयित्वा पवित्रे ब्रह्माणं[७] दक्षिणत आहवनीयस्योपवेश्य प्रणीताः प्रणयेत्। नात्र प्रणीता इत्यपरे। प्रणीताऽभावेऽपि यजमान वाचं यच्छ इत्युक्त्वा कर्मणे वाम् इति हस्तौ मार्जयित्वा प्रोक्षणीः संस्कृत्य पात्राणि प्रोक्ष्य प्रोक्षणीशेषं निधाय वेदं परिवासय इति ब्रूयात्। यदि न साधारणो वेद[८] प्रैषखण्डस्य विकल्पेनावस्कम्भनं चाथ स्थानं चाथ प्रोक्षणीः[९] स्फ्यस्य वर्त्मन् सादयित्वोत्तरेणाहवनीयमिध्माबर्हिरुपसाद्य प्रतिप्रस्थाता स्रुचः संमृज्य पूर्वया द्वारा निष्क्रम्योत्तरेण सदः परीत्योत्तरेणाग्नीध्रीयं परिहृत्यापरे[ण . . .][१०] तां प्रतीचीं[११] च पुरुषाणां द्रव्याणां चैष एव मार्गः। पत्न्यवेक्षितमाज्यमाहृत्याहवनीयेऽधिश्रित्योत्तरेण प्रोक्षणीः सादयित्वा अग्नेर्जिह्वासि इत्यवेक्ष्य यजमानमवेक्षमाणं वाचयित्वाऽऽत्मनश्छायामवेक्ष्य[१२] पुनराहृत्य [. . . .][१३]द्रौस्त [उपांशुपात्रं . . .][१४] सादयित्वा पूर्वया द्वारा हविर्धानं प्रपद्य

१-१. M Ad अथ; B अथ प्रथमः. २. M Ad B ववया. ३. M Ad B व्रता°. ४. M Ad B °तोवपाता°. ५. M Ad B सर्वर्त्वि°. ६. M Ad B °भृत्य इत्यसवा°. ७. M Ad B ब्राह्मणं. ८. M Ad B वेदा. ९. M Ad B प्रोक्षणी. १०. M Ad B broken. ११. M Ad B प्रतीचां. १२. M Ad B °क्ष्योद्य. १३. M Ad B broken. १४. M Ad B. Here the text dealing with उपांशुपात्र is broken; cf. VādhŚS ७.१.८.

पात्राणि युञ्ज्यात्। अन्तर्यामपात्रं सादयन् नेदीय उपांशुपात्रस्य सादयेद्, यथोभाभ्यां ग्रावा स्पृष्टः स्यात्॥ [१]

परिस्त्रजं यस्य परितः स्त्रुगाकारो[१] मध्यत उत्सेधात् द्विभृष्टि[२] यदस्य ध्रुवाकारौ द्वावुपर्युपर्युत्सेधो स्तनावा [३][. . . .] द्वौ स्त[नाका][३]रौ शुक्रामन्थिनोश्च पात्रे मिथो नेदीयसी युनक्ति। एवम् ऋतुपात्रे अश्वशफबुध्ने अश्वशफाकारे बुध्ने प्रस्थिते व्रतगमनपरतः प्रबाहुक् समीचीने। आज्यग्रहणानन्तरमेवाध्वर्युः शालामुखीये दर्विहोमिकमाज्यं संस्कृत्य प्रचरणीं संमृज्य गत्वाऽग्नीध्रीय आहुतिद्वयं जुहोति। अथोन्नेता[४] ग्रावादीनि प्रक्षालितानि प्रक्षालिते द्रोणकलशे समवधाय पूर्वया द्वारा हविर्धानं प्रपद्य दक्षिणस्य हविर्धानस्य पूर्वेण अक्षमध[५] ईषां[६] सादयेत्। एवं चमसान् पयःसक्तुहिरण्यस्त्रज[७] इति चोपकल्पयेत्[८] प्रचरणाय। आज्येष्वाहवनीयं प्रतिप्रणवेष्वध्वर्युरतिद्रुत्य[९] प्रोक्षणीरादायोत्तरेणाज्यानि परीत्याग्नीध्रीयं गत्वा तूष्णीं धरुणेऽवोक्ष्य पुनरेत्येध्मप्रोक्षणादि प्रतिपद्यते। प्रोक्षणादौ तु विशेष उक्तः। औपानुवाक्यैरभिमर्शनमाध्वर्यवं स्त्रुगभिमर्शनं च। [१०]ग्राव्णोऽभिमर्शनमधिषवणफलकयोर्निधाय तस्मिन् राजानं सादयेत्तूष्णीम्। फलकयोश्चर्म चर्मणि ग्राव्णो[११] ग्रावसु राजानमित्येके। अथाग्नीत् सर्वेभ्य एव सवनेभ्यः सवनीयं निर्वपेत्। उक्तः संप्रैषः। प्रातःसवनीयानेवात्र निरुप्य उपरम्य क्षुल्लकवैश्वदेवस्य स्तोत्रे माध्यन्दिनीयान् निर्वपेत्। माहेन्द्रस्य स्तोत्रे तार्तीयसवनीयानित्येके। तदेव ज्यायः। प्रातर्दोहादि प्रतिपद्यते॥ [२]

यद्यामिक्षा। पयस्यापक्षान्तरे पात्रसादनानि उत्तरेण शालामुखीयं दर्भानास्तीर्य तेषु पात्राणि सादयेद् एकादशकपालानि भर्जनमेकं द्वे वा अग्निहोत्रहवण्यादीन्यष्टौ। प्राशित्रहरणं चैके। मेक्षणं पिष्टोद्वपनीं च प्रणीताप्रणयनं चैकेषाम्। आमिक्षापक्षे वाजिनपात्रं च भर्जनपात्रं च यवान् व्रीहींश्चाहृत्य अपरेण शालामुखीयं निधाय पवित्रे आदाय यजमान वाचं यच्छ इत्युक्त्वा कर्मणे वाम् इति हस्तौ मार्जयित्वाऽग्निहोत्रहवणीं शूर्पमित्यादयः पृथक् धूः-मन्त्रं जपेत्। एत्येको[१२] धानाभ्यो यवान् निरुप्य। करंभाय च यवानेव निर्वपेत्। अथ परिवापाय व्रीहीन्। अथ पुरोडाशाय च व्रीहीन्। सर्वत्रेन्द्र एव देवता। अथ

---

१. M Ad B °स्त्रगारो. २. M Ad B °दृषि. ३-३. M Ad B text dealing with the placing of ऐन्द्रवायवपात्र, मैत्रावरुणपात्र and आश्विनपात्र is broken. ४. M Ad B °न्नता. ५. M Ad B °मधं. ६. M Ad B ईशं. ७. M Ad B °रण्यस्त्र°. ८. M Ad B °ल्पये कूपणाय. ९. M Ad B °रितिद्रु°. १०. M ग्राविह्णो Ad B ग्राविण्णो. ११. M Ad B ग्राविण्णः. १२. M Ad B एत्यके.

प्रोक्षणीः संस्कृत्य हवींषि प्रोक्ष्यातिशिष्टा निदध्यात् यदि च प्रणीताः। सतीषु प्रणीतासु सर्वाभिः प्रोक्षणप्रोक्षणीरतिशेषयेत्। पूर्वं यवानवघ्नन् अर्वाक् प्रैषान् कृत्वा सकृदवहतानेव। तानपनीय व्रीहीनवहन्यात्। अथ हविष्कृदाह्वानात् यवानवहन्यादित्येके। परिवापो भृष्टास्तण्डुलाः। पिष्टयवागूरित्येके। पिष्टा एव [१]प्रभ्वाज्यसंयुक्ता इत्यपरे। तेषु पक्षेषु तयोः पक्षयोस्तदर्थान् आज्यसंयुक्ता लाजा इत्यन्ये। तस्मिन् पक्षे तदर्थानां नावघातसंवापः। परिवाप इति ज्यायः, न पिष्टयवागूः। अथोपवेषमादाय प्रथमेन कपालमन्त्रेण भर्जनकपालमधिश्रयेत्। धाना करंभार्थान् भर्जयित्वा परिवापस्य लाजापक्षे स्थालीम्॥ [३]

अथैकादशकपालान्युपदध्यात्। अथ पयस्याया आमिक्षापात्रे तिरःपवित्रं पयः आनीय उत्तरत आमिक्षापात्रमधिश्रयेत्। अथ यवान् भर्जयेत्। घर्मस्य विश्वायुष **इत्यावपनम्। प्रथममर्थलुप्तमन्त्रेण आलोडनं[२] कुर्यादित्येके।** उरु प्रथध्वमुरु[३] वो यज्ञपतिः प्रथताम् **इति [४]त्वग्ग्रहणमर्थलुप्तं मेक्षणेनालोड्य भ्राष्टानुद्वास्य[५] तेषां त्रयः[६] फुल्लास्तान् धानार्थान् एकतः कुर्यात्। अफुल्लान् सक्त्वर्थान् पिष्ट्वा तण्डुलान्[७] पिनष्टि। तत्रोपलाधानात् तन्त्रमधिवप[८]नाद्यावर्तते।** यथाभागं व्यावर्तध्वम् **इत्येव पिष्टानि विभज्य,** प्रणीताभ्योऽध्याहर **इत्युक्त्वा** प्रोक्षणीभ्योऽध्याहर **इति वा। पुरोडाशीयानि समुप्य[९] पिण्डकरणान्तं कृत्वा धाना आज्येन संयुज्य तथा सक्तून् संयुज्य परिवापार्थानि पिष्टान्यावपेत्।** घर्माणि स्थ विश्वायूंषि **इति,** घर्मोऽसि विश्वायुर् **इति वा पुरोडाशमधिश्रित्य प्रथनत्वग्रहणे कृत्वा आमिक्षापक्ष आमिक्षां श्रपयित्वा उद्वासयेत्। पक्षान्तरे चोपनिदध्यात्। पर्यग्निकरणं यथा सर्वाणि हवींषि पर्यग्निकृत्वा** अविदहन्त श्रपयत **इत्युक्त्वा** देवस्त्वा **इत्यपूर्वं सर्वाणि हवींषि चाभिमृश्य अवज्वलनाद्यपोनिनयान्तं[१०] कुर्यात्। आप्यायनं प्राग्वंश एव वेद्यां परेणाहवनीयम्। महावेद्यामित्येके। प्रैषमुक्त्वा स्वयं चतुर्गृहीतं बर्हिरादाय गच्छेत्। मैत्रावरुणचमसाध्वर्युर्मैत्रावरुणचमसमादायानुगच्छेत्।[११] यथार्थमयुजस्त्ववमानैकधनं[१२] दशपरमानैकधनं वाऽऽदाय[१३] परिकर्मिणोऽनुगच्छेयुः। कुंभ्य एकधनस्थाल्ये [१४]वाऽऽनीतेषु सर्वेषु पत्न्यां च नेष्ट्राऽऽनीतायामग्निहोतृचमसं च वसती-**

१. M Ad B प्रभाज्य. २. M Ad B ॰डना. ३. M Ad B ॰मुर. ४. M Ad B ॰त्वग्र॰. ५. M Ad B भ्राष्टाद्वा॰. ६. M Ad B तय. ७. M Ad B लानि. ८. M Ad B ॰तन्त्रमवधि॰. ९. M Ad B च्य. १०. M Ad B ॰ज्वलनाद्याध्यनिन॰. ११. M Ad B ॰चमसादाया॰. १२. M Ad B ॰युजस्त्यवमानेकं॰. १३. M Ad B नादय. १४. M Ad B वातीते॰.

वरीश्चात्वाले होतृवसने संस्पृष्टाः सादयित्वोपास्ते। सर्व एकधनिनो मन्त्रेणोन्नयन्ते॥ [४]

होतृचमसं च मैत्रावरुणचमसं च संस्पृश्य होतृचमसे वसतीवरीभ्योऽधि प्रस्कन्दयति। ताभ्यां वसतीवरीः संस्पृश्येत्येके। तं होतृचमसमनक्ति सकृदेव। प्रति स्तोममित्येके। तथा सति प्रकृतौ चतुष्टोमे चतुः। सकृदेव मन्त्रमुक्त्वा ग्रहमभिमृशतोऽध्वर्युयजमानौ। वसतीवरीश्चैकधनाः। तांश्च पूर्वया द्वारा हविर्धानं प्रपाद्य दक्षिणेन होतारं परिगृह्य पुनर्निष्क्रमय्यापरया द्वारा प्रपाद्योत्तरस्य हविर्धानस्यापरेणाक्षं सादयेयुः। निग्राभ्यास्तु पूर्वया द्वारा प्रपाद्य दक्षिणेन होतारं[१] नीत्वा सादयेद् वा। यद्युक्थः[२] परिधौ निमार्ष्टि, न जुहोति। हुत्वाऽग्निमभिमृजेदित्येके। अस्मिन् पक्षे होमस्तूष्णीको निमार्जनं मान्त्रम्[३]। अतिरात्रे होमनिमार्जने तूष्णीकेऽग्निष्टोमस्य क्रतुकरणं तदत्यग्निष्टोमस्य, यदुक्थस्य तत् षोडशीवाजपेययोः, यदतिरात्रस्य तदप्तोर्यामस्य। उत्तरस्य हविर्धानस्य युगे प्रचरणीं सादयेत्। अपानाय त्वा इति व्रजति विश्वेभ्यस्त्वा भूतेभ्य इत्यन्तेन। यतः प्रजा इत्यादिना जुहोति। यथायतनमादित्यस्थाल्ये समीपे तृतीयमुद्देशेनाव-[४]नयतोऽध्वर्युयजमानौ। निग्राभ्यासु होतृचमसस्थासु वाचयित्वा[५] अभिमृशेदित्येके। निग्राभ्यासु वाचयित्वाऽर्धवेलां राज्ञश्चर्मणि न्युप्यान्तरेण एव नीडे उत्सादयति। न्युप्तस्यार्धं मन्त्रैर्मित्वा धिष्णियं[६] मिनुयात्। राज्ञः फलकयोश्चाभिमर्शनमुभावध्वर्युयजमानौ कुरुतः। सन्तर्पणं कलशात्, निग्राभ्या इत्येके। कलशादिति ज्यायः। हिरण्येन श्रीणाति। हिरण्यरजः प्रक्षिपति॥ [५]

हिरण्यशल्कप्रासन[७]माचार्येणाभिप्रेतमित्येके। न हिरण्यशल्के होतव्याः उदयनीयान्ते समुद्युत्याध्वर्यवे दद्यात्। सर्वत्रैव हिरण्यशल्कश्रवणे अनागसस्त्वा वयम् इति मन्त्रः, सकृदेवाभिषवः। अष्टौकृत्वः[८] सन्दर्शयन्निव शल्कैः प्रहृत्य पञ्चकृत्वो बलवदभिषुणुयात्। सव्येन हस्तेनांशून् पात्रं च धारयन् दक्षिणेन प्रथमनिक्षिप्तावंशू[९] आदाय पात्रस्योपरि निधाय अथ द्वाभ्यां हस्ताभ्यां पात्रमारभ्यांशून् प्रति सोमे संभृते पुनर्दक्षिणेन हस्तेनांशून् प्र[थममष्टौकृत्वः। तान् निष][१०]ज्य पुनरेव हस्तयोः कृत्वा च बलवदभिषुणुयात्। पात्रे[११] कृत्वोपासीत। तथा द्वितीयमेकादशकृत्वः,[१२] तथा तृतीयं द्वादशकृत्वः।

१. M Ad B होरं. २. M Ad B यद्युक्त. ३. M Ad B °र्जनमन्त्रः. ४. M Ad B °यन्तो° मानो. ५. M Ad B °यिता. ६. M धृष्णिं, Ad थिष्णिं. ७. M Ad B °प्राशन°. ८. M Ad B कृत्वा. ९. M Ad B °क्षिप्तावांशू. १०. M Ad B broken. ११. M Ad B पात्रं. १२. M Ad B कृत्वा.

तयोरप्यभिषवयोरादौ सकृन्मन्त्रः त्रिश्चामन्त्रमभिषुत्य अष्टौकृत्वो नवकृत्वश्च[१] बलवदभिषुणुयात्। अंश्वोरासाद[२]नान्तर्धाननिषजनानि दशापवित्रेण[३] परिमार्जन-मुत्तरेण[३] होत्रकव्रजनम्। दक्षिणतो ग्रहं[४] परिगृह्णाति। कर्तव्यवाक्यो[५] वाचनिकः। पात्रं सादयति यथायतनम्। सकृन्निगदः। अत्रापि विसर्गमन्त्रः षट्कृत्व आवर्तते॥ [६] इति प्रथमोऽनुवाकः॥

अथ द्वितीयोऽनुवाकः

॥ अथ प्रयोगकल्पना॥

अथ राजानं चत्वारोऽभिषोतारः पर्युपविशन्ति। पश्चात्प्राङ्मुखोऽध्वर्युः। तमपरेण परितः[६] परिक्रम्य पुरस्तान्नेष्टोत्तरत आग्नीध्रो [दक्षिणतो][७] अध्वर्यु-र्यजमानश्च। चत्वारोऽभिषोतार इत्येके। पूर्वोक्तमेव ज्यायः। दक्षिणेनाग्नीध्र-स्तमपरे[णाध्वर्यु][८]यजमानौ। परीत्य दक्षिणतो ब्रह्माऽऽस्ते। चतुरो ग्राव्ण[९] आदाय चत्वारोऽभिषातारो राजानं विभजन्ति। उन्नेता [तमपरस्मिन् कलश आनयति][१०]। अभिषोतारोऽभिषुण्वन्ति। निग्राभमुपयन्ति सर्वेऽभिषोतारः, अध्वर्युरेव वा कलशात्सदोपसर्गे[११] निग्राभ्याभ्योऽधि यजमानः, स एव सृजति। उन्नेता कलशादित्येके। कलशादेव सर्वदोपसृजेत्। उन्नेतैवेति ज्यायः। [सर्वेषु][१२] पर्यायेषु सम्यगभिषुणुयात्, यथा भूयान् सोमरसो निष्पद्येत। स सासृजति भूय उदकानासिञ्चति। तमुपसृज्य राजानं सर्वेऽभिषोतारोऽभिमृशन्ति।[१३] आप्यायना ब्रूयुः। वैश्यरथकारयोरपि आप्यायस्व इत्येव विशेष उक्तः। त्रिषु महापर्यायेषु यथा नीरसमृजीषं भवति तथाऽभिषुणुयुः। दशापवित्राभ्यां सुतरामभिषवण-चर्मावमृज्य दशापवित्रस्थं सम्यक् संभरण्यां संपीड्याधवनीयेऽवनयेयुः। समी-चीनमुखान् संगतमुखान्। ऋजीषमेभ्यो व्यपोहन्ति।[१४] ग्रावाणं दृढिम्णे यथैष्वध्यूढो द्रोणकलशो न पतितः[१५] स्यात्। पवित्रं प्रतायते[१६]। तस्य मध्ये शुक्लोर्णास्तुका बद्धाः स्यात्। राजक्रये यजमानाय प्रत्ता उदङ्केनाधवनीयादुदच्योन्नेता निग्रा-भ्यास्ववनयेत्। यथा न धारा विच्छिन्द्येत तथाऽवनयेत्। उत्तरेण होतारमागच्छन् दक्षिणेन पात्रं परिहरेत्। दशापवित्रेण

---

१. M Ad B कृत्वं. २. M B अंश्वोराद°, Ad अश्वोरादा°. ३-३. M Ad B से...रेण. ४. M Ad B ग्रहः. ५. M Ad B °वायो. ६. M Ad B परिनौ. ७. M Ad B broken. ८. M Ad B broken. ९. M Ad B ग्राविण्ण. १०. M Ad B broken; cf VādhŚS ७.५.१९. ११. M Ad B °सर्गो. १२. M Ad B broken. १३. M Ad B °शन्त. १४. M Ad B °हस्ति. १५ M Ad B वतित. १६. M Ad B व्रता°.

परिमृज्य नीचहस्तेन परिमृज्यात्। अत्र कर्तव्यवाचो वाचनिकः। मनसेत्युपांशुत्वे [1]पत्नीसंमनसैवेत्येके। आऽऽग्रयणा-दित्यभिविधिः। उपयामगृहीतोऽसि वायये त्वा जुष्टं गृह्णामि **इत्यपयच्छेत्।** वायवे त्वा **इत्येव ब्रूयात्,** न जुष्टं गृह्णामि **इत्यन्ते॥ [१]**

ग्रहणमन्त्रे, एष ते **इत्यादि सादनमन्त्रः। परिमार्गस्तूष्णीकः। पात्रस्योपरि पार्श्वतश्च ये सोमविप्रुषस्तान् परिमार्ष्टि। हिरण्येन श्रीणाति। हिरण्यरजः प्रत्यस्यति। हिरण्यशल्कं [2]प्रास्येदित्याचार्याभिप्राय इत्युक्तम्। प्रागग्रहणमन्त्रात्** भूः **इति ब्रूयात्, मन्त्रान्ते प्रागग्रहणात्** भुवः **इति, सादनमन्त्रान्ते प्राक्सादनात्** सुवर् **इति। पयःसक्तूनां श्रयणे हिरण्यं समुच्चीयते। द्विदेवत्यां दशापवित्रेण परिमृज्य द्विरूर्ध्वं मृज्यार्धस्तेन शुक्रामन्थिनौ तिर्यग् विमृजेत्। प्रस्थापयन्ति पृथक् स्थापयन्ति, धारयन्ति।** इन्द्रियेण वीर्येण भुव[3] **इति गृहीत्वा दक्षिणं जान्वाच्य[4] तस्योपरि उभाभ्यां हस्ताभ्यामभिपद्य हिङ् कृत्वा दशापवित्रेण त्रिः परिमृज्यात्।** एष त योनिर्विश्वेभ्यस्त्वा देवेभ्यः सुवर् **इति सादयति। पात्रस्य तृतीयवेलायामाग्रयणं च षोडशिनं च गृह्णीयात्। [5]ऊर्ध्वबिलमन्यान् पूर्णान् आमयाविनो वर्षकामस्य च वाचयत ऊर्ध्वं सशब्दं यथाऽन्यैरन्तिकस्थैरुपलभ्यते शब्दः। अतिग्राह्याः प्रकृतावनित्याः। नैव विश्वजिति सर्वपृष्ठे नियताः। तत्रोक्तास्तेषां धर्मानिहानुसन्दध्यात्। उक्थ्यं दशापवित्रेण परिमृज्य हस्तेन मध्यं द्विः परिमृज्य ध्रुवमधस्तादनूर्ध्वानेव[6]। अत ऊर्ध्वं सकृद् द्विस्त्रिर्वा यथादेवतमुन्मृज्यात्। उदङ्कं पर्यवस्यति[7] निदधाति। [8]पवमानाद्यावर्तते। निग्राभ्याया[9] द्रप्साभिमन्त्रणं मन्त्रोक्तिमात्रम्। द्रप्सानभिसन्धाय उत्तरयोरपि पवमानग्रहयोर्** उपयामोऽनुषज्याः, **नानुषङ्ग इति। एतदर्थमुन्नेता पूतभृद्बिले पवित्रं वितत्याधवनीयादेकं द्वे त्रीन्वा राज्ञ उदचनान्नयेत्॥ [२]**

अथाध्वर्युः विश्वेभ्यस्त्वा देवेभ्यः **इति पूतभृतमभिमृशेत्। निष्क्राम[10]त्यध्वर्यु-र्हविर्धानाभ्यां पवमानाय सर्पितुमन्वारभमाणः। उत्तरीयादिव्यतिषङ्गं मिथः कुर्युर्यथा न विच्छेदः स्यात्। तद्विच्छेदे महत्प्रायश्चित्तं स्यात्। तत उद्गातारो-ऽन्वारभेरन्। यस्य प्रायश्चित्तानामन्ये प्रशास्त्रादयो येषां वचनमस्ति ये च बहिष्पवमानस्य मार्जनं विजान[11]न्तस्तेनात्मानं पवयितुमिच्छन्तस्तमन्वारभन्ते। [12]होत्रध्वर्योर्ब्रह्मणश्च बृहस्पतिर्** इति च **स्रुवाहुतिः। सप्तहोतृहोमः सकृत्-**

---

१. M Ad B पलसंम°. २. M Ad B प्रोस्येदि°. ३. M Ad B भव. ४. M Ad B °न्वाप्य. ५. M Ad B अध्व°. ६. M Ad B अनेर्ध्वान्. ७. M B पर्यस्यति thus Ad. ८. M Ad B निग्राद्या. ९. M Ad B निष्क्रम°. १०. M Ad B विजना°. ११. M Ad B पवना°. १२. M Ad B होमाध्व°.

सकृत् स्रुवेणादाय प्रचरण्येतरे। सर्वत्रैवं स्रुचा प्रचरण्या वा यत्र चतुर्गृहीतं न विधीयते। स्रुवसाधनत्वं वा सर्वेषाम्। [१]विप्रुड्ढोमेऽनुचरीत्येके। सर्वाचार्याभिप्रायं पवमानेष्वन्यतमः। द्वितीयमपि बर्हिरादाय यत्ते[२] बर्हिर्विचालयन्नध्वर्युः प्रथमः सर्पेत्। प्रह्वास्ते जानूनि सन्धाय वीक्षमाणा नृत्यन्त इव प्रेयुः[३]। यदन्यत्तद् आस्तावे[४] प्रास्येत्। भूतमसि भूते मा धा इति प्रस्तोतुर्मुखमीक्षेत। प्रस्तरार्थं बर्हिः प्रदायोपाकरणं जपेत्। इन्द्रवन्त इत्येतावदुच्चैर्ब्रूयात्[५]। मुखमसि मुखं भूयासम् इति स्तुवत उद्गातुर्मुखमीक्षते। सामन्ननुद्रुते पूतभृति बिले दशापवित्रं वितत्योन्नेताऽऽधवनीयात् प्राञ्चं राजानं पूतभृति संपवयेत् ग्रहावकाशचर्यर्थम्। अथाध्वर्युर्दशहोतारं व्याख्याय मध्यमाया प्रस्तावे कृते[६] श्येनोऽसि इति वाचयेत्। स्तोत्रे परिसमाप्ते प्रस्तरीयं बर्हिरादाय यथास्थानमपिसृजेद्वा। सर्वेषु स्तोत्रेषूत्तरं स्तोमभागम्। अथाध्वर्युणा प्रेषितोऽग्नीद्[७] धिष्णियान् विहरिष्यन् सन्दंशं च सतं चादायाग्नीध्रीयात् सन्दंशेन[८] सतेऽङ्गारान् समुप्योत्तरेणाग्नीध्रीयं परीत्य प्रत्यङ्ङासीन आग्नीध्रीये विहृत्याङ्गारानादाय यथेतमेत्य पूर्वया द्वारा सदः प्रपाद्य प्रत्यङ्ङासीनोऽन्तःसदसि धिष्णियान् विहरेद् आवपनक्रमेण॥ [३]

अच्छावाकस्य धिष्णियं विहृत्यापसलैः पर्यावृत्य [९]प्राङासीनो मार्जालीयं[९] धिष्णियं विहरेत्। आग्नीध्रीय एवावशिष्टानङ्गारानन्ते निवपेत्। हृतान् धिष्णियानुप समादध्यात्, यथा [१०]प्राग्व्याघारणान्नानुगच्छेयुः। अथाध्वर्युस्तृतीयसवन इव तानभिजुहोति। तद् व्याघारणमाग्नीध्रीयं होत्रीयं मार्जालीयं च नाभिजुहुयादित्येके। नैवानयोः सवनयोः[१०] व्याघारणमाचार्याभिप्राय इत्यपरे। बर्हिःस्तरणं पृष्ठ्यामनु बर्हिर्भृष्टेः[११]स्तरणमोत्तरवेद्याः। पुरोडाशशब्देन सवनीयानि हवींष्युपलक्ष्यन्ते। अलङ्करणशब्देनोद्वासनम्। पात्र्यां पूर्वाधानाभ्य उपस्तृणीते दक्षिणतः करंभार्थं पश्चात् परिवापार्थम्। चरुविकारत्वेनोपस्तरणमनुद्धृत्य सादनं न चापि होममध्यतः पुरोडाशस्य पयस्याया उत्तरतस्तूष्णीम्। यद्यामिक्षा[१२] पयस्या स्यादामिक्षार्थमुपस्तरणम्। तानि यथाप्रकृत्युद्वास्य पूर्वया द्वारोपनिर्हृत्यापरया द्वारा सदः प्रपाद्य ब्रह्मसदनस्योपरि हविर्धानं प्रपाद्य दक्षिणेनाज्यानि परिहृत्य निष्क्रमय्य जघनेनोत्तरवेदिं स्तीर्णे बर्हिषि सादयेत्। आमिक्षापक्षे सादनम् इदम् इन्द्रियम् इति मन्त्रस्य भावः[१३]। शृतं मयि श्रयताम् इत्यभिमृशेत्॥ [४]

---

१. M Ad B पितृड्ढोमे. २. M Ad B यत्ते ?. ३. M Ad पेयुः. ४. M Ad B° °स्तोवे. ५. M Ad B इत्थेके ताव. ६. M Ad B कृतते. ७. M Ad B °ग्नीन्. ८. M Ad B सन्देशे°. ९-९. MB °मार्जीयं, Ad प्रासीना मार्जीयं. १०-१०. M Ad B text from व्याघरणान्नानुगच्छेयुः to सवनयोः repeated. ११. M Ad बर्हिमृष्टे, B °भ्रुष्टे. १२. M Ad B °मिक्षां. १३. M Ad B भावा.

तत्र सायंदोहत्वे यत्पृथिव्याम् **इत्यादि सादयेत्**। दध्यामिक्षामन्थिनस्तु[१] **इत्यभिमृशेत्। प्रतिप्रस्थाता सवनीयं पशुमाहृत्यान्तिके स्थापयेत्। अध्वर्युः** विष्णो त्वं नो अन्तम **इत्यादि प्रतिपद्यते। राजानं सुतमसुतं च कृत्स्नं यज्ञोपचार आग्नीध्रीयादीनामुपस्थानमन्त्रैरभिमृशेत्। उपस्थानपक्षे याजमानमेतदुपस्थानम्**[२]**। आश्विनं द्रोणकलशाद् गृह्णाति। परिपात्रेण सर्वत्रैवं द्रोणकलशाद् ग्रहणे।**[३] प्राणाय मे **इत्युपांशुपात्रमवेक्षते**। तस्य ते प्राणमुन्मृजे **इति**। इदम् **स्थाने प्राणादीन् निदध्यात्**। इदम् **इत्येवेत्येके। प्राणम् इत्येव ज्यायः। यत्कामो वा भवति यं कामं कामयते तं चतुर्थ्या निर्दिशेत्। मन्त्रान्ते** भूत्यै, ब्रह्मवर्चसाय, आयुषे, अभिचाराय **इत्येषां कामानां च चतुर्णामेकम्**। अपानाय मे **इत्यन्तर्यामपात्रम्**। चक्षुर्भ्यां मे वर्चोदौ वर्चसे पवेथां तस्य मे रासाथां तयोर्वां भक्षीय तयोर्वां चक्षुषी उन्मृजे ब्रह्मवर्चसाय **इति शुक्रामन्थिनौ**। आत्मने[४] मे वर्चोदा वर्चसे पवस्व तस्य ता आत्मानमुन्मृजे ब्रह्मवर्चसाय **इत्याग्रयणम्। एवमुत्तरेष्वपि पर्यायेषु**। वीर्याय मे **इत्यतिग्राह्येषु प्रत्येकमावर्तते**। वीर्याय मे वर्चोदा वर्चसे पवध्वं तस्य मे राध्वं तेषां वो भक्षीय तेषां वो वीर्यमुन्मृजे ब्रह्मवर्चसाय **इति सह सर्वानवेक्षेतेत्येके। ऋतुपात्रयोः** [५]**सोममासिच्यावेक्षेत। अनासिच्येत्येके। द्विषदत्र मन्त्रोक्तिः**। विष्णोर्जठरमसि वर्चोदा तस्य ते जठरमुन्मृजे **इति त्रिष्वनुषजति। यावदुक्तमित्येके। पृषदाज्यमवेक्षते** [विश्वेभ्यो मे रूपेभ्यो वर्चोदा वर्चसे पवस्व तस्य ते][६] विश्वानि रूपाण्युन्मृजे **[इति]**। पशुभ्य **इत्येके। यथा** अपां पशूनुन्मृजे **इति**। पशुभ्यः **इत्यपरे। यथापाठमिति ज्यायः**। पशुभ्यः **इत्यत्र यथाभीप्सितं कामं ब्रूयात्। ग्रहावकाशचरणं** [७]**याजमानमित्येके॥ [५]**

यजमानेनापि सर्वैः सह जपनीया इत्यपरे। स्रुचो[र्दशहोतारमध्वर्यु][८]**ब्रूयात्। अप उपस्पृश्य निष्क्रम्य यूपरशनामादाय** [९]परिवीयमाणायानुब्रूहि **इत्युक्त्वोदूह्य पूर्वां रशनां नाभिदयति। अध्वर्युः**[१०] **प्रवरिष्यन् द्वौ शकलावादायाश्रावयेत्। इतरेष्वेकैकम्**। [जुष्टो वाचो भूयासम् **इति प्रवृताहुतिं जुहुते होता। अध्वर्युः**][११] **प्रतिप्रस्थाता उभावपि द्वेद्वे इत्येके। ब्रह्मणः प्रति ब्रह्मसंस्कार इति संकल्प्य। एवं सर्वत्र होतुराहुतिं षष्ठीं** [१२][**जुहो**]**तीत्यत्र द्विर्दश होतुराहुतिं जुहुयात्। वपया प्रचर्य**[१३]

१. M Ad B °थिनो तु°. २. M Ad B °नमेषमु°. ३. M Ad °णेन. ४. M Ad B आत्मान. ५. M Ad B सामं. ६. M Ad B om; cf. *VādhŚS* 7.8.19. ७. M Ad B याजनि. ८. M Ad B broken; cf. VādhŚS 7.8.20. ९. M Ad B परिपीय°. १०. M Ad B °ध्वर्युं. ११. M Ad B broken; cf. VādhŚS 7.8.28-29. १२. M Ad B broken. १३. M Ad B पर्या°.

आपो हि ष्ठा मयोभुव **इति तृचेन मार्जयित्वा संप्रसर्पेयुः**[१]॥ [६] इति द्वितीयोऽनुवाकः॥

अथ तृतीयोऽनुवाकः

अत्र अग्नीत् पुरोडाशम् **इत्यध्वर्युः संप्रेष्येत्। पशुपुरोडाशाभावे** ब्रह्मन् पृषदाज्यम् **इत्यादि** हृदयजिह्व **इति प्रतिप्रस्थाता। अध्वर्युः प्रतिप्रस्थाता ब्रह्मा यजमान इत्युत्करोपस्थानादि प्रतिपद्येरन्। सदस्योऽपि महारात्र उत्थाय सदस्य-कल्पे उक्तेन प्रवरणाहुत्यन्तं कृत्वान्तर्वेद्यो वा** [२]**वपाहोमासादनादित्योत्करोप-स्थानाद्योऽन्तर देवतोपस्थानात् कृत्वा यथोक्तं प्रतिपद्यते। अध्वर्युर्यजमानश्च पूर्वया द्वारा प्रतिपद्येते इत्येके। परिसमाप्यान्ते** नमः[३] सदसस्पतये **इति यजमानो ह्यात्मानं प्रेक्षते। दक्षिणं द्वार्बाहुं निश्रयमाणोऽध्वर्युरुपविशति, उत्तरं प्रतिप्रस्थाता। संप्रसृप्तावपि ब्रह्मयजमानावैष्टिकेषु पाशुकेषु च पुनरेत्य दक्षिण आहवनीयस्यासाते। सौमिकेषु सदसि यथाद्रुत्याध्वर्युर्** यन्मे अग्ने **इत्यनुपूर्वं हवींष्यभिमृश्य** यस्ते शुष्म **इत्यभिघार्याज्यभागौ यजेत्॥** [१]

आज्यभागौ कृत्वा पुरोडाशैः सह कृद्भिश्चरित्वा हवींषि होत्र उपनिधाय द्विदेवत्यैश्चरेत्। दशापवित्रेण परिमार्गो हिरण्यशल्कश्रयणं च प्रतिग्रहेष्वित्येके। नेत्याचार्याभिप्रायः। अध्वर्युरेव मन्त्रेण निष्क्रामतीत्येके। उभावपीति ज्यायः। निष्क्रामन् पुनः प्रविशन्नपि प्रतिप्रस्थाताऽध्वर्युं परिगृह्णीयात्। अनुमन्त्रयेते अध्वर्युयजमानौ[४]**। द्वितीय इत्येके। होत्रे पात्रं प्रदातुं प्रत्यङ् द्रवन् प्रतिप्रस्थातारं प्रतिगृह्य प्रसलैः पर्यावृत्य द्रवेत्। प्राग् द्रवन्नपिसलैः प्रैषानन्तरमुन्नेता उत्तरवेद्यां च चमसान् निधाय होतृचमसमेव प्रथममुन्नयेत्। यथोपपादमितरान्**[५]**। द्रोण-कलशात् सोभयतः शुक्रता। पूर्वेण हविर्धाने अध्वर्युर्गत्वा जघनेनोत्तरवदिं तिष्ठेत्। प्रतिप्रस्थाता निष्क्रामन् मन्थिनाऽध्वर्युं परिगृह्णीयात्। अध्वर्युश्च सग्रहो दक्षिणेन यजमानं गत्वाऽऽयन्नु[त्तरवेदिमधितिष्ठति]**[६]**। उभावपि**[७] **उपस्पृशतः। चमसाध्वर्युभिश्चमसेष्वात्तेष्वाश्रावयेदध्वर्युरेव। वषट्कृतानुवषट्कृतयोर्मन्त्रे-णाध्वर्युः, तूष्णीं चमसाध्वर्यवः।** चिकित्वन्तस्मा **इत्यन्ते। उभयोः साधारणम्।** प्रयन्तु सदस्या **इत्येकत्वे बहुवचनम्। होत्रकाणां** चमसाध्वर्यवः **इत्युक्त्वा होतृ-चमसे यजमानचमसे च पर्यावृत्य स्वं स्वं चमसं सदः प्रापयन्ति। पात्रं सादयित्वा**

---

१. M Ad B °सर्पयुः. २. M Ad B °होमासादित्यो°. ३. M Ad B समनः. ४. M Ad B °मानो. ५. M Ad B °मितरा. ६. M Ad B broken. ७. M Ad B उभावप.

निष्क्रान्ते बहिरध्वर्यौ होत्रकाच्छावाकवर्जानां होत्रकाणां चमसाध्वर्यवः स्वं स्वं चमसं सकृत्-सकृत् द्रोणकलशादभ्युन्नीय वषट्कृतेऽध्वर्युणा हुतं-हुतं तथैव प्रापयन्ति॥ [२]

उभावध्वर्यू अग्निमभि पर्यावृत्तौ यथेतं परेत्य प्रत्यङ्ङाद्रवतः। ततोऽध्वर्युः सह पोत्रा[1] **हविर्धानं प्रविश्य तूष्णीमाग्रयणे संस्रावमवनीयापसलैः**[2] **पर्यावृत्य निष्क्रम्य दक्षिणेन यजमानं परिगृह्य मन्त्रेण होतृचमसे समवनयेत्। उभावपि यजमानचमसे प्रस्कन्दतः। होमाय प्रतिप्रस्थाताऽवशेषयेत्। इह होत्रादीनां चमसं प्रयन्ति। अनीकस्पृशमङ्गारं कृत्वा यथा परिधिर्न दहेत्तथा कृत्वा तस्मिन् मन्थिनः संस्रावं जुहोति। निधत्तः पात्रे यथायतनम्।** अग्नीदुपह्वयस्व **इति सर्वेषां वषट्कर्तृणां प्रदर्शनम्। ते सर्वे** उपहूत उपहूत **इति अदृष्टार्थे समुपहवः। दृष्टार्था इत्यपरे। अध्वर्युर्** अयाड् **इति प्रतिब्रूते। पुनः** स भद्रमकर्यो नः **इत्यादि होतैव प्रतिगृह्णाति। अस्मा अध्वर्यवे पुरोडाशशकलं सवनीयपुरोडाशस्य उपस्थ एनम् अध्वर्युः चक्षुषोः प्रत्येकं प्रतिनिधाय** चक्षुष्पा **इति मैत्रावरुणपात्रं भक्षयेत्। भक्षयित्वा पुनः प्रतिहरेत्। परिहृत्य होतृचमसमिडामादधाति। न चास्य** सुरूपवर्षवर्ण एहि **इतीदानीं यजमानो ब्रूयात्। अवान्तरेडामनवत्तेडानां पुरोडाशानामवद्येत्। उपोद्यच्छन्ति पुरोडाशान्। सह दारुपात्र्या उपप्रगृह्णन्ति। चमसानुपरि च निधाय सर्वे संविभजेरन्। यजमानस्तूभयश्चैतर्हि पत्नीशालायां यत् किञ्चिद्धविष्यं प्राश्नाति। अथ सर्वे निमित्तिनः सोमं समूपहूय भक्षयन्ति**[3]**। त्रीणि भक्षणनिमित्तानि वषट्कारौ होमाभिषवौ समाख्या चेति। वषट्कर्तुः प्रथमः, ततो होमाभिषवयोः कर्तुः॥ [३]**

ततः समाख्यातुः[4]**, ततः शुक्रामन्थिप्रचारे होतृवषट्कारे चमसाहुता इति। होतृचमसमवशिष्टाद्धोताऽग्रे भक्षयेत्। होता भक्षयन्नध्वर्योरुपहवमिच्छेत। प्रशास्त्रादिचमस उद्गातृचमसे त्रिषूद्गातृषु ब्रह्मयजमानसदस्यानां चमसेषु**[5] **चमसिभिरेव अध्वर्युर्होतारं मिथश्चोपहवमिष्ट्वा** वसुमद्गणस्य **इति होतृचमसं भक्षयते। अथ प्रशास्त्रादिचमसं स्वं चमसं वषट्कारनिमित्तेन स्वं चमसं तथा तथाऽध्वर्युस्तं तं चमसम्। अथाध्वर्युस्तमेव होतृप्रशास्त्रोरुपहवमिष्ट्वा, अथ ब्राह्मणाच्छंसी पोता नेष्ट्राग्नीध्रो** [6]**होताऽध्वर्योरुपहवमिष्ट्वा स्वं स्वं चमसम्। तथाऽध्वर्युस्तं तं चमसमुपहवमिष्ट्वा भक्षयति। होता पूर्वं स्वं समाख्यायैव सर्वे**

---

१. M Ad B सहपात्रो. २. M Ad B °मविनी°. ३. M Ad B °यत्विति. ४. M Ad B °ख्यातुं. ५. M B च समेषु. ६. M Ad B होत्रा°.

भक्षयन्ति। ग्रहसंस्रावनिमित्तं मिथः समुपहूय चमसमाप्यायस्व **इत्याप्यायन्ति। वैश्वरथकारयोरपि**[१] आप्यायस्व **इत्येवाप्यायनमन्त्रः। तृणैरुपसंगृह्य पुरोडाश-प्राशनानन्तरमेव वाजिनानन्तरमेव वाजिनचर्यादीनि कर्तव्यानि। अथ** अच्छावाक वदस्व यत्ते वाद्यम् **इति ब्रूयात्। वाद्य उत्तरे होतारं ब्रूयात्।** ब्राह्मणोऽयमुपहव-मिच्छते[२] **इत्युपहूतेऽध्वर्युर्** उन्नीयमानाय **इति प्रेष्येत्। अच्छावाकचमसाध्व-र्युरुन्नयन्नुभयतः शुक्रं**[३] **करोति। अथाध्वर्युरच्छावाकचमसमन्वारभेत्यादि करोति। अच्छावाके** 'अच्छावाक सीद' **इति प्रैषार्थं** [कृते][४] **सर्वैःक्रियते। अच्छावाको यथाक्रमं स्वे धिष्णिय उपसीदेत्। नेष्टा तु पत्नीमपरस्य द्वारस्य दक्षिणादाबाह्वोर्दक्षिणतः पन्नेजनीः सादयति।** पत्नी सादनकर्त्री असत् **इत्यग्नीत् ब्रूयात्॥** [४] इति तृतीयोऽनुवाकः समाप्तः॥

॥ इत्यग्निष्टोमाख्यः षष्ठः प्रपाठकः समाप्तः ॥

॥ इति आ[चा]र्य[५] शिवश्रोणस्य कृतिः प्रयोगक्लृप्तिः[५] समाप्ता ॥

---

१. B कारयोऽपि. २. M Ad B ऽयमुपनव. ३. M Ad B शक्रं. ३. M Ad B broken. ४. M Ad B आर्य. ५. M B प्रयोगकल्पना.

अनुक्रमणिका - I

व्याख्यात-पारिभाषिकपदानामनुक्रमणी

अच्चुकारम्—शब्दमकुर्वन्। १.४.४

अतिग्राह्याः—प्रकृतावनित्याः। नैव विश्वजिति सर्वपृष्ठे नियताः। ६.२.२

अतिवाचयति—पूर्वं मन्त्रमतीत्य वाचयति। ५.३.४

अत्यूहति–प्रयच्छति। ५.५.१

अधःशायी—खट्वादि प्रतिषेधः। प्रासादमञ्चादावपि न शयीतेत्येके। ३.६.१

अनतिदृश्नम्—अधिद्रष्टुमशक्यम्। २.२.३

अनुग्रन्थति–विस्रंसयति। ५.३.२

अनुपरमेण—शीघ्रम्। ५.४.१

अन्तःशालं—शालाभ्यन्तरम्। ५.१.७

अन्वर्जति–विसृजति। ५.३.३

अपर्यावर्तयन्—पर्यावर्तमानमकुर्वन्। ४.३.४

अपानग्रहाः—अपानभृन्मन्त्राः अपानग्रहाः। १.३.१

अपिव्रताः—पुत्रा दुहितरोऽप्रत्ता भ्रातरोऽविभक्ताः। सपिण्डा इत्येके। ५.६.१

अपोर्णुते—प्रावरणमपनयति। ५.३.३

अप्रस्तराय—अप्रतिस्तरणाय, ५.३.५

अभिघारयेत्—सर्वतः सन्तर्पयेत्। २.२.३

अभिवान्या—अन्यवत्सा, यस्या नास्ति स्ववत्सः। ३.४.१

अम्बरीषम्—भर्जनपात्रम्। ३.४.१

अर्धव्रतम्—अर्धस्तनव्रतम्। ५.४.६

अर्धस्तनव्रतम्–द्वेधा विभज्यार्धस्तनव्रतम्। ५.४.६

अलंकरणम्—अलङ्करणशब्देनोद्वासनम्। ६.२.४

अलंकारः—भूयसोपस्तरणं, स्वरूपापादनं वा सर्वेषां हविषाम्। अलङ्कुर्वन्त्यानुपूर्वं हवींषि गन्धपुष्पेणाज्येन वा। ३.१.१

अविवेकम्—विवेकवर्जः, सकृदेव वा वितुषीभावः। २.४.२

अश्वशफबुध्ने—अश्वशफाकारे बुध्ने। ६.१.२

असंवपन्ति—अमिश्रयन्ति। २.२.१

अस्यति—आस्यति परिव्यये रशनागुणे॥ ४.१.३

आपर्वणम्—पर्वदिवसात्प्रागित्यर्थः। १.५.१

आस्तावः—दक्षिणेन चात्वालं यत्र बहिष्पवमानेन स्तुवन्ति, यत्र ब्रह्माऽऽस्ते सदसि दक्षिणेन होत्रकान्, यत्र हारियोजनीभिश्चरति, यत्र धानाभिः पितृकार्यं कुर्वन्ति मार्जालीयसमीपे, यत्र निर्मन्थ्येन चरति। ५.८.१

उत्काशयति—उदीक्षयति। ४.१.३

उत्तुषान्—उन्मुक्ततुषान्, पृथग्गततुषान्। २.१.३

उदिङ्गयति–उत्कम्पयति, पाणिना चोर्ध्वं गमयति। २.१.३

उपचारणतः—उपस्तंभतः। ५.५.३

उपवसथः—उपवसथो नाम यजनीयेऽहनि प्रधानकर्म क्रियते, ततः पूर्वेद्युरुच्यते। यथा दर्शपूर्णमासयोर्यस्मिन् देवता यथा च सोमस्य यस्मिन्नैन्द्र आलभ्यते पशुः। एवमेवान्यत्रापि पूर्वेद्युरभिधीयत उपवसथशब्देन। १.१.२.

उपवेषः—उपधानार्थो नित्योऽन्यः शाखामूलम्। तेनाङ्गारनिर्वर्तनप्रतिनोदनावर्त्तनानि कुर्यात्। २.२.१,

उपव्याहरणम्—ऋत्विजां सकाशे करिष्यमाणस्य कर्मणो व्याहरणं सङ्कीर्तनम्। १.१.३.

उपस्पर्शनम्—अभिवादनं तत्तदभिमृश्य। १.५.२

एकस्तनव्रतम्—सकृद्दुग्धमेकस्तनव्रतम्। ५.४.६

ओन्नक्षत्राद्—उदितनक्षत्रकालात्। ५.१.७

कवोत्तानम्—ईषदुत्तानम्। ४.२.३

कुण्ड्या—जलप्रस्रवणार्थं सुषिरवती। १.४.४

क्लृप्तचषालः—प्रतिमुक्तचषालः। ४.१.२

क्षीरम्—दुग्धमात्रम्। ५.३.२

क्षुरगन्धिः—क्षुरपथं करोति। ५.१.५

गृह्याः—पिता पुत्रा भ्राता च अप्रत्ता दुहितारश्च। अविभक्ताः सपिण्डा इत्येके। कल्याणकर्मणः सपिण्डा इत्यपरे। ३.२.३

जोषंकृतेषु—तूष्णीमेव कृतेषु प्रारब्धेषु। तूष्णीं शब्दोऽत्र लक्षणयोपांशुत्वप्रकर्षवचनः। ६.१.१

तप्तव्रतः—उष्णव्रतः। ५.३.५

तप्त्वेति–व्रतोपलक्षणम्। तप्तं व्रतयित्वा। ५.१.८

तूष्णीम्—तूष्णीं शब्दोऽत्र लक्षणयोपांशुत्वप्रकर्षवचनः। ६.१.१

तृणग्लाभम्—तृणकलापीम्। ५.३.५

त्रिवृत्—त्रिगुणम्। ३.२.२

त्वग्ग्रहणम्—अद्भिरभिमर्शनम्। २.२.१

दृढीकरोति—अशिथिलीकरोति। ५.३.५

दृंहयति–दृढयति। ४.१.३

द्रुपदः—विष्टम्भनार्थं तिर्यक् स्थापितं काष्ठं, द्रुपदाख्यमनुष्ठानफलकम्। ५.३.३

नद्धकम्–बन्धनप्रतिबद्धा ५.१.८

नभ्यस्थे—नभ्यफलके स्थिते। ५.५.१

निघातः—निघातो नाम बलवद्विसार्य तस्यान्तेषु समन्ततः शङ्कूनां निघातः। ५.२.१

निपदःकाले—निपदनकाले, शयनकाले। ५.८.१

निपिचति—विकुञ्चति। ५.१.६

निबाधते—नीचैर्बाधते। ५.५.३

निवर्तयति—पृथक् प्रेरयति। ३.३.१

पयः–शान्तफेनं शीतम्। ५.३.२

परिचितम्—परिचिन्मन्त्रेण परिचितम्। २.२.१

परिपात्रेण—सर्वत्रैवं द्रोणकलशाद् ग्रहणेन। ६.२.५

परिप्रजनयति—परितो गमयति। आनीता अपः संयौति मेक्षणेन। २.२.१

परिवापः—परिवापः भृष्टास्तण्डुलाः। पिष्टयवागुरित्येके। पिष्टा एव प्रभ्वाज्यसंयुक्ता इत्यपरे। ६.१.३

परिवासयति—छिनत्ति। ४.१.१

परिव्यये—रशनागुणे। ४.१.२

परोक्षं मनुष्यनामकथनं —पर्यायशब्दैरभिधानम्। ५.१.६

परोप्तपुनराधानम्, परोप्तपुनराधेयं—इयन्तं कालमग्नीनुत्सृज्याधास्यमिति यदाधानं तत् परोप्तपुनराधानम्। १.४.१

पर्यस्यति—निदधाति। ६.२.२

पल्पूलनम्—रजकधवलिकरणम्। ६.२.२

पुनरुत्सृष्टोऽनड्वान्—जीर्णमुत्सृज्य पोषयित्वा कर्षणादिभिः पुनरपि जीर्णमुत्सृष्टः। १.४.१

पुनरुत्स्यूतम्—जीर्णं वासः प्रोतम् १.४.१

पुनर्निष्कृतः -जीर्णः पुनः संस्कृतः १.४.१

पुरोडाशम्—कूष्माण्डमात्रं कुक्कुटाण्डमात्रं वा ३.१.१; पुरोडाशशब्देन सवनीयानि हवींष्युपलक्ष्यन्ते। ६.२.४

पूर्वायतम्—प्रागायतम्। २.२.१.

पृश्नयः—'प्राचीदिशाम्' इत्येवमाद्याः (मन्त्राः) पृश्नयः। १.३.१; 'वायुरसि प्राणो नाम' इत्येवमाद्याः पञ्च समाः। १.३.१

पृष्टीर्धावतः—पृष्ठे शोधयतः, उन्नयति तीरत आगमयति। ३.२.७

प्रतिधुक्-पुनः प्रस्नुतोपात्तम् ५.३.२

प्रतिमोचयति—तत्पुत्रादावुपनयति। ५.१.४

प्रतियौति—अपिदधाति। ४.२.३

प्रतिवचनम्—अनुज्ञानादिकं वा स्यात् प्रतिवचनम्। अथवा तेषामेव सन्निधौ तथैवोपविश्य 'सर्वकामोऽग्नीनाधास्ये' इति मनसा त्रिः संकल्प्य तदेव वाचा त्रिर्व्याहरेत्। १.१.३

प्रधिकम् —प्रधावुपधेययोरन्यतरत्। २.२.१

प्रपतनम्—मरणम्। ५.१.७

प्रप्रापयति—पातयति। ४.१.१

प्रबाहुक्—समीचीने। ६.१.२

प्रम्णाय—प्रमृद्य हस्तेन। २.२.१

प्रस्थापयन्ति-पृथक् स्थापयन्ति, धारयन्ति। ६.२.२

प्राचः—प्रागपवर्गाम् २.२.२

प्राणग्रहाः—प्राणभृन्मन्त्राः 'अयं पुरोभवः' इत्येवमाद्याः, १.३.१

प्राशित्रप्राशनम्—आप्राणसंमर्शनाद्भिः प्राशनम्। २.५.३

बद्धमवस्यन्ति—बन्धनादि विस्रस्य सम्यक् निर्णिज्य। ५.५.१

भक्ताशनम्—सकृदशनम्, यथालाभमशनमित्यपरे। १.३.२

भक्ताशी-सकृदाशी। ३.६.१

मन्त्रमुष्टयः—मन्त्रवन्तः ५.३.४

महापरिधयः-द्राघिष्ठाः, परिकृष्टाः परिणाहेन च महान्तः। अत्र सवनीयार्थं गार्हपत्याहवनीययोरभ्याधाय शाखां छित्त्वा यजमानस्य व्रतदुहो वत्समपाकुर्यात्। ५.८.२

यावन्मूतं—यावत्क्लिन्नम्। ५.२.३

संकाशयति—समीक्षयति। ५.२.३

लोहितायसः—ताम्रमय अयो विकारः ३.१.२

वयांसि-निष्क्रयमाणानि, अधिदेयानीत्येके। ५.३.२

वर्तन्याम्—वर्त्मनि। ५.५.१

विगृह्णाति—विविधं गृह्णाति। ५.३.४

विशातयेत्—सन्ततमापरस्मात् तीरात् तेष्वपारे तीरे उदकान्त यदुच्छिष्येत तन्न्यसेत्। ५.१.७

विषूके—विशाखे स्थूणायाः कर्णयोरन्तराले। ५.५.२

विषूचीनाग्रम्—व्यस्ताग्रम्। ४.१.३

व्यन्तान् करोति—पृथक् करोति। १.४.२

शकलम्—अभिमन्थनशकलम्। ४.२.१

वृषणौ—वृषणस्थाणौ शकलद्वयमेव। ४.२.१

शरः—आविर्भूतस्नेहम् ५.३.२

शुल्बिणी—शुल्बिणी नामोत्तरनाभिच्छादनार्थं वाधूलकेषु प्रसिद्धः कश्चिदाकृतिविशेषः। ५.४.६

शृतम्—पक्वम्। ५.३.२

संतराम्—सम्यक्तरां समायच्छते। ५.३.५

संप्रगृह्णाति-सम्यक् प्रस्नावयन् गृह्णाति। २.३.६

संमिनोति—संगमयति। २.३.५

संवाहयेयुः-संप्रवाहयेयुः। ५.१.८

संशरणम्—सर्वसाधारण्येन व्याधिना मरणम्। अविज्ञातव्याधेर्निश्चेष्टीभूतस्य मरणम्। पौरुषो वा वधः पुरुषचैतन्यात्। ५.१.७

सांकाशिने—समीचीने, संकाशस्थिते वा। ५.५.१

समवशमनम्—सम्यगवधानम्। ५.६.१

समीचीनमुखान्—संगतमुखान्। ६.२.१

सशब्दम्—यथाऽन्यैरन्तिकस्थैरूपलभ्यते शब्दः। ६.२.२

साग्रम्—समाग्रम्। २.२.२

सासृजति—भूय उदकानासिञ्चति। ५.२.१

सीव्यति—छादयति ऊर्ध्वाग्रैर्दर्भैः कुशलतया ग्रन्थिरहितामेव। ५.५.२

सेभुम्—शिंघाणिकारे। ५.१.८

स्निहानम्—स्नेहमश्रुनिष्ठीवितमित्यपरे। नासिकाश्मश्रुनिष्ठीवितम्। ५.१.८

स्पन्द्या—शकटयोजन्यभिधानी, ५.३.३; मानरज्जुः। ५.४.४

हविर्धाने—शकटे प्रतियुक्तचक्रे यत्र हविर्धीयतेऽभिषुतोऽनभिषुतश्च सोमः। ५.५.१

—०—

अनुक्रमणिका - II

उद्धृतमन्त्रानुक्रमणी

अ

अक्रन् कर्म, **३**.२.४ (तैसं. १.८.३.५)

अगानग्नीत्, **१**.३.२; **२**.३.२ (तैसं. २.६.५.६)

अगा३नग्नीत् श्रावय स्वगा दैव्या होतृभ्यः, **३**.२.५ (तैसं. २.६.५.५)

अग्नय आज्यस्यावदीयमानस्यानुब्रूहि, **४**.२.५

अग्नये देवेभ्यः पितृभ्यः समिध्यमानाय, **३**.४.५ (तैब्रा. १.६.९.१)

अग्नये समिध्यमानायानुब्रूहि, **२**.३.१; **४**.२.१ (तैसं. ६.३.७.१)

अग्निं वैश्वानरम्, **१**.४.३ (तैसं. ४.१.५.५)

अग्निं होतारम्, **१**.३.१ : ७; **२**.४.३ : २१; **३**.१.१ (तैसं. १.५.१०.९)

अग्निं गृह्णामि, **३**.६.१ (तैब्रा. ३.७.४.३)

अग्निं देवानां प्रीणामि स मा प्रीतः प्रीणातु, **५**.४.३

अग्निर्ज्योतिर्ज्योतिरग्निः स्वाहा, **१**.४.३ (तैब्रा. २.१.९.२)

अग्निर्द्वेषांसि, **२**.४.४ (तैब्रा. ३.७.६.७)

अग्निर्भेषांसि, **३**.६.२

अग्निर्मा दुरिष्टात्पातु, **२**.४.६ (तैसं. १.६.३.१)

अग्नीदग्निम्, **३**.३.३

अग्नीदग्निं सकृत्सकृत् समृड्ढि, **३**.४.५

अग्नीदुपह्वयस्व, **६**.३.३

अग्नी देवौ होतारौ देवान् यजेतां विविद्वांसौ चिकित्वदा च वहताम्, **३**.२.४

अग्नीदौपयजानङ्गारानाहर, **४**.३.५ (वाधूश्रौ. ५.९.२७)

अग्नीनाधास्ये, **१**.१.३ (वाधूश्रौ. १५.५.१)

अग्नीभ्यां समिध्यमानाभ्याम् अनुब्रूहि, **३**.२.४

अग्नीषोमौ यज, **२**.३.३

अग्नेः स्विष्टकृतोऽहम् प्रतिष्ठां गमेयम् **४**.४.३

अग्ने देवेद्ध, **२**.४.४ (तैसं. १.६.२.१०)

अग्नेरहं देवयज्ययाऽऽयुष्मान् यज्ञेन प्रतिष्ठां गमेयम्, **२**.४.४; **४**.४.३ (वाधूश्रौ.३.८. ११)

अग्ने रेतः, **१**.१.५ (तैब्रा. १.२.१.४)

अग्नेर्जिह्वासि, **२**.२.२; **३**.२.४; ३.२; ४.३; **५**.६.३[२]; **६**.१.१ (तैसं. १.१.१०.१६)

अग्ने वाजजित्, **२**.४.४; **३**.६.३

अग्ने व्रतपते, **२**.४.१ (तैसं. ५.१०.८; वासं. १.५)

अग्ने हव्यं रक्ष, **२**.१.३ (वासं. १.११; तु.तैसं. १.१.४.१९)

अच्छावाक वदस्व यत्ते वाद्यम्, **६**.३.४

अच्छावाक सीद, **६**.३.४ (ऐब्रा. ६.१४.८)

अजिरे सा भृताङ्गे वहाथोम्, **३**.६.२

अथा सपत्नानिन्द्राग्नी, **२**.३.५ (तैसं. १.१.१३.२)

अदितेऽनुमन्यस्व, **१**.१.६ (तैसं. २.३.१.३)

अदितेऽनुमांस्थाः, **१**.१.६.५ (आपगृ. १.२.८)

अध्वर्यो किमत्र, **५**.५.३ (शब्रा. ३.५.४.१७)

अनागसस्त्वा वयम्, **६**.१.५ (तैब्रा. ३.७.९.१)

अनाज्ञातम्, **३**.१.१ (तैब्रा. ३.७.१२.२)

अनाधृष्टं देवपितृयजनम्, **३**.५.२ (मैसं. १.१.११ : ऊह)

अनुप्रहर संवदस्व, **३**.२.५ (वाधूश्रौ. २.१२.१७)
अनुब्रूहि, **२**.३.२, **३**.२.५ (शब्रा. १.५.२.८)
अनुमन्यस्व, **५**.३.४ (तैसं. ३.१.४.२)
अनुमन्ये, **५**.३.४
अनु स्वधाकुरु, **३**.४.५ (तैब्रा. २.७.८.२)
अन्तरिक्षाय त्वा, **४**.१.३ (तैसं. १.१.११.५)
अन्नादो भूयासम्, **३**.६.१ (शब्रा.११.२.७.११)
अन्यदेवायुवम्, **३**.५.१
अन्योऽन्यस्मै न द्रुह्याम:, **५**.३.४
अन्वपा रमयन्तु गाव:, **२**.५.३
अपानाय त्वा, **६**.१.५ (तैसं. १.१.६.८)
अपानाय मे, **६**.२.५ (तैसं. ३.२.३.३)
अपां परिगृह्णीतम्, **२**.५.२
अपां पशूनुन्मृजे, **६**.२.५
अपेत, **१**.१.३ (तै.सं. ४.२.४.१)
अपो देवास:, **५**.१.५
अब्धिरसि, **१**.३.१
अभिचाराय, **६**.२.५
अभिभवौ स्थ:, **३**.६.२
अमर्त्यस्य ते होतर्, **२**.४.४
अमुकेन यज्ञक्रतुना यक्ष्ये, **५**.१.१
अयं यज्ञ:, **२**.४.४
अयं यज्ञ: समसदद्धविष्मान्, **४**.४.३ (तैब्रा. **३**.७.९.१३)
अयं ते योनि:, **४**.३.५ (तैसं. १.५.५.२)
अयमात्मीयाद् गृहादनपायिनमिच्छन्तमुपवेषमाहर, **२**.४.७
अयं पुरो भुव:, **१**.३.१ (तैसं. ४.३.२.१)
अयाट्, **६**.३.३ (तैब्रा. ३.७.६.२३)
अरिष्ट्य विश्वान्यङ्गानि, **२**.५.१ (तैसं. ५.५.९.७)
अवर्धाते मा रिषम्, **३**.४.१
अवसृष्ट:, **२**.४.७ (तैब्रा. ३.७.६.२३)
अवस्यवे त्वा, **५**.१.४ (तैआ. ४.९.१)
अवाहं बाध, **४**.४.२ (तैब्रा. ३.७.६९)
अविदहन्त श्रपयत, ६.१.४ (तैब्रा. ३.२.८.७)
अश्मन्नूर्जम्, **१**.३.३ (तैसं. ४.६.१.१)
अश्मन्मे, **५**.१.५ (वाधूश्रौ १५.७.१)
अश्वं गोपायत, **१**.१.८
अश्वत्थाद्धव्यवाहात्, **५**.१.५ (तैब्रा. १.२.१.८)
अश्विनावध्वर्यू, **३**.३.३ (मैसं. १.९.१)
अश्वो रूपम्, **१**.१.५ (तैब्रा. १.२.१.५)
असौ मे जार:, **३**.२.४ (वाधूश्रौ. ४.६.२१)
अस्तु श्रौषट्, **२**.३.१ (तैब्रा. १.६.११.१)
अस्तु स्वधा, **३**.४.५ (तैब्रा. १.६.९-५१)
अस्मिन् यज्ञे, **२**.४.४ (तैब्रा. ३.७.६.१४)
अहं जोष्ट्रियो: **४**.४.३
अहं त्वदस्मि, **१**.१.८; **५**.३.५ (वाधूश्रौ. १.४.१)
अहं देव पशुमान् भूयासम् **४**.३.३
अहं देवयज्यया प्रजावान्, **४**.४.३
अहं देवेषु, **२**.४.५
अहं नराशंसस्य, **४**.४.३
अहं बर्हिषो वा ऋतीनाम्, **४**.४.३
अहम्, **४**.४.२
अहं भूपति:, **२**.५.१ (तैब्रा. ३.७.६.३)
अहं मनुष्येषु, **२**.४.५

आ

आकूतिं देवीम्, **१**.१.२ (तैब्रा. ३.५.३.२)
आकूत्यै त्वा, **१**.१.२ (तैसं. ३.४.२.२)
आ जुहोत, **२**.३.१ (तैब्रा. ३.५.२.३)
आज्यमसि, **२**.४.४ (तैब्रा. १.६.१.१)
आज्यायो यवमात्रात्, **२**.४.६ (तैब्रा. ३.७.५.६)
आज्येनोदेहि, **३**.३.२; **५**.६.२ (तैब्रा. ३.२.९.१४)
आत्मने मे वर्चोदा वर्चसे पवस्व तस्य ता आत्मानमुन्मृजे ब्रह्मवर्चसाय, **६**.२.५ (तैसं. ३.२.३.९)

आत्मनवत्यः सोम घृतवत्यो हि भूत्वा पितॄन् गच्छत सुवर्विन्दत=कामान्, **३**.४.३ (तु. तैब्रा. ३.७.५.३)

आत्मानं पशुषु प्रविष्टस्तमङ्ध्वम्, **३**.४.५

आत्मानं वर्षप्रविष्टस्तमङ्ध्वम्, **३**.४.३

आदित्यास्त्वा, **३**.४.२

आ देवपितृयजं वह, **३**.५.१ (तु. तैसं. १.१.७.४)

आद्य स्वधा नमः, **३**.४.५

आ नू ह, **३**.६.२

आ पितृयजं वह, **३**.५.१

आपो हि ष्ठा मयोभुवः, **२**.४.७; **६**.२.६ (तैसं. ४.१.५.२)

आप्यायस्व, **६**.२.१; **६**.३.४ (तैब्रा. ३.७.११.५)

आमिक्षा मयि श्रयताम्, **३**.१.१

आ यज, **२**.३.२

आ यान्तु पितरः सुमनस्यमानाः, **३**.५.१

आयुषः क्लृप्तिः, **२**.४.६

आयुषे, **६**.२.५ (तैब्रा. ४.३.७.२)

आयुष्पाः, **२**.३.६ (तैसं. १.१.१३.१०)

आर्द्राः प्रथस्तनवो भुवनस्य=जनयित्र्यो मतीनाम्, **३**.४.३ (तैब्रा. ३.७.५.३)

आशास्तेऽयं यजमानः, **२**.४.७

आ श्रावय, **३**.४.५ (तैसं. १.६.११.१)

आ स्वधा, **३**.४.५ (तैब्रा. १.६.९.५)

ओ३म्, **२**.४.६

इ

इदं हविः, **२**.४.७ (तैब्रा. २.६.३.५)

इदमहं सत्यादमृतमुपैमि, **२**.४.७

इदमहम्, **५**.६.५

इदमिन्द्रियम्, **४**.२.४; **६**.२.४ (तैब्रा. ३.७.६.१२)

इदम्, **६**.२.५

इदं पितृभ्यः, **३**.५.१ (तैसं. २.६.१२.१०)

इदं पितॄणाम्, **३**.५.१ (अवे. ७.६८.२)

इदं ब्रूहि, **३**.२.५

इध्माबर्हिरुपसादय **५**.६.२ (आपश्रौ. २.३.११)

इन्द्रं (यज), **२**.३.३ (आपश्रौ. ३.१६.१७)

इन्द्राग्निभ्यां छागस्य, **४**.२.५ (आपश्रौ. ७.२१.१)

इन्द्राग्निभ्याम्, **४**.२.५ (तैब्रा. ३.१.४.१४)

इन्द्राग्नी यज, **२**.३.३

इन्द्रियावी, **५**.७.१

इन्द्रियावी भूयासम्, **४**.४.२

इन्द्रियाव्यन्नादो भूयासम्, **३**.६.१

इन्द्रियेण वीर्येण भुवः, **६**.२.२

इन्धाना वां सुप्रजसः, **३**.६.२

इमं भोगं जुषस्व, **२**.३.४

इमां नराः, **२**.२.२ (तैब्रा. ३.७.७.१३)

इमामूर्जम्, **४**.४.१; **५**.१.४

इमामूर्जं चतुर्दशीं वहतु वरुणप्रघासा हविः, **३**.६.१

इमामूर्जं (पञ्च)दशीमारम्भणीयं वैश्वदेव-हविः, **३**.६.१ (तु. तैब्रा. ३.७.४.३)

इमामूर्जं प्रतिपदष्टमीं पञ्चदशम्, **४**.४.१२

इमां प्रणय, **२**.५.२

इमे नराः कृणुत वेदी एत्य, **३**.२.२ (तु. तैब्रा. ३.७.७.१३)

इमौ प्रस्तरावुभयस्य धर्तारौ प्रयाजानां तौ दधत, **३**.६.२

इमौ प्राणौ चापानौ च यजमानमपि गच्छताम्, **३**.६.२ (तु. आपश्रौ. १.६.१०)

इषे त्वोर्जे त्वा, **३**.१.१ (तैसं. १.१.१.१)

इह वो विश्वेदेवाः, **३**.१.१

इहैव सन् तत्र सतो वो अग्नयः, **१**.५.३ (तु. तैब्रा. १.२.१.२७)

उ

उग्रौ स्थः, **३**.६.२ (तु. तैसं. १.६.२.२)

उच्छुष्मा, **२**.४.४ (तैसं. ४.२.६.१०)

उच्छुष्मावग्नी यजमानाय स्तं निशुष्मावभि-दासते, **३**.६.३

उच्छुष्मो अग्ने, **३**.२.४; ४.५ (तैसं. १.६.२.१०)

उद्ग्राभं च निग्राभं च, **२**.३.५ (तैसं. १.१.१३.२)

उन्नीयमानाय, **६**.३.४ (शांश्रौ. ७.७.१; काश्रौ. ९.१२.१२)

उन्मुक्तो वरुणस्य, **५**.३.३

उप त्वाग्ने दिवेदिवे, **१**.५.१२; **३**.१.२; **४**.४.२ (तैसं. १.५.६.५)

उप प्रयन्तो अध्वरम्, **१**.४.५ (तैसं. १.५.५.१)

उप प्रेत, **२**.३.७; ४.७ (तैसं. ४.६.४.१२)

उपभृज्जुहूर्ध्रुवासि, **४**.१.२

उपयामगृहीतोऽसि (वायव्येन) वायवे त्वा जुष्टं गृह्णामि, **६**.२.१ (तु. तैसं. १.४.३.१)

उपहूतः, **२**.४.६ (आपश्रौ. ८.३.१४)

उपहूत उपहूतः, **६**.३.३

उपहूतः पशुमानसानि, **२**.४.६ (तैब्रा. ३.३.८.४)

उपहूता, **५**.२.१

उपहूता पृथिवी माता, **२**.४.६ (तैब्रा. ३.७.६.१५)

उपहूतो द्यौष्पिता, **२**.४.६ (वासं. २.११)

उरुं हि राजा, **३**.२.६ (तैसं. १.४.४५.१)

उरु प्रथध्वमुरु वो यज्ञपतिः, **६**.१.४ (तु. तैसं. १.१.८.९)

उरु यजमानाय, **३**.४.४

उरु यज्ञपतये, **३**.४.४

उरु यज्ञाय, **३**.४.४ (शांश्रौ. १२.२६.४)

उर्वन्तरिक्षमन्वित, **१**.३.३

उर्वन्तरिक्षमन्विहि, **२**.५.३; **४**.४.२ (तैसं. १.१.२.१८)

ऊ

ऊर्गस्यन्नाद्यमूर्जम्, **५**.१.८

ऊर्गाहुत्योरहं तिसृणां तिसृणां देवीनाम्, **४**.४.३

ऊर्जा पृथिव्याः, **१**.१.५

ऊर्जे सत्ये स्तम्, **३**.६.१

ऊर्णाम्रदसं त्वा, **३**.५.२ (तैसं. १.१.११.९)

ऋ

ऋतं त्वा सत्येन परिषिञ्चामि, **१**.४.२; ४ (तैब्रा. २.१.११.१)

ऋतस्य त्वा व्योमने, **१**.३.१ (तैसं. ३.३.५.७)

ऋतात्सत्यमुपैमि, **१**.५.२ (आपश्रौ. ४.१.६)

ऋत्वियवती स्थः, **१**.१.८ (तैब्रा. १.२.१.१४)

ए

एकदेवान् पितॄन्, **३**.५.२

एकस्फ्यया, **४**.१.२ (शब्रा. ३.५.२.२)

एतद्वः पितामहाः, **२**.४.२ (तु. तैसं. १.८.५.३)

एतद्वः प्रपितामहाः, **२**.४.२ (तु. तैसं. १.८.५.३)

एतशेन वां सूर्यो देवतां गमयतु, **३**.६.३ (तु. तैसं. १.६.४.३)

एता मरुतो वरुणश्च रमयन्तु गाः, **३**.२.१

एमा अग्मन्नाशिषः, **२**.४.७ (तैसं. १.६.४.१४)

एष ते, **६**.२.२ (तैसं. १.४.२.७)

एष ते योनिर्विश्वेभ्यस्त्वा देवेभ्यः सुवः, **६**.२.२ (तैसं. ६.४.११.४)

ऐन्द्रमसि, **५**.५.२ (तैसं. १.३.१.२०; ६.२.१०.१६)

क

कतरत्पूर्वं करिष्यामः, **५**.३.५

कर्मणी स्थः करणे स्थः क्रियासम्, **३**.६.३

कर्म[णे वः] पितृभ्यः शकेयम्, **३**.५.१

कर्मणे वां देवेभ्यः पितृभ्यः, **२**.५.२ (तु. तैसं. १.१.४.१)

कर्मणे वाम्, **३**.२.६; **६**.१.१; ३ (तैसं. १.१.४.१)

कविर्यज्ञस्य वितनुतः पन्थां नाकस्य=हव्यं वहथ याथ दूतावितः प्रचेता अमुतः

सनीयांसौ, **३**.६.१ (तु. तैसं. ३.५.५.३)
कव्यास्तृप्यन्तु, **३**.५.१
कव्याय च, **३**.५.२
कः स्वधितिहस्तम्, **३**.६.२; **४**.२.१
कामधुक्षः, **२**.१.२ (तैब्रा. ३.२.३.६)
कामाय त्वा, **१**.१.२ (तैसं. ३.४.२.२)

ख

खमङ्ध्वं त्वचमङ्ध्वम्, **३**.४.३ (तु. तैब्रा. ३.७.५.२)

ग

गायत्रिया ह्रियमाणस्य,**१**.१.५ (तैब्रा.१.२.१.५)

घ

घर्मस्य विश्वायुषः, **६**.१.४ (तु.तैसं. १.१.८.८)
घर्माणि स्थ विश्वायूंषि, **६**.१.४
घर्मोऽसि विश्वायुः, **६**.१.४ (तैसं. १.१.८.८)
(घृतवन्तं कुलायिनं रायस्पोषं सहस्रिणं) वेदौ दत्तां वाजिनम्, **३**.६.३ (तैसं. १.६.४.२४)
घृतेनाक्तौ, **४**.२.१ (तैसं. १.३.८.६)
घ्राता हवन, **२**.३.१

च

चक्षुर्भ्यां मे वर्चोदौ वर्चसे पवेथां **६**.२.५ (तु. तैसं. ३.२.३.७)
चक्षुष्पाः, **२**.३.६; **६**.३.३ (तु. तैसं. १.२.१.११)
चतुःशिखण्डे युवती सुपेशसौ, **३**.६.२[२] (तु. तैब्रा. १.२.१.२७; आपश्रौ. ७.५.१)
चमसमाप्यायस्व, **६**.३.४
चमसाध्वर्यवः, **६**.३.२
चिकित्वन्तस्मा, **६**.३.२
चित्रियादश्वत्थात्, **१**.१.५ (तैब्रा. १.२.१.७)
चिदसि, **५**.२.२ (तैसं. १.२.४.६)

ज

जातायानुब्रूहि, **४**.२.१ (तैसं. ६.३.५.११)
जिह्वा मयि श्रयताम्, **४**.३.३
जुष्टं गृह्णामि, **६**.२.१
जुष्टे जुष्टिं तेऽशीय, **२**.४.६ (तैसं. १.६.३.१)
जुष्टो वाचो भूयासम्, **६**.२.६ (तैसं. ३.१.१०.१)
जुह्वोराहतं पथः, **३**.६.२
जेमानं महिमानं गमेयम्, **३**.६.१
ज्योतिष्मन्तं त्वाऽग्ने, **१**.४.५; ५.१ (तैसं. ४.१.३.२)

त

तत्ते ऋध्यताम् = तत्ते संवर्धताम् कामः, **१**.१.३ (वाधूश्रौ. १५.५.१८)
तत्सवितुर्वरेण्यम्, **१**.५.१ (तैसं. १.५.६.१२)
तं त्वा, **१**.४.२
तं धूर्व, **३**.५.१ (तैसं. १.१.४.४)
तन्नौ सह, **५**.५.३[२]
तयोः स्रुचोर् असि, **३**.६.२
तस्य ते प्राणमुन्मृजे, **६**.२.५ (तु. तैसं. ३.२.३.१७)
तस्य मे रासाथां तयोर्वां भक्षीय तयोर्वां चक्षुषी उन्मृजे ब्रहमवर्चसाय, **६**.२.५ (तु. तैसं. ३.२.३.१६)
तूनिकुरुताद्, **२**.२.१
त्वमग्ने, **२**.४.३
त्वं मेऽध्वर्युरसि, **१**.१.३
त्वां गावोऽवृणुत राज्याय, **४**.४.२ (तैसं. ३.३.९.५)

द

दध्यामिक्षामन्थिनस्तु, **६**.२.५
दब्धिरसि, **३**.६.१२; **५**.४.३ (तैसं. १.६.२.२१)
दिवि जाताः, **१**.१.६ (तैब्रा. ३.७.१२.६)
दिवे त्वा, **४**.१.३ (तैसं. १.१.११.४)

दिव्यं नभो गच्छतु, **२.**३.६ (तैब्रा. ३.७.५.१७)
दृंहस्व, **४.**३.१ (तैसं. १.१.३.२)
देवंगमं स्थ, **१.**३.३ (तु. तैसं. १.१.२.१९)
देवपितॄन् गमयसि, **३.**५.१; २
देवपितृबर्हिः शतवलिश, **३.**५.१
देवपितृबर्हिर्भ्यर्स्त्वा, **३.**५.१
देवपितृयजनात् पृथिव्याः, **३.**५.२
देवपितृयज्यायै, **३.**५.२
देवपितृयुवः, **३.**५.१
देव सवितः, **२.**५.१ (तैब्रा. १.७.७.१)
देव सवितर् ओमहं मानुषः, **२.**५.२
देवस्त्वा सविता, **२.**२.१ (तैसं. १.१.८.१२)
देवस्य त्वा, **३.**४.१; **६.**१.४ (तैसं. १.१.४.९)
देवा गातुविदः, **२.**४.७ (तैसं. १.१.१३.१८)
देवानां पत्नीर्यज, **२.**३.६
देवानां पितॄणां परिषूतम्, **३.**५.१
देवान् पितॄन् हविषः, **३.**५.२
देवानां पितॄणां ब्रह्मणा देवा, **३.**५.१
देवानां ब्रह्मवादम्, **१.**१.५ (तैब्रा. १.२.१.६)
देवाः पितरः, **२.**४.५
देवा यज यज, **३.**४.५
देवीद्वारामहमुषासनक्तयोः, **४.**४.३
देवेभ्यः, **१.**४.२
देवेभ्य पितृभ्यः, **३.**५.२ (तैब्रा. ३.७.१४.४)
देवेभ्यः पितृभ्य ऊर्जे सीद, **३.**५.२
देवेभ्यः पितृभ्यो जुष्टं, **३.**४.१ : ३३; ५.१
देवेभ्यः पितृभ्यस्त्वोद्धर्वबर्हिभ्यः, **३.**४.१; ५.१
देवेभ्यः स्वाहा, **४.**२.५ (वाधूश्रौ. ५.७.२.९)
देवेभ्यो मह्यम्, **१.**५.३
देवेभ्यो हव्यं मह्यम्, **१.**४.५
देवौ यज यज, **३.**२.७
दैव्ययोर्होत्रोरहम् , **४.**४.३
द्यौरसि, **४.**३.१[२] (तैसं. १.१.३.२)
द्यौ स्थ पृथिवी स्थ, **४.**३.१

ध

धत्त, **२.**४.४; ५.२
धरीयांसौ, **३.**६.२
धरुणौ, **३.**६.२
धर्तारौ, **३.**६.२
धान्यमसि, **२.**२.१२ (तैसं. १.१.६.१)
धूरसि, **२.**४.३ (तैसं. १.१.४.४)
धृत्यः स्थ विधृत्यः स्थः, **३.**६.२
ध्रुवा, **४.**४.२ (तैसं. १.१.१.७)
ध्रुवाऽसदत्, **५.**४.३ (मैसं. १.१.१२)
ध्रुवा असदन्, **३.**२.४; ४.४; **५.**४.३ (मैसं. १.१.१२)
ध्रुवोऽसि, **२.**४.४ (तैसं. १.६.२.१)
ध्रुवौ स्थः, **३.**६.२

न

नमः सदसस्पतये, **६.**३.१ (तै. ३.२.४.२१)
नमो देवेभ्यः, **५.**६.५ (तैसं. १.३.४.११)
नयन्तु देवाः, **३.**५.१
नर्य प्रजां मे गोपाय, **१.**२.१ (तैब्रा. १.१.१०.२)
नाना प्राणः, **४.**४.२ (तैसं. ३.१.४.८)
निवपान्वाहार्यपचनस्य संभारान्, **१.**१.९
निर्वपामि देवपितृयज्यायै, **३.**५.२

प

पञ्चानां त्वा वातानाम्, **३.**६.२ (तैसं. १.६.१.३)
पत्नि कति ते जाराः, **३.**२.४ (वाधूश्रौ. ४.६.१६)
पत्नी सादनकर्त्री असत्, **६.**३.४
पयस्वती देवानां धेनुः, **३.**५.२
पयो वामग्नी, **३.**६.२
परित्वा गिर्वणो गिरः, **५.**५.३ (तैसं. १.३.१.१७)
परिवीयमाणायानुब्रूहि **६.**२.६ (वाधूश्रौ. ५.३.४०)
पर्यग्नयेऽनुब्रूहि, **४.**४.२ (वाधूश्रौ. ५.५.१७; ६.२१.२)

पवमानः सुवर्जनः, **१**.१.६ (तैब्रा. १.४.८.१)
पशुमनसानि, **२**.३.४
पशून् मयि धारयत, **३**.६.२ (तैब्रा. ३.७.६.८)
पितरः कव्यस्य मे, **३**.५.१
पितृन् गच्छ देवानाम्, **३**.५.२
पितृणामसि सस्नितमं पितृहूतमम्, **३**.५.१
पितृणां विष्ठामनु, **३**.५.२
पितृभ्यः शुन्धध्वम्, **३**.५.१
पृथिवि देवपितृयजनि, **३**.५.२ (आपश्रौ. ८.१३.६)
पृथिवीजन्मनाऽऽज्यस्थालीनाम्ना, **४**.१.२; ५.४. ३ (वाधूश्रौ. २.९.३७)
पृथिव्यै त्वा, **४**.१.३ (तैसं. १.१.११.१)
पृषदाज्याय दध्याहर, **५**.६.२
प्रजा ज्योतिः, **१**.४.४
प्रजापतिः प्राची दिक्, **१**.४.२; **२**.५.१; ३.१.१; ४.१.१
प्रजापतिराप्यायताम्, **२**.३.६
प्रजापतेर्भागोऽसि, **२**.४.७ (तैसं. १.६.३.३)
प्रजाभ्यस्त्वा, **५**.३.१ (तैसं. १.२.६.१)
प्रजां योनिं चक्षुः श्रोत्रं गोष्ठाद्रयिं मा निमृक्षं संमार्ज्मि, **४**.१.२
प्रजां मयि धारयत, **३**.६.२ (तु. तैब्रा. ३.७.६.८)
प्रजावान्पशुमानायुष्मान् यज्ञेन, **५**.४.४
प्रजा सृष्टानाम्, **१**.१.५
प्रणयतम्, **२**.५.२ (वाधूश्रौ. ३.१३.१०)
प्रणय यज्ञम्, **२**.५.१ (आपश्रौ. ३.१९.१)
प्रणय यज्ञं देवताः पितृन् वर्धयैतेन नाकस्य पृष्ठ अस्तु यज्ञं च धेह्योम् प्रणय, **२**.५.२
प्रणीताभ्योऽध्याहर, **६**.१.४ (वाधूश्रौ. २.६.३५)
प्रतिमा तिष्ठ, **२**.४.५
प्रयन्तु सदस्याः, **६**.३.२ (तु. आपश्रौ. १२.२३. १३)
प्रयाणः, **२**.४.५
प्रवेधसे, **१**.१.८ (तैब्रा. १.२.१.९)
प्रशास्तर्यज, **१**.१.९; ५.३ (वाधूश्रौ. ७.११. २८)
प्रह्वियमाणायानुब्रूहि, **४**.२.१ (तैसं. ६.३.५.४)
प्राची दिशाम्, **१**.३.१ (तैसं. ४.३.३.१)
प्राच्यां दिशि देवाः, **२**.३.६; ४.७३ (तैसं. १.६.५.१)
प्राणान् मयि धारयत, **३**.६.२ (तु. तैब्रा. ३.७.६.८)
प्राणाय मे, **६**.२.५ (तैसं. ३.२.३.२)
प्रियं देवानाम्, **३**.५.२ (तैब्रा. ३.१.१.४)
प्रियं देवानां पितृणाम्, **३**.५.२
प्रिया देवानाम्, **३**.५.२ (तैब्रा. ३.१.१.२)
प्रिया देवानां पितृणाम्, **२**.५.२
प्रियाय कर्मणे देवपितृयज्यायै पितृपीतये वः, **३**.५.१
प्रिया स्योना नो स्तम्, **२**.५.२
प्रोक्षणीभ्योऽध्याहर, **६**.१.४
प्रोक्षणीरासादय, **३**.३.२; ४.४ ; **५**.६.२ (वासं. १.२८; वाधूश्रौ. ४.२.११)

ब

बर्हिरूर्णाम्रदसं त्वा, **३**.५.२ (तु. तैसं. १.१.११. ९)
बर्हिषः, **२**.४.७ (तैसं. १.६.४.१)
बहु दुग्धि (वरुणाय), **३**.२.१ (तु. तैब्रा. ३.२.३)
बहु दुग्धि मरुद्भ्यो वरदाय हविः, **३**.२.१ (वाधूश्रौ. ४.५.१३)
बृहस्पतिः परिगृह्णीतम्, **२**.५.२
बृहस्पतिर्ब्रह्मा, **२**.५.१ (तैसं. २.६.९.३)
बृहस्पतिर्ब्रह्मा स यज्ञं पातु मां पातु यज्ञन्यम्, **२**.५.२ (तु. तैसं. २.६.९.३)
बृहस्पतिस्तनुताम्, **२**.४.७ (तैसं. १.५.३.७)
ब्रध्न पिन्वस्व, **२**.३.४; **२**.४.६२ (तैसं. १.६.३.६)
ब्रह्मन् पृषदाज्यम्, **६**.३.१

ब्रह्मन् प्रस्थास्यामः, **३**.२.५ (तैसं. २.६.९.६)
ब्रह्मन् हुतमसि, **१**.१.८
ब्रह्मन्नपः प्रणेष्यामि, **२**.१.२; **३**.४.१ (वाधू. ३.१३.१०)
ब्रह्मवर्चसाय, **६**.२.५ (तैब्रा. ३.१.४.६)
ब्रह्म देवाः पितरोऽवीवृधन्, **३**.५.२
ब्राह्मणस्योदरेण, **२**.५.१
ब्राह्मणा अयं व ओदनस्तं यथाभागं प्रतिगृह्णीध्वम्, **२**.३.५
ब्राह्मणान् भोजयत, **१**.१.८ (वाधूश्रौ. १५.८.१)
ब्राह्मणोऽयमुपहवमिच्छते, **६**.३.४

भ

भद्रम्, **५**.५.३[२]
भरतमुद्धर, **२**.३.२ (तैब्रा. ३.७.५.५; आपश्रौ. २.१८.९)
भुवः, **६**.२.२
भुवनमसि = नमः, **२**.३.१ (वाधू. २.१०.९)
भूः, **६**.२.२ (तैब्रा. १.१.५.२)
भूतमसि भूते मा धाः, **६**.२.३ (वाधू. ७.१९.४)
भूत्यै, **६**.२.५ (तैब्रा. ३.१.४.५; वाधूश्रौ. १३.१०.२)
भूपते, **२**.५.१ (तैब्रा. ३.७.६.१)
भूर्भुवः सुवर्देवस्य त्वा, **२**.१.२
भूर्भुवः सुवरग्नय आहोष्यमाणाः, **१**.५.३ (वाधूश्रौ. १.२२.८)
भूर्भुवोऽमीषाम्, **१**.१.८

म

मघवे स्वाहा, **५**.१.५ (मैसं. १.३.१६)
मनः स्थ प्राजापत्यं मनसा मा भूतेनाविशतम्, **३**.६.३ (तु. वाधूश्रौ. ७.११.४)
मनुना दृष्टाम्, **२**.४.६ (तैब्रा. ३.७.५.६)
मनोतायै हविषः, **४**.३.३ (तैसं. ६.३.१०.८; वाधूश्रौ. ११.२४.३२)
मनोऽसि, **२**.४.४ (तैसं. १.६.२.१२)
मनो ज्योतिः, **२**.४.७ (तैसं. १.५.३.७)
ममाग्ने, **१**.१.६ (तैसं. ४.७.१४.१)
मयि श्रपयताम्, **४**.२.४; **६**.२.४
मरुतो यद्ध वो दिवः, **५**.२.२ (तैसं. १.५.११.१५)
महेन्द्रं (यज), **२**.३.३ (तु. वाधूश्रौ. ३.७.३६)
मातरिश्वनो धर्मोऽसि, **४**.२.३ (तैसं. १.१.६.२)
मां धिनोतु, **३**.१.१
मार्जयस्व, **३**.४.५
मुखमसि मुखं भूयासम्, **६**.२.३ (तैब्रा. ३.२.८.५)
मेक्षय चरून्, **३**.१.१
मे दुहाताम्, **३**.६.२
मैत्रावरुणेन सह यज, **४**.३.४

य

यं वामग्नी पितरौ चरन्तौ अग्नीयोनौ द्वेष्टि सौतानग्नीन् सन्दहताम्, **३**.६.२
यज, **२**.३.२; ४.५; **३**.४.५ (तैसं. १.६.११.१)
यजमान किमत्र, **५**.५.३ (शब्रा. ३.५.४.१६)
यजमान वाचं यच्छ, **३**.२.६; ४.१; **४**.१.२; ३.१; **५**.४.२; **६**.१.१; ३ (वाधूश्रौ. ३.१०.१०)
यज्ञं तनुवै देवानां पितृणामात्मना, **३**.५.१
यज्ञाय रमताम्, **३**.६.१; **४**.४.१
यज्ञे ह्यभूवन् पोतारः पवित्राणि हव्यशोधनानि, **३**.६.२ (तैब्रा. ३.७.४.१२)
यतः प्रजाः, **६**.१.५ (तैसं. ३.५.८.२)
यतो अग्ने अस्य यज्ञस्य रिष्यात्, **३**.६.३ (तैसं. १.६.२.६)
यत्ते तान्तस्य, **१**.१.५ (तैब्रा. १.२.१.७)
यत्ते सृष्टस्य, **१**.१.५ (तैब्रा. १.२.१.७)

यत्पर्यपश्यत्, **१**.१.५ (तैब्रा. १.२.१.४)
यत्पृथिव्याम्, **६**.२.५
यथाभागं देवता, **२**.४.५ (तु. मानश्रौ. १.४.१.२६)
यथाभागं व्यावर्तध्वम्, **३**.१.१; **६**.१.४
यथाभागं व्यावर्तेथाम्, **३**.१.१ (वाधूश्रौ. २.६.४४)
यद्ग्रामे यदरण्ये, **३**.२.४ (तैसं. १.८.३.४)
यददश्चन्द्रमसि कृष्णं तदिहास्तु, **१**.१.४ (सामब्रा. १.५.१३; आपश्रौ. ५.९.७)
यदिदं दिवः, **१**.१.४ (तैब्रा. १.२.१.२)
यद्देवा देवहेडनम्, **१**.१.७ (तैब्रा. २.४.४.८)
यं त्वा समभरं जातवेदः, **१**.१.५ (तैब्रा. १.२.१.९)
यं देवाः पितरः कल्पयन्, **३**.५.२
यं देवा मनुष्येषु, **२**.४.७ (तैब्रा. ३.३.११.१; आपश्रौ. ३.१३.६)
यन्मे अग्ने, **१**.३.१; **२**.४.४[२]; **३**.१.१; ३.३; ४.४; ६.२; **४**.३.२; ४.३; **६**.३.१ (तैसं. १.६.२.६)
यन्मे अग्ने पञ्चहोता, **३**.२.४
यया ते सृष्टस्य, **१**.१.५ (तैब्रा. १.२.१.६)
यवानां मेधाः सुमनस्यमानाः, **३**.४.३ (माश्रौ. १.२.६.२२)
यस्ते शुष्म, **४**.२.४; ३.२; **६**.३.१
यस्य रूपं बिभ्रद्, **१**.१.५ (तैब्रा. १.२.१.३)
या ते धामानि, **५**.३.४ (तैसं. ४.६.२.१३)
या पुरस्तात् प्रस्रवन्तीः, **१**.१.२
याभिरदृंहज्जगतः, **१**.१.५ (तैब्रा. ४.६.२.५)
यास्ते अग्ने शिवास्तनुवस्ताभिस्त्वामादधे, **१**.१.९ (तैब्रा. १.१.७.३)
युनज्मि वां ब्रह्मणा जातवेदसौ, **३**.६.२ (तु. तैसं. १.६.२.१)
ये देवाः, **५**.३.५
येन संप्र, **२**.४.७
ये यजामहे, **२**.४.५ (तैसं. १.६.११.१)
ये स्वधा, **३**.४.५ (वाधूश्रौ. ४.१४.२१)
यो अश्वत्थः, **१**.१.५ (तैब्रा. १.२.१.८)
यो मा वाचा, **४**.४.२ (तैब्रा. ३.७.६.९

र

रक्षायै त्वा नारात्यै, .१.३ (काठसं. १.४)
रन्तिरसि, **२**.४.६ (तैसं. १.६.३.१)
रुद्राय गाम्, **१**.३.३
रेवतीः, **२**.५.३ (तैसं. १.३.८.११)
रोहितेन त्वा, **२**.४.७ (तैसं. १.६.४.३)
रोहितेन वामग्निर्देवतां गमयतु, **३**.६.३ (तु. तैसं. १.६.४.१५)

व

वत्सेभ्यो देहि, **३**.२.१ (तैसं. ३.७.४.१७; वाधूश्रौ. २.३.२८)
वनस्पतेरहं देवयज्ययाऽऽयुष्मान्, **४**.४.३ (मानश्रौ. १.४.२.६)
वपे प्रवपे देवेन सवित्रा प्रसूतो ब्रह्मणा शंसितोऽहं यानि म इत ऊर्ध्वं लोमानि ते सन्तु, **१**.१.६
वयुनानि वसतात्, **३**.६.२
वरुणो गृह्णातु, **३**.२.४
वर्धयतम्, **२**.५.२
वसन्तमृतूनाम्, **२**.४.५ (तैसं. १.६.२.१४)
वसुमद्गणस्य, **६**.३.४
वस्व्यसि, **५**.२.३ (तैसं. १.२.५.१)
वाक् स्थ ऐन्द्री सपत्नक्षयणी वाचा मेन्द्रियेणाविशतम्, **३**.६.३
वागसि, **२**.४.४ (वासं. ५.३३)
वाचं यच्छ, **२**.४.३ (शब्रा. १३.४.१७)
वाचा त्वा होत्रा, **१**.३.२ (वाधूश्रौ. १.२३.१; आपश्रौ. ६.१.६)
वायवः स्थोपायवः स्थ, **३**.१.१ (तैसं. १.१.१.३)
वायवे त्वा, **६**.२.१ (तैसं. १.२.३.१४)

वायुरसि प्राणो नाम, **१**.३.१ (मानश्रौ. ७.२.६)
वायुष्टेऽवतु, **२**.४.६
विद्युदसि विद्य मे पाप्मानम्, **२**.४.१ (तैब्रा. ३.१०.९.२)
विशो यन्त्रा नुदमाना अरातीः, **३**.६.२ (तैब्रा. ३.७.६.७)
विशो यन्त्राभिः, **३**.६.७ (तु. तैब्रा. ३.७.६.७)
विश्वजनस्य छाया, **५**.५.२ (तैसं. १.३.१.१६)
विश्वधाया, **४**.३.१ (तैसं. १.१.३.२)
विश्वेभ्यस्त्वा देवेभ्यः, **६**.२.३ (तैब्रा. ३.८.७.२)
विश्वेभ्यस्त्वा भूतेभ्यः, **६**.१.५ (तैसं. ३.५.८.३)
विश्वेभ्यो मे रूपेभ्यो वर्चोदा वर्चसे पवस्व तस्य ते विश्वानि रूपाण्युन्मृजे, **६**.२.५ (तु. तैसं. ३.२.३.१७)
विष्णवे(ऽनुब्रूहि), **२**.३.३ (शब्रा. ३.४.४.१३)
विष्णुं देवानाम्, **५**.४.३
विष्णुं (यज), **२**.३.३ (शब्रा. ३.४.४.१३)
विष्णोः क्रमः, **२**.४.७
विष्णो त्वं नो अन्तमः, **६**.२.५ (तैसं. ३.१.१०.९)
विष्णो पाहि, **३**.३.३
विष्णोर्जठरमसि वर्चोदा तस्य ते जठरमुन्मृजे, **६**.२.५ (तैसं. ३.२.३.१३)
वीर्याय मे, **६**.२.५
वीर्याय मे वर्चोदा वर्चसे पवध्वं तस्य मे राध्वं तेषां वो भक्षीय तेषां वो वीर्यमुन्मृजे ब्रह्मवर्चसाय, **६**.२.५ (तु.तैसं. ३.२. ३.१३)
वृत्रहा भूयासम्, **३**.६.१; **४**.४.२; **५**.१.५
वृष्टिरसि वृश्च मे पाप्मानम्, **१**.५.२; **२**.४.१ (तैब्रा. ३.१०.९.२)
वेदं परिवासय, **५**.६.२; **६**.१.१
वेदिमभिमृशामि, **१**.५.२
वेदोऽसि विन्द पुष्टिम्, **३**.४.१ (तु. तैसं. १.६.४.२३)
वेदौ स्थः वित्ती स्थ विदेय, **३**.६.३ (तु. तैसं. १.६.४.२३)
वेषाय त्वा, **२**.१.३ : १४; **४**.३.१ (तैसं. १.१.४.२)
वैश्वदेवस्यान्नादो भूयासम्, **३**.६.१
वैश्वानरं ज्योतिः, **३**.४.२
वैश्वानर्ये रूपम्, **१**.१.४

श

शमितार उपेतन, **२**.५.३; **४**.४.२ (तैसं. ३.१.४.१०)
शिवा च मे, **२**.४.१; **४**.४.१ (तैब्रा. ३.७.६.६)
शिवे च मे शं च मे स्तम्, **३**.६.१
शुन्धध्वं दैव्याय कर्मणे देवयज्यायै, **२**.१.२ (तैसं. १.१.३.१)
शृतं मयि श्रयताम् **६**.२.४ (तैब्रा. ३.७.६.१२)
श्येनोऽसि, **६**.२.३ (तैसं. ३.२.१.३)
श्रीरसि, **४**.३.३ (तैसं. १.३.१०.१)
श्रोत्रपाः, **२**.३.६ (तैसं. ३.२.१०.१०)

स

सं यजत्रैः, **४**.२.१ (तैसं. १.३.८.८)
सं यज्ञपतिः, **४**.२.१ (तैसं. १.३.८.९)
संवपत पिष्टानि, तूनिकुरुताद्, **२**.२.१
सं वर्चसा, **२**.४.७ (तैसं. १.४.४४.३)
स इदं पितृभ्यः कव्यं शमिष्व, **३**.५.१
सजूर्देवैः, **१**.४.३ (तैसं ४.३.४.१०)
स ते माऽऽस्थात्, **१**.३.३ (तैसं. १.१.२.१५)

सत्यं त्वर्तेन परिषिञ्चामि, **१**.४.२ (तैब्रा. २.२.११.१)

[सदसि सन्मे] भूयाद्, **२**.४.७ (तु. तैसं. १.६.५.३)

सनी स्थः सनितारौ स्थः सनेयम्,

स भद्रमकर्यो नः, **६**.३.३

समिधावाधायाग्नीदग्नी सकृत् सकृत् समृड्ढि, **३**.२.५

समङ्क्ता बर्हिर्हविषा घृतेन, **२**.३.६ (तैब्रा. ३.७.५.१०)

समङ्गानि (गच्छन्ताम्), **४**.२.१ (तु. वासं ७.१०)

समायुषा, **२**.३.६ (तैसं. १.१.१०.१०)

समिन्द्र णः, **२**.४.७ (तैसं. १.४.४४.२)

सं त आकुर्वन्तु, **१**.४.५

सं ते प्राणः, **४**.२.१ (तैसं. १.३.८.७)

सं ते मनसा, **४**.३.३ (तैसं. १.३.१०.१)

संभारान् संनिधत्त, **१**.१.८

संमृज्याज्येनोदेहि, **३**.२.६

स यज्ञं पाहि स पाहि मां पाहि यज्ञन्यम्, **२**.५. २ (तैसं. २.६.९.८)

सर्वकामोऽग्नीनाधास्ये, **१**.१.३ (वाधूश्रौ. १५. ५.२)

सविताघशंसात्पातु, **२**.३.४; ४.६ (तैसं. १.६. ३.१)

सविता माऽघशंसात् पातु, **२**.४.६

स विन्दति लोकम्, **३**.४.३; ४.४ (तु. तैब्रा. ३.७.६.१३)

सा मे सत्याशीः, **२**.३.३; ४.६ (तैसं. ३.२.७.३)

सीद, **३**.४.५ (तैसं. ३.५.११.२)

सीदन्त्यो देव्यः सुकृतस्य लोके, **३**.६.२

सीदं योनिम्, **४**.१.२

सीद होतर्, **५**.४.३ (तैसं. ३.५.११.६)

सुब्रह्मण्योम्, **५**.३.३ (तैब्रा. १.१२.३)

सुभूर्देवानां पितृणां धाम्ने-धाम्ने, **३**.५.२

सुरूपम्, **२**.२.३ (तैब्रा. ३.७.५.२)

सुरूपवर्षवर्ण, **२**.३.३; ४.६; **६**.३.३ (तैसं. १.६.३.३)

सुरूपा वो वसुविदः पशूनां तेजसा पितृभ्यो बर्हिषद्भ्यो जुष्टा अभिघारयामि, **३**.४.३ (तु. तैब्रा. ३.७.५.२)

सुवीर्याय त्वा, **४**.४.१; **५**.४.३ (तैसं. १.६.१.११)

स्रुवः, **६**.२.२

स्रुवं च स्रुचश्च संमृड्ढि, **३**.२.६ (आपश्रौ. २.३.११)

सूर्यमग्निमादधे, **१**.१.९

सूर्यो ज्योतिर्ज्योतिरग्निः स्वाहा, **१**.४.३ (तैब्रा. २.१.२.१०)

सोमं देवानाम्, **५**.४.३

सोमं यज, **२**.३.३ (शब्रा. २.५.२.३२)

सोममाज्यम्, **४**.२.५

सोमायानुब्रूहि, २.३.३ (शब्रा. २.५.२.३२)

स्तृणीत बर्हिः, **२**.२.२

स्योनं वः सदनं करोमि=सीदतामृते प्रतिष्ठित, **३**.४.३ (तु. तैब्रा. ३.७.५.२)

स्योने च मे सुषदे च स्तम्, **३**.६.१

स्वगा दैव्या होतृभ्यः, **२**.३.६ (तैब्रा. ३.३.८. ११

स्वधा नमः, **३**.४.५ (तैब्रा. १.६.९.५)

स्वधा पितृभ्यः, **५**.६.५ (तैसं. १.१.११.१)

स्वधितिरसि, **४**.१.२

स्वासस्थं देवेभ्यः पितृभ्यो युनज्मि त्वा, **३**.५.२ (तु. तैब्रा. २.६.१०.६)

स्वाहा, **३**.४.५

स्वाहा देवेभ्यः, **४**.२.५ (तैसं. ३.१.४.१५)

स्वाहा द्यावापृथिवीभ्याम्, **५**.६.५ (तैसं. १.१.३.५)

स्वाहा यज्ञं मनसा, **५**.१.६ (तैसं. १.२.२.१७)

स्वाहा वाते धाः, **२**.३.६ (तैसं. १.१.१३.२०)

स्वाहोरोरन्तरिक्षात्, **४**.६.५ (तैसं. १.२.२.१९)

ह

हर, **३**.२.२

हरिभ्यां वामिन्द्रो देवतां गमयतु, **३**.६.३ (तु. तैसं. १.६.४.१६)

हविषां देवान्, **२**.४.५

हविष्कृदेहि, **२**.१.३ (तैब्रा. ३.२.५.८)

हुवे पितॄन् यज्ञियान्, **३**.५.१

हृदय जिह्व, **६**.३.१

हृदयं मयि श्रयताम्, **४**.३.३

होत्राध्वर्योर्ब्रह्मणश्च बृहस्पतिः, **६**.२.३

— ० —

अनुक्रमणिका - III
उद्धृतपदानुक्रमणी

अंशू, ६.१.६
अंशून्, ५.३.२; ५; ६.१.६[३]
अंश्वोः, ६.१.६
अंसम्, ५.६.२
अंसे, ३.४.४
अंसौ, १.१.४
अकवारम्, ५.१.१
अकामः, १.१.६
अकामतः, १.१.६
अकामानाम्, ५.५.२
अकिलासिनम्, ५.१.१
अकुनखिनम्, ५.१.१
अक्रिम्णम्, ४.१.१
अक्लिष्टानि, ६.१.१
अक्षम्, ५.५.१[२]; ६.१.२; ५
अक्ष्णया, ४.२.१; ५.४.५
अखण्डम्, ५.१.१
अग्नयः, १.३.२
अग्निग्रहणप्रभृति, १.१.८
अग्निग्रहणमन्त्रद्वयम्, २.५.१
अग्निग्रहणम्, १.१.८
अग्निचित्यायाम्, ५.५.४
अग्निजघनेन, ३.२.४
अग्निनयनान्ते, ३.२.३
अग्निनिवपनम्, १.१.९
अग्निपावमानीभिः, १.५.१
अग्निप्रणयिनीयौ, ३.२.१
अग्निप्रथमाः, ५.६.४
अग्नियोगम्, २.४.४; ३.३.२
अग्नियोगे, ३.६.२
अग्निवेश्यगुरुः, १.१.१
अग्निशालायाम्, १.२.१
अग्निष्टोमम्, ५.१.१
अग्निष्टोमस्य, ६.१.५
अग्निष्ठामन्त्रेण, ४.१.३
अग्निष्ठायाः, ४.१.१
अग्निष्वात्तेभ्यः (पितृभ्यः), ३.४.२
अग्निस्थाल्याम्, १.४.२
अग्निहोतृचमसम्, ६.१.४
अग्निहोत्रद्रव्यम्, १.४.२; ४
अग्निहोत्रम्, १.५.३; २.१.१; ३.३३
अग्निहोत्रशालाम्, १.४.२
अग्निहोत्रशेषम्, १.३.२
अग्निहोत्रस्य प्रयोगः, १.४.२
अग्निहोत्रहवणीः, ३.२.१
अग्निहोत्रहवणीम्, १.४.२; ३.२.६; ३.१; ४.१.२; ३.१; ५.४.२; ६.१.३
अग्निहोत्रहवण्यादीनि, २.१.३; ३.४.१; ६.१.३
अग्निहोत्राभावः, १.३.३
अग्निहोत्रार्थकम्, १.३.२
अग्निहोत्रे, १.२.१; ३.१.१; २.१
अग्निहोत्रोच्छिष्टम्, २.१.१; ३.१.१[२]; २.१
अग्निहोत्रोच्छिष्टव्रतत्वम्, १.३.२
अग्नीत्, १.३.१; २.२.२; ३.१; २, ४[३], ५[१]; ३.२.३[२], ४, ५[२]; ४.५; ४.२.२[२]; ३.१; २, ३; ५.४.१, २[२]; ६.२[६]; ८.२; ६.१.२, २; ३.१, ४; २.३

अग्नीत्सहितः, **३**.२.६
अग्नीधः, **२**.३.४, ६; **५**.६.३[२]
अग्नीधे, **२**.३.४, ५, ६; **३**.३.३; **४**.३.२; ४; ५; **५**.३.४; ६.३
अग्नीध्रः, **२**.२.२; **५**.४.६
अग्नीध्राणाम्, **५**.४.५
अग्नीध्रियावदाने, **२**.४.६
अग्नीध्रिये, **५**.६.२
अग्नीन्, **१**.१.१; ४.१, २, ५; ५.१; **२**.१.१[३]; ३.५; **३**.३.१; **४**.४.१[२]; **५**.१.४[२]
अग्नीवरुणाभ्याम्, **३**.२.६
अग्नीषोमीयः, **५**.७.१
अग्नीषोमीयविकारः, **१**.३.३
अग्नीषोमीयार्थः, **५**.४.७
अग्न्यनुवीक्षणादि, **१**.४.४
अग्न्यभिधायिनाम्, **३**.२.४
अग्न्यागारपरिशोभनम्, **२**.१.१
अग्न्यागारम्, **१**.१.३; **१**.१.३
अग्न्यागारस्य, **१**.१.५
अग्न्याधेयदक्षिणा, **१**.१.१
अग्न्याधेयदक्षिणाम्, **१**.३.२
अग्न्याधेयस्य, **१**.१.१[२]
अग्न्यायतनम्, **१**.३.२
अग्न्युत्पत्तिसामर्थ्याय, **१**.१.२
अग्न्युद्धरणकालम्, **१**.५.३
अग्रविलानि, **५**.१.३
अङ्गप्रधानार्थाः, **५**.४.१
अङ्गप्रधानार्थेषु, **३**.५.१
अङ्गविकारः, **३**.५.२
अङ्गारनिरूहणम्, **१**.४.२; ५.२; **४**.२.४
अङ्गारनिर्वर्तन-, **२**.२.१
अङ्गारप्रत्यूहणम्, **१**.५.२
अङ्गारान्, **१**.४.२; **६**.२.३
अङ्गारे, **१**.४.४; **४**.२.४
अङ्गारेषु, **१**.१.७; ४.२
अङ्गार्थाः, **५**.४.१
अङ्गार्थे, **३**.५.१
अङ्गित्वात्, **३**.५.१
अङ्गिरसः, **५**.१.१
अङ्गुलीः, **५**.१.६; ६.५
अङ्गुलीयकादि, **५**.२.२
(सौवर्णम्) अङ्गुलीयम्, **५**.३.१
अङ्गुलैः, **२**.३.४
अङ्गुल्यग्रेण, **५**.३.१
अङ्गुष्ठाग्रम्, **५**.३.१
अङ्गुष्ठे, **५**.३.१
अङ्गुष्ठोपकनिष्ठिकया, **२**.५.१
अङ्गुष्ठौ, **५**.१.६
अङ्गेज्याः, **५**.४.१
अच्चुकारम्, **१**.४.४
अच्छावाक-(धिष्णियम्), **५**.५.४
अच्छावाकः, **६**.३.४
अच्छावाकचमसमन्वारभेत्यादि, **६**.३.४
अच्छावाकचमसाध्वर्यु, **६**.३.४
अच्छावाकस्य, **५**.४.५; **६**.२.४; ३.४
आच्छावाके, **६**.३.४
अच्छावाक्, **६**.३.४
अच्छवाक् (धिष्णियम्), **५**.५.४
अजस्रपक्षे, **५**.१.४
अजस्राः, **१**.३.२
अजस्रैः, **५**.१.४; ८
अजाम्, **५**.३.३
अजिनम्, **२**.५.१
अञ्जनम्, **४**.२.१
अञ्जनाभ्यञ्जनादिभिः, **३**.३.३
अञ्जनेन, **१**.१.६
अञ्जलिम्, **५**.६.५
अञ्जलिमात्रेण, **५**.६.३

अञ्जलिस्थम्, **१**.१.८
अञ्जलौ, **१**.१.८; **२**.३.६; ४.७; **३**.४.५; **४**.३.५
अतिगमयेत्, **५**.३.३
अतिग्राह्याः, **६**.२.२
अतिग्राह्येषु, **६**.२.५
अतिचङ्क्रम्य, **३**.४.५
अतिद्रुत्य, **६**.१.२
अति प्रथयेत्, **२**.२.१
अतिप्रयन्ति, **१**.१.९
अतिमुक्तयः, **३**.२.३
अतिमुक्तीः, **४**.१.२
अतिमुक्त्यन्ते, **३**.३.३
अतिरात्रः, **५**.१.१; ४.१
अतिरात्रस्य, **६**.१.५
अतिरात्रे, **६**.१.५
अतिरिक्तम्, **३**.३.२
अतिवाचयति, **५**.३.४
अतिवालयतः, **५**.२.२
अतिवाल्य, **१**.४.४
अतिशिनष्टि, **१**.१.७
अतिशिष्टाः (अपः), **२**.३.६; ४.७; **५**.४.२; ६.२; **६**.१.३
अतिशिष्यात्, **३**.४.५
अतिशेषयेत्, **६**.१.३
अतिहरणम्, **२**.३.४; ५
अतिहरेत्, **२**.३.४
अतिहाय, **२**.३.३; ५.१; **३**.४.५
अतिहृत्य, **२**.३.४; ५; ८.१
अतीकाशवत्, **५**.२.२
अतीकाशवन्तम्, **५**.१.२
अत्यग्निष्टोमस्य, **६**.१.५
अत्याक्रम्य, **२**.३.३; ४; ६
अत्याक्रामति, **३**.४.५
अत्याक्रामन्, **२**.३.१[३]
अत्याक्राम्य, **२**.३.१
अत्यूहति, **५**.५.१
अत्यूहेत्, **२**.३.२
अत्यूह्य, **२**.४.७
अदः, **१**.३.३
अदधानंकृत्वा, **३**.३.२
अदानाधिश्रयणे, **४**.३.१
अदितिम्, **५**.२.२
अदीक्षितव्रते, **५**.१.८
अदीक्षिष्टा, **५**.१.७
अदृष्टार्थः (मन्त्रः), **५**.३.५
अदृष्टार्थे, **६**.३.३
अधःशायी, **३**.६.१
अधरारणिम्, **४**.२.१
अधरारण्याम्, **४**.२.१
अधर्मकत्वे, **३**.२.३
अधर्मकम्, **३**.२.२; ३; **५**.८.२
अधःप्रमाणम्, **५**.५.३
अधिकमात्रेण, **५**.४.५
अधिकृतेन, **५**.४.३
अधितिष्ठति, **६**.३.२
अधिदेयानि, **५**.३.२
अधिधाय, **१**.४.४
अधिनिरस्यति, **२**.१.३
अधिप्रस्कन्दयति, **६**.१.५
अधिलोमकस्याम्, **५**.३.१
अधिवपनादि, **६**.१.४[२]
अधिवृक्षसूर्ये, **१**.१.७
अधिश्रयणम्, **१**.५.२; **४**.२.४
अधिश्रयणमात्रम्, **५**.४.२; ६.२
अधिश्रयणान्तम्, **५**.६.२
अधिश्रयति, **१**.४.२
अधिश्रयन्ति, **२**.२.१

अधिश्रयान्तम्, **५.२.१**
अधिश्रयेत्, **२**.२.१; **५**.६.२; **६**.१.४
अधिश्रिते, **३**.४.२
अधिश्रित्य **१**.५.२; **२**.४.२; **३**.४.३
अधिषवणचर्म, **५**.५.३
अधिषवणफलकयोः, **६**.१.२
अधिषवणफलके, **५**.१.३
अधोअक्ष, **५**.५.३
अध्यर्धप्रादेशव्यासे, **५**.१.३
अध्याहृता, **२**.२.१
अध्यूढः, **६**.२.१
अध्यूध्निम्, **४**.३.१
अध्यूहन्, **२**.३.१
अध्यूहितः, **५**.१.६
अध्वर्यवे, **१**.३.२; ४.१; **२**.३.४, ५; **३**.२.१; **४**.३.२; ३; **५**.६.३; ४[२]; **६**.१.६; ३.३
अध्वर्युः, **१**.१.८, ९; ३.१; ४.२; ४[२], ५; ५.३; **२**.२.२[२], ३; ३.२; ४, ५, ६; **३**.२.२, ३, ४, ६, ७; **४**.१.२, ३; २.२, ३, ५; ३.२[२], ३, ४[३]; **५**.१.३, ४, ६; २.१, २; ३.३; **४.१**, २, ३; ५.३[४]; ६.२[२], ३[२], ४[३]; ८.१; **६**.१.२[२]; २.१[३]; ३[३]; ४, ५, ६[२]; ३.१[३], २[२], ३[३], ४
अध्वर्युणा, **२**.३.१; **३**.२.४; **५**.४.२[२]; ५.२; **६**.२.३; ३.२
अध्वर्युणोक्तेन, **२**.२.२
अध्वर्युपरताम्, **२**.५.२
अध्वर्युपुरुषाः, **५**.६.२
अध्वर्युप्रवरे, **२**.४.४
अध्वर्युम्, **३**.२.२; **५**.१.१[२]; ८.१; **६**.३.२[२]
अध्वर्युयजमानौ, **३**.३.३; **४**.१.३; २.२; **५**.२.२[२]; ३.३[२]; ५.२; **६**.१.४; ५[२];
२.१; ३.२
अध्वर्यू, **३**.२.७; **५**.५.२; **६**.३.३
अध्वर्योः **३**.२.२, ४, ५[२], ६; ६.२; **५**.३.५; ६.२[२]; **६**.३.२, ४[२]
अध्वर्यौ, ६.३.२
अनः, **५**.६.१
अनक्ति, **२**.३.४; **४**.१.३[५]; २.१; **६**.१.५
अनक्षसङ्गम्, **४**.१.१
अनखः, **५**.१.४
अनग्नाम्, **४**.१.२
अनड्वान्, **१**.४.१
अनड्वाहम्, **५**.३.३; ४
अनतिदृश्नम्, **२**.२.३
अनत्याक्रम्याश्रावणेति, **४**.३.४
अनध्वर्यवः, **२**.३.४
अननुसृजेत्, **३**.२.१
अननूपात्तपूर्वान्, **१**.१.५
अनन्तर्गर्भा, **५**.१.१
अनन्यव्यापार-, **५**.४.४
अनपसर्पणार्था, **५**.५.१
अनभिप्रेतमिव, **२**.३.४
अनभिषुतः (सोमः), **५**.५.१
अनवत्तेडानाम्, **६**.३.३
अनवहताः, **३**.४.२
अनवेक्षितेन (आज्येन), **३**.४.३
अनवेक्ष्य, **२**.५.३
अनशनेन, **१**.५.३
अनसी, **५**.१.३
अनस्थिके, **४**.३.३
अनाग्निकेन, **१**.१.५
अनाज्यकेन, **४**.३.२
अनादीप्तायाम्, **१**.४.३
अनाधाय, **१**.४.४
अनामग्रहणात्, **१**.४.५

अनाराधीयमानयोः, ३.६.२
अनावृत्तिः, २.१.३; ३.२.१
अनित्याः, ६.२.२
अनित्यौ, ५.७.१
अनिधाय, १.४.४
अनियतमाः, ५.१.१
अनियतवृक्षाणि, ५.१.३
अनियतानि, ५.५.२
अनियमः, ३.१.१
अनीकवतस्य, ३.३.१
अनीकस्पृशम्, ६.३.३
अनुकल्पितदक्षिणस्य, ५.१.७
अनुगमनम्, २.५.३
अनुग्रन्थति, ५.३.२
अनुचरी, ६.२.३
अनुच्छिन्दन्, ३.२.४
अनुजपेद्, २.३.६
अनुजानाति, १.४.२; ५
अनुजानीते, ५.२.१
अनुज्ञानम्, १.५.३; ५.२.१
अनुज्ञानादिकम्, १.१.३
अनुज्ञाने, ५.२.१
अनुज्ञापयितुम्, ५.१.४
अनुज्ञापयीत, १.१.१
अनुज्ञापयेत्, ५.१.४
अनुदिशति, ५.८.१
अनुदिशन्ति, ५.५.४
अनुदिशम्, ४.१.२
अनुदिशेत्, ५.८.१
अनुदेशयति, ५.८.१
अनुद्धृत्य, ६.२.४
(मन्त्राम्) अनुद्रुत्य, १.४.४; २.३.६
अनुद्वासितायाः, १.१.७
अनुनिर्वपेत्, १.३.२
अनुपदासात्, १.१.५
अनुपरमेण, ५.४.१
अनुपलक्षितायाम्, ५.४.४
अनुपलब्धे, ५.५.१
अनुपसदम्, ५.३.४; ५
अनुपस्तीर्णाभिघारिताम्, ३.३.३
अनुपस्थाय, १.५.३
अनुपहतः, ५.१.१
अनुपूर्वम्, २.२.३; ६.३.१
अनुपूर्वोपसत्सु, ५.३.५
अनुपेत्य, ४.४.१
अनुप्रहरणाः, ३.३.१
अनुप्रहरेत्, ५.४.२
अनुप्रहृत्य, २.३.६[२]
अनुप्रास्य, २.३.६
अनुब्रूयात्, ५.१.८
अनुमदतः, ५.२.२
अनुमन्त्रणतन्त्रम्, ३.२.१
अनुमन्त्रणमन्त्रः, १.३.१; ३.४.५
अनुमन्त्रणम्, ३.१.२; २.५; ६.१, २; ५.१.८; ४.३, ४; ७.१
अनुमन्त्रणानि, २.४.६; ३.६.१; ५.४.३; ४
अनुमन्त्रयते, ३.४.५; ४.२.३
अनुमन्त्रयेत, २.३.२; ५.५.१
अनुमन्त्रयेते, ६.३.२
अनुमन्त्र्य, २.१.१
अननुमन्त्र्यमाणः, ४.४.२
अनुयजति, ३.२.६
अनुयज्ञैः, ३.१.२
अनुयाजेषु, २.५.२
अनुयुंक्त्वा, २.४.४
अनुरब्धेषु, ५.६.४
अनुलेखने, ४.१.२
अनुलोमम्, १.३.३

अनुवर्तयन्ति, ५.५.४
अनुवर्तयेत्, २.३.६
अनुवर्त्य, ४.३.५
अनुवाकद्वयम्, १.५.२
अनुवाकद्वयेन, १.४.५; ५.१
अनुवाकशेषम्, १.४.४
अनुवाकेन, १.१.६[२]; ७; ५.१
अनुवादयोः, २.३.४
अनुवित्तिहोमम्, १.१.७
अनुवित्तिहोमाय, १.१.७
अनुवीक्षणेन, १.४.५
अनुवीक्षते, ५.६.५
अनुवेष्ट्य, ५.२.२[२]
अनुषक्तव्यः, ५.३.४
अनुषङ्गः, २.३.४; ६.२.२
अनुषजति, ६.२.५
अनुषज्य, २.३.१
अनुषज्यते, २.२.१
अनुषज्याः, ६.२.२
अनुष्ठानफलकम्, ५.३.३
अनुष्ठेयम्, १.१.१
अनुसन्दध्यात्, ६.२.२
अनुसृजेत्, ४.४.२
अनूकशब्दम्, ५.५.४
अनूक्तायाम्, २.३.२
अनूचः, १.४.२
अनूचानान्, ५.१.१
अनूचीनानि, ५.१.३
अनूह्यमाने, १.३.२
अनूपात्तपूर्वान्, १.१.५
अनूयाजविकारत्वे, ५.४.३[२]; ४
अनूयाजविकाराः, ५.४.१
अनूयाजसमिधम्, ३.४.५
अनूयाजस्य, ५.५.४
अनूयाजान्, २.४.७; ४.३.४; ५
अनूयाजार्थम्, ३.२.६
अनृतम्, १.३.२
अनृत्विजे, ५.१.८
अनोप्रवर्तनम्, ५.६.१[२]; ५.६.१
अन्तरदेवतोपस्थानात्, ६.३.१
अन्तरालः, ५.५.४
अन्तरालबहुना, १.१.५
अन्तरालानाम्, ५.४.५
अन्तराले, ५.५.२
अन्तरालेषु, ५.४.२
अन्तर्यामपात्रम्, ६.१.१; २.५
अन्तर्वर्ताद्, ५.५.२
अन्तर्वर्तान्, ५.५.२
अन्तर्वर्तिनः, ३.४.५
अन्तर्वेदि, २.१.३; २.२[२]; ३.५–६; ४.७; ३.१.२
अन्तर्वेद्यः, ६.३.१
अन्तर्हनु, २.५.१
अन्तःपरिधि, २.३.३
अन्तःशालम्, ५.१.७
अन्तःसदसि, ६.२.३
अन्तिकस्थैः, ६.२.२
अन्नदक्षिणा, १.१.१
अन्नदानार्थानि, १.१.१
अन्नदाने, १.१.२
अन्यत्रर्तोः, ३.६.१
अन्यदेवायुवम्, ३.५.१
अन्यपक्वम्, ३.३.३
अन्यप्राकृतानाम्, ३.६.१
अन्यवत्सा, ३.४.१
अन्यात्मदासात्, ३.६.१
अन्यार्थः, ३.५.१
अन्युप्तधिष्णियानुदेशेन, ५.८.१

अपाकृत्य, ३.२.१
अन्वगिव, ५.६.४
अन्वपेत्, २.३.२
अन्वर्जति, ५.३.३
अन्ववस्त्रावयेत्, ५.५.२
अन्वाख्यातिम्, ४.१.२
अन्वाघातम्, ५.२.१
अन्वाधाना, १.३.३
अन्वाधाय, २.१.१; ४.१
अन्वारभन्ते, ६.२.३
अन्वारभमाणः, ५.६.३; ६.२.३
अन्वारभमाणम्, ४.४.२
अन्वारभमाणाः, ४.२.४
अन्वारभेत, ४.१.२
अन्वारभेरन्, ६.२.३
अन्वारभ्य, २.३.५; ४.२.२
अन्वारम्भः, २.५.३
अन्वासङ्गः, २.५.२; ३.५.१, २
अन्वासङ्गपक्षे, ३.५.२
अन्वासंजयेत्, ५.४.१
अन्वासञ्जयेयुः, ३.५.१
अन्वाहारम्, २.४.७
अन्वाहार्यः, ४.३.२[२]
अन्वाहार्यपचनम्, १.१.७; २.४.१; ३.२.१; ४.२
अन्वाहार्यपचनस्य १.३.२
अन्वाहार्यपचनस्यान्ते, ३.४.३
अन्वाहार्यपचनस्यायतनम्, १.१.४[२]
अन्वाहार्यपचनस्यायतने, १.१.५
अन्वाहार्यपचनस्यार्धम्, ३.४.३
अन्वाहार्यपचनस्योद्धते, १.१.७
अन्वाहार्यपचने, २.३.७; ४.३; ३.४.३
अन्वाहार्यम्, २.३.५
अन्वाहार्यस्थालीम्, २.१.२
अन्वाहार्यहरणम्, ५.१.५
अन्वाहार्यात्, २.३.५
अन्वाहार्ये, २.३.५
अन्वाहार्येण, ४.४.३
अन्वाहितेषु, ४.१.२
अन्वेक्षते, २.२.१
अपकृष्येत, ४.१.२
अपक्षाय, ४.३.१
अपनयति, ५.३.३
अपनयन्, ५.५.३
अपनेतुम्, ५.१.४[२]
अपयच्छन्, ३.१.१
अपयच्छति, ५.२.१
अपयच्छेत्, ६.२.१
अपरतः, १.१.४[२]
अपरम्, ४.१.३[२]; २.१; ५.१.१
अपराधः, १.१.१
अपराह्णिक्यौ, ५.४.४
अपराह्णे, २.१.१; ६.१.१
अपरिमितम्, १.१.२
अपरिमितावकाशम्, १.१.४
अपरिमिते, १.१.४
अपरे, १.१.७, ९
अपरेण, १.१.५; ४.२; ४; ५.२
अपरेणात्मानम्, १.४.४
अपर्यावर्तयन्, ४.३.४
अपवनीयरात्रेः, ६.१.१
अपवर्जयेत्, ५.४.६
अपसर्पतः, ५.५.३
अपसलैः, २.३.६; ३.२.२; ४.४; ४.२.२; ५.६.४; ६.२.४; ३.२[२]
अपसव्यम्, ३.४.५
अपाकुर्यात्, २.१.२; ५.८.२
अपाकृत्य, २.१.१

अपानग्रहाः, १.३.१
अपानग्रहान्, १.३.१
अपानभृन्मन्त्राः, १.३.१
अपानिति, १.४.४
अपानेन, २.४.७
अपान्य, २.३.५
अपारे (तीरे), ५.१.८
अपां प्रत्यानयनम्, १.५.२[2]; ३
अपिदधाति, ४.२.३
अपिपृष्ठम्, ३.१.१
अपिव्रताः, ५.६.१; ३
अपिश्रित्य, ३.१.१
अपिसृजति, २.३.७
अपिसृजन्, २.३.४
अपिसृजेत्, २.२.२; ६.२.३
अपिसृज्यमानयोः, २.४.४
अपूर्वत्वे, ५.४.३[2], ४
अपूर्वपक्षे, ५.४.२; ३[2]
अपूर्वम्, ५.४.१
अपूर्वसान्नायविकारः, ३.६.१
अपूर्वाज्यस्थाल्याः, ४.३.३
अपूर्वाम्, ४.३.३
अपूर्वेण, ३.२.६
अपेक्षते, ३.६.२
अपेक्षणम्, ३.१.१
अपोनिनयान्तम्, ६.१.४
अपोप्ते, १.४.४
अपोर्णुते, ५.३.३
अपोहति, २.३.५
अपोहेत्, ३.४.१; ३; ४[2]; ५[2]
अप्तोर्यामस्य, ६.१.५
अप्रकाशाम्, ४.१.२
अप्रणीय, ५.४.२
अप्रतिषिद्धैः, १.४.२
अप्रतीक्षम्, २.३.७; ४.७
अप्रताः, ३.२.३
अप्रयताः, ६.१.१
अप्रस्तराय, ५.३.५
अप्रस्तरणाय, ५.३.५
अप्राकृतमन्त्रकम्, ५.३.४
अप्सुदीक्षा, ५.१.५
अप्सुदीक्षापूर्वकत्वे, ५.१.६
अप्सुदीक्षायाः, ५.१.४
अप्सुदीक्षायै, ५.१.२
अप्सुन्यस्ताभ्याम् (वासोभ्याम्), ३.२.७
अप्सुमित्र (चनसित), ५.१.६
अफले, ४.४.३
अफुल्लान्, ६.१.४
अभावः, ५.२.२
अभावे, १.१.२; ५.२[2]
अभिक्रम्याभिक्रम्य, २.३.२
अभिगृह्णाति, ५.२.३
अभिगृह्य, ५.१.५
अभिघारणमन्त्रः, ४.३.३
अभिघारणम्, ३.४.३
अभिघारणात्, ३.२.५
अभिघारम्, २.२.३
अभिघारयति, ३.२.५
अभिघारयन्, १.३.१
अभिघारयन्ति, २.३.४
अभिघारयेत्, २.२.३[2]; ४.३.३[2]
अभिघार्य, २.२.३; ३.२.३; ४.२.४; ३.२
अभिच्छादयति, ३.४.४
अभिच्छाद्य, २.३.७
अभिजुहुयात्, २.३.२; ४.१.२; ५.५.१
अभिदयति, ६.२.६
अभिद्योतनम्, १.४.२[2]
अभिद्योतनप्रत्यानयने, ३.२.१

अभिद्योतनपर्यधिकरणे, **१**.५.२

अभिद्योतनस्य, **१**.४.२

अभिधानतन्त्रम्, **३**.२.१

अभिधानम्, **५**.१.६

अभिधानी, **५**.३.३

अभिधानीम्, **५**.३.३

अभिधाय, **२**.३.१

अभिधीयते, **१**.१.२

अभिध्यायति, **३**.४.२

अभिध्यायन्, **५**.६.५

अभिनवम्, **१**.१.५

अभिनिवर्तनम्, **१**.१.८

अभिनिर्वेष्टयेत, **३**.२.७

अभिपर्यावृत्य, **२**.४.३

अभिपूजिताः, **३**.३.३

अभिपूरयन्ति, **२**.२.१

अभिपूर्य, **२**.२.२

अभिप्रथयति, **२**.२.१

अभिप्रयाति, **५**.१.४

अभिप्राणिति, **५**.१.७

अभिप्रेतम्, **२**.३.४; **६**.१.६

अभिभवन्निव, **५**.३.२

अभिमन्त्रण-, **५**.८.२

अभिमन्त्रणम्, **२**.१.२; ४.३; **४**.४.२; **५**.२.२

अभिमन्त्रणे, **३**.६.३

अभिमन्त्रयते, **२**.१.१

अभिमन्त्रयेत, **४**.४.३; **५**.८.२

अभिमन्त्रयेते, **५**.२.२

अभिमन्त्र्य, **२**.१.१[२],३; **३**.३.१[२]

अभिमन्थनशकलम्, **४**.२.१

अभिमन्थनस्य, **४**.२.१

अभिमर्शनम्, **२**.१.३; २.१[२]; **६**.१.२; ५

अभिमुखः, **१**.५.३

अभिमृजेत्, **६**.१.५

अभिमृशतः, **५**.५.२; **६**.१.५

अभिमृशति, **१**.४.३; **२**.२.३

अभिमृशन्ति, **६**.२.१

अभिमृशेत्, **२**.२.१; ३; **३**.१.१; **४**.२.३; ३.२; ४.३; **६**.१.५; २.४, ५

अभिमृश्य, **१**.५.२; **२**.१.३; २.३; **३**.३.३

अभिवादनम्, **१**.५.२

अभिवान्या, **३**.४.१

अभिवान्यायै, **३**.४.२

अभिविधिः, **३**.२.५; **६**.२.१

अभिवृष्टः, **५**.१.८

अभिव्यनिति, **२**.४.३

अभिषवः, **६**.१.६

अभिषवणचर्म, **६**.२.१

अभिषिच्य, **४**.२.३

अभिषिञ्चेत्, **४**.२.२

अभिषुण्वन्ति, **६**.२.१

अभिषुतः (सोमः), **५**.५.१

अभिषेकाद्याञ्जनावन्तम्, **५**.१.५

अभिषोतारः, **६**.२.१[४]

अभिष्टव्यवहारः, **५**.६.१

अभिसन्धाय, **६**.२.२

अभिहितः, **१**.१.१[२]; २

अभिहितानि, **१**.१.१

अभिहोमः, **३**.१.२; २.६

अभिहोमप्रतिषेधः, **२**.३.३

अभिहोमान्तेन, **३**.१.२

अभिहोमेषु, **५**.५.३

अभ्यक्तः, **५**.१.४

अभ्यगारे, **४**.१.१

अभ्यज्य, **१**.१.५; ६

अभ्यधिकम्, **५**.१.७

अभ्यन्तरः, **५**.६.४

अभ्यन्तराः, ४.६.४
अभ्यपहा?, ३.६.१
अभ्यादधाति, २.३.१[३]
अभ्यादधातीत्यदि, १.५.३
अभ्यादध्यात्, ५.४.२[२]
अभ्याधानप्रभृति, ३.३.१
अभ्याधाय, १.१.६; २.३.१; ३.३.१; ४.१; ४.१.२
अभ्याधायात्, २.३.१
अभ्याधीयमानयोः, २.४.४
अभ्याधेयानि, २.३.१[२]
अभ्याशे, ५.१.५; ३.१, २
अभ्याहितौ, ५.८.२
अभ्युत्क्रामन्त्याः, ५.२.३
अभ्युन्नीय, ६.३.२
अभ्युपायेन, १.१.१; ८
अभ्रप्रभृत्यनुवाकम्, ६.१.१
अभ्रिम्, ३.४.१
अमन्त्रकम्, १.५.३
अमात्यपरिचरणं नाम, १.१.६
अमात्यहोमम्, १.१.७
अमात्यहोमशेषेण, १.१.७
अमात्याग्निम्, १.१.७
अमांसम्, ३.६.१
अमात्यात्, १.३.२
अमावास्याम्, ४.१.१
अमावास्यायाम्, २.३.३[३]; ४.१
अमिश्रयन्ति, २.२.१
अमृन्मयपायी, ३.६.१
अमेध्यम्, ५.१.८[२]
अम्बरीषम्, ३.३.४[२]; ४.२; ५.१.२
अम्बरीषाधिश्रयणमात्रम्, ३.४.२
अम्बरीषान्, ३.४.३
अम्बरीषे, ३.४.२
अयास्यम्, ५.१.१
अयुजः, २.१.१
अयुजस्त्ववमानैकधनम्, ६.१.४
अयोदर्व्यादीनि, २.१.२
अयोविकारः, ३.१.३
अरणी, १.१.५, ८
अरणीषु, ५.१.८
अरण्यस्य, ५.१.४
अरण्योः, १.१.२, ८; २.३.२
अरत्नयः, ५.४.५[२]
अरत्निप्रमाणाः, ५.५.४
अरत्निमात्रः, ५.५.४
अरत्निमात्रपृष्ठ्याया, ५.५.१
अरत्निमात्राणि, ५.१.२
अरत्निकमात्रे, ५.५.१
अरत्निमात्रे, ५.५.१[२]; ५.४
अरत्निषु, ५.४.४
अरत्न्यन्तरालाः, ५.५.४
अरुणपिशङ्गलैकहायनी, ५.२.१
अर्घ्यादिभिः, १.१.३
अर्थः, १.१.४; ५.५.२
अर्थत्वेन, १.१.६
अर्थलुप्तमन्त्रेण, ६.१.४
अर्थलुप्तम्, ३.४.३; ४.३.१; ६.१.४
अर्थलुप्तानि, ४.२.४
अर्थलुप्ते, ३.४.३; ४.३.१
अर्थलोपः, ४.२.४[२]
अर्थवचसः, १.१.१
अर्थविरुद्धम्, ५.१.५
अर्थान्तरेण, ५.१.७
अर्धकक्षम्, ३.२.१
अर्धचतुर्दशमात्रेण, ५.४.५
अर्धचन्द्राकृतिः, १.१.४
अर्धपञ्चमप्रक्रमाः, ५.४.५

अर्धप्रक्रमम्, ५.४.५[२]
अर्धप्रक्रममात्रम्, ५.४.५
अर्धप्रक्रमे, ४.१.२
अर्धम्, १.१.४
अर्धवेलाम्, ५.३.१; ६.१.५
अर्धव्रतम्, ५.४.६
अर्धसमिद्भिः, ५.४.७
अर्धस्तनव्रतम्, ५.४.६; ६.२
अर्धस्रुवैः, ३.२.६
अर्धाष्टककिष्कुक्षेत्रः, ५.४.६
अर्धिनः (ऋत्विजः), ५.६.४
अर्धिभ्यः (ऋत्विग्भ्यः), ५.६.४
अर्हयेत्, १.१.३
अलक्षणम्, ३.२.१
अलक्षधियाम्, प्रस्ता: १
अलङ्करणशब्देन, ६.२.४
अलंकरणानि, १.२.१
अलंकारः, ३.१.१
अलंकुर्वन्ति, ३.१.१
अलंकृत्य, २.३.१; ४.१.२; ३.२
अवकाशानि, १.१.४
अवखण्ड्य, २.३.३; ४.३.२
अवगाहेत, ५.१.८
अवगूहनार्थः, ५.३.३
अवघातः, ३.४.२
अवघातपक्षे, ३.४.२
अवघातसंवापः, ६.१.३
अवघार्य, १.१.७
अवघ्नन्ति, ३.४.२
अवघ्रातानि, ३.४.५[२]
अवजिघ्रति, २.४.३
अवज्वलनादि, ६.१.४
अवज्वलनाभिवासने, २.२.२
अवटम्, ५.५.२
अवतु, १.१.१
अवतृणैः, ३.२.२
अवत्तप्रदेशानाम्, २.३.३
अवत्तम्, ४.३.३[२]
अवत्ताम्, ४.३.२
अवदधाति, ५.२.२
अवदातुम्, २.३.२
अवदानक्रमेण, २.२.३
अवदानम्, ३.४.५
अवदानानि, २.३.२; ३; ४.३.२[२]
अवदानेषु ४.३.३
अवदानैः, ६.१.१
अवदाय, ३.२.५; ६; ४.३.२[३], ३
अवदीयमानायाम्, २.४.६
अवदेये, २.२.१
अवद्येत्, ३.१.२; २.५; ३.३; ४.३.२; ६.३.३
अवधाय, १.१.७
अवधारणम्, ३.२.६
अवधृतनिश्चयः, ५.१.८
अवनयतः, ६.१.५
अवनयति, २.३.६; ५.२.२
अवनयेत्, ४.३.१; ५.३.४
अवनयेयुः, ६.२.१
अवनिनयनम्, ५.६.५
अवनीय, ६.३.३
अवभृथपात्रसादनादि, ३.२.६
अवभृथम्, ३.२.६
अवमार्जयते, २.४.६
अवयातान्, ५.२.२
अवशिष्टः, १.१.४
अवशिष्टम्, ४.३.२
अवशिष्टात्, १.४.४; ६.३.४
अवशिष्टान्, ५.३.२

अवशिष्य, ५.४.५[२]
अवशेषयेत्, ५.३.५; ५.१; ६.३.३
अवश्यदेयम्, ५.१.४
अवसरः, ५.१.६
अवसानमन्त्रम्, ५.१.८
अवसाय, ४.१.१
अवसृज्य, २.४.७
अवस्कन्दयेत्, ५.२.१
अवस्कभ्य, ३.२.६; ५.४.७; ६.२
अवस्कम्भनम्, ३.२.३; ६.१.१
अवस्तरण-, ५.५.३
अवस्तरणात्, ४.१.३
अवस्थापयितव्याः, १.१.१
अवस्थितानि, १.१.१
अवस्थितायाः, १.१.७
अवस्यति, ५.१.४
अवस्राव्य, ५.२.१
अवहत्य, २.४.२; ५.३.२
अवहितैः, ३.३.१
अवान्तरदीक्षायाम्, ५.३.५
अवान्तरदीक्षाविसर्गकाले, ५.३.५
अवान्तरदीक्षाव्रते, ५.३.५
अवान्तरदीक्षोपादानविसर्गाभ्याम्, ५.३.५
अवान्तरावकाशः, २.२.२
अवान्तरावकाशेन, २.२.२
अवान्तरेडाम्, २.४.६; ४.३.२; ६.३.३
अविकारः, ३.५.१[३]; ४.४.२
अविकृतः (प्रैषः), ५.६.२
अविकृत्या, ३.१.१
अविज्ञातव्याधेः, ५.१.७
अविभक्ताः, ३.२.३; ५.६.१
अविमुक्तानि, ४.४.३
अविरुद्धम्, ५.६.३
अविरोधम्, १.१.१
अविवेकम्, २.४.२
अविशेषाद्, १.१.१
अविशेषेण, १.४.३, ४
अवेक्षणम्, ३.२.६
अवेक्षते, ६.२.५
अवेक्षमाणम्, ३.३.२; ४.३
अवेक्षयेत्, ३.२.६
अवेक्षेते, २.२.२
अवेक्षेत्, ३.२.४; ६.२.५[२]
अवेक्ष्य, २.२.२
अवेक्ष्यमाणम्, १.१.६
अवोक्षति, १.१.४
अव्यवेत्य, २.३.४
अशक्यम्, १.३.३; ५.१.४[३]
अशक्या, प्रस्ता. १
अशक्याः, ५.१.८
अशक्यानि (कर्माणि), १.५.३
अशनिहतम्, १.१.५
अशूद्रोच्छिष्टम्, ३.६.१
अश्नाति, ३.६.१
अश्वत्थम्, १.१.२
अश्वत्थस्य, १.१.२
अश्वमेधे, १.१.३
अश्वम्, १.३.२
अश्वशफबुध्ने, ५.१.३; ६.१.२
अश्विभ्याम्, ३.३.३
अषाढाभिः, ३.२.१
अष्टग्रहणम्, ४.१.२
अष्टमभागः, ५.३.२
अष्टर्चेन, ५.१.६
अष्टाकपालमुखानि, २.३.४
अष्टाकपालम्, २.३.४; ४.६
अष्टाशीतितमाङ्गुलपार्श्वमानीम्, ४.१.१
अष्टौकृत्वः ६.१.६[३]

असंयाज्य, ३.४.५
असंवपन्ति, २.२.१
असंवेशने, ५.१.७
असकृत्, २.२.३
असकृन्मन्त्रः, २.२.१
असंगमयन्, ४.३.४[२]
असञ्चरे, २.३.५
असति, १.१.९; ५.८.२
असन्नयतः, २.३.३
असन्नोपस्नानम्, ३.२.३
अस्कन्दयन्, २.१.२
अस्तमनवेलायाम्, १.१.७
अस्तमिते, ६.१.१
अस्तु श्रौषट्, २.३.२
अस्पर्शयन्निव, ५.६.५
अस्मद्विधैः, १.१.१
अस्माकम्, प्रस्ता. १
अस्माभिः, प्रस्ता १[२]
असमारूढेषु, ५.१.४
असंभवे, ५.१.१[३]
असंभिन्दन्, ४.३.४
असहनादिकम्, ५.३.५
असिदादानादिना, ५.३.५
असुत्यस्य, ५.१.८
असुषिरम्, ४.१.१
अस्तु श्रौषट्, २.३.२
अस्यति, ४.१.३
अस्यन्निव, ५.४.४
अहतंवासः, ५.१.५
आकर्मपरिसमाप्तेः, ५.३.४[२]
आकाशम्, ५.६.५
आकांक्षेत्, ३.३.१
आकूतिं (देवीम्), १.१.२
आकूत्यावेदनम्, १.१.२
आकृतिविशेषः, ५.४.६
आक्रान्तम्, १.३.२
आखरम्, ५.५.३
आख्याताः, २.४.४
आगमः, १.१.९; २.१
आगुः, २.३.२
आगृहमेधीयसमाप्तेः, ३.३.१
आग्नीध्रः, ४.१.२; ५.६.३; ६.२.१[२]
आग्नीध्रागारम्, ५.५.३; ४.५; ६.४
आग्नीध्रागारस्य, ५.५.४
आग्नीध्राहृताभिः, ५.३.५
आग्नीध्रीयः, ५.१.२
आग्नीध्रीयम्, ५.६.३, ४; ६.१.१, २; २.३, ४
आग्नीध्रीयात्, ६.२.३
आग्नीध्रीयादीनाम्, ६.२.५
आग्नीध्रीये, ५.४.५; ५.४; ६.१.१; २; ३; २.४
आग्नीध्रे, ५.८.१[२]
आग्नेयविकारः, १.३.३
आग्नेयविकारस्य, ३.४.३
आग्नेयविकारेषु, ३.१.१
आग्न्याधेयिकम्, १.३.१
आग्न्याधेयिकाः, १.४.१
आग्रयणात्, ६.२.१
आग्रयणादीनाम्, १.१.१
आग्रयणम्, ६.२.२, ५
आग्रयणे, ६.३.३
आघारः, ५.४.१[२]
आघारप्रभृति, ३.४.५
आघारम्, २.३.१; ४.४
आघारयेत्, २.३.१
आघाराभिमन्त्रणम्, ३.६.३
आघारेण, ५.४.१

आङ्गिरसम्, ५.१.१
आऽङ्गुलीनां विसर्जनात्, ५.६.५
आचमननिमित्तेषु, ५.१.८
आचमय्य, १.१.६
आचमसप्रदानात्, ५.१.६
आचम्य, २.१.१; ५.१.३
आचम्याचम्य, १.४.४
आचान्तः, २.५.१
आचान्ताः, ५.५.२
आचार्याभिप्रायः, ४.२.२; ५.२.२; ८.२; ६.२.२; ४; ३.२
आचार्याभिप्रेतः, ५.२.२
आचार्याभिहितम्, ५.१.५
आचार्यस्य, २.३.४^{2}
आचार्येण (इष्टम्), १.२.१; ६.१.६
आच्छिद्रिकोपादानपक्षे, ३.१.२; ४.१.२
आच्छिद्रिकोपादानम्, २.३.४; ३.४.३
आच्छिनत्ति, ३.१.१; ४.१
आच्छ्यति, ४.२.३
आज्यग्रहणम्, ४.१.२; ४.१
आज्यग्रहणादि, २.२.२
आज्यग्रहणानुमन्त्रणेषु, ३.६.२
आज्यग्रहणान्तम्, ५.६.३^{2}
आज्यग्रहणानन्तरम्, ६.१.२
आज्यग्रहान्, २.४.४
आज्यध्रुवा, ४.१.२
आज्यभागम्, ४.२.५
आज्यभागयोः, ३.२.५; ६
आज्यभागादि, ३.३.३^{2}
आज्यभागाघारयोः, २.३.२
आज्यम्, १.५.२; ५.२.१
आज्यभागाभ्याम्, ४.३.२
आज्यभागौ, ४.२.४; ५.२.२; ७.१; ६.३.१; २
आज्यम्, १.१.७
आज्यस्थालीः, ३.२.१; ४.१.२
आज्यस्थालीद्वयम्, ४.३.३
आज्यस्थालीम्, १.१.७; २.१.२; ३.२.३; ६; ३.१; ४.१.२; ५.४.२^{2}, ३^{2}
आज्यस्थालीस्थम् (आज्यम्), २.३.६
आज्यस्थाल्याज्यम्, ३.२.६
आज्यस्थाल्याम्, १.३.१; ५.२.१; ४.३
आज्यस्थाल्याः, १.३.१^{2}; २.३.२; ४; ४.१.२; ४.२
आज्यस्थाल्ये, ३.२.६
आज्यहविष्काणाम्, १.३.१
आज्यानि, ३.४.३; ५.६.३; ४
आज्याधिश्रयणमात्रम्, ५.४.१; ६.३
आज्याधिश्रयणान्तम्, ५.६.३
आज्येन, ३.१.१
आञ्जनम्, ५.३.५
आञ्ज्य, १.१.६
आण्डीबलत्वादिगुणयुक्तः, ५.७.१
आतच्य, २.१.१; ३.१.१; २.१
आतञ्चनम्, ३.२.१; ५.८.२
आतनोति, ५.४.५
आतनुयात्, ५.१.२
आतमितोः, २.४.३
आतिथ्यानन्तरम्, ५.४.१
आतिथ्यान्ते, ५.४.१
आतिथ्यार्थम्, १.१.६
आतिथ्यायाम्, ५.२.२
आत्तेषु, ६.३.२
आत्मनश्छायाम्, २.२.२; ३.२.६; ४.३; ५.१.७; ६.१, ३; ६.१.१
आत्मानम्, १.१.१; ४.४; २.२.२; ३.४, ५, ६; ३.२.२
आत्मीयमण्डलम्, १.१.६

आत्मीयात् (गृहात्), १.१.६
आददीत्, १.१.८; ४.३; २.३.१; ६; ५.५.३
आदधानः, २.३.१
आदध्यात्, २.३.३; ४.४
आदरेण, ५.४.४
आदशहोतुर्व्याख्यानात्, ५.६.४
आदित्यग्रहाय, ५.८.२
आदित्यप्रक्षेपणार्थम्, ५.२.१
आदित्यम्, ४.४.१
आदित्यस्थाल्ये, ६.१.५
आदित्योदयम्, ३.३.१
आदिशेत्, २.२.१
आदीपयन्ति, ५.४.७
आदीप्तायाम्, १.४.३
आदीप्ते (इध्मे), २.३.१
आदीप्य, १.१.७
आद्रवतः, ६.३.३
आद्यौ (स्वरौ), २.३.२
आद्रियेरन्, ५.४.४
आधत्ते, १.१.८; ५.१
आधवनीयपूतभृतोर्योगः, ५.८.१
आधवनीयपूतभृतौ, ५.१.२
आधवनीयपूतभृदाख्यौ, ५.८.१
आधवनीयात्, ६.२.१; २; ३
आधवनीये, ६.२.१
आधातुम्, १.३.२
आधानक्रमेण, १.४.२; ४
आधानम्, १.४.१
आधानमन्त्रः, १.१.८[२]
आधानमन्त्रम्, १.१.८
आधानादीनाम्, १.१.१
आधानानन्तरम्, १.३.२
आधाय, १.४.४; २.३.५
आधास्यमानः, १.१.१
आधास्यमानस्य, १.१.२, ६, ८
आधास्यमाने (ने), १.१.८
आधास्यम्, १.४.१
आधीयमानम्, २.४.४
(इध्मौ) आधीयमानौ, ३.६.३
आधेयः, १.१.४
आध्वर्यवम्, १.१.८; २.१.३; ३.१.१; ४.५;
४.१.२; ५.१.७; ३.५; ६.१.२
आध्वर्यवाः (मन्त्राः), २.२.३
आध्वर्यवे, १.१.८; २.४.४
आध्वर्यवौ, १.१.९
आनयन्ति, ५.२.२
आनीताः (आपः), २.१.२; २.१
आऽनुवचनात्, २.३.२
आन्तःसरः, ५.२.१
आपन्नात्, ५.१.७
आपरिसमाप्तेः, १.१.८
आपर्वणम्, १.५.१
आपस्तम्बः, प्रस्ता १
आपादयितुम्, ५.३.४
आपादयेत्, १.१.१
आपीड्य, १.४.२
आपूर्विकेण विधानेन, १.१.७
आपोहिष्ठीयाभिः (ऋग्भिः), २.५.१; ३
आपोहिष्ठीयेन (तृचेन), २.३.७
आप्यम्, १.१.६
आप्यायते, ४.२.२
आप्यायनकाले, ५.२.१
आप्यायनमन्त्रः, ६.३.४
आप्यायनमन्त्रान्, ४.२.३
आप्यायनम्, ३.४.५; ६.१.४
आप्यायनाः, ६.२.१
आप्यायनार्थम्, ४.२.२
आप्याययन्ति, ६.३.४

आप्याययेत्, **४**.२.४
आप्याय्य, **१**.३.२; **२**.४.७
आप्येन (पुरुषेण), **५**.१.८
आप्रतीक्षम्, **२**.४.७
आप्रणीताभ्याम्, **३**.३.१
आप्राणसंमर्शनाद्भिः (प्राशनम्), **२**.५.३
आबध्य, **५**.३.१
आभाति, **१**.४.३; **४**.१.२; २.५; **५**.६.२
आभाषेत, **२**.५.१
आभिमन्त्रणाद्, **१**.१.८
आभ्यन्तरौ, **५**.६.४
आमन्त्र्य, **२**.३.१
आमयाविनः, **६**.२.२
आमहीयवेन, **१**.१.९
आमात्, **३**.१.२
आमिक्षा, **५**.८.२; **६**.१.३; २.४
आमिक्षापक्षे, **६**.१.३, ४; २.४
आमिक्षापात्रम्, **३**.१.१; २.३; **६**.१.४
आमिक्षापात्रयोः, **३**.२.४
आमिक्षापात्रे, **६**.१.४
आमिक्षाम्, **३**.१.१[३]; **६**.१.४
आमिक्षायाम्, **३**.६.१
आमिक्षार्थम्, **६**.२.४
आमिक्षाश्रपणीम्, **३**.२.३
आमुष्यायणन्त्या, **५**.१.७
आमुष्यायनः, **५**.१.७
आम्नाताः, **१**.१.२
आम्नातेन, **१**.१.७
आम्नानभेदात्, **१**.३.३
आयतनप्रदेशाभ्यधिकविस्ताराणि, **५**.५.१
आयतनम्, **१**.१.३, ४
आयतने, **१**.१.८; **३**.२.५
आयतीः, **२**.१.१; **३**.२.१
आयुधानि, **२**.४.३
(प्राणान्) आयम्य, **२**.४.१; **५**.४.४; ५
आयामविस्ताराभ्याम्, **५**.४.५
आयुष्कामस्य, **१**.३.२
आयूपावरीयात्, **५**.४.७
आरण्येन, **१**.१.५
आरभेत, **२**.३.२; **३**.२.१; ३.१
आरम्भणीयम्, **३**.६.१
आरम्भणीयवैश्वदेवयोः, **३**.६.१
आरम्भणीयायै, **३**.१.१
आरम्भणीये, **३**.६.१
आरम्भणीयेष्ट्याम्, **३**.१.१
आराधितानाम्, **१**.१.३
आरेचनेन, **२**.४.१
आर्जवे, **२**.३.२; **५**.४.४; ५
आर्षेयाः, **१**.१.८
आलम्, **५**.४.३
आलब्धव्याः, **१**.१.२
आलभ्य, **६**.१.१
आलभ्यते, **१**.१.१
आलोडनम्, **६**.१.४
आलोड्य, **२**.२.१
आवर्तते, **२**.१.२; ३.२; **३**.२.१; **४**.२.३; **५**.१.७; **६**.१.६
आवर्तनानि, **२**.२.१
आवपते, **२**.२.१
आवपन्, **२**.१.३
आवपनक्रमेण, **६**.२.३
आवपनम्, **६**.१.४
(अङ्गार)-आवर्त्तनानि, **२**.२.१
आवषट्कारात्, **२**.३.२
आऽवान्तरदीक्षाविसर्गात्, **५**.३.५
आवृता, **३**.२.२
आवृत्य, **२**.३.७; **५**.३.१
आवृत्तया, **५**.३.२

आवृत्तिः, **२**.१.३; **३**.१.१; ४.३; **५**.५.३
आवेदनात्, **२**.४.३
आवेद्यन्तात्, **५**.१.४
आवेद्यासादनात्, **१**.४.२
आवेद्युपवेशनात्, **१**.४.२
आशकलावगूहनम्, **४**.१.३
आशंक्येत, **१**.१.२
आशयन्, **५**.१.५
आशयपात्रम्, **३**.१.१
आशास्य, **१**.५.१
आशितः, **५**.१.४
आशिताः, **३**.३.३
आशिरे, **५**.१.२
आशिषः, **१**.५.१
आश्रावणात्, **२**.३.२[२]
आश्रावणादयः, **२**.४.६
आश्रावणादि, **३**.४.५
आश्रावणे, **२**.३.२
आश्रावयेत्, **२**.३.२[२]; ५; **३**.१.२; **६**.२.६; ३.२
आश्राविते, **२**.३.१; ४.५
आश्लेषयतः, **३**.२.३
आश्वत्थम्, **१**.१.५
आश्वत्थे, **५**.१.३
आश्विनम्, **६**.२.५
आसंक्षालननिनयात्, **४**.३.१
आसजति, **१**.१.८
आसदनम्, **५**.५.२
आसनम्, **२**.५.३
आसन्द्याम्, **५**.३.४
आसन्नम्, **५**.४.७
आसन्नां (हविः), **४**.४.३
आसन्नोपस्थानान्तम्, **५**.३.३
आसमाप्तेः, **२**.५.१
आसाते, **६**.३.१
आसादनसंमर्शनाभिघारणमन्त्राः, **४**.३.३
आसादनान्तम्, **२**.२.२
आसादनान्तर्धाननिषजनानि, **६**.१.६
आसादने, **२**.२.१
आसादितासु, **२**.४.७
आसाद्य, **२**.३.५
आसाद्यमानम्, **२**.४.४
आसिच्य, **२**.१.३; **३**.३; ५
आसीनः, **२**.४.३
आऽस्तमयात्, **१**.४.१
आस्तावः, **५**.८.१
आस्तावे, **६**.२.३
आस्यति, **४**.१.३
आस्रावयेत्, **५**.२.२
आस्रुग्व्यूहनात्, **३**.४.४
आस्वरोरवगूहनात्, **४**.४.२
आहरणम्, **१**.३.२
आहरन्नेतीत्यादि, **२**.१.३
आहरेत्, **२**.२.२
आहवनीयः, **१**.३.२
आहवनीयमार्गः, **१**.५.२
आहवनीयम्, **१**.४.४; ५.१[३]; **२**.१.२; ३.१, ४, ४; ४.३; ५.१; **३**.२.१; ४.२, ३; **४**.१.१; २.५; ३.३[२]; ४.२; **५**.१.६, ७, ८; ३.४[३]; ४.२; ५.१; २; ६.३–४[४]; ८.; **६**.१.१[२], २; ४
आहवनीयसमीपे, **४**.२.४
आहवनीयस्य (आयतनम्), **१**.१.४; ३.२; **५**.६.४; **६**.१.१; ३.१
आहवनीयस्यायतने, **१**.१.५
आहवनीयस्यार्धम्, **३**.४.५
आहवनीयाग्निसमिन्धनार्थाय, **५**.४.७
आहवनीयात्, **१**.१.४[२]; **४**.२.२; **५**.३.३

आहवनीये, १.१.७; ४.४; २.३.१; ६; ४.१.३; ५.१.६; ६.३; ६.१.६; ६.३

आहवनीयोपासनम्, ३.१.२

आहार्यः, १.३.२; २.२.२

आहितः, १.४.१

आहितम्, ५.२.३

आहिरण्यप्रासनात्, १.१.८

आहुतिम्, १.१.७

आहुतिः, २.३.२

आहुतिषाहम्, १.१.९

आहूय, ५.१.१

आहृतः, १.३.२

आहृत्य, २.१.१; २; २.१

आहोतुर्व्याख्यानात्, ४.१.२

इक्षुपत्रे, ५.३.४

इक्षुशलाका, ३.४.१

इच्छन्ति, १.४.४[२]

इच्छेत, ५.३.२; ६.३.४

इडापात्रम्, २.१.२; ३.३.१; ४.३.३

इडाम्, २.३.३, ४; ४.६[२], ७[३]; ३.१.२; २.५; ३.३; ४.३.२[२], ५; ६.३.३

इडायाः, १.३.१

इडायाम्, २.३.३; ४.६; ३.३.३

इडार्थम्, ४.३.२

इडालेपाद्, २.३.४

इडावदाने, २.२.१

इडसूनम्, ४.१.२[२]

इतरे, १.४.१

इतरेषु, १.३.३

इति केचित्, see Intro. p. xiii

इत्यन्ये, see Intro. p. xiv

इत्यपरे, see Intro. p. xv ff.

इत्यातः, २.१.१

इत्येके, see Intro. p. xvii ff.

इध्मः, ५.६.२; ८.२

इध्मकाष्ठानि, २.१.१; ५.३.४; ५.४.२

इध्मद्वयम्, ३.२.१

इध्मपश्वाज्योलूखलमुसलम्, २.३.६

इध्मप्रवृश्चनानि, ३.२.५

इध्मप्रोक्षणः, ६.१.२

इध्मम्, १.१.७; २.२.२; ४.१.२[२]

इध्मसदने, २.५.१

इध्मसन्नहनानि, २.३.६

इध्मात्, २.३.१

इध्माबर्हिः, २.२.२; ३.४.३–४; ५.४.२; ५.६. ३; ६.१.१

इन्द्रियकामः, १.१.६

इयन्तम्, १.४.१

इष्टिपक्षे, ४.१.१

इष्टिपूर्वकम्, ५.१.६

इष्टिम्, १.३.३

इष्टिषु, १.३.२

ईषदति (गता), २.१.२

ईषदुत्तानम्, ४.२.३

ईषाम्, ५.५.१; ६.१.२

उक्तक्रमेण, १.५.२

उक्तेन, १.२.१; १.५.३

उक्थः, ६.१.५

उक्थस्य, ६.१.५

उक्थ्यम्, ६.२.२

उचीनानि, ५.१.३

उच्चैः, २.३.३; ४; ५.१; ५.१.१; २

उच्चैस्तरम्, ५.१.३

उच्छिनष्टि, ३.१.२

उच्छिष्टाः, ४.१.३

उच्छिष्येत, ५.१.८

उच्छेषयेत्, ३.१.२

उच्छ्रयति, ५.५.१

उच्छ्रयणेन, ३.३.३
उच्छ्रियमाणाम्, ५.५.२
उज्जितीः, २.४.७
उत्कम्पयति, २.१.३
उत्करः, ३.४.३; ४.१.१
उत्करम्, १.४.२; ४; २.३.४; ५; ५.१
उत्करस्य, २.३.४
उत्करस्यार्जवे, २.२.२
उत्करे, १.१.३; ३.१; ३.१.१
उत्करोपस्थानादि, ६.३.१
उत्काशयति, ४.१.३
उत्क्रमयते, ५.२.२
उत्क्षुभ्य, ५.६.१२
उत्तमर्णत्वनिमित्तेन, १.१.१
उत्तमर्णम्, ५.१.४
उत्तमर्णाय, ५.१.४
उत्तमविकारेषु, ४.४.३
उत्तरतः, १.१.४; ७
उत्तरनाभिच्छादनार्थम्, ५.४.६
उत्तरनाभिम्, ४.१.२[२]
उत्तरपरिग्रहादि, ४.१.२
उत्तरम्, २.३.१; ४.४; ३.३.३
उत्तरलोम, ५.२.१
उत्तरविहारम्, १.५.२
उत्तरविहारस्थः, १.५.१
उत्तरवेदिकस्या, ३.२.२
उत्तरवेदिः, ४.१.२; ५.४.५
उत्तरवेदिम्, २.५.२; ३.२.३, ४; ५.४.५; ६.४; ८.१; ६.२.४; ३.२[२]
उत्तरवेदेः, ५.४.२[३], ६
उत्तरवेद्याः ४.१.२; ५.४.५; ५.६.५
(आ) उत्तरवेद्याः, ६.२.४
उत्तरवेद्याम्, ५.४.६; ६.३.२
उत्तरसिचौ, ३.२.७
उत्तरस्याः, १.३.१
उत्तरा (वेदिः), ३.२.२
उत्तराम् (वेदिम्), ३.२.५
उत्तरांसः, ५.४.५
उत्तराग्नीध्रीयम्, ५.६.४
उत्तरारणिम्, ४.२.१
उत्तरीयादि (व्यतिषङ्गम्), ६.२.३
उत्तरीये (वाससी), ३.२.७
उत्तानम्, २.१.२; ४.३.५; ५.६.५
उत्तानहस्तेन, २.४.६
उत्तानानि (पात्राणि), १.४.२; २.१.२
उत्तानेन (पाणिना), १.५.२; ५.५.१
उत्तारयेत्, ५.१.८
उत्तुषान्, २.१.३
उत्थाय, २.१.२
उद्धृत्य, १.१.८
उत्पूय, २.२.२; ३.२.६; ४.३; ५.१.८
उत्सत्वात्, ५.४.५
उत्सरुमन्तः, ५.१.३
उत्सर्जनप्रायश्चित्तम्, ५.५.१
उत्सर्जने, ५.५.१
उत्सादनप्रदेशेभ्यः, ४.३.३
उत्सादयति, ६.१.५
उत्सिद्य, ५.२.२
उत्सृज्य, १.४.१
उत्सृष्टः, १.४.१
उत्सेधः, ६.१.२
उत्सेधात्, ६.१.२
उत्सृष्टव्यः, १.३.२
उदकपृष्ठ्यायाः, ५.४.५
उदकम्, २.१.३
उदकान्ते, ५.१.८
उदकुम्भम्, २.४.२; ३.४.४[२]
उदगपवर्गम्, १.४.२; २.३.३; ५.६.२

उदगायतम्, ५.४.५; ५.२
उदगावृत्तसप्तम्, १.४.४
उदगावृत्तः, १.४.४
उदगावृत्तानि, २.३.४
उदगुद्वासयति, १.४.२
उदङ्कः, ५.१.३
उदङ्कद्रोणकलशौ, ५.१.३
उदङ्कम्, ६.२.२
उदङ्केन, ६.२.१
उदचन, ६.१.२
उदचनान्, ६.२.२
उदच्य, ६.२.१
उदजेत्, १.१.३
उदञ्चनः, ५.१.३
उदञ्चम्, २.३.१; ५[२]; ४.४.२
उदपात्रम्, १.१.५; ६; २.३.७; ४.१.१; ५.२.२
उदपात्रेण, १.३.१
उदयनीयान्तेः, ६.१.६
उदयनीयार्थम्, ५.२.१
(पुराऽऽदित्यस्य) उदयात्, १.४.२
उदस्तात्, ५.५.३
उदस्य, १.१.३; २.२.२
उदस्यमाने, २.४.३
उदस्येत्, २.३.५; ५.४.२
उदात्ताः, ५.२.२
उदिङ्गनम्, २.१.३
उदिङ्गयति, २.१.३
उदितहोमी, १.४.३
उदितनक्षत्रकालात्, ५.१.७
उदितनक्षत्राणाम्, ५.४.४
उदीक्षयति, ४.१.३
उदीचीनकर्णा, ५.५.१
उदीचीनम्, ५.१.२
उदीचीनाग्रम्, २.१.२; २.२
उदीचीनाग्राभ्याम् (पवित्राभ्याम्), ३.४.३
उदूहति, २.३.५
उदूह्य, ३.३.२; ६.२.६
उदेत्य, ३.४.३
उद्गाता, ५.६.४
उद्गातारः, ६.२.३
उद्गातारम्, ५.१.१
उद्गातुः, १.१.२
उद्गातुर्मुखम्, ६.२.३
उद्गातृचमसे, ६.३.४
उद्गातृपञ्चमाः, १.१.१
उद्गातृषु, ६.३.४
उद्गात्रकाः, १.१.१
उद्गात्रा, १.१.९; ५.५.२
उद्गूह्य, २.१.१
उद्गृह्णाति, ४.१.२
उद्दध्युः, ५.५.१
उद्देशेन, ६.१.५
उद्धननकर्मवर्जम्, ३.३.२
उद्धननम्, ५.४.२
उद्धननादि, १.१.५
उद्धन्ति, १.१.३
उद्धन्यमानम्, १.१.३
उद्धरणसमर्थाम्, १.१.७
उद्धरणम्, १.३.२[२]
उद्धरणपक्षे, १.३.२
उद्धरणादि, १.३.२
उद्धरणोपसमेधपक्षयोः, १.३.२
उद्धरति, ३.३.२
उद्धाय, ३.२.१; ५.५.२
उद्धृतः, १.३.२
उद्धृतमाग्निम्, १.१.७
उद्यच्छति, १.४.३

उद्यच्छन्ते, **४**.१.२
उद्यता, **३**.३.१
उद्वपनानि, **५**.५.३
उद्वादने, **२**.१.३
उद्वासनकाले, **४**.४.३
उद्वासनम्, **१**.५.२; **२**.२.३; **३**.४.३; **६**.२.४
उद्वासनानन्तरम्, **५**.४.७
उद्वासने, **२**.२.३
उद्वासने मार्गः, **२**.३.५
उद्वासयति, **३**.१.१
उद्वासयन्ति, **३**.४.१
उद्वासयेत्, **२**.२.३; ३.४; **६**.१.४
उद्वास्य, **२**.२.३; **३**.१.१; **४**.३.२
उद्वृह्य, **५**.५.१
उद्व्यूहनम्, **२**.३.१
उन्नयति, **१**.४.२; ५.२, ३; **३**.२.७; **५**.६.५
उन्नयन्ते, **६**.१.४
उन्नयेत्, **६**.३.२
उन्नीतः, **१**.४.३
उन्नीतम् **१**.४.३
उन्नेता, **६**.१.२; २[२].१, २, ३; ३.२
उन्मुक्ततुषान्, **२**.१.३
उन्मृज्य, **१**.२.१
उन्मृज्यात्, **६**.२.२
उपकनिष्ठिके, **५**.६.५
उपकल्पनीयम्, **५**.१.२
उपकल्पनीयाः, **१**.१.१
उपकल्पयन्, **५**.१.२
उपकल्पयेत्, **५**.१.२; ८.२; **६**.१.२
उपकल्पितदक्षिणः, **५**.१.१
उपकल्पिताभिः, **५**.१.७
उपकल्प्य, **१**.१.१; **४**.१.२
उपकारिणः, **५**.४.१
उपक्रमः, **५**.४.४
उपक्रमकाले, **५**.८.२
उपगूहति, **१**.३.३
उपगूहनान्तम्, **३**.१.१
उपचारणतः, **५**.३.३
उपतिष्ठते, **१**.१.८, ९; ५.१; **२**.३.१
उपतिष्ठमानः, **४**.४.१
उपतिष्ठमाने, **१**.५.१
उपतिष्ठेत, **१**.२.१[२]; ४.५; ५.१
उपदधाति, **२**.२.१
उपदध्यात्, **२**.२.१
उपधाय, **३**.४.२
उपधि, **४**.३.१
उपधेययोः, **२**.२.१
उपनयति, **५**.१.४
उपनह्य, **५**.२.२
उपनिधाय, **४**.१.२
उपनिधेयम्, **२**.२.१
उपनिनीय, **२**.२.२
उपनिवपन्, **५**.४.७
उपनिषदः, **५**.१.६
उपनिषदनुपनिषदौ, **५**.४.३
उपनिष्क्रमय्य, **१**.१.६
उपनिहिताम्, **५**.५.२
उपन्यस्यति, **५**.३.२
उपपरिक्रम्यः, **४**.३.५
उपपात्रे, **३**.४.५
उपप्रगृह्णन्ति, **६**.३.३
उपबर्हणम्, **१**.१.१[२]; ३.२; **३**.४.१
उपबर्हणानि, **१**.३.२
उपभृतः, **४**.१.२
उपभृतम्, **२**.१.२; २.३; ३.५, ६; **३**.३.१; **४**.१.२; **५**.४.२
उपभृति, **२**.३.१; **३**.४.३, ५[२]; ५.२; **४**.१.२; ३.३

उपभृतैः, ४.३.४
उपभृतोः, ३.६.२; ३
उपभृत्स्थानीयः, २.३.६
उपभृन्मन्त्रेण, ४.१.२
उपमथ्य, ३.४.२
उपमार्ष्टि, १.४.४
उपयच्छन्ति, ४.१.२
उपयत्य, २.३.१
उपयन्ति, ६.२.१
उपयमनी, ३.२.३
उपयमनीहरणम्, ३.२.३
उपयमन्यः, ४.१.२
उपयष्टा, ४.३.४
उपरमति, ४.१.१
उपरमा, ३.२.५
उपरवकाले, ५.४.७
उपरवाद्, ५.५.२
उपरवान्, ५.५.३
उपरवार्थम्, ५.५.२
उपरविभागान्वयात्, ४.१.१
उपरि, १.१.४
उपरिष्टात्, १.१.३
उपलक्षणम्, १.३.३; ३.६.१
उपलक्षयेत्, ४.२.१; ३.१
उपलक्षिते, ४.२.१
उपलक्ष्यन्ते, ६.२.४
उपलाधानात्, ६.१.४
उपलिम्पति, १.४.२
उपवसथः, १.१.२
उपवाजनमन्त्रस्यावृत्तिः, २.३.१
उपवाजनम्, ५.४.३
उपवाजयन्, ३.४.५
उपवाज्य, ३.३.३
उपविशति, ५.४.६; ६.३
उपविशेत्, २.३.४; ५.२
उपविश्य, १.४.४
उपवीजनेन, १.४.४
उपवीज्य, १.४.४
उपवीज्यमानम्, २.४.४
उपवीतविपर्यासे, ५.६.५
उपवेशनम्, ३.२.५; ६.१; ५.१.६
उपवेशने, २.३.४
उपवेशयेत्, ३.३.१
उपवेश्य, २.१.२; ४.१.२; ५.४.२
उपवेषः, २.२.१
उपवेषम्, १.४.२; २.१.२; ३.७ ; ४.७; ४.३.१; ६.१.३
उपवेषोद्वासनम्, ५.१.५
उपव्याहरणम्, १.१.३
उपसंह्रियन्ते, १.१.१
उपसंगृह्णाति, ४.२.३
उपसंगृह्य, २.३.६
उपसत्सु, ५.२.२[२]; ४.२
उपसदङ्गम्, ५.४.४
उपसदन्तानाम्, ५.२.२
उपसदम्, ५.४.४
उपसदि, ५.४.२; ४[२]
उपसद्भिः, ५.४.४[२]
उपसन्नह्य, ५.३.५
उपसमूहति, ५.३.१
-उपसमाधान-, १.२.१
उपसमाधाय, १.१.७, ९; ४.१.२
उपसमेधपक्षः, १.३.२[२]
उपसमेधपक्षे, १.३.२
उपसादनीयम्, १.४.२
उपसादयति, २.२.२
उपसिञ्चति, १.१.८
उपसिञ्चेत्, ३.३.२

उपसीदति, **१**.३.१
उपसीदेत्, **६**.३.४
उपस्तभ्नाति, **५**.३.३
उपस्तंभतः, **५**.३.३
उपस्तंभनस्य, **५**.५.३
उपस्तंभनाभिमर्शनम्, **५**.३.३
उपस्तंभनीम्, **५**.३.३
उपस्तरणमन्त्रः, **२**.२.३
उपस्तरणम्, **२**.२.३; **६**.२.४^{२}
उपस्तरणाभिघारणद्वयोः, **२**.३.४
उपस्तरणाभिघारणार्थाय, **२**.४.२
उपस्तरणाभिघारणे, **२**.३.२; **३**.२.६
उपस्तरणाभिघारणेनोपारंभ, **३**.१.२
उपस्तरणाभिघारिते, **४**.३.४
उपस्तीर्णानाम्, **२**.५.१
उपस्तीर्णाभिघारितम्, **३**.१.१
उपस्तीर्णाभिधारितान्, **३**.३.२
उपस्तीर्य, **१**.१.७
उपस्तृणन्ति, **२**.३.४
उपस्तृणानाः, **१**.३.१
उपस्तृणीते, **१**.३.१; **६**.२.४
उपस्थात्, **४**.२.३
उपस्थानद्वयम्, **१**.१.८
उपस्थानपक्षे, **६**.२.५
उपस्थानम्, **१**.१.९; २.१; **४**.१.२; **६**.२.५
उपस्थानमन्त्रैः, **६**.२.५
उपस्थानानि, **१**.५.३
उपस्थापयति, **३**.२.७; **५**.५.४; ६.३^{२}
उपस्थापयेत, **५**.१.६
उपस्थाय, **१**.१.६; ४.५; ५.१^{४}; ३^{४}; **२**.४.१
उपस्थास्यमानः, **१**.५.१
उपस्थे, **५**.६.३; **६**.३.३
उपस्पर्शनम्, **१**.५.२
उपस्पृशतः, **६**.३.२
उपस्पृशति, **२**.४.१
उपस्पृशेत्, **२**.२.२
उपहत्य, **१**.१.७; ४.४; **२**.३.१
उपहवम्, **६**.३.४^{७}
उपहूतः, **२**.३.४
उपहूतायाम्, **३**.३.३
उपहूते, **६**.३.४
उपहूयमानायाम्, **२**.३.३, ४
उपांशु, **२**.३.२, ३, ६; ४.६; ५.१; **५**.२.२^{४}
उपांशुतराः, **२**.३.६
उपांशुत्वप्रकर्षवचनः, **६**.१.१
उपांशुत्वे, **६**.२.१
उपांशुधर्मः, **३**.१.२
उपांशुपात्रम्, **६**.१.१; २.५
उपांशुपात्रस्य, **६**.१.१
उपांशुयाजनपक्षे, **५**.४.२
उपांशुयाजविकारत्वे, **५**.४.२, ३^{३}; ४.४
उपांशुयाजविकाराः, **५**.४.१
उपांशुयाजविकारवर्जम्, **३**.६.१
उपाकरणम्, **६**.२.३
उपाकरोति, ५.१.७
उपाकुर्यात्, **५**.१.८
उपाञ्जनम्, **३**.४.३
उपात्तः, **५**.६.२
उपात्तनाय, **५**.५.१
उपात्ता, **४**.१.२
उपादद्यात्, **१**.१.६
उपादातव्यम्, **५**.४.७
उपादानम्, **१**.१.२
उपादाय, **२**.१.२
उपादीयते, **५**.४.७
उपाधानार्थः, **२**.२.१
उपानक्ति, **५**.५.१

उपारम्भः **३**.१.२
उपावरोप्य, **५**.३.४
उपावरोहेत्, **२**.३.१
उपावर्तनमन्त्रः, **५**.६.५
उपावहरणीयकूर्चे, **१**.४.२
उपावहरणीयम्, **१**.४.२
उपावहृत्य, **२**.१.१
उपाशीयमानाम्, **२**.४.६
उपेयात्, **२**.२.३; **४**.१.२; ४.१
उपैति, **३**.३.२
उपोद्यच्छन्ति, **६**.३.३
उपोषति, **३**.२.१
उपोष्य, **३**.१.१
उपोहेत्, **३**.३.३
उपौषत्, **३**.२.१
उप्त्वा, **२**.१.३
उप्य, **३**.४.२
उभयतः, **१**.१.४
उभयतःपाशाम्, **१**.१.४
उभयतोमुखे, **५**.१.३
उलूखलम्, **२**.२.२
उलूखलमुसलम्, **२**.४.१, ३; **४**.३.२; ४.२
उलूखलमुसले, **१**.१.७; **४**.४.३
उलूखलाकाराणि, **५**.१.३
उलूखले, **२**.१.३
उल्मुकप्रथमाः, **४**.२.४
उल्मुकम्, **४**.२.२^{३}, ४
उल्मुकादानम्, **५**.३.३
उल्मुकान्, **४**.२.३
उल्मुके, **४**.२.३
उषित्वा, **५**.१.८; **६**.१.१
उष्णीषचतुर्थानि, **५**.२.१
उष्णोदकेन, **१**.४.२
उस्रादयः, **५**.१.७
ऊरौ, **५**.३.३
ऊर्णासूत्रमये, **३**.२.६
ऊर्णास्तुका, **४**.१.२
ऊर्णास्तुकाम्, **५**.३.३
ऊर्ध्वपात्राणि, **५**.१.३; ६.१
ऊर्ध्वमुपराद्, **५**.१.३
ऊर्ध्वलोम, **५**.५.३
ऊर्ध्वविलम्, **६**.२.२
ऊर्ध्वाग्रे, **२**.२.३
ऊर्ध्वाग्रैः, **५**.५.२
ऊषाम्, **१**.१.४
ऊहः, **२**.५.२; **३**.१.१; ४.३^{२}, ४; ६.१
ऊहित्वा, **३**.२.१; **४**.१.२; ४.१
ऊहेत्, **२**.५.२; **३**.१.१; २.३, ४; ६.१^{३}; **४**.४. २; **५**.१.५
ऊहेन, **२**.५.२; **३**.४.१
ऋजीषम्, **६**.२.१^{२}
ऋजु, **३**.३.३
ऋजुधा, **३**.४.५
ऋजुम्, **२**.३.१^{५}
ऋणम्, **५**.१.४
ऋणानि, **१**.१.१
ऋतुदीक्षासु, **५**.१.६
ऋतुपात्रयोः **६**.२.५
ऋतुपात्रे, **६**.१.२
ऋत्विजः, **१**.१.१; **२**.३.५; **३**.३.३; **५**.१.३; ६.१; **६**.१.१^{२}
ऋत्विजाम्, **३**.४.४; **५**.१.१
ऋषभः, **५**.३.२
ऋषिः, प्रस्ता. **१**
एककपालः, **३**.१.२
एककपालके, **३**.१.२
एककपालम्, **३**.४.२
एककपालस्य, **३**.१.२; ६.१

एकचरम्, ४.३.१
एकतयाधिकानि, ३.२.१
एकत्वे, ६.३.२
एकधनाः, ६.१.४; ५
एकधनार्थाः, ५.१.२; ८.१
एकधनिनः, ६.१.४
एकपवित्रा (अपः), २.४.२
एकपवित्राम्, २.४.२
एकमतिरिक्तम्, ३.२.३
एकमन्त्रत्वम्, २.१.३
एकविंशतिपक्षे, २.३.१
एकसराभिः, ५.१.३
एकस्तनमात्रम्, ५.३.५
एकस्तनम्, ५.४.४[२]
एकस्तनव्रतम्, ५.४.६
एकस्तनानि, ५.३.५
एका, १.१.१
एकहायनी, ५.३.३
एकातिरिक्तानि, ३.२.४
एकादशकपालानि, ६.१.२, ४
एकादशकृत्वः, ६.१.६
एकादशकृत्वम्, ४.३.४
एकादशाग्रबिलानि, ५.१.३
एकान्ततः, १.१.१[२]
एके, २.४.२; ३.१.१; ४.१; ५.४.२; ६.१.३[२]
एकेषाम्, ६.१.३, ४
एकैकशः, ३.४.१
एधा, ५.४.७
एधान्, १.३.२; २.२.१; ३.१
एवंजातीयकानि, ४.१.२
एवंजातीयकेषु, ५.५.१
एवंविधाः, ५.१.५
ऐडः, २.३.२
ऐन्द्रः (पशुः), १.१.२
ऐन्द्राग्नकपालोपधानान्तरम्, ३.२.३
ऐन्द्राग्नात्, ३.२.५
ऐन्द्राग्ने, ३.२.३; ६.३
ऐषीकम्, ३.२.१
ऐष्टिकेषु, ६.३.१
ओदनम् १.१.७; ५.२; ३.३.२
ओदनादि, १.५.३
ओदनान्, ३.३.२
ओदने, १.५.३
ओदनोद्धरणाय, ३.३.१
ओन्नक्षत्रात्, ५.१.७
ओप्य, २.३.६; ३.२.५; ५.२.२
ओषधीभ्यः, १.४.४
औत्तरविहारिकम्, ३.२.५
औत्तरवेदिकम्, ३.२.७
औत्तरवेदिके, ४.४.१
औदकीम्, ५.६.१
औदुम्बरम्, १.१.५
औदुम्बरी, ५.१.२; ४.६
औदुम्बरीम्, १.१.३; ५.५.२
औदुम्बरीस्थूणामध्यम्, ५.५.२
औदुम्बरे, ५.१.३
औदुम्बरौ, ५.१.३
औपभृतान्, ४.४.१
औपयजान्, ४.३.४
औपवसथिकया, १.१.७
औपवसथिकस्य, १.३.३
औपानुवाक्यैः, ६.१.२
औप्तापेक्षम्, ५.४.५
औषसमग्निहोत्रम्, ३.३.३
कंसादिमयीम्, १.१.७
ककुदि, ४.२.१
कक्षम्, ३.२.१

कण्डूयनसमर्थः, ५.१.१
कदमन्तरेण, ४.२.१
कनिष्ठिके, ५.६.५
कनीयस्या, ५.३.१[६]
कपालमन्त्रेण, ३.४.२; ६.१.३
कपालादीनि, ४.३.१
कपालानाम्, २.२.१; ४.३
कपालानि, २.२.१; ३.१.१; ४.१, २; ४.३.१, २; ४.३; ५.१.२
कपालोपधानादि, ३.२.३
कपालविमोकः, २.३.७
करणम्, ३.२.२
करण्या, ५.४.६
करम्भपात्रम्, ३.२.१
करम्भपात्राणि, ३.२.३, ४
करंभाय, ६.१.३
करंभार्थम्, ६.२.४
करिष्यन्, २.२२
करंभार्थान्, ६.१.३
करिष्यमाणस्य (कर्मणः), १.१.३
करीरफलानि, ३.२.१
करीरसक्तवः, ३.२.१
करीरसक्तूनाम् ३.२.५
करीरसक्तून्, ३.२.४
करोति, १.१.८; २.१
कर्तव्यवाक्यः, ६.१.६
कर्तव्यवाचः, ६.२.१
कर्तव्याः, १.१.१
कर्तृषु, ५.६.४
कर्तॄन्, २.३.५
कर्ते, १.४.४
कर्मकरणाः, २.२.३
कर्मकलापस्य, १.३.३
कर्मणि, १.३.२
कर्मवशाद्, २.२.३
कर्मशेषम्, ६.१.१
कर्षणादिभिः, १.४.१
कलशयोः, ५.१.३
कलशाः, ५.१.२; ८.१
कलशात्, ६.१.५[२]; २.१[२]
कलशे, ६.२.१
कलशौ, ५.८.१
कला, ५.३.२
कल्पकाराभिप्रायः, ५.८.१, २
कल्पकारेण, १.१.२
कल्पपक्षे, ५.४.५[२]
कल्पयेत्, १.१.४; ५.५.३
कल्पवाक्यानि, २.३.१
कल्पसूत्रकाराणाम्, प्रस्ता.
कल्पे, १.१.७
कल्याणकर्मणः, ३.२.३
कवोत्तानम्, ४.२.३
कशिपुः, ३.४.१
कांसे, ३.१.१
कामण्डलुकाभिः(अद्भिः), १.४.२; २.१.२
कादृशः, ५.१.२
कामयते, ६.२.५
कामिनाम्, ५.५.२
कार्ष्मर्यमयाः, ५.१.३
कार्ष्मर्यमयान्, ५.३.४
कालम्, १.४.१
काले, १.१.२; ३.४.२; ५.८.२
काशमयम्, ५.३.४
कश्चित्, २.२.१
काष्ठकला, ५.१.३
काष्ठानि, ५.१.३
काष्ठस्यान्ते, ४.३.१
काष्ठैः, १.४.२

किन्दून्विन्दून्, ३.२.७
किमङ्ग, प्रस्ता. १
किष्कुभिः, ५.४.६
किष्कोः, ५.४.६
कुक्कुटाण्डमात्रम्, ३.१.१
कुट्टयित्वा, १.५.२
कुडुम्बभारविला, ५.१.३
कुडुम्बभारबिलानि, ५.१.३
कुड्याः, १.४.४
कुड्ये, १.४.४
कुम्भः, ५.६.१
कुम्भम्, ३.४.४
कुम्भाः, ५.१.२
कुम्भीम्, ४.१.२; ३.१
कुम्भ्यः, ५.१.२; ६.१.४
कुम्भ्याम्, ४.३.१; २
कुरुत, ५.३.२
कुर्वीत, प्रस्ता. १
कुशलतया, ५.५.२
कुशलाः, ४.२.१
कूपे, ५.२.२
कूर्चम्, १.४.२
कूर्चापिहितेन, ५.६.१
कूर्चे, १.२.१; ४.४[२]
कूर्माकृतिम्, २.२.१
कूष्माण्डमात्रम्, ३.१.१
कृतकर्ते (?), १.४.४
कृतमन्वीक्षमाणः, २.५.२
कृतानुकरः, ५.१.५
कृतानुकरणपक्षे, ५.१.५, ६
कृतेण्ड्वम्, ५.८.१
कृत्तिकाद्यानाम् ५.४.४
कृत्वा, १.४.२
कृद्भिः, ६.३.२
कृष्णविषाणा, ५.१.१, ६
कृष्णाजिनस्तरणमात्रम्, ५.३.३
कृष्णाजिना, ५.१.६
कृष्णाजिनात्, ५.१.६
कृष्णाजिनादानात्, ३.४.२
कृष्णाजिनादानादि, ३.४.२
कृष्णाजिनानि, ५.१.३
कृष्णाजिने, ५.१.६
क्लृप्तचषालः, ४.१.२
केचित्, १.१.३, ८[२], ९; ४.४; ५.२; २.२.१[२]; ३.४; ५.२; ३.२.३; ४.२.२; ५.५.४; ६.२, ३[२]
केनचिद्, १.१.१
केशश्मश्रू, १.१.६
कैशिनी, ५.१.६
कैशी (दीक्षा), ५.१.६
कौण्डिन्यानाम्, १.१.९
क्रतुकरणम्, ६.१.५
क्रत्वर्थम्, ५.५.२
क्रत्वर्थानि, ५.५.२
क्रयदेशे, ५.३.१
क्रयसंबन्धम्, ५.३.२
क्रयाय, ५.१.२
क्रयार्थाः, ५.१.३
क्रियापदम्, ४.२.१
क्रियेरन्, १.३.३
क्रीडमानाः, ३.३.३
क्रीते (राजनि), ५.६.५
क्लन्निम्, ५.२.३
क्लीबम्, ५.१.८
क्षत्रियम्, ५.१.४
क्षत्रियस्य, १.१.४
क्षिप्रम्, ५.३.२
क्षीरम्, ५.३.२

क्षुरगन्धि, ५.१.५
क्षुरपथम्, ५.१.५
क्षुल्लकवैश्वदेवस्य, ६.१.२
क्षेमा, ३.६.१
क्षेमे, १.४.४
क्षौमाभावे, ५.१.५
क्षौमे, ५.१.१
खटवादि (प्रतिषेध:), ३.६.१
खण्डत:, ५.६.३
खननम्, ५.२.३
खनन्ति, ४.१.१
खात्वा, ५.२.३
खादिरा:, २.१.१
गतश्रिय:, १.३.२
गन्धपुष्पेन, ३.१.१
गन्धपुष्पै:, २.३.१
गभस्तिमता, ३.३.१
(प्राग्) गमयित्वा, १.४.४
गवां दुग्धे, ३.३.१
गवालम्भम्, १.१.६
गा:, २.१.१[२]; ३.२.१
गाने, १.१.९[२]
गायन्त:, ३.३.३
गार्हपत्नीम्, ३.२.४
गार्हपत्यम्, १.४.२[२], ४; ५.१[२], २; २.१.१; ३.५; ४.७; ३.२.१, ३; ४.१; ५.६.१, २, ३
गार्हपत्यस्य, १.१.४[३], ६; ३.४.२
गार्हपत्यस्यायतनम्, १.१.४[३]
गार्हपत्यस्योद्धते, १.१.७
गार्हपत्यहोमम्, १.४.५
गार्हपत्यान्वाहार्यपचनयो:, ३.४.१
गार्हपत्यान्वाहर्यपचनाहवनीयान्, ५.६.२
गार्हपत्याभिमन्त्रणम्, २.१.३
गार्हपत्याहवनीययो:, ५.४.२; ८.२
गार्हस्थ्याश्रमप्रभृति, १.२.१
गुणात्, २.२.३
गुणेन, २.२.३
गुदतृतीयम्, ४.३.३
गुदतृतीयस्य, ४.३.४
गृहमेधीयतण्डुलाभ्यादानम्, ३.३.१
गृहमेधीयस्य, ३.३.१
गृहे, १.१.६
गृह्णन्ति, १.३.३
गृह्या:, ३.२.३; ३.३
गो:, २.३.२, ५.३.२
गोमतीम् (ऋचम्), २.४.७
गोदाने, ५.१.५
गोमयेन, १.४.२
गोष्ठे, ५.१.८
गो: समुच्चय:, ४.४.३
गौ:, १.३.२; ४.३.२[२]; ४.३
ग्रन्थिरहिताम्, ५.५.२
ग्रन्थे, ५.३.५
ग्रहणकाले, ५.६.१
ग्रहणमन्त्र:, ६.२.२
ग्रहणमन्त्रा:, ४.१.२
ग्रहणाभावात्, ४.४.२
ग्रहणे, २.२.३
ग्रहम्, ६.१.५; ६
ग्रहवर्जम्, १.४.३
ग्रहसंस्रावनिमित्तम्, ६.३.४
ग्रहावकाशचरणम्, ६.२.५
ग्रहावकाशचर्यर्थम्, ६.२.३
ग्रामस्य, ५.१.४
ग्रामे, ५.१.४
ग्रावसु, ६.१.२
ग्रावा, ६.१.१

ग्रावाणः, ५.६.१; ५.६.४
ग्रावाणम्, ६.२.१
ग्रावादीनि, ६.१.२
ग्राव्णः, ६.१.२; २.१
ग्राव्णोऽभिमर्शनम्, ६.१.२
ग्रीष्मे, ३.२.१
घर्मवान्, ५.४.१
घर्मोद्वासनाय, ५.१.२
घृताक्तम्, १.१.५
घ्राणभक्षम्, ३.१.२
चक्रम्, ५.५.१[३]
चक्षुर्निमितः, १.१.४
चतुरतत्निम्, ४.१.१
चतुरश्राणि, १.१.४
चतुर्गृहीतम्, २.३.६; ३.३.२; ४.१.२; ६.२.३
चतुर्गृहीतानि, ५.४.३
चतुर्गृहीते, ३.२.६; ५.२.२
चतुर्दशीमुपात्तदिगन्तरेण, ५.१.१
चतुर्धाकरणे, २.३.४
चतुर्धाकृतम्, २.३.४
चतुर्धाक्रियापक्षे, २.३.४
चतुर्होतारम्, ३.३.३
चतुर्होतुःस्थाने, १.३.१; ४.१.२
चतुर्होत्रर्थम्, ३.१.१
चतुःशताङ्गुलपश्चिमबाहुम्, ४.१.१
चतुःशरावः (ओदनः), ५.२.१
चतुष्टयानि, ५.१.२
चतुष्टोमे, ६.१.५
चतुष्पथे, १.१.६
चतुस्तन-, ५.३.५
चतुःस्रक्तिः, ३.४.१; ४.१.२
चनसित, ५.१.६
चनसितेन, ५.१.६
चमसम्, ५.३.४; ६.३.२, ३, ४[४]
चमसाः, ५.१.३
चमसाध्वर्यवः, ६.३.२[२]
चमसाध्वर्युभिः, ६.३.२
चमसान्, १.१.७; ६.१.२; ३.२, ३
चमसाहुताः, ६.३.४
चमसाध्वर्यु, ६.१.४
चमसिभिः, ६.३.४
चमसे (अधि), ३.१.१; ५.१.६
चमसेषु, ६.३.२
चमसौ, ५.१.२
-चरतन्त्र-, प्रस्ता., १
चरति, ५.८.१
चरव्यान्, २.२.१; ३.१.१
चराचरम्, १.१.१
चरितार्थता, १.३.३
चरित्वा, ४.३.२[२]; ६.३.२
चरुः, ३.१.१
चरुम्, २.२.१, ३; ५.२.१
चरुरूपात्, १.३.३
चरुविकारत्वेन, ६.२.४
चरुस्थालीम्, २.१.२; ३.१.१; ३.१
चरुस्थाल्याम्, २.४.३
चरूणाम्, ३.६.१
चरेत्, ५.८.२
चरोः, २.३.३; ३.६.१
चरौ, ५.२.१; २.२
चर्म, ६.१.२
चर्मणि, ५.३.२[३]; ६.१.२
चर्मानुडुहम्, १.१.७
चषालच्छेदने, ४.१.१
चषालशकलाभ्याच्छादने, ४.१.१
चातुर्मास्येषु, २.५.२; ३.६.१
चात्वालकालम्, ४.१.१

चात्वालकाले, **५**.४.६
चात्वालप्रदेशे, **४**.२.५
चात्वालम्, **५**.८.१
चात्वालस्य, **४**.२.२
चात्वालात्, **४**.१.१
चात्वाले, **४**.२.५; **६**.१.४
चात्वालोत्करौ, **३**.२.२; **४**.२.१, २; **५**.४.५
चान्द्रमसं लक्ष्यं, **१**.१.४
चूर्णीकृतानि, **३**.२.१
च्छदिः, **५**.३.३; ५.१, २; ५.१
छदिःसन्धिषु, **५**.५.२
छदींषि, **५**.५.१[२], २
छेदः (मन्त्रस्य), **२**.१.३
छागादयः, **५**.१.३
छादनीयाः, **१**.३.२
छादयति, **२**.२.१; **५**.५.२
छित्वा, **१**.५.२; **२**.१.१[२]; **५**.८.२
जघनेन, **२**.३.२; **५**.१.२; **६**.३.२
जपः, **२**.२.२
जपति, **१**.१.८; **२**.१.२
जपनीयाः, **२**.२.३; **६**.२.६
जपित्वा, **२**.३.४
जपेत्, **१**.५.३; **३**.६.२
जम्बू, **५**.१.३
जलप्रस्रवणार्थम्, **१**.४.४
जलम्, **१**.५.२
जहाति, **५**.५.३
जागरयति, **३**.३.३
जातवेदसे, **१**.१.५
जातिवचनम्, **५**.१.७
जानूनि (सन्धाय), **६**.२.३
जान्वाच्य, **६**.२.२
जामदग्न्यः, **२**.३.२
जाराः, **३**.२.४
जारान्, **३**.२.४
जिह्वामूले, **२**.५.१
जीर्णः, **१**.४.१
जीर्णं वासः, **१**.४.१
जीवपिता, **२**.४.२
जुष्ट्यावचनमन्त्रस्य, **२**.१.३
जुहुयात्, **२**.३.२[२], ३, ५
जुहूगतेन (आज्येन), **४**.२.१
जुहूपभृतोः, **४**.३.३[२]; ४.२
जुहूपभृतौ, **२**.३.१; **४**.१.२; **५**.४.३
जुहूम्, **२**.१.२; **२**.३.१[२], ३, ५, ६[२]; **४**.१.२; ३.३; ४.२
जुहोति, **१**.१.७, ९; ४.३, ४; **२**.३.२; **३**.२.६; ३.१; **४**.२.१
जुह्वा, **२**.३.१; **३**.२.६; **४**.२.१; **५**.१.५
जुह्वाम्, **२**.३.६; **४**.१.२; ३.५
जुह्वोः, **३**.६.२, ३
जोषंकृतेषु, **६**.१.१
जौहवेः, **३**.२.६; **५**.४.३
जौहवान्, **४**.४.१
जौह्वैः, **५**.४.३
ज्ञानाभिमानेन, प्रस्ता. **१**
ज्यायः, **१**.३.२; **२**.३.२; **३**.४.१[२], ४; ५.२; **४**.३.२, ३; ४.२; **५**.२.२; ४.५[२], ७; ५.३; ६.१, २, ५; **६**.१.२, ३, ५; २.१[२], ५[२]; ३.२
ज्याय इव, **४**.१.२[२]; **५**.६.२[२]
ज्यायान्, **३**.२.४, ५, ६; ३.२; ४.२, ३; **४**.२.४; ४.२; **५**.१.७; ६.३
ज्यायान् इव, **४**.२.५; ३.२
ज्योतिष्टोमेन, **५**.१.१[२]
तज्जातीयैः, **२**.३.५
तण्डुलम्, **१**.५.२
तण्डुलाः, **१**.५.३

तण्डुलान्, **२**.४.२; **५**.२.१, २
तण्डुलानि, **६**.१.४
तण्डुलैः, **२**.२.१; ३.५; **३**.३.१
तत्परिमाणम्, **५**.४.५
तत्प्रमाणा, **३**.४.१
तथा सति, **१**.३.३
तथेति, **१**.१.३
तथोपात्तया, **५**.४.४
तद्गतमानसौ, **१**.१.२
तद्वशान्, **५**.१.१
तन्त्रम्, **३**.२.१, ५; ४.२; **५**.२.२; ४.१; ६.३; **६**.१.४
तन्त्रतावचनाद्, **१**.३.३
तन्त्रस्वरभिन्ना, **५**.२.२
तन्त्राणाम्, **३**.४.३
तन्त्रे, **५**.८.२
तन्त्रेण, **२**.३.४; **३**.६.१; **४**.२.४
तपन्ति, **२**.२.१
तप्तम्, **५**.१.८
तप्तव्रतः, **५**.३.५
तप्तायाम्, **२**.२.१
तप्त्वा, **५**.१.८
तरांसि, **५**.८.१
तरित्र्याकारः, **३**.४.१
तरुणदर्भेषु, **३**.१.१
तर्पयेत्, **२**.४.७
तल्प्यावकाशा, **३**.४.१
तानूनप्त्रम्, **५**.३.४^{२}
तानूनप्त्राज्येन, **५**.३.४
तार्तीयसवनीयान्, **६**.१.२
ताः, **१**.१.४
तिथौ, **५**.१.५
तिरःपवित्रम्, **३**.१.१; **६**.१.४
तिरश्चीषु, **३**.६.२
तिरश्च्यर्थे, **५**.३.४
तिरश्च्योः, **२**.४.४; **३**.४.४
तिरश्च्योर्ग्रहणम्, **२**.२.३
तिर्यञ्चम्, **२**.३.१
तीरात्, **५**.१.८
तीर्थे, **१**.१.६; **६**.१.१
तीर्थेन, **१**.४.२^{३}; **२**.१.१; **३**.१.१; **४**.१.१, २; २.२, ४; ३.३; ४.२; **५**.५.१, २^{२}
तुषात्, **३**.२.७
तूष्णीकः, **५**.३.४ ; ५.१; **६**.१.५; २.२
तूष्णीकत्वम्, **३**.२.२
तूष्णीकम्, **१**.१.९; **५**.१.६, ३; २.२, ३; ४.७
तूष्णीकाः, **४**.१.३; **५**.४.७
तूष्णीकानि, **४**.२.१
तूष्णीके, **६**.१.५
तूष्णीम्, **१**.१.६^{३}, ७, ८; २.१; ३.२^{२}; ४.२, ४; **२**.१.१, २; २.१, २^{२}; ३.३, ५^{२}; **३**.१.१, २.१, २, ६^{२}; ३.२, ३; ४.२, ४; **४**.१.१, २; २.४; **५**.१.५; ३.१, ५; ४.३^{२}; ६; ५.२^{२}; ६.२; **६**.१.१^{२}, २^{२}; ३.२, ३
तृचेन, **२**.४.७
तृणकलापि, **५**.४.७
तृणकलापिमन्त्रेण, **५**.४.२
तृणकलापीम्, **५**.३.५
तृणकलाप्यः, **५**.१.३; ४.३
तृणग्लाभम्, **५**.३.५^{२}
तृणजातम्, **५**.२.१
तृणमुष्टिम्, **२**.४.२
तृणहस्ताः, **१**.३.३
तृणादीनि, **२**.१.३
तृणानि, **२**.१.१, २; ३.५, ६; **३**.४.१
तृणावर्तान्, **५**.५.२

तृणैः, ६.३.४
तृतीयवेलायाम्, ६.२.२
तृतीयसवने, ६.२.४
तृतीयिनः (ऋत्विजः), ५.६.४
तृतीयिभ्यः (ऋत्विग्भ्यः), ५.६.४
तैलम्, १.५.२
तैले, १.५.२
त्रयोदशाङ्गुलान्तराले, ३.२.१
त्रिगुणम्, २.१.१; २.२
त्रित्वसंकल्पः, ४.३.१
त्रिप्रवरकम्, ५.१.७
त्रिप्रादेशाः, २.१.१
त्रिप्रादेशाम्, १.५.३
त्रिप्रादेशायामविस्तरम्, ५.५.३
त्रिप्रादेशे, ५.१.३
त्रिभागः, १.१.४
त्रिभागेन, १.१.४
त्रिरहान्तात्, १.४.२
त्रिवली, ५.१.१
त्रिवृतत्वम्, ३.४.४
त्रिव्रतम्, ५.३.५
त्रिवृत्, २.२.२
त्रिवृच्छ्रितम्, २.१.१
त्रिवृद्गृह्णतः, २.१.२
त्रिवेणी, ५.१.१
त्रिवेदिम्, २.१.१
त्रिष्कम्, २.२.१
त्रिष्फलीकृत्य, २.१.३
त्रिष्फलीक्रियमाणानाम्, २.४.३
त्रिष्फलीक्रियाम्, ३.४.२
त्रिष्वंसार्थम्, ५.४.५
-त्रिस्तन-, ५.३.५
त्रिस्तनव्रतम्, ५.४.४
त्र्यङ्गाणाम्, ४.३.३
त्र्यम्बकैः, २.५.२
त्र्यरत्निम्, ४.१.१
त्र्यवत्तः, ३.१.२
त्वग्ग्रहणम्, २.२.१; ६.१.४
त्वचः, ४.२.३
त्वचम्, ४.२.३
त्वरध्वम्, ५.३.२
त्वा-शब्दस्य, ३.६.२
दक्षिणजानु, २.५.१
दक्षिणबाहुद्विगुणम्, १.१.४
दक्षिणबाहुम्, १.१.४
दक्षिणमग्निम्, ३.२.३
दक्षिणमवाञ्चम्, ५.६.५
दक्षिणमुखः, ५.६.५
दक्षिणमुखत्वम्, ४.१.३
दक्षिणम्, १.१.४; ३.३.३
दक्षिणया द्वारा, १.१.३; ४.२
दक्षिणविहारम्, १.५.२
दक्षिणविहारार्थानि, ३.२.१
दक्षिणविहारे, ३.२.३
दक्षिणस्यां वेद्याम्, ३.२.२
दक्षिणस्याः (वेदेः), ३.६.१
दक्षिणा(वेदिः), ३.२.२; ४.४.३; ५.१.१[२]
दक्षिणाग्निः, १.३.२
दक्षिणाग्निप्रणयनस्य, ३.६.१
दक्षिणाग्निम्, १.५.२; २.५.२; ५.४.२
दक्षिणाग्नेः, १.५.२; ३.४.१, २
दक्षिणाग्नौ, ५.४.२
दक्षिणापवर्गम्, २.३.३
दक्षिणापवर्गाः, २.४.२
दक्षिणापायम्य, १.१.४
दक्षिणापिण्डम्, ३.१.१
दक्षिणाभिः, ५.१.७; १.८
दक्षिणाभूतैः, ५.१.८

दक्षिणाम्, १.३.२
दक्षिणाविकल्पः, ५.१.१
दक्षिणार्धे, ३.४.२
दक्षिणेन, १.४.४
दक्षे, ५.३.५
दण्डः, ५.१.१, ७
दतः, १.१.६
ददाति, १.१.१; १.२; ३.२[२]
दद्यात्, १.१.१; ३.२
दधनि, २.२.१
दधि, १.५.२; ४.१.२, ५.८.२
दधिग्रहाय, ५.८.२
दधिघर्माय, ५.१.२
दधिपूर्वम्, २.२.१
दधिवर्जम्, ४.४.१
दधिसंसृष्टम्, ४.१.२
दधिसोमतण्डुलानाम्, १.५.२
दध्ना, १.१.४; २.२.१
दध्यामिक्षामन्थिनः, ६.२.५
दम्पती, १.१.२; २.३.५; ३.२.५; ५.६.३[४], ४; ६.१.१[२]
दम्पत्योः, ३.२.७; ५.१.५; २.१, २
दर्भपुञ्जीलानि, ५.१.५
दर्भपुञ्जीलैः, ५.१.५[२]
दर्भमयम्, २.१.१
दर्भमये, ३.४.१
दर्भमय्या, ५.४.५
दर्भाग्रे, १.५.२
दर्भान्, ६.१.३
दर्भेषु, १.१.२, ३; २.१.३
दर्भैः, १.१.४, ६; २.१.३; ५.१.७; ५.२
दर्विसादनान्, २.४.२
दर्विहोमिकम् (आज्यम्), ३.३.३; ६.१.२
दर्वीम्, १.१.७; २.४.२; ३.३.३
दर्व्या, १.१.८
दर्व्याम्, १.१.७
दर्शपूर्णमासयोः, १.१.२
दर्शपूर्णमासविकाराणाम्, २.५.२
दर्शपूर्णमासारंभनिमित्ताः, १.३.३
दर्शयितुम्, ५.१.८
दशकम्, ५.४.५
दशकृत्वः, ५.३.१
दशपदा, ५.४.५
दशपरमानेकधनम्, ६.१.४
दशव्यासम्, ५.४.५
दशहोता, ४.१.२
दशहोतारम्, १.३.१; ४.३; ३.१.१; ६.२.३, ६
दशहोतुराहुतिम्, १.४.४
दशादिना, ५.३.२
दशान्, २.४.३
दशापवित्रम्, ६.२.३
दशापवित्रस्थम्, ६.२.१
दशापवित्रस्य, ५.३.३
दशापवित्राभ्याम्, ६.२.१
दशापवित्रेण, ६.१.६; २.१, २[३], ३; ३.२
दशायाम्, ५.१.६
दहेत्, ६.३.३
दानम्, ५.१.४
दानात्, १.१.१[२]
दारुः, ५.१.३
दारुपात्रीम्, २.१.२; ३.३.१; ४.३.१
दारुपात्र्या, ६.३.३
दारुपात्र्याम्, ३.१.१; ३.२
दारुमयाणि, ५.१.२
दारूणि, २.३.१[२]; ३.२.५
दार्शिकी (वेदिः), ३.२.२
दासी, २.२.१

दिक्षु, ५.१.२
दिगुपलक्षणम्, ५.४.४
दिश्यात्, प्रस्ता. १
दिष्टम्, ४.१.२
दीक्षणीया, ५.१.६
दीक्षणीयाध्रौवम्, ५.१.६
दीक्षणीयादीनाम्, ५.२.२[२]
दीक्षणीयायाम्, ५.२.२
दीक्षयेत्, ५.१.५; २.१
दीक्षा, ५.१.५
दीक्षादिवसे, ५.२.१
दीक्षाम्, ५.३.५
दीक्षायाः, ५.१.६
दीक्षायाम्, ५.१.९; २.१[२]
दीक्षाहुतयः, ५.१.६
दीक्षाहुतिषु, ५.१.६
दीक्षितः, ५.१.४
दीक्षितवसने, ५.१.१
दीक्षितस्य, ५.१.४, ६, ८
दीक्षिते (वादः), ५.१.६
दीक्षिष्यमाणः, ५.१.४
दीक्षिष्यमाणे, ५.१.४
दुर्जननिरोधः, ५.१.३
दृंहणवर्जम्, ४.२.४
दृंहणानि, ४.२.४
दृंहयति, ४.१.३
दृढयति, ४.१.३
दृढिम्ने, ६.२.१
दृढिष्ठः, ५.६.१
दृढीकरोति, ५.३.५
दृशीकवः, ५.५.२
दृषदुपलम्, २.४.३
दृष्टार्थाः, ६.३.३
देया, १.१.१; ३.२
देवता, १.१.२; ३.६
देवताकल्पम्, ५.२.२
देवतापरिग्रहार्थत्वे, ५.२.१
देवताम्, २.३.१
देवतासौविष्टकृते, ४.३.२
देवतोपांशुत्वात्, १.३.१
देवदत्तः, ५.१.७
देवदत्त, ५.१.६
देवपत्नी, ५.१.६
देवपितृयज्यायै, ३.५.२
देवयजनम्, १.१.६; ५.१.३, ४[३]; ६.१
देवयजनाभिमन्त्रणादि, ५.१.८
देवयजने, ५.१.४
देवव्रतानि, ३.६.१
देवशब्दः, ३.५.१
देवशब्दे, ३.५.१[२]
देविकाहविर्भ्यः, ५.१.२
देवोपसदनम्, ५.३.४
देशे, ५.१.१
दैक्षणीयं (हविः), ५.१.५
दैक्षम्, ५.३.५
दैक्षयज्ञविचारपक्षे, ४.४.३
दैववत्, ३.४.५
दोषः, १.१.२; ५.३
दोहनार्थाः, ३.२.१
दोहम्, ३.२.१
दोहयन्, २.१.२
दोहयित्वा, ३.२.१
दोहयेत्, २.१.२; ५.८.२[२]
दौघटकटौ, ५.१.३
द्यावापृथिवीभ्याम्, ५.३.५
द्रप्सान्, ६.२.२
द्रप्साभिमन्त्रणम्, ६.२.२
द्राघिष्ठाः, ५.८.२

द्राघीयान्, ३.४.१
द्रुपदाख्यम्, ५.३.३
द्रोणकलशः, ६.२.१
द्रोणकलशम्, ५.६.४
द्रोणकलशात्, ६.२.५[२]; ३.२[२]
द्रोणकलशे, ६.१.२
द्वन्द्वम्, १.१.७; २.१.१, २
द्वन्द्वशः, १.४.२; २.१.२
द्वादशकृत्वः, ६.१.१
द्वादशप्रक्रमायाम्, ५.१.२
द्वादशम्, १.१.२
द्वादशाहः, १.३.२
द्वादशाहम्, १.३.२[२]
द्वादशाहे, १.३.२[२]
द्वारः, ५.२.१
द्वारम्, ५.५.३
द्वारोः, ५.५.१
द्वार्बाहू, ५.५.२[२]
द्वार्बाहुम्, ६.३.१
द्वितर्यः, ५.१.३
द्विदेवत्याम्, ६.२.२
द्विदेवत्यैः, ६.३.२
द्विपत्नीवते, २.३.६
द्विप्रादेशाः, २.१.१
द्विभृष्टि, ६.१.२
द्विर्दैक्षम्, ५.३.५
द्विवत्, ३.६.२
द्विषत्, ६.२.५
द्वेष्यस्य, २.४.६
द्वेष्यान्, ३.२.४
–द्विस्तन–, ५.३.५
–द्विस्तनव्रतम्, ५.४.४
द्वयङ्गुले, १.४.३
धनधान्यसमृद्धस्य, १.१.६
धनुरिव, ५.४.४
धरुणप्रोक्षणवर्जम्, ३.४.४
धरुणे, ५.६.४; ६.१.२
धर्मः, ५.४.७
धर्मपदविधानम्, २.१.२
धर्मवत्, ५.८.२
धर्माः, ५.४.१, ६
धर्मान्, ५.४.६; ६.२.२
धानाः, ३.४.१, २, ३; ६.१.३, ४
धानान्, ३.४.२
धानापात्रम्, ३.४.१
धानाभिः, ५.८.१
धानाभ्यः, ६.१.३
धानार्थान्, ६.१.४
धानासु, ३.४.४
धारणम्, १.२.१
धारयित्वा, २.३.२
धारा, ६.२.१
धार्यः, १.३.२
धावतः, ३.२.७
धावते, १.१.६
धिष्णियः, ५.५.४
धिष्णियम्, ५.४.५; ६.३, ४[२]; ६.१.५; २.४[२]
धिष्णियाः, ५.५.४
धिष्णियानाम्, ५.४.५
धिष्णियान्, ५.५.४; ६.२.३[२], ४
धिष्णियाम्, ५.५.४
धिष्णिये, ६.३.४
धिष्णियोत्तरवर्जम्, ५.६.२
धूर्मन्त्रम्, २.४.३; ६.१.३
धेनुव्रतदुहौ, ५.१.१
ध्यायेत्, १.१.४; २.३.१
ध्रुवम्, ६.२.२

ध्रुवया, **२**.३.६
ध्रुवा, **३**.४.५
ध्रुवाकारौ, **६**.१.२
ध्रुवात्, **५**.२.१
ध्रुवाऽऽप्यायनम्, **५**.३.४
ध्रुवाऽऽप्यायनात्, **३**.२.५
ध्रुवाऽऽप्यायनादि, **३**.२.५
ध्रुवाभाजनम्, **३**.३.२, ३
ध्रुवाभाजने, **३**.३.२
ध्रुवामन्ते, **३**.३.२
ध्रुवामन्त्रे, **४**.१.२; **५**.४.३
ध्रुवाम्, **२**.१.२; २.३; ३.१, ६; ४.७; **३**.६.३; **४**.१.२; २.४; ३.५
ध्रुवायाः, **१**.३.१[२]; **२**.३.१
ध्रुवायाम्, **१**.३.१; **२**.३.६[३]; **३**.४.४; ५.२; **४**.१.२;
ध्रुवायै, **४**.३.४
ध्रुवासंस्काराः, **४**.१.२
ध्रुवासन्नाम्, **३**.३.३
ध्रौवम्, **५**.१.६
ध्रौवैर्मन्त्रैः, **३**.३.२; **५**.४.३
नक्षत्रे, **१**.५.१
नक्षत्रेषु, **१**.१.२
नखानि, **१**.१.६
नद्धः, **५**.४.२
नद्धकम्, **५**.१.८
नभ्यफलके, **५**.५.१
नभ्यस्थे, **५**.५.१
नमस्कारः, **३**.३.३
नमस्काराञ्जलिम्, **५**.३.५
नमस्कृत्य, **१**.१.१; **३**.१.१; ३.३
नयवतीम्, **५**.६.४
नवकम्, **५**.४.५[२]
नवकृत्वः, **६**.१.६
नवच्छदीत्यादीनाम्, **५**.५.२
नवनीतेन, **१**.१.६
नवव्यासम्, **५**.४.६
नवाजिनद्वयम्, **३**.२.४
नस्कूजनी, **५**.१.१
नानावाक्ष्यः, **५**.१.३
नाभिदघ्नाः, **५**.१.२
नाभिम्, **४**.२.३
नामानि, **५**.१.६
नारिष्ठः, **२**.३.६
नारिष्ठहोमानन्तरम्, **२**.३.५
नारिष्ठहोमानाम्, **३**.२.५
नारिष्ठहोमान्, **२**.३.६
नासिकाश्मश्रु, **५**.१.८
नास्तित्वम्, **५**.१.८
निकृत्य, **१**.१.६
निगदः, **६**.१.६
निगमेषु, **५**.३.४
निग्राभम्, **६**.२.१
निग्राभ्याः, **६**.१.५; १.५
निग्राभ्याभ्यः, **६**.२.१
निग्राभ्यायाः, **६**.२.२
निग्राभ्यासु, **६**.१.५; २.१
निघातः, **५**.२.१
नित्यौ, **५**.७.१
निदधाति, **१**.४.२; ५.२; **२**.१.२; २.१[२], २
निदधातीत्यादि, **२**.२.२; **३**.१.१
निदध्यात्, **२**.१.३
निदेशविहितैः (मन्त्रैः), **१**.१.३
निधत्तः, **६**.३.३
निधाय, **१**.१.७; ३.२; ४.२; ५.२, ५; **२**.१.१, ३; ३.४
निनयति, **४**.२.३
निनयेत्, **२**.५.१

निनीताः (अपः), **४**.२.३
निनीय, **१**.१.५; ४.४; **२**.१.३; २.२; **३**.२.२
निपदःकाले, **५**.८.१
निपदनकाले, **५**.८.१
निपाय्य, **४**.२.१
निपिचति, **५**.१.६
निबध्नीयात्, **५**.५.३
निबाधते, **५**.५.३
निबाधनम्, **५**.५.३
निमार्जनम्, **६**.१.५
निमार्ष्टि, **१**.४.४
निमित्तिनः, **६**.३.३
निमिनुयात्, **५**.८.१
निमीलयन्निव, **२**.४.४
निमृज्य, **१**.२.१
निमृज्यात्, १.२.१
निम्नतः, **४**.१.१
नियतः, **१**.३.२
नियताः, **६**.२.२
नियमः, **५**.५.२
नियमव्रतचारिणः, **५**.१.१
नियमाः, **१**.३.२
नियमेन, **१**.१.८
नियोगतः, **३**.३.३; ५.२; **५**.१.६; ४.४; ६.१, ५
निरञ्छता, **५**.४.५
निरञ्छनम्, **५**.४.४; ५
निरञ्छनेन, **५**.४.५
निरन्तरम्, **५**.४.५
निरसीयन्, **२**.१.३
निरस्यति, **१**.४.२; **५**.१.५
निरावधम्, **५**.१.८
निरुक्तायाम्, **४**.१.२
निरुप्तस्य, **५**.४.२
निरुप्तानाम्, **२**.४.३
निरुप्तेषु (हविःषु), **१**.३.१
निरुप्य, **३**.३.१
निरूहणादि, **१**.४.२; ५.२
निर्गतकृष्णाजिनः, **५**.१.७
निर्णिज्य, **५**.२.२
निर्दिशेत्, **३**.२.४; **५**.१.५
निर्मन्थ्यः, **३**.२.४
निर्मन्थ्येन, **३**.१.१; **५**.८.१
निर्यौषीत्, **५**.१.६
निर्वर्तनप्रतिनोदने, **२**.२.१
निर्वपणसमर्थम्, **१**.१.७
निर्वपति, **२**.१.३
निर्वपेत्, **१**.१.७; **५**.२.१; ५.४
निर्वर्तनमन्थनम्, **४**.२.१
निर्वापकाले, **५**.३.४
निवपति, **१**.१.४; **४**.१.२
निवपनमात्रेण, **१**.१.४
निवपन्, **१**.१.४
निवपेत्, **५**.१.४
निवर्तनम्, **३**.१.३
निवर्तयति, **३**.३.१
निवर्तयते, **३**.१.३; **४**.२.१
निश्चिनुयात्, **५**.४.४
निश्चीयते, प्रस्ता. १
निश्चेतुम्, प्रस्ता. १
निश्चेष्टीभूतस्य, **५**.१.७
निश्रयमाणः, **६**.३.१
निश्रये, **५**.१.८
निष्कलिवनिष्ठुवर्जम्, **४**.३.३
निष्क्रमणम्, **४**.१.२
निष्क्रयमाणानि, **५**.३.२
निष्क्रयाय, **५**.१.१

निष्कासेन, ३.३.३
निष्कासतुषान्, ३.२.६
निष्क्रामन्, ६.३.२
निष्क्रामति, ६.३.२
निष्टपयति, १.४.२
निष्टप्य, १.४.४ ; २.३.३
निष्ठीवितम्, ५.१.८[२]
निस्तक्षणीयः, ४.१.१
निस्तूष्णी, ४.२.१
निहत्य, १.१.४; २.२.२; ५.४.४[३]
निहन्यात्, ५.४.४, ५
निहिताग्नेः, १.३.२
निह्नुवते, ५.३.५
नीचहस्तेन, ६.२.१
नीचैः, ४.३.५
नीडे, ५.३.३; ८.१; ६.१.५
नीयमानस्य, २.५.३
नृत्यन्त इव, ६.२.३
नेदिष्ठतमम्, ५.१.१
नेदीयसी, ६.१.२
नेदीष्टः, ५.१.१
नेष्टा, ६.२.१; ३.४
नेष्टृधिष्णियम्, ५.५.४
नेष्ट्रा, ६.१.४
नैरन्तरेण, ५.६.२
नैय्यग्रोधाः, ५.१.३
नैय्यग्रोधान्, ५.१.३
न्यञ्चि, २.१.१, २
न्यसे, २.३.१
न्यसेत्, ५.१.८
न्यस्यतः, ३.२.७
न्यायप्रसिद्धम्, ४.१.२
न्यायशास्त्रग्रन्थादिषु, प्रस्ता. १
न्यासे, २.३.१
न्युप्तेन, ४.१.२
न्युप्य, १.१.७; २.४.७; ३.२.२
न्युब्ज्य, १.४.२
पक्षः, १.४.३; ४.३.२; ५.१.७; ६.३
पक्षप्रोक्षण–, ४.२.१
पक्षयोः, ५.४.६
पक्षान्तरत्वाय, १.३.२
पक्षान्तरे, ४.३.१, २२, ५; ४.१, ३२, ४; ५.४.४; ६.१.४
पक्षान्तरेषु, ५.४.२२
पक्षे, १.३.२; ५.३; २.५.२; ३.२.३; ५.१.७; ४.१, ६; ६.१.३, ५
पक्षेषु, १.१.३; २.२.३; ३.७
पंकम्, १.१.५
पचनाग्निकार्ये, १.१.६
पचनाग्नेः, १.१.६
पचन्ति, १.५.२
पच्यन्ते, १.५.३
पञ्चकृत्वः, ५.३.१२; ६.१.६
पञ्चगृहीतम् (आज्यम्), ४.१.२
पञ्चदशीम्, ३.६.१
पञ्चदश्याम्, ३.१.१
पञ्चममुन्नयनम्, १.४.२
पञ्चवली, ५.१.१
पञ्चहोता, ३.२.४
पञ्चहोतारम्, ४.३.३, ४
पञ्चहोतुः, ३.२.३
पञ्चारत्नि, ५.४.५
पञ्चावत्तिनः, २.३.२
पञ्चावतिनाम्, २.३.२
पञ्चावत्तिनाम्, १.४.२
पटुधियः, प्रस्ता. १
पत्निया, ५.१.२
पत्नियै, ५.१.२

पत्नी, १.४.५; २.१.३; २.१; ३.३.३; ४.३, ५; ५.२.२, ३२; ३.४; ४.३; ५.१
पत्नीम्, १.१.६; २.३.५, ६; ३.२.४, ६; ४.२.३; ५.१.५; २.१; ४.३; ६.३.४
पत्नीयजमानौ, ३.२.६; ५.६.३
पत्नीवर्जम्, ३.४.३
पत्नीशालम्, ५.१.२
पत्नीशालायाः, ५.१.२
पत्नीशालायाम्, ६.३.३
पत्नीसंबन्धे, ३.२.३
पत्नीसंमनसा, ६.२.१
पत्नीसंयाजनम्, ५.८.१
पत्नीसंयाजमन्त्राः, २.३.६
पत्नीसंयाजान्, २.४.७
पत्नीसंयाजान्तायाम्, ५.१.५
पत्नीसंयाजादि, ३.२.५
पत्नीसन्नहनम्, २.१.२; ४.१.२, ५.२.२
पत्नीसन्नहनादि, २.२.२
पत्न्यवेक्षितम् (आज्यम्), ५.६.३[२]; ६.१.१
पत्न्यवेक्षितेन (आज्येन), ३.३.२; ५.४.३
पत्न्याः, २.३.२; ४.२.३; ५.१.५, ६, ९; ६.१
पत्न्याम्, ६.१.४
पथ्या स्वस्त्याहार्यम्, ५.२.२
पथ्ये, १.५.३
पदम्, ५.२.३
पदपांसवः, ५.२.२
पदाङ्गुष्टाभ्याम्, ५.५.३
पदिबन्धनम्, ५.२.२
पदे, १.४.१
पद्धरणी, ५.१.२
पद्धरणीम्, ५.२.२
पन्नेजनीः, ६.३.४
पयः, १.४.२२; ५.३.२
पयःसक्तूनाम्, ६.२.२
पयसी, ५.१.१
पयस्या, ५.८.२; ६.२.४
पयस्यातञ्चनम्, ५.८.२
पयस्यापक्षान्तरे, ६.१.३
पयस्यायाः, ६.१.४; २.४
पयस्यायै, ५.१.२; ८.२[२]
परतः, १.१.४
परमेष्ठी, २.३.६
परसूत्रप्रसिद्धः, ५.६.३
परागिनहोमम्, १.५.३
पराञ्चम्, ४.१.३
परिकर्मिणः, २.२.३; ४.१.२; २.१; ५.१.३; ५.२; ६.२; ६.१.१, ४
परिकर्मी, ५.२.२
परिकृष्टवासतीवरः, ५.६.१
परिकृष्टाः, ५.८.२
परिक्रमय्य, ५.३.४
परिग्रहणयोः, २.४.३
परिग्रहणयोयोपने, ३.२.३
परिग्रहात्, ३.२.२, ४.१.१
परिग्राहप्रसवम्, २.५.२
परिग्राहम्, ५.४.७
परिग्राहे, २.४.१; ५.२; ३.६.१, २; ४.४.१
परिगृह्णन्ति, ५.५.१
परिगृह्णीयात्, ३.२.२; ६.३.२[२]
परिगृह्य, २.१.२, ६.१.५
परिचरेद्, १.१.६
परिचितम्, २.२.१
परिचितान्, २.२.१
परिचिन्मन्त्रकाणि, २.२.१
परिचिन्मन्त्रेण, २.२.१
परिणाहः, ५.३.३
परिणाहतः, ४.१.१

परिणाहाभ्याम्, **४**.१.१
परिणाहेन, **५**.८.२
परितनोति, **४**.१.१
परिदध्यात्, **२**.२.३
परिदेशनात्, **१**.३.३
परिदेशनातन्त्रम्, **३**.१.१
परिधयः, **२**.१.१; **४**.१.२; **५**.१.३; ६.२
परिधानारंभे **२**.४.४
परिधानीयोपलक्षणम्, **२**.३.१
परिधिः, **६**.३.३
परिधिभिः, **५**.४.७
परिधिम्, **२**.२.३; ३.५
परिधिषु, **३**.४.४
परिधीनाम्, **५**.३.५
परिधीन्, **३**.३.१, २, ३; ४.४; **५**.३.४; ४.७
परिधीयमानेषु, **२**.४.४; **३**.६.२
परिधौ, **६**.१.५
परिध्यनुमन्त्रणानि, **३**.६.२
परिनह्य, **५**.४.५
परिपात्रेण, **६**.२.५
परिपालयिष्यामः, **५**.३.२
परिप्रजनयति, **२**.२.१
परिप्लावयेत्, **१**.१.४
परिप्लाव्य, **१**.१.४
परिभोजनीयम्, **२**.१.१
परिभोजनीयात्, **२**.२.३
परिभोजनीयान्, **२**.३.२
परिमण्डलाकारम्, **१**.१.१
परिमण्डलानि, **१**.१.४
परिमार्गः, **६**.२.२; ३.२
परिमार्ष्टि, **६**.२.२
परिमितैः, **१**.१.६
परिमिनुयात्, **१**.१.४
परिमृज्यात्, **६**.२.१
परिलिखति, **१**.१.४; **५**.२.३
परिलिखेत्, **१**.१.४
परिवर्तनम्, **३**.१.३; **४**.२.१
परिवापः, **६**.१.३२
परिवापाय, **६**.१.३
परिवापार्थम्, **६**.२.४
परिवासनम्, **४**.२.३
परिवासनानि, **५**.४.३
परिवासयति, **४**.१.१
परिवासिता, **४**.२.३
परिवास्य, **६**.१.३
परिव्यये, **४**.१.३
परिश्रयणमन्त्रेण, **५**.५.३
परिश्रयणस्य, **३**.४.५
परिश्रयन्ति, **३**.४.५; **५**.१.३; ५.१, २, ५
परिश्रयेत्, **३**.२.३
परिश्रिते, **२**.३.६; **५**.१.२
परिषिच्य, **१**.१.६; **२**.३.७; ४.७
परिषिञ्चति, **१**.४.२, ४
परिषेक्ता, **३**.४.४
परिष्वङ्गपरार्ध्यप्रादेशावरपरिमाणम्, **४**.१.१
परिसंख्याता, **५**.४.१
परिसमापयेत्, **३**.४.४
परिसमाप्ते, **५**.१.८
परिसमाप्य, **६**.१.१
परिसमूह्य, **१**.१.७, ९; ४.२
परिसमूहन-, **१**.२.१
परिस्तरण-**१**.२.१
-परिस्तरणादेः, **३**.१.१
-परिस्तरणानि, **५**.८.२
परिस्तीर्य, **१**.१.७, ९; ४.२; **२**.१.१[२]; **३**.३.१; **४**.१.२; **५**.६.२; ८.२
परिस्तृणीतः, **३**.२.३

परिस्तृणीयात्, २.१.१; ३.२.३; ४.१.२; ५.४.२
परिस्त्रजम्, ६.१.२
परिहरणपक्षे, २.३.४
परिहरणम्, २.३.४; ४.३.१[२]; ५.३.४
परिहरति, ३.३.३; ४.२.१
परिहरेत्, २.३.४[२]
परिहाप्य, ३.४.४; ५.४.७; ५.१, २
परिहृतस्य, २.५.३
परीक्षितौ, ५.८.१
परीक्ष्य, ५.१.१
परीत्य, १.४.४
परीयुः, ५.५.२
परेक्षते, ३.४.२
परेक्ष्य, ४.३.२
परोक्षम्, ५.१.६
परोप्तपुनराधानम्, १.४.१
परोप्तपुनराधेयं नाम, १.४.१
पर्णसूनम्, ४.३.३
पर्णसूने, ४.३.३
पर्यग्निकरणम्, ३.२.१; ६.१.४
पर्यग्निकुर्यात्, ३.२.३; ४.२; ४.२.२
पर्यग्निकृत्वा, ३.२.६; ३.१; ४.१.२; ३.३; ५.४.२
पर्यस्यति, ६.२.२
पर्यस्येते, ३.२.६
पर्यातुम्, ५.१.८
पर्यानीय, ५.३.३
पर्याय, ५.१.८[२]
पर्यायशः, ५.३.१
पर्यायशब्दैः, ५.१.६
पर्यायेषु, ६.२.५
पर्यावर्तनयजुः, ५.१.७
पर्यावर्तमानम्, ४.३.४
पर्यावृत्तम्, ३.१.२
पर्यावृत्तौ, ६.३.३
पर्यावृत्य, १.४.४; २.३.६; ३.२.२
पर्याहरणम्, २.३.५
पर्याहर्तव्यानि, ५.५.२
पर्याहृत्य, २.२.३[२]; ३.५; ५.५.१, २
पर्युक्षण-, १.२.१
पर्युक्ष्य, १.१.७
पर्युपविशन्ति, ६.२.१
पर्युपविश्य, १.१.८
पर्यूहनम्, ५.५.३
पर्वणि, १.१.२; २.३.४
पलाशम्, १.१.५
पलाशमात्रम्, २.३.२
पलाशशाखाम्, ३.१.१; ५.३.२
पल्पूलनम्, ३.६.१
पल्पूलयित्वा, ५.२.१
पवनादि, ६.२.२
पवमानग्रहयोः, ६.२.२
पवमानाय, ६.२.३
पवमानेषु, ६.२.३
पवमानेष्टिः, १.३.१
पवमानेष्टिकम्, १.३.१
पवमानेष्टिषु, १.३.१
पवमानेष्टिर्हवि, १.३.१
पवयितुम्, ६.२.३
पवित्रम्, २.१.२; ३.२.१; ६.२.१
पवित्रादानम्, ३.४.१
पवित्रान्तर्हिताः (आपः), ५.४.७
पवित्राभ्याम्, ३.४.३
पवित्रे, २.१.२, ३; २.२[३]; ३.२.३, ६; ३.१; ४.३.१; ५.४.२; ६.३; ६.१.१, ३
पवित्रेण, ३.२.७

पशाविव, ३.२.७
पशुपुरोडाशम्, ४.३.२
पशुपुरोडाशस्य, २.५.३; ४.४.२
पशुपुरोडाशस्विष्टकृतः, ४.४.७
पशुपुरोडाशाभावे, ६.३.१
पशुबन्धस्येव, ३.२.२
पशुबन्धेन, ४.१.१
पशुम्, २.५.३; ४.२.१[3], २; ३.१, ३[5]; ४.२; ६.१.१
पशूखा, ५.१.२
पशोः (वेदिः), ३.२.२; ४.२.१[3], ३
पशोरुपायनम्, २.५.३
पशौ, २.५.२; ४.३.२; ५.२.२
पश्चाद्बाहुम्, १.१.४
पश्वाज्यशेषेन, ५.८.१
पांसून्, ५.५.३
पाटलिची, ५.१.३
पाणिद्वयम्, २.३.४; ५.६.५
पाणी, १.१.५
पातयति, ४.१.१
पात्रत्रये, ३.३.२
पात्रप्रक्षालनम्, २.१.१
पात्रयागकाले, ५.८.१
पात्राणि, १.१.७; ४.२; २.१.१; २; ३.२.३; ५.६.३
पात्राभ्याम्, ३.२.१
पात्रसादनानि, १.१.४; ६.१.१, ३
पात्रासादनकाले, ३.१.१
पात्रियाम्, १.१.७; २.३.४
पात्रीम्, १.१.७
पात्र्याम्, २.२.३; ३.४.१; ४.३.२; ६.२.४
पादप्रक्षालनम्, ३.६.१
पादिभ्यः (ऋग्विग्भ्यः), ५.६.४
पाद्यत्वेन, १.१.५
पान्नेजनम् (उदकम्), ४.२.२
पाप्मनः (विनिधयः), १.१.६
पाययित्वा, ४.२.१
पाराशर्यः, ५.१.७
पार्थिवानाम्, १.१.५
पार्श्वम्, १.१.४
पार्श्वे, ४.३.४; ५.३.१
पालाश-, २.१.१
पालाशम्, ४.१.१
पालाशी, ५.१.३
(अष्टर्चेन) पावमानेन, ५.१.६
पाशद्वयम्, १.१.४
पाशप्रतिमोचने, ४.४.२
पाशम्, १.१.४; ५.४.५
पाशात्, ५.४.४
पाशान्तरम्, ५.४.५
पाशुकम्, ५.६.२, ५
पाशुकानि (पात्राणि), ५.६.२; ६.१.१
पाशुकेषु, ६.३.१
पाशुक्या (वेदिः), ३.२.२
पिण्डकरणान्तम्, ६.१.४
पिण्डत्रये, २.४.३
पिण्डदानम्, २.४.२
पिण्डद्वयम्, २.४.२
पिण्डपितृयज्ञः, ५.१.४
पिण्डपितृयज्ञम्, १.१.७; ५.३; ४.१.१
पिण्डपितृयज्ञयोः, १.१.७
पिण्डपितृयज्ञेन, २.४.१
पिण्डानाम्, २.४.२
पिण्डान्, २.४.३
पितृकार्यम्, ५.८.१
पितृभ्यः, १.१.७; २.१.१; ३.४.२; ५.१.४; ६.५
पितृमते, ३.४.१

पितृयज्ञे, **२**.५.२
पितृवेदिम्, **२**.५.२
पितृशब्दः, **३**.५.१; २[२]
पितृशब्दम्, **३**.४.१; ५.१[३]
पिनष्टि, **२**.२.१[२]; **३**.४.२[२]; **६**.१.४
पिबन्तः, **३**.३.३
पिंषेत्, **३**.४.२
पिंष्यात्, **३**.१.१
पिष्टपात्रीम्, **२**.२.२
पिष्टयवागूः, **६**.१.३[२]
पिष्टलेपम्, **२**.३.६
पिष्टलेपनम्, **४**.३.२, ५
पिष्टलेपानुवर्तते, **४**.४.३
पिष्टानि, **२**.२.१[२]; **६**.१.४[२]
पिष्टेन, **१**.१.६
पिष्टोद्वपनीम्, **२**.१.२; २.१[२], २; **४**.३.१; **६**.१.३
पिष्टोद्वपन्याम्, **२**.२.१
पुञ्जीलैः, **१**.१.६
पुत्रादौ, **५**.१.४
पुनःसंस्कृतः, **१**.४.१
पुनन्ति, **५**.३.३
पुनरुत्सृष्टः, **१**.४.१
पुनरुत्सृष्टादीन्, **१**.४.१
पुनरुत्स्यूतम्, **१**.४.१
पुनरुद्धृत्य, **१**.१.४
पुनर्निष्कृतः, **१**.४.१
पुनर्निष्क्रमय्य, **६**.१.५
पुनर्बद्धाम्, **५**.५.१
पुरस्तात्, **१**.१.३
पुरस्ताद्बाहुम्, **१**.१.४
पुराकर्मसमाप्तेः, **५**.३.४
पुराणगार्हपत्यम्, **५**.६.३
पुराऽऽदित्यस्यास्तमयात्, **१**.४.२
पुरीषम्, **४**.१.२
पुरीषेण, **२**.२.२; **४**.१.२
पुरुषचैतन्यात्, **५**.१.७
पुरुषम्, **५**.४.४
पुरुषसंमिता, **३**.४.१
पुरुषसंस्कारम्, **३**.१.१
पुरुषाः, **५**.५.२; ६.४
पुरोडाशगणे, **३**.१.१
पुरोडाशप्राशनानन्तरम्, **६**.३.४
पुरोडाशमात्रम्, **३**.१.१
पुरोडाशमेक्षणम्, **२**.१.२
पुरोडाशम्, **२**.२.१[२], ३; **३**.१.१, २; ४.२, ३; **४**.३.२[३]; **६**.१.४; ३.१
पुरोडाशयवान्, **३**.४.२
पुरोडाशविषयम्, **२**.२.१
पुरोडाशशकलम्, **६**.३.३
पुरोडाशशब्देन, **६**.२.४
पुरोडाशस्य, **२**.२.२; **४**.३.१; २; **६**.२.४
पुरोडाशात्, **२**.३.४
पुरोडाशान्, **६**.३.३
पुरोडाशानाम्, **३**.६.१; **६**.३.३
पुरोडाशाय, **६**.१.३
पुरोडाशार्थाः, **५**.६.२
पुरोडाशार्थान्, **३**.१.१; ४.३
पुरोडाशीयपेषणानन्तरम्, **३**.४.२
पुरोडाशीयान्, **२**.१.२; **३**.४.२; **४**.३.१[२]
पुरोडाशीयानि, **६**.१.४
पुरोडाशीयेभ्यः, **२**.१.३
पुरोडाशीयेषु, **२**.४.३
पुरोडाशेडान्ते, **५**.८.२
पुरोडाशोद्वासनानन्तरम्, **३**.४.३
पुरोडाशैः, **६**.३.२
पुष्करपर्णान्, **१**.१.५
पुष्टिकामः, **१**.१.६

-पूतभृत् (कलशः), ५.८.१
पूतभृतम्, ६.२.३
पूतभृताकारः, ५.८.१
पूतभृति (बिले), ६.२.३[२]
पूतभृते, ५.८.१
पूतभृद्बिले, ६.२.२
पूरणेन, २.४.१
पूर्णपात्रे, २.३.६; ४.७
पूर्णमासे, २.४.१
पूर्णान्, १.४.२
पूर्वतनपक्षः, ३.४.२
पूर्वत्वोपलक्षणाम्, ५.१.४
पूर्वपरिग्राहम्, ४.४.१
पूर्वमाघारम्, २.४.४
पूर्वया द्वारा, ६.१.१[२], २, ५
पूर्वरज्ज्वोः, ४.१.१
पूर्ववत्, २.२.१; ५.८.२
पूर्वह्रदये, ४.३.३
पूर्वाधानाभ्यः, ६.२.४
पूर्वां (रशनाम्), ६.२.६
पूर्वायतम्, २.२.१
पूर्वावदेये, २.२.१
पूर्वाहुतिः, २.३.३
पूर्वाहुतेः, १.४.४
पूर्वोपात्तान्, १.१.५
पृथग्गततुषान्, २.१.३
पृथिवीम्, २.३.६
पृश्नयः[२], १.३.१
पृश्नीन्, १.३.१[२]
पृषदाज्यग्रहणम्, ४.१.२; ४.४.२
पृषदाज्यग्रहण्याम्, ३.६.३
पृषदाज्यरक्षणम्, २.५.३
पृषदाज्यम्, ४.३.३; ४.२; ६.२.५
पृषदाज्यस्य, ४.३.३, ४
पृषदाज्याय, ५.६.२
पृषदाज्यावेक्षणे, २.५.३
पृषदाज्ये, ४.४.१
पृष्टीः, ३.२.७
-पृष्ठप्रोक्षण-, ४.२.१
पृष्ठे, ३.२.७
पृष्ठ्याः, ५.४.७
पृष्ठ्याम्, ५.४.५; ६.२.४
पृष्ठ्यायाः, ५.४.५, ६; ५.१, २, ३
पृष्ठ्यायाम्, ५.५.४[२]
पृष्ठ्यास्तरणार्था, ५.४.७
पैतृयज्ञिकाः, ३.४.१
पैतृयज्ञिकान्, २.४.१
पैतृयज्ञिकानि, ३.४.१
पोता, ६.३.४
पोतृ(धिष्णियम्), ५.५.४
पोषयित्वा, १.४.१
पौतुद्रवाः, ४.१.२
पौरुषः (वधः), ५.१.७
पौर्णमासान्ते, ३.१.३
पौर्णमासी, ३.१.१; २.१
पौर्णमासे, ३.१.३
पौर्णमास्याम्, २.१.१; ४.१
पौर्णमास्यायाम्, २.३.३
पौर्वाह्णिक्यौ, ५.४.४
पौष्णस्य, ३.१.१
पौष्णान्, ३.१.१
प्रउगे, ५.८.१
प्रकृतिभिः, ५.४.४
प्रकृतौ, ५.४.१[२]; ६.१.५; २.२
प्रकृत्यर्थाः, २.३.७
प्रक्रमत्रये, ५.५.४
प्रक्रमाः, ५.४.५[२]
प्रक्रमे, ४.१.२

प्रक्रमेत्, १.१.७
प्रक्रमेषु, ५.४.४[२]
प्रक्षालनम्, २.१.३
प्रक्षालयति, २.२.२; ४.२.३
प्रक्षालयेत्, १.१.८; ३.६.१
प्रक्षालितः, ४.१.२
प्रक्षालितपादाः, ५.५.२
प्रक्षलितम्, १.१.५
प्रक्षालितौ, ५.८.१
प्रक्षाल्य, १.१.७; ४.२; २.१.३; ३.३
प्रक्षिपति, ६.१.५
प्रक्षिपन्, २.३.२
प्रक्षिपन्ति, २.२.१
प्रक्षिप्य, १.३.२; ४.४; २.३.१
प्रक्षेप्ता, २.३.१
प्रक्षेप्तुम्, २.३.२
प्रगृहाण, ५.३.२
प्रचरणाय, ६.१.२
प्रचरणी, ५.१.३
प्रचरणीम्, ६.१.२; ५
प्रचरण्या, ६.२.३[२]
प्रचरद्भिः, २.५.२
प्रचरेत्, ५.२.१
प्रचरेयुः, ५.४.४
प्रचर्य, ६.१.१[२]; २.६
प्रच्छिन्द्यात्, ४.३.४
प्रच्छेदनाभिमर्शनम्, ३.४.१
प्रच्छेदम्, ४.३.४
प्रजातिभिः, ४.२.१
प्रजापतये, २.३.१
प्रजापतिः, २.३.६
प्रज्वाल्य, १.५.३
प्रज्ञप्ते, ४.२.१
प्रज्ञातम्, ४.३.३
प्रणयनात्, ५.८.२
प्रणयिष्यामि, २.१.२
प्रणयेत्, ५.४.२
प्रणवादि, २.५.१
प्रणवे, २.३.१
प्रणवेषु, २.३.१
प्रणीतयोरग्नयोर्मन्त्रेण, २.५.२
प्रणीताः, २.२.२[२]; ४.१.२; ३.१, ५; ५.५.२[२]; ६.१.१, ३
प्रणीतानाम्, ४.१.२[२]
प्रणीतानिनयनम्, ३.२.६; ५.२.२
प्रणीतापात्रम्, २.१.२
प्रणीताप्रणयनम्, २.१.२; ४.१.२; ३.१; ५.४.२; ६.१.३
प्रणीताभावे, ४.१.२; ६.१.१
प्रणीताभ्यः, २.२.१
प्रणीतासु, २.४.७; ५.२
प्रणीतेऽग्नौ, २.५.२
प्रतपति, ५.१.६
प्रतापे, ३.१.१
प्रतायते, ६.२.१
प्रतिगृह्णाति, ५.१.७
प्रतिग्रहीतुम्, १.३.२
प्रतिग्रहेषु, ६.३.२[२]
प्रतिच्छन्नाः, ५.६.३
प्रतिच्छाद्य, १.१.७[२]; २.१.३
प्रतिच्छिन्नाग्रम्, २.५.१
प्रतिजानीयुः, ५.१.१
प्रतिदोहम्, २.१.२
प्रतिधुक्, ५.३.२
प्रतिनोदन-, २.२.१
प्रतिन्यासम्, २.३.१
प्रतिपत्तिम्, १.१.१
प्रतिपथम्, ३.४.४[२]; ५.१.७

प्रतिपद्यते, **१**.४.२; **२**.१.३; २.२; **४**.३.४, ५[२]; ४.३; **५**.१.४

प्रतिपद्यन्ते, **३**.१.१

प्रतिपद्येरन्, **६**.३.१

प्रतिपर्यावर्तनम्, **५**.१.७

प्रतिपुरुषम्, **१**.१.१; **३**.२.३; ४.२[२]

प्रतिप्रणवम्, **२**.३.१[४]

प्रतिप्रणवेषु, **६**.१.२

प्रतिप्रस्थाता, **३**.२.२[२], ३, ४, ५; **४**.२.४, ५[२]; ३.१, २, ३, ४[३]; **५**.१.५; २.१; ६.२; **६**.१.१; २.५, ६; ३.१[२], २[२], ३

प्रतिप्रस्थातारम्, **३**.२.२[२]; **६**.३.२

प्रतिप्रस्थातुः, **३**.२.२; ६.२; **४**.३.३; **५**.६.३[२]

प्रतिप्रस्थातृकर्मणा, **३**.२.२

प्रतिप्रस्थात्रा, **४**.२.५[३]; ३.३;

प्रतिप्रस्थात्रे, **५**.६.२

प्रतिप्रैषम्, **५**.२.२

प्रतिब्रूते, **६**.३.३

प्रतिब्रूयुः, **१**.१.३[२]

प्रतिभाति, **४**.२.२

प्रतिमुक्तचषालः, **४**.१.२

प्रतिमुच्य, **१**.१.४

प्रतिमुञ्चय, **५**.४.५

प्रतिमुष्टि, **२**.२.१

प्रतिमोचयति, **५**.१.४

प्रतियुक्तचक्रे, **५**.१.३; ५.१

प्रतियौति, **४**.२.३

प्रतिवचनम्, **१**.१.३

प्रतिवचनाश्रावणप्रैषाः **३**.२.२

प्रतिवर्षम्, **५**.१.१

प्रतिशिष्य, **१**.१.८

प्रतिषिद्धवर्जम्, **२**.१.२

प्रतिष्ठापनम्, **३**.२.१

प्रतिष्ठाप्य, **१**.१.६

प्रतिसंवपनम्, **५**.२.३

प्रतिसन्धाय, **४**.३.३

प्रतिस्तोमम्, **६**.१.५

प्रतिहरेत्, **६**.३.३

प्रतीकग्रहणम्, **१**.२.१

प्रतीकग्रहणानि, **१**.२.१

प्रतीक्षते, **३**.२.१; **५**.३.३

प्रतीक्ष्य, **२**.१.२

प्रतीचीम्, **१**.२.१

प्रतीयात्, **१**.५.२

प्रत्ताः, **५**.६.१; **६**.२.१

प्रत्यक्षम्, **३**.१.२

प्रत्यक्षवचनानि, **५**.१.६

प्रत्यगावृत्तः, **४**.१.२

प्रत्यगाशिषः (मन्त्राः), **२**.२.३

प्रत्यग्गत्वा, **१**.१.७

प्रत्यग्रम्, **१**.४.४

प्रत्यङ्ङासीनः, **५**.५.४

प्रत्यङ्मुखम्, **४**.२.१

प्रत्यञ्चम्, **१**.२.१

प्रत्यञ्जनम्, **२**.३.२; ३

प्रत्यञ्जलिम्, **२**.३.१

प्रत्यभिमृशते, **२**.३.६

प्रत्यभिषिक्तस्य, **१**.१.६

प्रत्यवदानम्, **४**.३.३

प्रत्यवस्यति, **५**.५.२

प्रत्यवेक्ष्य, **१**.४.४

प्रत्यस्यति, **६**.२.२

प्रत्याख्यास्यति, **५**.१.७

प्रत्यागत्य, **१**.४.२

प्रत्यानयनम्, **१**.५.२[२]

प्रत्यानयने, **१**.५.३

प्रत्यानयनकाले, १.५.२
प्रत्यानयेत्, ३.१.२
प्रत्यानह्य, ५.५.१
प्रत्यभिमर्शनम्, ५.१.५
प्रत्याम्नातः, ३.१.१
प्रत्याश्रावणादौ, ३.२.५
प्रत्याश्रावयेत्, २.३.१
प्रत्याश्राविते, २.३.२; २.४.५
प्रत्याहृत्य, २.३.२
प्रत्युत्थाय, २.४.३
प्रत्युदयनम्, ५.६.१
प्रत्युदीर्णम्, ५.३.१
प्रत्युपवसथम्, १.३.३
प्रत्यृचम्, ३.१.२
प्रथनत्वग्रहणे, ६.१.४
प्रथमनिहताच्छङ्कोः, ५.४.६
प्रथमनिहतात्, ५.४.६; ५.१
प्रथमनिहते, ५.४.५
प्रथमविकारेषु, ४.४.३
प्रथमानुमन्त्रणम्, ४.४.३
प्रथमाहः, ५.१.१
प्रथमोद्धृतम्, ३.३.२
प्रदक्षिणम्, १.१.४; २.३.१, ७; ४.३.४; ४.२; ५.२.२; ४.३; ६.४
प्रदर्शनम्, २.३.५; ६.३.३
प्रदर्शनार्थम्, ५.४.६
प्रदानात्, २.३.२
प्रदानेषु, २.४.४
प्रदेशम्, २.२.२
प्रदेशान्तरे, ५.३.१
प्रदेशिन्या, २.३.४; ५.३.१[३]
प्रदेशिन्यौ, ५.१.६
प्रधानयाग-, २.४.१
प्रधानयागात्, ५.२.२
प्रधानविषयः, ५.२.२
प्रधानार्थाः, ५.४.१
प्रधानार्थे, ३.५.१; २
प्रधानाहुतीः, २.३.२; ३.४.५
प्रधिकम्, २.२.१
प्रधौ, २.२.१
प्रपतनम्, ५.१.७
प्रपतिता, ५.१.८
प्रपतितान्, २.२.१
प्रपद्य, १.१.३
प्रपद्यते, २.२.२
प्रपादयेत्, ५.१.५; ५.६[२].५
प्रपाद्य, १.१.६; ४.२; ५.८.१
प्रप्रापयति, ४.१.१
प्रबध्नाति, ५.१.६
प्रबाहुक्, २.१.२; ५.१; ३.४.१; ६.१.२
प्रबाहुत्वम्, २.३.२
प्रबोधने, ५.१.७
प्रब्रूयात्, २.१.३
प्रभवे, ५.४.६
प्रभुः, १.१.१
प्रमार्ष्टि, १.४.४
प्रमृद्य, २.२.१[२]
प्रम्णाय, २.२.१[२]
प्रम्णायन्, २.२.१
प्रयच्छति, १.१.८; ५.३.४
प्रयच्छेत्, २.३.४; ६; ३.६.१
प्रयताः, ६.१.१
प्रयाजत्रयावशिष्य, २.३.१
(उत्तमं) प्रयाजम्, ३.४.५
प्रयाजमन्त्रम्, ५.१.८
प्रयाजविकारत्वे, ५.४.३
प्रयाजविकाराः, ५.४.१
प्रयाजशेषाभिघारणे,

प्रयाजान्, २.३.२; ३.४.५; ४.२.१; ४.२
प्रयाजानूयाजौ, ३.४.५
प्रयाजाय, ४.२.१
प्रयाजे, २.४.५; ३.४.५
प्रयाजेषु, २.४.६
प्रयाणावसानमन्त्रौ, ५.१.४
प्रयाणे, ४.४.२
प्रयाति, ५.१.८
प्रयायात्, ५.१.८
प्रयुञ्जीरन्, ३.५.१
प्रयुत्य, ४.३.३
प्रर्युक्ष्य, १.१.९
प्रयोगः, प्रस्ता. १; १.४.२
प्रयोगक्लृप्तिः, प्रस्ता. १[३]
प्रयोजनवन्तः, ५.५.२
प्रयोजनमनसाम्, ५.६.२
प्रवणा, ३.४.१
प्रवयति ४.१.३
प्रवरः, ३.४.५
प्रवरम्, ३.२.४; ३.३
प्रवरणाहुत्यन्तम्, ६.३.१
प्रवराय, ५.४.३
प्रवरिष्यन्, ६.२.६
प्रवर्ग्यत्वम्, ५.४.१
प्रवर्ग्यम्, ५.८.२
प्रवर्ग्याः, ५.१.४
प्रवर्ग्यानन्तरम्, ५.४.२
प्रवर्ग्योपसदौ, ५.४.४
प्रवर्तनम्, ५.६.१
प्रवत्स्यतः, ३.२.६
प्रवत्स्यन्, १.५.३
प्रवसतः, १.५.३
प्रवसदुपस्थानम्, १.५.३[२]
प्रवसन्, १.५.३
प्रवाचनम्, २.३.४
प्रवासविधिना, १.५.३
प्रविशन्ति, ५.६.४
प्रवृणीते, ३.२.४
प्रवृताहुतिम्, ६.२.६
प्रवृत्तिः, ५.१.६
प्रवृद्धभस्मापनया, १.३.३
प्रवृश्चति, ४.४.१
प्रवेशयेयुः, ५.५.२
प्रव्रजति, १.५.३
प्रशास्तुः (धिष्णियम्), ५.५.४
प्रशास्त्रादिचमसम्, ६.३.४
प्रशास्त्रादिचमसे, ६.३.४
प्रशास्त्रादयः, ६.२.३
प्रशिष्यः, प्रस्ता., १
प्रश्चोत्य, २.३.६
प्रसङ्गेन, १.५.२
प्रसलैः, २.३.६; ५.५.२; ६.३, ४; ६.३.२
प्रसर्पकाय, ५.१.८
प्रसवानन्तरम्, २.३.५
प्रसवम्, २.५.१
प्रसवे, २.५.२
प्रसवेषु, २.५.१
प्रसारय, ५.३.२
प्रसारयति, ५.१.६
प्रसिद्धम्, २.१.२; ३.१.१; ४.१.२[१०]; ४.१, २, ३[३]
प्रसिद्धान्, ४.४.२
प्रसिद्धाः, १.४.१
प्रसुनियमः, ३.२.१
प्रसूदयति, ४.१.१
प्रसूमयम्, ३.१.१
प्रसौति, २.५.२
प्रस्कन्दतः, ६.३.३

प्रस्कन्दन्, ५.५.३
प्रस्तरतिरश्ची, ५.६.२
प्रस्तरतृणकलाप्या, ५.४.१
प्रस्तरप्रहरणानुमन्त्रणौ, ३.६.३
प्रस्तरम्, २.३.५; ४.७
प्रस्तरमात्रम्, ३.१.१
प्रस्तरयोः, ३.६.२
प्रस्तरस्य, ५.३.५
प्रस्तरात्, २.१.१; ५.५.३
प्रस्तराय, ५.३.५
प्रस्तरार्थम्, ६.२.३
प्रस्तरीयम्, ६.२.३
प्रस्तरे, ४.४.२
प्रस्तरेण, ५.३.५; ५.३.५
प्रस्ताव-(कृते), ६.२.३
प्रस्तूयते, १.१.१
प्रस्तोतुर्मुखम्, ६.२.३
प्रस्थानम्, ५.१.८
प्रस्थापयन्ति, ६.२.२
प्रस्थिते, ६.१.१
प्रहरणकाले, ३.३.१
प्रहरणमन्त्रः, २.१.३
प्रहरति, २.१.३; २.२; ३.५
प्रहरिष्यमाणम्, ३.४.२
प्रहरेत्, २.२.३; ३.३; ५
प्रहृत्य, २.२.२; ३.६
प्रह्रियमाणम्, २.४.७
प्रह्वः, २.३.५
प्रह्वाः, ६.२.३
प्राकृतः, ३.४.३; ५.४.७
प्राकृतत्वे, ३.४.३
प्राकृतम्, ३.१.२; ५.६.२
प्राकृतं तन्त्रम्, ५.६.२
प्राकृतमन्त्रम्, ४.१.२
प्राकृतस्य (आज्यस्य), ५.६.२
प्राकृतस्योपलक्षणम्, ३.१.१
प्राकृतात्, ३.४.१
प्राकृतीम्, ४.३.३
प्राक्तनमन्त्रम्, ५.३.५
प्राक्तना, ५.६.२
प्राक्तने, ५.६.२
प्राक्प्रवणात्, ५.६.५
प्राक्प्रेषणात्, ३.४.२
प्राक्सादनात्, ६.२.२
प्राक्स्विष्टकृत्संस्रावाभिहोमात्, ३.३.३
प्रागग्निप्रणयनात्, ३.४.१
प्रागग्राः, १.४.३
प्रागग्राम्, १.४.४
प्रागधिवपनात्, ३.४.२
प्रागपवर्गम्, १.१.३; ४.२; ५.१.४; ५.२
प्रागपवर्गाः, २.३.२
प्रागपवर्गाणि, ४.१.२
प्रागपवर्गान्, २.२.२
प्रागपवर्गैः, २.२.२
प्रागायतम्, २.२.१
प्रागाघाराद्, २.३.२
प्रागावपनात् (तन्त्रम्), ३.४.२
प्रागावृत्तः, ५.६.३
प्रागावृत्तउपस्थम्, ३.६.१
प्रागावृत्य, १.४.४
प्रागाहवनीयस्य, ५.८.२
प्रागाहुतिम्, २.२.२
प्रागुदक्प्रपन्ने, ५.१.१
प्रागुदक्संस्थानि, २.२.१
प्रागुपवेशात्, २.३.२
प्राग्ग्रहणमन्त्रात्, ६.२.२
प्राग्दीक्षायै, ५.१.४
प्राग्द्विगुणम्, ५.१.२

प्राग्याजमाने, १.५.१
प्राग्वंशः, ५.१.२
प्राग्वंशकाले, ५.१.२
प्राग्वंशम्, ५.१.१, २[२]
प्राग्वंशस्य, ५.४.४
प्राग्वंशार्थम्, ५.४.४
प्राग्वंशे, ५.६.३; ६.१.४
प्राग्व्याघारणात्, ६.२.४
प्राङ्मार्जनाद्, २.३.४
प्राङ्मुखः, १.१.३; ५.४.४; ६.२.१
प्राङ्मुखौ, १.१.२
प्राङ्मेखलादि, ५.१.६
प्राचः, २.२.२; ३.२
प्राचा, ५.५.१
प्राचीनकर्णास्थूणा, ५.५.२
प्राचीनावीतत्वम्, १.४.४
प्राचीनावीतम्, २.४.१
प्राचीनावीतित्वम्, ४.१.३
प्राचीनावीती, १.१.३; ३.४.१; ५.६.५
प्राचीम् (दिशम्), ५.५.४[२]
प्राचीराहुतिः, ५.४.३
प्राजापत्यम्, ४.३.५
प्राजापत्यया, ३.४.५
प्राञ्चम्, १.२.१
प्राणग्रहाः, १.३.१
प्राणग्रहादयः, ३.१.१
प्राणग्रहान्, १.३.१[१]
प्राणभृन्मन्त्राः, १.३.१
प्राणायामत्रयम्, १.१.२
प्राणिति, १.४.४
प्राण्यापान्य, १.४.२; २.१.१; ४.७; ५.१; ३.१.१; ४.१.१; ५.१.३
प्रातराहुतिम्, १.४.१
प्रातर्दोहम्, २.१.२; ३.१.१; २.१; ५.८.२
प्रातर्दोहादि, ६.१.२; २.१.२
प्रातःसवनीयान्, ६.१.२
प्रादर्शये, ४.२.१
प्रादेशः, ५.५.३
प्रादेशपरिणाहानि, ५.१.३
प्रादेशप्रमाणः, ५.५.४
प्रादेशप्रमाणात्, ३.४.१
प्रादेशमात्रगताम् (शाखां), २.१.१
प्रादेशमात्राः, ४.१.२
प्रादेशमात्राणि, ५.१.३
प्रादेशान्तरालाः, ५.५.४
प्रापयन्ति, ६.३.२[२]
प्रायणीयस्थालीम्, ५.२.२
प्रायणीयस्य, ५.२.१
प्रायणीयाज्यशेषम्, ५.२.२
प्रायणीयायाः, ५.२.२
प्रायणीयायाम्, ५.२.२
प्रायणीयारम्भः, ५.२.१
प्रायणीयोदयनीययोः, ५.१.२
प्रायश्चित्तहोमः, २.५.३
प्रायश्चित्तादिभिः, १.१.१
प्रायश्चित्तानाम्, ६.२.३
प्रायश्चित्ते, १.३.२
प्रारब्धेषु, ६.१.१
प्रार्थनामन्त्रम्, १.१.३
प्रावरणम्, ५.३.३
प्राशनवाचने, १.१.८
प्राशित्रपक्षे, ४.३.२[२]
प्राशित्रप्राशनम्, २.५.३
प्राशित्रप्राशनानन्तरम्, २.३.४
प्राशित्रम्, २.५.१; ४.३.२[३]
प्राशित्रस्य, ५.३.४
प्राशित्रहरणम्, २.१.२; ४.३.१; ६.१.३
प्राशित्रात्, २.३.४

प्राशित्राभिघारणम्, **२**.३.३
प्राश्नन्ति, **१**.१.८; **४**.३.२; ४; **६**.३.३
प्राश्नीयात्, **३**.३.३
प्राश्नीयाताम्, **३**.३.३
प्राश्नीयुः, **१**.१.८; **२**.३.४
प्राश्य, **१**.४.४
प्रासादमञ्चादौ, **३**.६.१
प्रास्य, **१**.१.८
प्रास्येत्, **६**.२.३
प्रियात्, **१**.१.६
प्रेयात्, **२**.३.२
प्रेयुः **६**.२.३
प्रेषणीयान्, **२**.२.१
प्रेषम्, **१**.५.३
प्रेषार्थम्, **६**.३.४
प्रेषितः, **४**.३.३; ४.१; **५**.२.२; ६.२
प्रेषिता, **२**.१.३; २.१
प्रेष्यति, **४**.२.१
प्रेष्येत्, **३**.२.६; ४.३; **६**.३.४
प्रैषः, **१**.१.९; **३**.३.२; ४.५²; **५**.६.२⁵; ३
प्रैषखण्डः, **५**.४.७; **५**.६.१
प्रैषखण्डम्, **५**.६.२
प्रैषखण्डस्य, **६**.१.१
प्रैषम्, **२**.१.२, ३; २.१; **३**.२.३; **४**.१.२; ३.४²; **६**.१.४
प्रैषादि, **४**.३.४
प्रैषानन्तरम्, **६**.३.२
प्रैषानुपूर्वा, **५**.८.२
प्रैषान्, **३**.२.३; **६**.१.३
प्रैषार्थः, **५**.६.३
प्रैषार्थान्, **२**.२.२
प्रैषे, **२**.२.२; **४**.२.२; ३.१
प्रैषैः, **२**.२.१
प्रैषौ, **१**.१.९
प्रोक्षणप्रोक्षणीः, **६**.१.३
प्रोक्षणमन्त्रः, **३**.१.१
प्रोक्षणम्, **५**.४.३; ५.३
प्रोक्षणात्, **४**.४.१
प्रोक्षणानि, **४**.२.१
प्रोक्षणाय, **५**.४.७
प्रोक्षणीः, **१**.१.७; **२**.२.२; **३**.२.३, ६; ३.१, २; ४.३, ४³; **४**.३.१; **५**.४.२²; ६.२², ३, ४; **६**.१.१³, २, ३
प्रोक्षणीकत्वम्, **५**.४.७
प्रोक्षणीनाम्, **४**.१.३; २.१
प्रोक्षणीपात्रम्, **१**.१.७; **३**.२.३; ३.२
प्रोक्षणीशेषम्, **२**.२.२; **३**.२.३; ३.२; **६**.१.१
प्रोक्षणीषु, **२**.२.२
प्रोक्षण्यः, **४**.१.२; **४**.१.३; **५**.४.७; **५**.५.१
प्रोक्षति, **१**.१.३; **२**.१.३
प्रोक्षितः, **५**.६.२
प्रोक्षेत्, **३**.२.३
प्रोक्ष्य, **१**.१.७; ४.२; **२**.१.२²; ३
प्रोतम्, **१**.४.१
(वाससा) प्रोर्णवन्, **५**.१.६
प्रोर्णोति, **४**.३.३
प्रोष्ठपद्याम्, **४**.१.१
प्लक्षशाखाम्, **४**.१.२², ३²
प्लवते, **३**.४.५
फलकयोः, **६**.१.२
फलीकरणहोमम्, **३**.२.५; **४**.३.२, ५; **५**.१.५; २.२
फलीकरणहोमानन्तरम्, **५**.१.६
फलीकरणहोमे, **३**.२.५; **४**.४.३
फलीकरणादि, **३**.४.५
फलीकरणे, **४**.३.५
फलीकरणान्, **२**.३.६
फलीकृत्य, **२**.४.२

फाल्गुनशुक्लचतुर्दश्याम्, ३.१.१
फुल्लाः, ३.४.२; ६.१.४
फुल्लान् (धानार्थान्), ३.४.२
बद्धः, ५.१.७
बध्नीयात्, ५.३.२; ३; ५.३
बन्धनप्रतिबद्धा, ५.१.८
बन्धनमात्रम्, ५.२.२
बन्धनादि, ५.१.६
बन्धुसम्पन्नान्, ५.१.१
बर्हिः, १.५.२; २.१.१; २.२[२]; ३.२, ६; ३.१.१; ३.१; ४.१; ४.१.२, ५.४.२; ७[२]; ५.३; ८.२; ६.१.१, ४; २.३[४]
बर्हिःकार्याणि, २.३.२
बर्हिःखण्डम्, २.२.२; ४.२.४
बर्हिरनुप्रहरणाभ्युपायः, ३.२.५
बर्हिर्द्वयम्, ३.२.१
बर्हिर्भृष्टेः, ६.२.४
बर्हिर्मुष्टिम्, ५.५.३
बर्हिर्विचालयन्, ६.२.३
बर्हिषः, २.२.३; ५.४.२
बर्हिःषदम्, २.३.४; ४.६; ४.३.२
बर्हिःषद्भ्यः (पितृभ्यः), ३.४.२
बर्हिषा, २.३.६; ४.२.३; ५.५.३
बर्हिसंहरणे, १.३.३
बर्हिस्तरणम्, ६.२.४
बर्हिस्तीर्णा, २.३.१
बलवद्विसार्य, ५.२.१
बलवन्तः, ४.२.१
बल्बजस्तुकानाम्, ५.२.१
बहुकालेन, १.५.३
बहिःपरिधि, २.३.३
बहिष्पवमानस्य, ६.२.३
बहिष्पवमानेन, ५.८.१
बहुपर्णम्, ४.१.१
बहुवचनम्, ६.३.२
बहुवचनश्रवणे, ३.४.५
बहुशाखम्, ४.१.१
बहुसमित्प्रमाणाम्, ३.२.७
बह्वाज्यम्, १.१.८
बाधेत, ५.३.२
बाहुद्विगुणेन, १.१.४
बाहुमात्रम्, १.१.४
बाहुल्येन, ५.६.२
बृहस्पतिशब्दस्य, २.५.२
बैल्वम्, ५.१.३
ब्रह्मणः, २.३.२; २.५.३
ब्रह्मणे, १.३.२; २.३.५; ५.३.४
ब्रह्मण्यात्, ५.१.७
ब्रह्मत्वम्, २.५.२
ब्रह्मदत्त, ५.१.६
ब्रह्मपत्नीम्, ५.१.६
ब्रह्मभागम्, २.३.४
ब्रह्मयजमानयोः, २.३.२
ब्रह्मयजमानसदस्यानाम् (चमसेषु), ६.३.४
ब्रह्मयजमानाभ्याम्, ४.२.२
ब्रह्मयजमानौ, ३.४.१; ६.३.१
ब्रह्मवरणे, १.१.२
ब्रह्मवर्चसकामः, १.१.६
ब्रह्मवर्मेण, १.४.५
ब्रह्मवर्मोपस्थानम्, १.५.२
ब्रह्मसंस्कारः, ६.२.६
ब्रह्मसदनस्य, ६.२.४
ब्रह्मसदस्यन्ते, ६.१.१
ब्रह्मसदस्ययोः, ६.१.१
ब्रह्मा-, २.५.१[२]; ४.३.४; ५.६.४[३]; ६.३, ४[३]; ८.१; ६.२.१; ३.१
ब्रह्माणम्, २.१.२, २.२; ३.५; ३.३.१;

४.१.१, २; **५**.१.१[२]; ४.२; **६**.१.१
ब्रह्मौदनम्, **१**.१.८[२]
ब्रह्मौदनाग्निम्, **१**.१.६
ब्रह्मौदनाय, **१**.१.७
ब्राह्मणः, **१**.४.४; **२**.३.५; **५**.१.७[२]; ३.१; **६**.३.४
ब्राह्मणाः, **३**.३.३
ब्राह्मणस्य, **१**.१.४; **१**.१.६
ब्राह्मणाच्छंसिनः, **५**.५.४
ब्राह्मणाच्छंसी, **६**.३.४
ब्राह्मणान्, **२**.४.७; **५**.१.१
ब्राह्मणाय, **१**.१.६
ब्राह्मणे (ग्रन्थे), **१**.१.२
ब्राह्मणेन, **२**.५.१
ब्राह्मणेभ्यः, **३**.३.३
ब्राह्मणोक्तयोः, **१**.४.४
बीक्षमाणाः, **६**.२.३
ब्रीहीन्, **१**.१.७
ब्रूयु, **१**.१.९
भक्ताशनम्, **१**.३.२
भक्ताशी, **३**.६.१
भक्षणनिमित्तानि, **६**.३.३
भक्षयते, **६**.३.४
भक्षयन्ति, **६**.३.३
भक्षयित्वा, **१**.४.४
भक्षयेत्, **३**.१.२; **६**.३.३, ४
भक्षयेयुः, **३**.१.२
भक्षाय, **३**.१.२
भगवते (जातवेदसे), **१**.१.५
भद्रम्, **५**.५.३
भर्जनकपालम्, **६**.१.३
भर्जनपात्रम्, **३**.४.१; **६**.१.३
भर्जनम्, **६**.१.३
भर्जनान्तरम्, **३**.४.३
भर्जनीयाः, **३**.४.२[२]
भर्जयति, **३**.४.२
भर्जनपात्रम्, **३**.४.१; **६**.१.३
भर्जयति, **३**.४.२
भर्जयेत्, **६**.१.४
भस्मनि, **५**.४.७
भस्मोदूहनम्, **३**.४.३
भस्मोद्धरणस्य, **१**.३.३
भस्मोद्वपनम्, **२**.१.१
भाक्ते, **३**.४.१
भागः, **२**.३.४; **३**.३.२
भावः, **३**.३.२
भावात्, **३**.४.२
भावाश्रृतम्, **६**.२.४
भुञ्जाना, **३**.३.३
भूमिगते (आज्ये), **५**.५.२
भूमिम्, **१**.५.२; **५**.५.३
भूयः, **१**.४.४
भूयसोपस्तरणम्, **३**.१.१
भूयिष्ठदानात्, **१**.१.१
भूयिष्ठान्नदानम्, **१**.१.१; **१**.१.२
भृगून्, **५**.१.१
भृत्याः, **३**.३.३
भृष्टाः, **६**.१.३
भृष्टास्तुण्डुलाः, **६**.१.३
भृष्ट्वा, **३**.४.२
भेदः, **५**.२.२
भेदेन, **१**.३.३
भ्राष्ट्रान्, **६**.१.४
मण्डलाकारम्, **२**.३.२; **३**.४.५; **५**.४.३
मण्डले, **५**.१.४
मथित्वा, **५**.१.५
मदन्तीः, **२**.२.१
मदन्तीभिः, **५**.३.५[२]; ४.२

मदन्तीभ्यः, २.२.१; ५.१.२; ३.५[२]; ४.२
मदन्तीषु, ५.४.२
मदन्तीस्थालीम्, २.१.२; ४.३.१
मधुमिश्रेण, १.१.४
मधुपर्कदर्शनम्, १.१.३
मध्यन्दिनमध्यरात्रयोः, ५.१.८
मध्यमया, ५.३.१[३]
मध्यमवर्जम्, ४.१.२
मध्यमविकारेषु, ४.४.३
मध्यमिके, ५.६.५
मध्यरात्रे, ५.४.४
मध्यसूत्रम्, ५.४.७
मध्यापवर्गाणि, ४.१.२
मध्ये, १.१.४
मनसा, २.३.१; ४.२.१
मनाक्, ४.१.१; ५.३.२; ६.१.
मनुष्यनामकथनम्, ५.१.६
मनुष्यसंबन्धम्, २.३.२
मन्त्रखण्डान्, २.३.३
मन्त्रजातम्, ५.२.२
मन्त्रः, २.२.३
मन्त्रपात्रम्, ३.४.१
मन्त्रब्राह्मणसमानतन्त्र-, १.१.१
मन्त्रमुष्टयः, ५.३.४
मन्त्रम्, ५.३.१
मन्त्रवतीः (समिधः), १.१.७
मन्त्रवत्कर्मसु, २.५.१
मन्त्रवत्पर्यग्निकरणद्वयम्, ४.२.४
मन्त्रवन्तः, ५.३.४
मन्त्रवन्तौ, १.१.७
मन्त्रवर्जम्, १.२.१
मन्त्रविकल्पः, २.४.२
मन्त्रविपरिणमनम्, ३.१.१
मन्त्रलिङ्गविरोधः, ५.६.३
मन्त्रलिङ्गोपपत्तिः, ५.३.४
मन्त्रसन्नामः, ३.२.३
मन्त्रस्य, ३.४.३
मन्त्रस्योपस्तरणम्, ३.४.३
मन्त्रान्तया, २.३.६
मन्त्रान्ते, १.१.४ ; ५.५.२
मन्त्रावृत्तिः, ५.२.३
मन्त्रेण, १.१.५; ५.२; २.१.१; ३[२]; २.१, २[२], ३; ३.५; ३.३.१; ४.३.३[४]
मन्त्रैः, ३.२.६; ४.४
मन्त्रोक्ति, १.५.२; ५.२.२; ६.२.५; २.२
मन्थति, ४.२.१[२]
मन्थम्, ३.४.३
मन्थिनः, ६.३.३
मन्थिना, ६.३.२
मन्थीत, १.४.२
मन्दतमम्, ५.२.२
मन्दादुच्चरितम्, ५.२.२
मन्दम्, ५.२.२
मन्यते, ५.२.२
महत्प्रायश्चित्तम्, ६.२.३
महर्त्विजः, १.१.२
महादेवः, ५.१.७
महादेवानुचरभूतावेशः, ५.१.७
महानाम्न्या, ५.३.१[३]
महापरिधयः, ५.१.३; ८.२
महापरिधीन्, ५.८.२
महापर्यायेषु, ६.२.१
महारात्रे, ६.३.१
महावेदिकम् (बर्हिः), ५.४.७
महावेदिम्, ५.६.२
महावेदिस्तरणार्थम्, ५.४.७
महावेद्याम्, ५.४.६; ६.१.४
महावेद्यै, ५.४.६

महाहविषस्तन्त्रम्, **३**.३.३
महेन्द्रयाजिनः, **२**.३.३; **३**.६.१
मांसम्, **१**.१.२; ५.२
माघ्याम् (अमावास्यायाम्), **४**.१.१
मातृभिः, **३**.३.३
मादृशाम्, प्रस्ता. १
माध्यन्दिनीयान्, **६**.१.२
मानम्, **५**.४.५
मानरज्जुः, **५**.४.४
माने, **५**.३.१
मान्त्रम्, **६**.१.५
मारुतम्, **३**.१.१; २.१
मारुतस्य, **३**.१.१
मारुती, **५**.२.२
मारुतीम् (आमिक्षाम्), **३**.२.३
मारुत्यर्थम्, **३**.२.३
मारुत्याः, **३**.२.१; ६.३
मार्गः, **२**.३.५; **६**.१.१
मार्जनम्, **१**.५.२; **२**.३.४; ५.३; **४**.४.३; **६**.२.३
मार्जनादि, **५**.१.७
मार्जनान्तम्, **५**.१.७
मार्जयति, **१**.१.६; **४**.२.३
मार्जयित्वा, **१**.१.६; **२**.२.२[२]
मार्जयेत्, **१**.१.६
मार्जालीयम्, **५**.४.५; **६**.२.४
मार्जालीयम् (धिष्णियम्), **६**.२.४
मार्जालीयसमीपे, **५**.८.१
मार्जालीयस्य, **५**.५.३, ४
मार्जालीये, **५**.८.१
माहाचमसेन, **१**.४.५; ५.१; ३
माहाचमसोपस्थानाख्यम्, **१**.५.१
माहेन्द्रस्य (स्तोत्रे), **६**.१.२
मित्वा, **१**.१.४
मिथः, **५**.६.४
मिथुनम्, **१**.३.३
मिनुयात्, **३**.२.१; **६**.१.५
मिमानः, **५**.३.१
मिमाय, **३**.२.२
मिमीते, **४**.१.१; **५**.३.१, २; ४.५[२]
मिश्रयेत्, **५**.१.८
मुक्तानि, **४**.३.२
मुखसंमिताः, **२**.१.२
मुख्याः (ऋत्विजः), **५**.६.४
मुख्यानुपूर्व्या, **५**.६.५
मुष्टिक्रमः, **५**.३.१
मुष्टिना, **३**.४.४; **५**.३.१
मुष्टीनाम्, **२**.२.१
मुष्टीन्, **२**.१.१; **५**.३.१
मुष्टिभिः, **२**.२.२
मूतकार्यम्, **२**.१.१
(यावन्) मूतम्, **५**.२.३
मूत्रपुरीषकारणेषु, **५**.१.८
मूलकल्पाभिहिते, **५**.१.६
मूलच्छिन्ना, **३**.४.१
मूलमध्याग्रेषु, **४**.१.३
मृदितेन, **३**.२.३
मृन्मयीम्, **१**.४.२
मेक्षणम्, **२**.१.२; ३.३; ४.२; **३**.३.१; **४**.३.१; **५**.२.२; **६**.१.३
मेक्षणेन, **२**.२.१; **६**.१.४
मेखला, **५**.१.१
मेखले, **३**.२.६
मेथी, **५**.५.१
मेदः, **४**.३.१; ३.३
मेषम्, **३**.२.३
मेषमेष्यार्थाः, **३**.२.१
मेषमेष्योः, **३**.२.१

मेषमेष्यौ, ३.२.४; ५
मेषस्य, ३.२.१
मेषीम्, ३.२.३
मेष्यै, ३.२.१
मैत्रावरुणचमसम्, ६.१.४; ५
मैत्रावरुणचमसाध्वर्युः, ६.१.४
मैत्रावरुणदण्डम्, ४.१.२
मैत्रावरुणदण्डे, २.५.३; ४.१.३
मैत्रावरुणपात्रम्, ६.३.३
मौञ्जम्, ५.१.१
मौञ्जीभिः, ५.१.३
म्रियेत, ५.१.७[२]; ८[३]
यक्ष्यमाणः, ५.१.१
यक्ष्यमाणस्य, ५.१.१[२]
यच्छेत्, ४.४.१
यज, २.३.२; ४.५; ३.४.५
यजमानः, १.१.५, ६, ७, ८, ९; ४.२[२], ४[२]; २.२.३[२]; ३.२, ४; ३.१.२; २.६, ५; ३.३; ४.१.२[२], ३; ३.१; ३.३; ४.२; ५.१.१; ३.३[२]; ४.२, ६[२]; ५.३[३]; ६.३, ५[२]; ८.१; ६.१.१, ३; २.१[२]; ३.१[२], ३
यजमानचमसे, ६.३.३[२]
यजमानपुरुषाः, ६.१.१
यजमानभागप्राशनम्, ४.४.३
यजमानभागप्राशनवर्जम्, २.३.७
यजमानभागम्, ४.४.३
यजमानम्, २.१.१[२]; ३.२; ४, ५[२]; ३.२.४, ६; ३.२; ४.३, ४; ६.२; ४.२.१; ३.२, ४, ५; ५.५.४; ६.१.१; ३.२, ३
यजमानमात्रीम्, १.१.४
यजमानशब्दम्, ३.४.१, ३, ४[२]; ४.५
यजमानस्य, १.१.८; २.१.१; २.३; ३.२; ६, ७; ४.७; ३.३.३, ५; ४.४; ४.३.५; ४.२; ५.३.३[२]; ४.१; ८.२
यजमानायतनम्, ३.२.४
यजमानायतने, १.४.५; २.४.६; ३.६.१
यजमानावेक्षितः, ५.६.३
यजमाने, २.३.५
यजमानेन, २.२.३; ३.६; ५.१; ३.२.४; ५.१.३; २.३; ६.२.६
यजमानेनामन्त्रितम्, २.३.६
यजुः, १.१.९; ५.१.७
यजुरादिवचनम्, ५.४.६
यज्जातीयम् (हविः), २.३.५
यज्ञदत्त (विचक्षण), ५.१.६
यज्ञपतिशब्दम्, ३.४.५
यज्ञपुरुषः, २.३.६
यज्ञपुरुषनमस्कारम्, १.४.२
यज्ञपुरुषाय, ३.१.१
यज्ञम्, २.२.३
यज्ञवाट्, ६.१.१
यज्ञविदः, ५.१.३
यज्ञविमोकः, २.३.७
यज्ञविमोककपालविमोकौ, ५.१.५
यज्ञशालम्, ५.१.२
यज्ञसादनात्, २.४.३
(अन्यत्र) यज्ञसादनात्, ३.६.१
यज्ञसादनानि, २.४.४
यज्ञसाधनेषु, २.२.३
यज्ञसिद्ध्यर्थम्, २.५.१
यज्ञायुधानाम्, ३.२.१
यज्ञायुधानि, २.१.२; ३.४.१
यज्ञोपचारे, ६.२.५
यज्ञोपवीतम्, २.५.१; ४.१.१
यज्ञोपवीती, २.१.१; ४.१; ३.१.१; ४.१
यत्कामः, ६.२.५

यथाकथंचित्, १.१.२
यथाकामम्, ३.३.३; ५.५.२
यथादिशम्, २.४.७
यथादेवतम्, २.२.३; ६.२.२
यथापाठम्, १.५.१; २.१.१; २.३; ३.४; ५; ६.२.५
यथाप्रकृति, ३.१.१; २.४; ४.१, ५[३]; ४.४.२; ५.४.२[२], ३; ६.२.४
यथाबुद्धि, १.१.१
यथाभीप्सितम्, ६.२.५
यथामति, १.१.१
यथायतनम्, ३.४.४; ४.३.२; ६.१.५; ३.३
यथार्थप्रमातम्, ५.५.३
यथार्थम्, १.१.४; २.५.१; ३.४.३
यथार्थानि, १.१.४
यथार्हम्, ३.२.१
यथालाभमशनम्, १.३.२
यथालिङ्गम्, २.५.१; ४.१.२
यथालिङ्गनम्, ४.२.३; ४.३[४]
यथावकाशम्, १.१.४
यथावर्णम्, १.१.२
यथाशक्ति, १.१.१
यथाश्रुतम्, २.३.६
यथासंभवम्, १.१.१; ३.२.१
यथासमाम्नातम्, ४.१.२
यथास्तीर्णम्, ३.३.१
यथास्थम्, ३.२.४; ३.२.३
यथास्थानम्, ३.३.२; ४.४; ५.१.४
यथेतम्, १.४.४; ३.२.२
यथोक्तः, १.४.१
यथोक्तकाले, ३.६.४
यथोक्तम्, १.४.१; २[२]; ४.४[२]; ५.१; ३
यथोत्साहम्, ५.१.४
यथोक्तसमुदिते, ४.३.३
यथोपपादम्, २.३.४; ४.१.२; ६.३.२
यवमयेषु, २.२.३
यवाः, ३.२.१; ५.१.३
यवागूः, १.५.२
यवान्, ३.४.२[२]; ६.१.३[५], ४
यवानाम्, ३.४.२
यवोदनम्, ३.२.३
यवोदनेन, ३.२.३
यागहोमेषु, २.३.६
यागानाम्, १.३.१
याचेत्, ५.१.४
याजः, ५.४.७
याजमानम्, १.१.८[३], ९[६]; ५.३; २.१.३; ४.१, ७; ३.४.५; ६.१; ४.१.२; ५.१.५[२], ६; ४.४; ६.२.५
याजमानानि, १.१.९; ३.६.१
याजमानोक्तेन, १.५.३
याजयेत्, २.३.२
याजविकारत्वे, ५.४.३
याजविकाराः, ५.२.२
याजान्त, २.३.२
याजुषे (माने), ५.३.१[२]
याज्यानुमन्त्रणेषु, ४.४.३
याज्यानुवाक्याभ्याम्, ३.१.२
याज्याम्, ३.२.४
याज्येत्, २.३.२
याज्ञिकानि (काष्ठानि), १.४.४
यावत्प्रयोगम्, ३.६.१
युक्तइव, १.४.३
युगपद्, ३.२.१
युगे, ६.१.५
युज्यात्, ६.१.१
युनक्ति ४.२.१
यूपकालम्, ५.४.४

यूपकालात्, ५.४.५
यूपम्, ४.१.१, ३; २.१, ५; ३.३[३]; ४.२; ५.१.४
यूपरशनाम्, ६.२.६
यूपरशनायाम्, ४.२.१
यूपशकलौ, ४.१.३
यूपार्थत्वात्, ४.१.१
यूपार्थम्, ५.५.२
यूपावटखननम्, ५.६.५
यूपावटम्, ४.१.२; ५.३.२
यूपावटीयः, ४.१.१
यूपावटीयम्, ५.१.२
यूपावटीयात्, ४.१.२
यूपावटीये, ५.४.५
यूपावटे, ४.१.१
यूपाहवनीयम्, ४.२.४
यूपाहवनीयाभ्याम्, ४.२.२
यूपाहुत्या, ४.१.१
यूपे, ४.२.१; ५.६.५
यूषन्, ४.३.३
यूष्णा, ४.३.३
यूष्णोपसेचनादि, ४.३.३
येनकेनचिद् विधानेन, १.१.१, ३
योक्त्रम्, ५.१.१
योगः, ५.१.८
योगतः, ३.५.२
योनिभिः, १.१.८[२]
योयुपित्वा, ५.४.७
योयोपनम्, ५.४.२
योयोपने, ३.६.२
यौष्णः, ४.३.३
रक्षिणः, ६.१.१
रक्षितुम्, ५.१.८
रजकधवलिकरणम्, ३.६.१
रज्जुः, ५.२.१
रज्जुभिः, ५.१.३
रज्जुम्, १.१.४
रज्ज्वा, ५.१.७
रत्नम्, २.१.१
रथप्रमाणाम्, ४.१.१
रथावकाशाम्, ४.१.१
रराटीयम्, ५.५.१; ५.५.२
रवथे, ३.३.३
रशनया, ४.१.३
रशनागुणे, ४.१.३
रशनाद्वयम्, ४.१.२
रशनाम्, ६.२.६
रसग्रहणपक्षे, १.५.२
(सोम) रसम्, १.५.२
राजक्रयणानि, ५.३.३
राजक्रयणीम्, ५.२.२
राजक्रये, ६.२.१
राजन्यस्य (गृहात्), १.१.६
राजा, ५.३.१; ६.४
राजानम्, ५.३.२, ३[३], ४[३]; ६.३[२], ४[३], ५; ८.१; ६.१.१, २[२]; २.१[३], ३, ५
राजासन्दी, ५.२.१
राज्ञः, ५.३.१, २; ६.१.५
राज्ञश्चर्मणि, ६.१.५
राज्ञा, ५.६.३, ४
रात्रीम्, ३.३.३
राशीन्, ३.३.२
रु-शब्देन, ३.३.३
रोहिण्यादिषु, १.१.२
रोहितम् (चर्म), १.१.७; ५.१.३; २.१
रोहिते चर्मन्, ५.३.१
लक्षणशङ्कुम्, ५.४.५
लक्षणद्वादशसु, ५.४.५

लक्षणम्, १.१.४; ५.४.५
लक्षणेन, १.१.४
लक्षयित्वा, ४.४.१
लक्षयेत्, २.२.२
लताग्रहणपक्षे, १.५.२
लताम्, १.५.२
लप्स्यते, ५.१.६
ललाटम्, ४.२.१[२]
ललाटे, ४.२.१
लाजाः, ६.१.३
लाजापक्षे, ६.१.३
लिप्यते, १.४.४
लुनीयात्, ३.२.१
लुप्यते, २.२.३; ३.४.२, ५; ५.१.५; २.२
लूताः, २.३[३].१
लूत्वा, २.१.१
लेपम्, १.४.४
लोके, ५.१.८
लोपः, ५.१.६
लोमानि, ३.२.१[२]
लोहितायस्ताम्रमयः, ३.१.३
लोहिते, ४.२.३
लौकिकत्वम्, १.३.२
लौकिकम्, १.१.३
वंशान्, ५.५.१; २
वक्षः, ४.३.४
वक्षप्रोक्षण-, ४.२.१
वक्ष्यते, प्रस्ता. १
वचनात्, १.१.९; ३.२.१
वचनाद्यनुक्रमणम्, ५.१.४
वर्तेत, ५.१.८
वर्त्मनि, ५.५.१
वत्सज्ञुम्, २.१.१
वत्साः, ३.३.३
वत्सान्, २.१.१, २; ३.२.१
वत्सापाकरणम्, ५.८.२
वत्साय, ५.३.५
वदरे, ५.१.३
वनस्पतिभागम्, ४.४.३
वनस्पती, ४.१.२
वपते, १.१.६
वपनम्, ३.१.३
वपनमन्त्रान्, ३.६.१
वपयति, १.१.६
वपया, ६.१.१; २.६
वपा, ४.२.३
वपागमनम्, २.५.३
वपात्, ४.४.३
वपाद्रव्यम्, ४.२.३
वपानुमन्त्रणम्, ४.४.२
वपान्ते, २.५.३; ४.३.२
वपान्तेन, ४.४.३
वपाम्, १.१.५; ४.२.४[३]
वपामन्त्रेण, ४.२.४
वपायाः, ४.२.५; ५.७.१
वपायोगः, ३.३.१
वपावत्, ४.४.३
वपाश्रपणी, ४.२.४, ५
वपाश्रपणीभ्याम्, २.५.३; ४.२.२; ४.२
वपाश्रपण्योः, २.५.३
वपाश्रपण्यौ, ४.१.२
वपाहोमान्तम्, ४.२.४
वपाहोमासादनादि, ६.३.१
वयांसि, ५.३.२
वरणस्य, १.१.३
वरणाय, १.१.१
वराहेण, १.१.५
वरुणप्रदेशे, २.२.२

वरुणप्रघासानाम्, ३.६.१
वरुणप्रघासार्थम्, ३.२.१[२]
वरुणप्रघासेषु, २.५.२
वरुणविमोकम्, २.३.७
वरुणविमोचनम्, २.५.२
वर्गक्रमेण, ५.४.३
वर्जयित्वा, ३.४.४; ४.२.३; ५.६.२
वर्तन्याम्, ५.५.१
वर्षकामस्य, ६.२.२
वल्यौ, ५.१.७
वश्याः, ५.१.३
वषट्कर्तुः, ६.३.३
वषट्कर्तॄणाम्, ६.३.३
वषट्कारनिमित्तेन, ६.३.४
वषट्कारप्रदाने, २.३.२
वषट्कारप्रदानेषु, २.४.६
वषट्कारम्, २.३.२
वषट्कारौ, ६.३.३
वषट्कृतानुवषटकृतयोः, ६.३.२
वषट्कृते, २.४.५; ४.२.५[२]; ३.४[२]; ६.३.२[२]
वसतीवरीः, ५.६.३; ४[२]; ८.१; ६.१.४, ५[२]
वसतीवरीभ्यः, ५.१.२, ५
वसतीवर्यः, ५.६.४
वसन्तादिषु, १.१.२
वसन्ताद्या देवताः, २.३.२
वसाम्, ४.३.३
वसाहोमम्, ४.३.४
वसाहोमहवनीम्, ४.१.२
वसाहोमीयम्, ४.३.३; ४.३.३[२]
वहन्तीः (अपः), ५.१.८; ६.१
वां-शब्दम्, ३.६.२
वाक्यपरिपूरणाय, ४.२.१
वाक्यशुक्लशुद्धवाससौ, १.१.२
वाक्यशेषम्, ५.५.४
वाङ्मनःपरौ, ३.६.३
वाग्यतः, २.४.३
वाग्यमः, २.५.१
वाग्यमनकाले, २.५.१
वाचनम्, २.५.३
वाचनिकः, ५.४.१, ७; ६.१.६; २.१
वाचनिकत्वे, १.३.१
वाचनिकम्, ५.३.५
वाचनेषु, २.२.२
वाचम्, ४.४.१
वाचयिता, ४.३.४
वाचयित्रा, २.२.२
वाचयित्वा, १.३.१; २.२.२; ३.४, ५[२]; ३.२.६; ४.३, ४; ४.३.२
वाचयेत्, २.३.३, ४; ४.२.३; ५.१.५; ५.१
वाच्यमानः, ३.६.१
वाजवतीभ्याम्, ४.३.५
वाजिनचर्यादीनि, ६.३.४
वाजिनपात्रम्, ३.१.१[२]; ६.१.३
वाजिनभक्षान्ते, ३.२.५
वाजिनम्, ३.१.१
वाजिनयागः, ३.६.१
वाजिनस्य, ३.१.२
वाजिनानन्तरम्, ६.३.४
वाजिनेन, ५.८.२
वाजिभ्यः, ३.१.२
वादः, ५.१.६
वाधूलकस्य, प्रस्ता. १
वाधूलकाचार्यसन्दर्भम्, प्रस्ता. १
वाधूलकेषु, ५.४.६
वामदेव्यम्, १.१.९
वामदेव्येन, १.१.९
वामलकी, ५.१.३

वायव्यानि, ५.६.१; ६.४
वारयतः काले, ५.५.१
वारुणीश्रपणादि, ३.२.३
वारुण्याः, ३.२.१
वारुण्याम्, ३.६.३
वासः, ५.३.१
वासयेयुः, ३.३.३
वाससः (अन्तान्), ५.३.२
वाससा, ५.६.३
वासिष्ठः, ५.१.७
वासिष्ठम्, ५.१.१
विकर्षेत, ४.२.१
विकल्पः, १.१.७; ३.२; २.३.४; ३.१.१; ५.१.७
विकल्पना, २.४.३; ३.३.५
विकल्पाः, १.१.२
विकल्पनामात्राभिधायी, ५.३.५
विकल्पेन, १.१.१; ३.२; ६.१.१
विकल्पोपादाने, १.३.२
विकल्प्यानि, १.५.३
विकल्प्येते, ५.१.६; ५.३.५
विकारः, ३.५.१; २
विक्रियेत, ३.५.२
विकृतिविषयौ, ५.३.५
विकृत्यर्थाः, २.३.७
विक्रममाणश्च, २.४.१
विक्रियेत, ३.५.२
विगतशाखम्, ४.१.१
विगृह्णाति, ५.३.४
विघातः, ५.२.१
विघ्नन्ति, ५.२.१
विचक्षण, ५.१.६
विचार्य, प्रस्ता. १
विचितः, ५.३.१
विच्छिन्द्येत्, ६.२.१
विच्छेदः, ६.२.३
विच्छेदे, ६.२.३
विजानन्तः, ६.२.३
वितुषीकृत्य, २.१.३
वितुषीभावः, २.४.२
विदले (काष्ठे), ४.३.१
विदितवेदितव्यानाम्, प्रस्ता. १
विधानेन, १.१.२, ३, ६, ७; ५.३[२]; २.५.२
विधाय, १.४.४
विधिः, १.३.२; ४.१
विधिना, १.३.३
विधीयते, ६.२.३
विनयन्ते, ५.३.४
विनिधयः, १.१.६
विनियोगतः, ५.५.१
विनियुक्ते, ४.१.२
विनियुज्य, १.१.६
विनियुञ्जीत, ५.५.१
विनिविष्टः, २.३.४; ४.२
विपर्यन्ति, ३.४.५
विपर्ययेण, २.५.२
विप्रुड्ढोमे, ६.२.३
विप्रुषाम्, ३.२.१
विभजन्ति, ६.२.१
विभृज्यात्, १.२.१
विमाय, २.२.२
विमितः, १.१.४
विमितम्, १.१.३
विमितायाम्, ५.५.१
विमिते, ५.५.१
विमुञ्चेत्, ४.३.२; ५.३.३
विमोकः, २.४.३
विराजक्रमैः, १.५.३

विरोधः, १.१.१
विविक्ते (प्रदेशे), १.१.२
विविधम्, ५.६.१
विवेकम्, २.१.३
विवेकवर्जः, २.४.२
विषुवति, १.१.९
विषूके, ५.५.२
विषूचीनाग्रम्, ४.१.३
विषूचीनाग्रे, ४.२.१
विष्टम्भः, ५.३.३
विष्टम्भनार्थम्, ५.३.३
विष्टम्भान्वारोहान्, ३.१.२
विष्णुक्रमादयः, २.३.७
विष्णुक्रमान्, २.४.७; ४.४.३
विष्णुक्रमैः, ४.३.२
विष्णुशब्दः, ५.३.४
विशदद्रव्यम्, १.५.३; २.३.२
विशये, ३.१.१
विशसनात्, ४.३.१
विशसनादिश्रपणान्तम्, ४.३.१
विशसनाय, ४.३.१
विशसितव्यम्, ४.२.१
विशाखे, ५.५.२
विशातयेत्, ५.१.८
विशास्ति, ४.३.१
विश्वजिति, ६.२.२
विसर्गः, ५.३.५
विसर्गमन्त्रः, ६.१.६
विसर्गे, ३.६.२
विसृजति, ३.२.७; ५.३.३; ६.५
विसृजेत्, २.३.७
विसृज्य, ४.२.४
विस्रंसयति, ३.२.७; ५३३.२
विस्रंसयन्, ४.२.५
विस्रंसयेते, ३.२.७
विसंस्रयेत्, २.३.६
विस्रंस्य, ५.५.१
विस्राव्य, २.२.१[२], ३.२
विस्तारार्थम्, ५.४.५
विस्मरणीयः, ५.१.७
विस्राव्य, २.२.१[२]; ३.२
विहताम्, १.१.५
विहरिष्यन्, ६.२.३
विहरेत्, ५.१.४; ६.२.३
विहारार्थम्, ३.२.१
विहिता, १.१.१; १.१.२
वीक्षमाणः, २.२.१
वीक्षमाणाः, ६.२.३
वीतकल्मषम्, १.१.१
वीतकल्मषाणाम्, प्रस्ता. १
वृक्णे, ५.६.५
(यज्ञियस्य) वृक्षस्य, ५.३.५
वृणीयात्, १.१.३
वृतानाम्, १.१.३
वृतेषु, ५.६.४
वृश्चति, ४.३.१
वृषणस्थायौ, ४.२.१
वृणीत, ५.१.१
वृणीयात्, १.१.३
वृणीयाताम्, १.१.२
वृषाणौ, ४.२.१
वृषारवम्, २.१.२; ४.३.१
वेदः, २.१.१; ३.६
वेदकरणम्, ४.१.२
वेदकरणाभिमन्त्रणेन°, ५.८.२
वेदप्रोक्षणम्, ५.४.२
वेदम्, २.१.१, २; २.३; ३.६; ३.१.१;
३.१, २, ६; ४.४; ४.१.२[२]; ५.२.२

वेदस्य, २.३.६; ५.४.२
वेदानुमन्त्रणम्, ३.६.३
वेदाभ्याम्, ३.२.२
वेदार्थान्, १.१.१
वेदिः, १.१.४; ३.४.१^{२}
वेदिकरण, ५.८.२
वेदिकरणम्, ३.३.२
वेदिकरणाभिमन्त्रेण, ५.८.२
वेदिकरणे, ३.३.१
वेदित्वापादनार्थाः, ५.४.६
वेदिपरिधितिरश्ची, ५.४.२
वेदिप्रदेशम्, ५.४.६
वेदिमध्ये, ३.४.१
वेदिम्, १.१.४; २.१.१^{२}, २^{२}; ३.७; ५.१; ३.२.१, २; ३.१, २; ४.१; ४.१.१^{२}; ५.४.६^{२}; ६.२, ३
वेदिशब्दवाच्यायाम्, ५.४.६
वेदिस्तरणम्, २.३.२
वेदिस्तरणाय, ५.४.२
वेदी, २.५.२; ३.२.२
वेदेः, ३.४.१; ४.१.१
वेदेन, २.२.१; २; ३.१; ४; ३.४.१, ५; ५.४.२
वेदौ, ३.२.१
वेद्यन्तरा, ४.१.२
वेद्यन्तात्, ४.१.१; ५.४.५
वेद्यन्तार्थम्, ५.४.४
वेद्यन्ते, ५.४.५
वेद्यम्, २.३.६
वेद्याः, ४.३.३; ५.४.६
वेद्याम्, १.४.२; २.३.४; ४.३.२; ६.१.४
वैकङ्कतः, ३.२.१
वैकङ्कतम्, १.१.५
वैकङ्कतीम्, १.१.३
वैकल्पिकम्, १.४.४
वैकल्पिकौ, ५.२.२
वैदिके, ५.१.४
वैश्यरथकारयोः, ६.२.१; ३.४
वैश्यस्य, १.१.४, ६
वैश्वदेवः, ३.१.१
वैश्वदेवस्य (काले), ३.१.३
वैश्वदेवहविः, ३.६.१
वैश्वदेवे, ३.२.१
वैश्वानरीयेष्टिः, ५.१.१
वैश्वामित्रम्, ५.१.१
वैसर्जनहोमानन्तरम्, ५.६.३
वैसर्जनहोमार्थम्, ५.६.२
व्यतिषज्य, २.३.२
व्यतिहरणम्, ३.२.५
व्यतीते, १.३.२
व्यन्तान्, १.४.२
व्यपगतोष्माणः, २.४.३
व्यपोहन्ति, ६.२.१
व्यवच्छिन्नेध्मम्, ५.४.७
व्यवधाने, ५.१.७
व्यवस्थितः, ५.१.७
व्यवहारोच्छित्तिः, प्रस्ता. १.
व्यवेत्य, २.३.४
व्यवेत्योपवेशने, २.३.४
व्यस्तदक्षिणोत्तरम्, २.३.४
व्यस्ताग्रम्, ४.१.३
व्यस्ताभिः (व्याहृताभिः), १.१.६
व्याख्यातम्, ३.४.२
व्याख्याय, ३.३.३; ४.४; ४.३.३; ६.२.३
व्याख्येयः, २.२.३
व्याख्येयाः, ३.१.१
व्याघरणानि, ४.१.२
व्याघारणम्, ६.२.४^{२}
व्याचष्टे : १.३.१^{३}

व्यादिष्टम्, २.३.४[२]
व्यादिष्टे, २.३.५
व्यापारात्, ३.२.५
व्याप्रियमाणाः, ५.५.२
व्यावर्त्य, २.२.१
व्यावर्तने, ३.१.१
व्याहरणम्, १.१.३
व्याहरेत्, १.१.३; ५.१.१
व्याहृतिभिः, १.१.६; २.५.१
व्युदजेत्, ५.१.४
व्यूहम्, ३.३.२
व्यूहेत्, ३.६.३
व्यूह्य, १.१.४, ८; ३.६.३; ५.४.२
व्यृद्धम्, १.३.३
व्रतकालः, २.२.३
व्रतकाले, ५.३.५
व्रतगमनपरतः, ६.१.२
व्रतचमसम्, ५.१.७
व्रतचर्या, ३.६.१
व्रतदुहः, ५.८.२
व्रतनम्, ५.३.५
व्रतप्रदानौ, ५.१.१
व्रतम्, १.३.२; २.२.३, ७; ४.७; ३.३.२; ४.१.२; ३.२; ४.१[२]; ५.१.८; ३.४[२]
व्रतयन्, ५.४.४
व्रतयित्वा, ५.१.७ ; ८
व्रतयोः, ५.१.२[२]
व्रतयेत्, १.३.२
व्रतविधानम्, ५.१.७
व्रतविसर्गः, २.३.७
व्रतविसर्गकालः, २.३.७
व्रतविसर्जनम्, ५.१.५
व्रतोपलक्षणम्, ५.१.८
व्रतोपायनम्, ५.१.५; २.२
व्रश्चनम्, ५.६.५
व्रीहयः, ५.१.३
व्रीहीन्, ४.३.१; ६.१.३[३]
शँव्वन्तम्, ४.३.५
शकटम्, ५.३.३; ४
शकटयोजनी, ५.३.३
शकटस्य, ५.३.३; ५.१
शकटे, ५.५.१
शकलद्वयम्, ४.२.१
शकलम्, ४.१.१; २.१; ५.४.३[२]
शकलयोः, ३.२.७
शकलादानादिना, ३.१.२
शकलानि, ५.३.४
शकलीकृत्य, ५.२.२
शकलेषु, ४.२.१
शकलौ, २.५.१; ६.२.६
शक्याः, ५.१.८
शङ्कुः, ४.१.१; ५.१.१
शङ्कुद्वयेन, १.१.४
शङ्कुम्, १.१.४; ५.१.२; ४.४[२]
शङ्कूनाम्, ५.२.१
शङ्कोः, ४.१.२; ५.४.५[२]; ५.१
शतमानम्, १.१.५
शतादधिकानि, ३.२.४
शपथम्, ५.३.४
शफः, ५.३.२
शमितारम्, ४.३.१
शमितृकर्म, ४.३.१
शमित्रम्, ४.२.४; ३.१; ३.३
शमित्रे, ४.२.१[२]
शमित्रेण, ४.२.२
शमित्रौ, ४.२.२
शमीगर्भाभावे, १.१.२
शमीगर्भारण्यो, १.२.२
शमीपर्णानि, ३.२.१; ४
शमीम्, १.१.५

शमीवर्जम्, ३.२.५
शम्या, १.१.५
शम्यानिधाने, ४.१.२
शम्यामात्रम्, ४.१.१
शम्यामात्री, ४.१.२
शयनकाले, १.१.८; ५.८.१
शयम्, ३.३.१
शरः, ५.३.२
शरदि, ३.२.१
शरमयम्, ३.२.१
शरमयी, ५.१.१
शरावाः, ५.१.२
शरेषीकया, १.१.६
शरेषीकशरतरुणाञ्जनसमर्था, ५.१.१
शर्कराः, १.१.४, ५
शलल्या, ३.१.३
शलाकया, ३.४.२
शल्कैः, ६.१.६
शाकलः, ५.४.७; ६.२[२]
शाकलत्वम्, ५.४.७
शाकलानि, ५.४.२
शाक्त्यः, ५.१.७
शाक्वोस्पन्द्याम्, ५.४.४
शाखान्तरे, १.१.२
शाखापवित्रम्, २.१.१; ३.२.१
शाखामूलम्, २.२.१
शाखामूलेन, २.४.७
शाखाम्, २.१.१; ३.५; ३.२.१; ५.८.२
शाखाहरणम्, ५.८.२
शाखे, १.१.३; ५.१.४
शामित्रदेशः, ४.२.२
शामित्रदेशम्, ४.२.३
शामित्रम्, ४.२.५; ३.१, ३
शामित्रे, ४.२.१[२]
शामित्रेण, ५.२.२
शामित्रौ, ४.२.२
शाययन्ति, ४.२.२
शाययितस्य, ३.३.१
शालाप्रपदनम्, ५.१.६
शालाप्रयाणे, ५.१.६
शालाभ्यन्तरे ५.१.७
शालामुखीयम्, ५.६.३[२]; ६.१.३[२]
शालामुखीये, ५.१.२; ६.१.२
शालाम्, ५.१.४, ५[२]; ४.७; ६.२, ३
शालार्थे, १.१.२
शासयति, ४.३.१
शास्त्रप्रसिद्धम्, ४.१.२
शिंशपा, ५.१.३
शिंघाणिकारे, ५.१.८
शिरसोऽधस्तात्, ५.१.६
शिरोपधानम्, ३.४.१
शिशिरादौ, ३.१.१
शिष्टम् (आज्यम्), २.३.५
शिष्यः, १.४.५
शीर्षण्यम्, ५.१.३
शुक्रता, ६.३.२
शुक्रपात्रम्, ५.१.३
शुक्रम्, ६.३.४
शुक्रामन्थिनौ, ६.२.२
शुक्रामन्थिप्रचारे, ६.३.४
शुक्रमन्थिनौ (पात्रे), ६.१.२; २.५
शुक्लोर्णस्तुका, ६.२.१
शुग्बन्धनम्, ५.३.३
शुचिवासः, २.५.१
शुचियाजविकारः, १.३.३
शुद्धान्तःकरणौ, १.१.२
शुद्धे, ५.१.१
शुनासीरीयम्, ३.६.४
शुनासीरीयाय, ३.२.१
शुल्बपक्षे, ५.४.५[२], ६[२]

शुल्बिणी, ५.४.६
शुष्काग्रम्, २.५.१
शूर्पम्, १.१.७; २.४.२; ३.२.१; २.४; ४.३.१; ६.१.३
शूर्पादानमन्त्रम्, २.१.३
शूर्पादिना, १.१.७
शूर्पेण, ३.२.२
शूलम्, ४.१.२
शृङ्गम्, ४.२.१
शृङ्गयोः, ४.१.२
शृङ्गे, ४.२.१
शृतम्, २.२.१; ३.१.१; ५.३.२
शृताप्ये, ३.१.१
शृते, २.२.१[२]
शेषकार्याणि, ३.२.५
शेषपक्षापेक्षम्, १.३.२
शोधयतः, ३.२.७
श्रद्धायुक्तः, १.१.२
श्रपणम्, ३.३.१
श्रपणार्थम्, १.५.२
श्रपयति, १.५.३[२]
श्रपयित्वा, ३.१.१; ६.१.४
श्रपयेत्, २.३.५; ३.४.२; ४.३.२
श्रप्यते, १.४.२
श्रप्यमाणानि, १.१.४
श्रप्यमाणाम्, ४.२.४
श्रप्यमाणायाम्, ४.२.४
श्रयणे, ६.२.२
श्रावय, २.३.२
श्राविते, २.३.२
श्रिते, ४.३.२
श्रीणाति, ६.१.५; २.२
श्रुतमन्त्राभ्याम्, ३.१.१
श्रूयमाणैः, १.२.१
श्रोण्यर्थम्, ५.४.५
(सव्यायाः) श्रोण्याः, ४.३.३
श्रोण्यात्, १.१.४
श्रोण्याम्, १.१.४; ४.२.४
श्रोण्योः, ४.२.३; ५.६.५
श्लक्ष्णाम्, ४.१.२
श्लक्ष्णीकृत्य, ३.३.२
श्वोभूते, ५.२.१
षट्कृत्वः, ६.१.६
षट्तयानि, ५.१.३
षडशीत्यङ्गुलपूर्वरज्जुम्, ४.१.१
षड्ढोतारम्, ३.४.४; ४.१.२
षड्ढोतृहोमवर्जम्, ३.२.२
षष्ठप्रणवे, ५.४.३
षोडशां, ५.३.२
षोडशिनम्, ६.२.२
षोडशीवाजपेययोः, ६.१.५
संयुवन्ति, ३.४.२
संयुत्य, ४.३.१
संयौति, २.२.१
संवत्सरम्, १.५.१
संवत्सरे, ३.६.१
संवपन्ति, २.२.१
संवपेत्, ५.२.३
संवाहयेयुः, ५.१.८
संवापेदम्, २.१.१
संविधूय, ४.२.३
संविभजरेन्, ६.३.३
संवृण्वन्ति, ५.२.१
संवेशनयजुः, ५.१.७
संवेष्ट्य, ४.२.३
संशरणम्, ५.१.७
संशितव्रतान्, ५.१.१
संशेरते, प्रस्ता. १
संसन्नम्, २.२.३; ३.६.३
संसन्नयज्ञम्, २.४.४

संसादयति, २.४.३
संसृज्यमाने, २.४.४
संस्कारम्, ५.३.५
संस्कृतिः, ४.२.१
संस्कृताभिः (अद्भिः), २.१.२
संस्कृत्य, १.१.७; ५.३.५
संस्तीर्य, २.१.१; २
संस्थामनु, ३.१.३
संस्पर्शनम्, २.२.२
संस्पर्शयति, २.३.६
संस्पर्शयन्तीव, १.४.२
संस्पृष्टाः, ६.१.४
संस्रावणानि, २.३.२
संस्रावम्, २.३.६; ६.३.३[२]
संस्रावेण, ५.४.३
सकामः, १.१.६
सकाम्यम्, १.१.६
सकाशे, १.१.३
सकृत्, १.३.१, ३, ३.२.६
सकृदवहतान्, ६.१.३
सकृदवहत्य, ३.४.२
सकृदशनम्, १.३.२
सकृदारंभाभावः, १.३.३
सकृदाशी, ३.६.१
सकृदुपमथ्य, ३.४.२
सकृद्गृहीतेन, ५.१.५
सक्तु-, ६.१.२
सक्तून्, ३.४.२[२]; ६.१.४
सक्त्वर्थान्, ३.४.२; ६.१.४
सक्थ्नः, ५.२.३
सग्रहः, ६.३.२
संकल्पयेत्, १.१.३; २.४.४
संकल्पितव्रतः, ५.१.१
संकल्पितव्रतस्य, ५.१.१
संकल्प्य, १.१.३, ५, ६; ४.३[३]; २.३.१[२]; ४.२; ४.३.१; ५.१.१; ३.२; ६.२.६
संकाशयति, ५.२.३
संकाशस्थिते, ५.५.१
संकीर्तनम्, १.१.३
संक्षालनम्, २.२.२
संक्षालनान्तम्, ३.२.१
संक्षालम्, २.५.१
संक्षालानयनम्, २.१.२
संक्षाल्य, १.४.४
संगमयति, २.३.५
संगमय्य, ५.३.२
संग्रहम्, ३.३.३
सज्येत, ४.१.१
सञ्चरे, २.२.२
सञ्चाराणाम्, ५.४.६
संचारेण, ५.४.५
संजातेषु, ३.१.१
संज्ञपनाय, ४.४.२
संज्ञप्तहोमपेषलैः, ४.४.२
संज्ञप्ते (पशौ), २.५.३
संज्ञप्यमाने (पशौ), २.५.३
संज्ञानम्, ५.३.४
सतम्, १.१.७; ६.२.३
सतस्य, १.१.५
सति, १.१.९
सतूलया, १.१.६
सतूलाः, ५.१.१
सते, १.१.५, ७; ६.२.३
सत्त्रीन्, ५.१.४
सत्ये, ५.१.६
सदः, ५.४.५; ५.५.२; ६.३, ४; ६.१.१; ६.३.२
सदस्यः, ६.३.१
सदस्यकल्पे, ६.३.१
सदसि, ५.८.१; ६.३.१

सदोपसर्गे, ६.२.१
सदोहविर्धानाग्नीध्रसंमानाय, ५.१.३
सद्भिः, १.१.१
सद्योनिर्वापपक्षे, १.३.२
सधर्मकत्वे, ३.२.३; ६.१
सधर्मकम्, ३.२.२
सनिरुपकल्पितः, ५.१.७
सनिलब्धम्, ५.१.७
सनीडम्, ५.१.३
सन्ततमृजु, २.३.१
सन्ततम्, २.३.१; ५.१.८
सन्ततिम्, २.३.५; ४.३.४
सन्ततिम् (आहुतिम्), ३.१.२
सन्ततेः, २.३.५
संतराम्, ५.३.५
सन्तर्पणम्, ६.१.५
सन्तर्पयेत्, २.२.३
सन्दंशम्, ६.२.३
सन्दंशेन, ६.२.३
सन्दध्यात्, २.३.२
सन्दिग्धेषु, ३.१.१
सन्धाय, ५.३.१
सन्धीन्, २.३.३
सन्नता, १.१.४
संनमयन्, ३.२.२
सन्नमयन्ति, ४.२.२
सन्नमयेत्, २.५.३; ४.४.१, २
सन्नयतः, २.३.३
सन्नय्य, ३.२.१
सन्नहनम्, ३.१.१; ५.१.६
सन्नह्यादि, ३.२.५
सन्नाम, ३.२.४
सन्निधाय, ४.२.३
सन्निपत्य, ५.४.१
सन्निहिताम्, ५.१.८
सपिण्डाः, ३.२.३; ५.६.१
सप्तदशकृत्वः, २.३.५
सप्तर्षिनमस्कारानन्तरम्, १.५.२
सप्तहोतृहोमः, ६.२.३
सप्ते, १.४.४
सप्राशाः (स्थालीप्राशाः), १.१.८
सभागृहे, १.२.१
सभ्यावसथीययोः, १.२.१
समग्निहोत्रम्, ३.३.१
समचतुरश्रम्, १.१.४[२]; ५.४.५[२]; ५.२
समञ्जनम्, २.३.२
समनक्ति, २.३.१; ४.२.१
समन्ततः, ५.२.१; ४.५
समन्तरेण, ४.२.१
समन्त्रकम्, १.३.२, ३; २.२.३; ३.१.१
समन्त्रकाम्, २.१.१; ४.२.१
समन्त्रकैः, २.२.२
समभिघार्य, ३.१.१
समवधाय, ६.१.२
समवनयेत्, ६.३.३
समवशमनम्, ५.६.१
समवस्यन्ति, ५.१.८
समवहितात्, २.३.४
समस्तनिष्कासान्, ३.२.६
समस्तसन्नहनम्, ३.१.१
समस्ताङ्गुलिना, ५.४.४
समस्ताभिः (व्याहृतिभिः), १.१.६
समस्यति, २.४.३
समाः, १.३.१
समाकृतम्, १.५.३
समाख्या, ६.३.३; ६.३.४[२]
समाख्याय, ६.३.४
समाग्रम्, २.२.२
समादध्यात्, ४.२.३; ६.२.४
समानः, ५.१.२

समान्वेक्षणा, ३.४.१
समापयन्ति, १.१.९
समायत्य, ५.३.२
समारब्धेषु, १.१.७
समारूढाः, ५.३.५[२]
समारूढाग्निभिः, ५.१.४
समारोपणम्, ५.१.८; ३.५
समारोपणविसर्गौ, ५.३.५
समारोपणे, ५.१.४
समारोप्य, ५.१.४
समारोहन्तम्, २.४.१
समारोहयते, ५.१.७
समासन्ने, १.३.१, ७
समिच्चोदनायाम्, ५.३.५
समिद्धाः, १.३.२[२]
समिधः, १.१.६; २.३.१; ४.१.२
समिधम्, १.४.२, ३, ४; ५.३; २.१.२; ३.१, ५; ५.३.५
समिधि, १.४.३; ४
समिधौ, २.२.३
समिन्धनम्, १.५.२
समिन्धनीयाः, १.३.२
समिष्टयजुः, २.३.६; ४.७; ५.२
समिष्टयजुषः, २.३.५
समिष्टयजुषा, ३.३.१
समिष्टयजुर्वर्जम्, ३.४.५
समिष्टयजूंषि, ४.३.५
समीक्षयति, ५.२.३
समीचीनमुखान्, ६.२.१
समीचीने, ५.५.१[२]; ६.१.२
समुच्चये, ३.१.२
समुच्चीयते, ६.२.२
समुच्चीयेते, ५.३.५
समुच्च्य, ६.१.४
समुच्छ्रयन्ति, ५.५.३
समुदिताः, २.४.७
समुद्धननम्, २.२.२
समुद्युत्य, ६.१.६
समुपनद्धम्, ५.३.२
समुपहवः, ६.३.३
समुपहूय, ६.३.३, ४
समुप्य, १.१.७; ४.३.१; ६.२.३
समूलम्, ३.४.१
समूहः, ५.१.१
समूह्य, १.४.२
समृद्धहोमानि, ३.४.५
संपवयेत्, ६.२.३
संपादवर्जम्, ५.३.२
संपीड्य, ६.२.१
संप्रकिरति, ३.२.७; ४.५
संप्रकृष्टेषु, ४.४.२
संप्रकृष्य, ४.२.३
संप्रगृह्णाति, २.३.६
संप्रदानादि, ५.६.५
संप्रप्लुता, ४.२.५
संप्रलुम्पन्, ४.२.५
संप्रवाहयेयुः, ५.१.८
संप्रसृप्तौ, ६.३.१
संप्रसर्पेयुः, ६.२.६
संप्रेष्येत्, ६.३.१
संप्रैषः, ६.१.२
संप्रैषम्, ३.२.४
संबोधयन्ति, ६.१.१
संभरणकाले, ५.४.७
संभरण्याम्, ६.२.१
संभरेत्, १.१.५; ५.८.२
संभर्तुकामः, १.१.५
संभवः, ५.५.४
संभवेयुः, १.१.४
संभाराः, १.४.१; ५.१.३

संभारान्, १.१.५; २.१.१; ४.१.२; ५.१.२
संभारे, ३.२.७
संभाषेत, २.५.१
संभिद्य, २.३.३; ४.३.२
संभिन्द्यात्, ५.४.३
संभृतसंभारः, ५.१.१
संभृत्य, २.१.१, ५.१.४
संभेदनम्, ४.३.४
संभेदनानि, २.३.३
-संमर्शनमन्त्र, ४.३.३
संमार्गः, ५.४.२
संमार्जनम्, २.२.२
संमार्जनानि, २.२.२
संमार्ष्टि, २.१.१; ३.५; ४.१.२
संमितः, ५.१.१
संमितौ, ५.१.३
संमिनोति, २.३.५
संमृज्य, १.१.७; २.२.२[२]; ३.५
संमृशति, ५.५.३
संमृष्टः, ३.२.२
संमृष्टौ, ५.५.१
सम्यगवधानम्, ५.६.१
सम्राडासन्दी, ५.१.३
सम्राडासन्द्याम्, ५.३.४
सर्पणादि, ५.१.६
सर्पय, २.२.१
सर्पितुम्, ६.२.३
सर्पिषा, १.१.५
सर्पेत्, ६.२.३
सर्वदोपसदः, ५.४.१
सर्वदोपस्थानादि, १.३.३
सर्वपृष्ठे, ६.२.२
सर्वफलीकरणान्, ३.२.५
सर्वमन्त्रान्ते, ५.६.५
सर्वाचार्याभिप्रायम्, ६.२.३
सर्वोपस्थानानि, १.१.९
सर्वाधानपक्षे, १.५.१
सर्वार्थत्वे, ४.१.२[२]
सर्वालयाम्, १.१.१
सवनीयपुरोडाशस्य, ६.३.३
सवनीयं (पशुम्), ६.२.५
सवनीयार्थम्, ५.१.२; ८.२
सवविधपक्षम्, ४.३.२
सवविधपक्षे, ४.३.१[२]
सवविधे, ४.४.३[२]
सव्यम्, ५.६.५
सव्यायाः, ४.३.३
सशब्दम्, ६.२.२
ससंस्रावान्, ४.१.२
सहक्रियाम्, ३.२.२; ३.२.५
सहक्रियायाम्, ३.२.२
सहपात्रः, ६.३.३
सहोपस्थानाधिवदनान्तम्, १.५.२
साकमेधार्थम् ३.२.१
साग्निपावमानिकेन, १.५.१
साग्रम्, २.२.२
सांकाशिने, ५.५.१
साज्यस्रुवायाम्, २.२.३
सादनमन्त्रः, ६.२.२
सादनमन्त्रान्ते, ६.२.२
सादनम्, २.३.४[२]
सादनान्तम्, ५.३.२
सादनान्तरम् (कर्म), ३.१.१
सादयतः, ५.३.३
सादयति, १.१.५, ७, ८, ९; ४.४; २.१.२; ३.६
सादयित्वा, १.१.७; ४.२; २.१.३; २.२[२]; २.२[३]
सादयेत्, २.१.१; २; २.३[२]
सादयेयुः, ५.८.१

सादितस्य (अग्नेः), ३.४.१
साद्यमानयोः, २.४.४
साद्येरन्, ५.५.३
साधनानि, १.१.१
साधारणकर्मणि, ३.२.५
साधारणे, ५.८.२
सान्याय्यपात्राणि, २.१.१
सान्नाय्यमन्त्रद्वयेन, ३.१.१
सान्नाय्यम्, २.१.२
सान्नाय्ययोः, २.३.३
सान्नाय्याङ्गुष्ठप्रदेशिन्यौ, २.३.२
सान्नाय्यान्तानि, २.३.४
सान्नाय्ये, २.२.३
सामन्ननुद्रुते, ६.२.३
साममन्त्रम्, १.१.९
सामान्यरूपो...?, ५.१.६
साम्नाम्, १.१.९
साम्नि, १.१.९
सायंदोहः, ५.८.२
सायंदोहत्वे, ६.२.५
सारम्, ५.४.७
सार्वकालम्, १.३.२
सावित्रः, ३.१.२; ५.३.४
सासृजति, ६.२.१
सिकता, १.१.४; ४.१.२
सिञ्चेत, ४.२.१
सीव्यतः, ५.५.२[३]
सुपर्णम्, ५.२.१
सुभिक्षताः, १.१.१[३]
सुभिक्षतार्थैः, १.१.१
सुयोज्यानि, २.३.१
सुवृत्ताः, ५.१.३
सुव्यक्तानि, २.३.१
सुशृतम्, १.१.७
सुषिरवतीम्, १.४.४
सुष्ठु, ४.१.२
सूक्तवाकान्ते, २.३.५
सूक्तवाकाय, ३.२.५
सूदम्, १.१.५
सूत्रान्तरत्वात्, ३.६.१
सृष्टिम्, ५.३.२
सेभुम्, ५.१.८
सोदञ्चनः, ५.१.२[२]
सोभयतः, ६.३.२
सोमः, १.५.२
सोमम्, ५.३.३[२]; ६.३.३
सोमचमसवत्, ५.१.७
सोमचमसापिधानम्, ५.८.१
सोमपात्राणि, ५.५.३
सोमयाजिनः, १.१.६
सोमरसः, ६.२.१
सोमवाहनम्, ५.१.३; ३.३[२]
सोमवाहनयोजनार्था, ५.२.१
सोमवाहनस्य, ५.३.३[३]
सोमविक्रयिणः, ५.३.२
सोमविक्रयिणम्, ५.३.२[२]
सोमविक्रयी, ५.३.३
सोमविप्रुषः, ६.२.२
सोमस्थाल्यः, ५.१.२
सोमाधाने, १.१.३[२]; १.३.३
सोमाय, ३.४.१
सोमार्थानि, ५.२.१
सोमांशुसवनाः, ५.६.१
सोमासन्दी, ५.१.२
सोमे, १.५.२
सौमिकेषु, ६.३.१
सौम्यस्य, ५.१.२
सौरीम्, ५.४.७
सौविष्टकृतम्, २.३.२
स्तनचतुष्के, ५.३.५

स्तनाः, ६.१.२
स्तनाकारौ, ६.१.२
स्तम्बयजुः, ३.३.२; ४.३; ४.१.१; ५.४.२
स्तम्बयजुर्नाम्ना, ५.४.६
स्तम्बयजुषः, ४.१.२; ५.४.१
स्तम्बयजुराज्यग्रहणम्, ३.२.२
स्तम्बयजुषी, ३.२.२
स्तरणम्, ६.२.४
स्तरणबर्हिष्ये, ५.४.३
स्तरणाभिघारणे, ३.१.२
स्तीर्णम् (बर्हिः), ५.२.२
स्तीर्णयोः, ३.६.२
स्तीर्णस्य, २.२.३
स्तीर्णेन, २.३.६
स्तीर्त्वा, २.३.२
स्तीर्यमाणे, ३.६.२
स्तुवन्ति, ५.८.१
स्तृणन्ति, २.२.२; ५.६.२^{२}
स्तोत्रे, ६.१.२
स्तोत्रेषु, ६.२.३
स्तोत्रोपकरणाय, ५.५.३
स्तोत्रोपकरणार्थम्, ५.५.३
स्तोमभागम्, ६.२.३
स्त्रियम्, ३.६.१
स्त्रीवृक्षी, ५.१.३
स्त्र्यम्बकान्, ३.४.२
स्थविमखण्डस्य, ४.२.३
स्थाणुम्, ५.४.४; ६
स्थानपक्षः, ४.१.१
स्थालीः, ५.१.२; ८.१; ६.१.४
स्थालीगतम्, १.४.३
स्थालीपाकम्, २.४.३
स्थालीम्, १.१.७; ४.२^{२}; ६.१.३
स्थाल्यः, ३.२.१; ५.१.२; ४.३.३
स्थाल्यामवशिष्टम्, ३.३.३
स्थाल्यामवशिष्टसंभवात्, १.३.२
स्थाल्याम्, १.४.४; ५.२.२
स्थाल्या विलम्, १.१.७
स्थित्युत्पत्तिलयाः प्रस्ता., १
स्थूणा, ५.५.१
स्थूणाम्, ५.३.३
स्थूणाराजन्, ५.४.४
स्थूणाराजे, ५.२.२
स्थूणायाः (कर्णयोः), ५.५.२
स्थूणौ, ५.१.३
स्नातः, ५.१.४
स्नाननियमः, ५.६.१^{२}
स्नानविधिना, १.१.६
स्नानाय, ५.६.१
स्नापयित्वा, १.१.६
स्निहानम्, ५.१.८
स्नेहमश्रु, ५.१.८
स्पन्द्यया, ४.१.१; ५.४.५
स्पन्द्या, ५.२.१; ३.३; ४.४, ५
स्पन्द्याम्, ५.८.३
स्पष्टः, ५.१.७
स्पाशयन्ते, ५.४.४
स्पृणन्, ५.१.७
स्फ्यः, ३.२.१
स्फ्यदानात्, ३.२.२
स्फ्यम्, १.१.१, ४^{२}; २.२.२^{३}; ३.२.३, ५, ६; ३.१; ४.१.१, २; ५.२.२; ४.२
स्फ्यस्य, २.२.२; ५.६.२; ६.१.१
स्फ्यादीनि, २.१.२
स्फ्यान्तया, २.३.६
स्फ्ये, २.३.६; ४.३
स्फ्येध्मसन्नहनम्, ३.२.४
स्फ्येन, ३.२.६, ५.४.६
स्मरेत्, १.५.३
स्रगार, ६.१.२

स्रुक्, **५**.१.३; **३**.२.६
स्रुकसंस्रावहोमान्तम्, **३**.४.५
स्रुक्सादनकाले, **५**.४.३
स्रुक्स्रुवौ, **५**.५.१
स्रुक्षु, **५**.३.५
स्रुगभिमर्शनम्, **६**.१.२
स्रुगाकारः, **६**.१.२
स्रुग्गतम्, **१**.४.४
स्रुग्गताद् (आज्यात्)
स्रुग्द्वयम्, **४**.३.३
स्रुग्धारणार्थात्, **५**.५.३
स्रुग्व्यूहनादि, **४**.४.३; **५**.३.५
स्रुचः, **१**.४.४; **२**.२.२[२]; **३**.२.३, ५; ४.३, ४; ६.३; **४**.१.२; **५**.५.३; ६.३; **६**.१.१
स्रुचम्, **१**.२.१; ४.२, ४[२]; **२**.३.२, ३; **४**.१.२
स्रुचा, **२**.३.५; **२**.३.६; **३**.१.२; **६**.२.३
स्रुचि, **१**.४.४
स्रुचोः, **२**.२.३; ३.२, ५, ४; **३**.४.४; ६.२; **४**.३.२[२], ३; **६**.२.६
स्रुवदण्डेन, **२**.३.३
स्रुवमन्त्रेण, **४**.१.२
स्रुवम्, **१**.१.७[२]; ४.२; **२**.१.२; २.३; ४.२; **३**.२.३; **३**.२.६[२]; ३.१, २[२], ३; **४**.१.२[२], ३; ३.३; **५**.४.२[२]
स्रुवसाधनत्वम्, **६**.२.३
स्रुवस्वधिती, **४**.१.२
स्रुवाहुतिः, **६**.२.३
स्रुवाहुतीः, **२**.३.५; **३**.१.२; ४.५; **४**.३.४
स्रुवाहुत्याम्, **५**.६.५
स्रुवे, **३**.३.२
स्रुवेण, **१**.४.४; ५.२, ३; **२**.२.१; ३.१; **४**.३.४
स्वगृहाभिमुखः, **१**.५.३
स्वधितिना, **४**.२.१
स्वधितिम्, **४**.१.२[२]; २.१[३]; ४.३
स्वनाम, **२**.३.२
स्वभागम्, **२**.३.४
स्वं भागम्, **२**.३.४
स्वमन्त्रैः, **२**.५.१
स्वयंहोमपक्षे, **१**.४.५
स्वरु, **४**.१.१
स्वरुणा, **४**.१.३
स्वरुम्, **४**.२.१[३]; ३.५
स्वरुसमीपम्, **४**.३.५
स्वरूपापादनम्, **३**.१.१
स्वरौ, **२**.३.२
स्वर्गलोकम्, **५**.६.५
स्वाद्योनेरूढम्, **४**.१.१
स्वाद्वन्नम्, **५**.३.३
स्वार्थे, **३**.५.१
स्वाहा, **३**.२.५
स्वाहाकारान्ते, **३**.२.४
स्वाहाकृत्यानुमन्त्रणादि, **४**.४.२
स्विष्टकृतः, **२**.२.१
स्विष्टकृतम्, **३**.२.५
स्विष्टकृदनुमन्त्रणम्, **४**.४.३
स्विष्टकृदर्थम्, **४**.३.३
स्विष्टकृदवदानम्, **२**.३.३
स्विष्टकृदवदानस्य, **२**.३.३
स्विष्टकृदवदाने, **२**.२.१
स्विष्टकृदिडार्थयोः, **४**.३.३
हरणम्, **२**.२.२
हविः, **१**.३.१; **२**.३.५; ४.२
हविरभिमन्त्रणम्, **२**.१.३; **५**.१.५
हविरासादनस्थानम्, **५**.६.२
हविरुद्वासनोत्तरम्, **१**.३.१
हविर्धानम्, **५**.४.५, ६; ८.१, २; **६**.१.१, २, ५; २.४; ३.३

हविर्धानस्य, **५**.५.१, ३; **६**.१.२, ५
हविर्धानाभ्याम्, **६**.२.३
हविर्धाने, **५**.१.३; ५.१; ६.२; **६**.३.२
हविर्यज्ञविधपक्षे, **४**.३.१, ५; ४.१
हविर्विधपक्षे, **४**.३.२
हविःषु, **१**.५.३; **२**.२.३; **३**.६.३
हविष्कृतम्, **२**.४.३
हविष्कृदन्ते, **४**.३.१
हविष्कृताह्वानात्, **२**.४.३; **३**.४.२; **६**.१.३
हविष्यम्, **६**.३.३
हविष्यासादयन्, **२**.२.३
हविःसादनप्रदेशः, **५**.६.५
हवींषि, **१**.१.४ ; २.३, ४
हव्याय, **३**.५.२
हसन्तः, **३**.३.३
हस्तप्रक्षालनम्, **५**.६.५
हस्तम्, **१**.२.१
हार्योजनीभिः, **५**.८.१
हिंसायाम्, **१**.१.२
हिंकृत्वा, **६**.२.२
हिरण्यपक्षे, **३**.६.२
हिरण्यम्, **१**.५.२; ५.२; ३[३]; **६**.२.२
हिरण्यरजः, **६**.१.५; २.२
हिरण्यशल्कप्रासनम्, **६**.१.६
हिरण्यशल्कम्, **१**.१.७, ८, ९; **४**.२.५[२]; **६**.२.२
हिरण्यशल्कश्रयणम्, **६**.३.२
हिरण्यशल्कश्रवणे, **६**.१.६
हिरण्यशल्कान्, **१**.१.५, ७, ८, ९; **४**.१.२; २.५[२]; **५**.१.२, ४; **६**.२.२
हिरण्यशल्के, **६**.१.६
हिरण्यशल्कौ, **१**.१.७
हिरण्यस्य, **५**.५.२; **६**.१.२
हिरण्ये, **५**.२.३
हिरण्येन, **६**.१.५, २.२
हृत्वा, **२**.२.२
हृदयदेशम्, **२**.३.६
हृदयमुत्तमम्, **४**.३.३
हृदयशूलप्रचारः, **२**.५.३
हृदयशूलेन, **४**.३.३
हृदयादीनाम्, **४**.३.३
हृदयाभिघारणे, **४**.१.२
हृदयाभिघारितम्, **४**.१.२
हेमन्तशिशिरौ, **२**.३.२
होतव्यः, **५**.१.५, ६
होता, **२**.३.२[३], ४; **५**.६.४; **६**.२.६; ३.३, ४[४]
होतारम्, **२**.३.१, ४; **५**.१.१; **६**.१.५[२]; २.१; ३.४
होतुराहुतिः, **५**.३.४
होतुराहुतिम्, **२**.३.५; **६**.२.६[२]
होतुरुत्थानम्, **५**.६.३
होतुर्धिष्णियम्, **५**.४.६; ५.४
होतुर्वचनम्, **३**.४.५
होतृकवचनम्, **६**.१.६
होतृकव्रजनम्, **६**.१.६
होतृचमसः, **६**.१.५[३]
होतृचमसम्, **६**.१.५[२]; ३.२; ३, ४[२]
होतृचमसे, **६**.१.५; ३.२; ३
होतृवषट्कारे, **६**.३.४
होतृवसने, **६**.१.४
होतृषदने, **२**.३.२
होतृषदनैः, **२**.३.७
होत्रकाच्छावाकवर्जानाम्, **६**.३.२
होत्रकाणाम्, **६**.३.२[२]
होत्रकान्, **५**.८.१
होत्रध्वर्यू, **५**.६.३
होत्रादीनाम्, **६**.३.३

होत्रीयम्, **६**.२.४
होत्रे, **२**.३.३, ४, ५, ६; **३**.२.५; **४**.३.२; **६**.३.२[3]
होमः, **२**.३.३; **६**.१.५
होमनिमार्जने, **६**.१.५
होमम्, **२**.३.२
होमवर्जम्, **४**.३.५
होमविधिः, **२**.२.३
होमाः, **१**.३.३
होमाभिषवयोः (कर्तुः), **६**.३.३
होमाभिषवौ, **६**.३.३
होमाय, **६**.३.३
होमेषु, **२**.३.१
ह्रदात्, **१**.१.५
ह्रदौ, **५**.८.१
ह्त्वा, **२**.२.२

—०—